Mothering for Capital

Mothering for Capital

Labor, Race, and Child "Value" in Neoliberalism

MARIA KROMIDAS

Vanderbilt University Press
Nashville, Tennessee

Library of Congress Cataloging-in-Publication Data

Names: Kromidas, Maria, 1974- author
Title: Mothering for capital : labor, race, and child "value" in neoliberalism / Maria Kromidas.
Description: Nashville, Tennessee : Vanderbilt University Press, 2026. | Includes bibliographical references and index.
Identifiers: LCCN 2026012546 (print) | LCCN 2026012547 (ebook) | ISBN 9780826500564 paperback | ISBN 9780826500571 hardcover | ISBN 9780826500588 epub | ISBN 9780826500595 pdf
Subjects: LCSH: Motherhood--Economic aspects | Human capital | Neoliberalism
Classification: LCC HQ759 .K77 2026 (print) | LCC HQ759 (ebook)
LC record available at https://lccn.loc.gov/2026012546
LC ebook record available at https://lccn.loc.gov/2026012547 Library of Congress Cataloging-in-Publication Data

To my mom, in all her boundless generosity

CONTENTS

INTRODUCTION

Neoliberal Motherhood and the Middle Class Project

> Appearances and reality intertwine. Appearances graft themselves onto reality, encompassing it, replacing it. The "alienated" world—social appearances, the theories and abstractions which express these appearances—seems the only reality.
>
> —*Henri Lefebvre*

> Everybody must have projects all the time. The maximum must be extracted from leisure . . . The whole of life must look like a job.
>
> —*Theodor Adorno*

The Three-Faced Spectacle of Neoliberal Motherhood

CONSIDER A TRIPTYCH of current motherhood.

The first panel is a video posted on social media of a cheerful and energetic mother reading with expression and delight to her ten-week-old baby, who is propped upright and facing her. The accompanied text tells viewers: "Read to your newborn." The baby's "developing brain" "forms new neural connections at an estimated 1 million per SECOND." This mother is "giving us a master class on how to do it right," "setting her baby up for a lifetime of success." The second is a collage of illustrations culled from influential media outlets such as NPR, *The Atlantic*, and *The Wall Street Journal* of overbearing mothers hovering in the air over children, the whirring blades of a helicopter attached to the mothers' backs. Accompanying the caricature of the "helicopter mother" is that of her "overprotected child"—overwhelmed, confused, and sad children stare off into space or dangle from marionette strings. The third panel is a bloodred screen with audio of a woman's bloodcurdling scream: "Aaaah! Aaaah! I'm so sick of my goddamn kids" that appeared in a *New York Times* series examining the pandemic's effects on "working" mothers. The mass closure of schools and childcare facilities and the mandate to "stay at home" during the COVID-19 public health emergency created exceptional circumstances, but the more general image of the overwhelmed and exhausted mother, for whom caring for her children has become an unmitigated misery, provides an apt third panel in this triptych.[1]

These three panels signify, respectively, the ideal, the scapegoat, and the real. All three are spectacles, exemplifying emotionally laden representations of motherhood that have saturated public culture for the past decade or more. Educational and child experts, economists, policymakers, politicians, and pundits love the ideal—they extol and exalt her sacrifices—and mothers are incessantly and painstakingly taught how to become more like her. Others love how no actual mother can live up to the Madonna-like reverence she is accorded. Sociologists, feminists, liberals, and conservatives alike love to hate the scapegoat (the derisive nicknames alone are revealing: helicopter, snowplow, lawnmower, and bulldozer mom)—they blame America's growing class inequalities and amplified competition for middle class life on her selfishness, and they similarly attribute the surge of psychopathologies in both childhood and the purportedly "stunted" adulthoods of millennials to her excesses. Flesh-and-blood mothers love the real because it affords them a small measure of comfort as the only representation that approximates their actual lives, bringing to light and almost normalizing heretofore taboo feelings of maternal rage, loss of autonomy and sense of self, and fantasies of abandonment. Meanwhile, others love, sadistically, to consume content of suffering mothers perpetually "in crisis," paragons of maternal self-sacrifice. Rather than understand them as three competing images, we might better see them as one entity with three different faces, much like Cerberus, the three-headed dog that prevents the dead from escaping the underworld in Greek mythology.

The three-faced mother performs multiple equally important functions in the political and libidinal economy of neoliberal capitalism. The ideal taps into mothers' fears and insecurities about their children's futures in the deteriorating prospects of capitalism's current crises and goads them to "invest" in their child; for others it provides hope that our collective circumstances are redeemable, at least to those virtuous enough to dutifully play the game. The scapegoat allows mothers to express their ambivalence and resentment toward the ideal and to assure themselves that their own mothering is not excessive and overbearing but just right and done out of love rather than vanity and selfishness. Meanwhile, for others, it is the punching bag that allows a release of pent-up frustration at the current generalized deterioration of social conditions and opportunities, and thus provides a convenient diversion from capitalism's perpetual crises. The real provides a safety valve for mothers, with its apparent recognition and sympathy for their plight and its implicit promises of reform; for the rest, it provides the perverse pleasure of satisfying a deep-seated, if misdirected, aggression at the sanctified paragon of the mother, as well as our current crises of rising inequality and deepening misery: If someone should carry the burden of collective suffering, why not mothers?

This is what I call *the tripartite spectacle of neoliberal motherhood*. The nature of a spectacle is that it draws our attention, dazzles our senses, resonates with our emotions and vulnerabilities, so that we are unable to grasp it beyond its surface form. The shimmer of the spectacle buries and disguises the relations of struggle that constitute it. First, it is imperative to note that the triple image of neoliberal motherhood is composed of images of pronouncedly *middle class* mothers, figures that are historically racialized as white. Indeed, the specifically middle class characteristics of these iconic mothers that make up the three-faced spectacle tend to subsume *all* mothers, regardless of the actual class, racialized, and other differences among them. How does the spectacle institute what is understood to be middle class mothering as its standard and norm? Why are we bombarded with representations of middle class mothers—and why now? After more than half a century of hysterical finger wagging and moralistic blaming of racialized and poor or working class mothers for practically every social ill, why have middle class mothers eclipsed them in public culture? What "work" does this figure perform for the collective psyche?

The three-faced mother guards the gates of the underworld that is neoliberal capitalism, conscripting subjects into its reign through what I call the middle class project. The middle class project purports to rehabilitate the proverbial American dream by helping mothers do what they do best—"make a difference" in their child's future prospects for success. "Common sense" is manufactured so that most only see mothers making more or less of a difference. Instead, this book argues that the middle class project represents a radical restructuring of expectations and aspirations for a decent life into a culture of endless work, sacrifice, and devotion to capital; one that crucially depends on orienting human subjectivity toward capital. In this project, mothers are absolutely crucial. The project begins at birth by capturing mothers to see, interact, and labor for their child from the standpoint of capital—actively working to convert the child's life into a bundle of living value with near-infinite potential to generate more value. The spectacle of the three-headed mother disguises and legitimizes these processes through the middle class project. All we are left to see is good mothers, bad mothers, and suffering mothers.

From Crisis to Catastrophe: Mothering in Capitalism

The current crisis of motherhood is indisputable. So much so that the US surgeon general declared parents' stress and mental health an "urgent public health issue" in 2024.[2] This crisis is so vast and enduring that attempts to diagnose it get caught in its abyss, inadvertently reproducing one of the visages of the three-faced spectacle. What distinguishes my analysis from extant scholarship is that I posit, and concretely situate, the current crisis as a paroxysm of the permanent catastrophe of mothering in capitalism. Maternal labors are crucial for capital's reproduction, and so a strategic object of its unprecedented life-destructive power. Mother's agonies are the visible manifestation of capital's bottomless appetite for human life within the crucial arena of social reproduction. These are the social relations of struggle—life against capital—that constitute the spectacle of motherhood. Making these links discernible in the analysis is so absolutely critical that missing them renders critique hollow. In the most common diagnosis, feminist scholars and popular feminist critics trace the major source of mothers' agonies as arising from the growing hegemony of "intensive parenting" since its emergence in the 1990s.[3] Where I agree with these interpretations of the links between sociocultural features of neoliberalism and mothering—the growing list of impossible work demands, the rule of so-called experts, its entrepreneurial spirit and working on the self, its commodification—I go further to insist that the ideal mother is not only another expert-backed ideal in a series of socially and historically shifting patriarchal ideals. Rather, the intensive mother is capital's latest and most intricately regulated demands for mothers, apparent ideals that morph according to the needs of its accumulation and carrying the force of capital's arsenal of power.

In parallel ways, my analysis diverges from the predominant strand of sociological work representing "intensive parenting" as a "style" emerging from middle class ways of being that functions as a vector of class reproduction.[4] Middle class mothers can access and bequeath money and networks, as well as particular knowledge, dispositions, and skills that advantage their children. This is incontrovertibly true. While I have many objections to this interpretive vein (particularly because it is hegemonic in "applied" fields such as education and in the parenting public sphere), my strongest disagreements are its political implications. By representing parenting as a zero-sum game in which mothers continually ramp up their strategic interventions to ensure their child's access to increasingly scarce middle class slots, mothers are implicitly held responsible for amplifying neoliberalism's race and class inequalities. Even when such accounts emphasize how institutions unfairly reward parenting effects, parenting practices are unintentionally held up as the ideal.[5] Even in their most critical registers, traditional sociology's normative and moral standpoints are derived from the system that it both takes for granted and purports to critique—capitalism. That is, the object of critique is fairness within the ideal of a pure meritocracy—an unrigged system in which rewards (inequalities) would be achieved uncorrupted by the circumstances of one's birth or parental advantage. In this frame, our collective struggles should thereby be aimed at eliminating "all artificial inequality leaving the *natural inequalities* to find their true level."[6] By ignoring the particular ways that mothers are subject to capital's arsenal of power, a power whose massive force is unprecedented in human affairs, such work is unwittingly complicit in ideologically legitimating capitalism, albeit one closer to its ideal form—study hard, work hard, play by the rules, and win. Domination, oppression, expropriation, and exploitation—all inherent, necessary, and core systemic features of the capitalist mode of production—are excused as long as equality of opportunity can reign. Inequality through fair competition, for these analysts, is the ultimate goal.

More recently, feminist scholars have rightly shifted their gaze to "the economy" as exacerbating the weight of mothers' struggling to bear the weight of intensive parenting's impossible demands.[7] They argue that the increasing unsustainability of work demands and their encroachment on nonwork life, the decreasing availability of support for childcare, and the increased difficulties of accessing and providing the basics of care (e.g., health, housing, schools) make it harder to mother. Dovetailing with this interpretation is recent work focusing on the "economization" of parenting children who are increasingly seen as "investments."[8] Some popular feminist writing has even begun to name capitalism, somehow structuring the visceral descriptions of various symptoms of mothers' social, psychic, and physical damage.[9] Childcare is work, and the growing demands of that work amid intensified economic polarization, individualism, and privatization make it difficult, if not impossible, to do that work. All of this is true. Yet this is a partial view that obscures the source, nature, and magnitude of the problem. This is an inherently political problem whose stakes are much more dire than such accounts portray.

The Battleground of Subjectivity

Mothering for Capital intervenes in these conversations to illuminate the prevailing force structuring mothering and its agonies—capital's insatiable drive to valorize value penetrates motherhood as never before. Capital's pervasive power is at once amorphous and changing forms, disguised and lurking in plain sight, pervasive and enshrouded in dissimulation. It is not a neutral cost-benefit logic that influences parents' decisions, nor is it rational. It is a profoundly irrational force that in its blind fury for value seeks to dominate the human subject who is its only source. The transformations within motherhood, childhood, and the family that so many have described but have inadequately traced and theorized are wrought by capital's unquenchable drive to subsume maternal labors of shaping children as subjects, a complex set of processes glossed as socialization. Mothering in late neoliberalism has become the key site of capital's protracted struggle to subordinate the human subject. The current crisis of motherhood is the distorted refraction of this radical restructuring of social reproduction.

Mothering for Capital traces how capital more intensely and stealthily subsumes mothering, transforming women's work of caring for children into labor for capital by tethering their care, relations, and socialization of children, as well as their wishes, fears, and understandings of themselves as mothers to the rule of value. I purposefully foreground mothering rather than the mother to signal its analytic and political importance in this project. This book is of course about mothers—real life, flesh-and-blood women—yet its focus is *mothering* as a verb (per Knott's titular phrase), specifically the work assigned and associated with this role.[10] Mothering is disaggregated from any essentialized grounding in birthing or biology, whether of sex or race, a stance that needs to be made explicit in both the historical association of ideal motherhood with whiteness and the current transphobia in which motherhood is used to uphold "cisness," the "sanctity of sex as an ordained social order," or what Emma Heaney aptly refers to as "feminism's counterrevolution."[11] As such, a feminist politics delinks mothering from the "female" while recognizing how the work and responsibility of mothers is tethered to the feminine, a gendering that is inherently political in terms of how the work and the people doing it are devalued and subordinated to the rule of patriarchal racial capitalism. With these provisos, I use *women* throughout the text when referring to mothers, people who carry the burden of "primary responsibility" of a child.

Yet this book is just as much about capital as it is about mothering—sharp new insights into each emerging through the other. More so, I propose that focusing on capital's subsumption of mothering in everyday life helps grasp the most intractable problems in neoliberal society. Neoliberalism is distinguished by capital's intensified hold on subjectivity, deepening forms of class, gender, and race domination, and a pervasive but largely concealed upending of motherhood and childhood as they are imagined and lived. We come to better appreciate the contemporary crisis of childcare by reckoning with mothering as labor for capital, just as we arrive at a more incisive critique of neoliberal capitalism by recognizing motherhood and childhood as absolutely critical, central, and truly foundational for capital's drive to subsume human subjectivity.

Marxist theory has long articulated that the stakes of abolishing capitalism are emancipation from capital's domination of the human subject and its "organized suppression of individual vitality, freedom, and independence."[12] In its drive for value, capital does not simply seek raw, brute strength embodied in labor, but the thinking, feeling, creative, active human subject. The human subject is both the source of new value and where capital finds its "natural limits" in the "willfullness of people," and so is "animated by the drive to reduce the resistance offered by human beings."[13] For Marx and Marxist theory, what is unprecedented in capitalist society is both the magnitude of capital's power and its peculiar combination of force that includes violence, ideology, and the unique, impersonal way that capital dominates subjects—"in the ordinary run of things the worker can be left to the 'natural laws of production'" where the "silent compulsion of economic relations sets the seal on the domination of the capitalist over the worker."[14] In this conception, subjects must act in ways that accord with capital's inexorable thrust to accumulate value, willingly or unwillingly, knowingly or unknowingly, whether it is in their favor to do so or decidedly not in their favor.

Marx had an insightful term for how the drive of capital coerces subjects to act in ways that personify their categorical role in capital's inexorable thrust to accumulate value—"economic actor masks" or character masks (*Charaktermasken*).[15] Said differently, the abstract power of capitalist society constructs subjects who are compelled to reproduce a system that maims and depletes them as subjects.[16] To survive in capitalism means to exist as a "value-thing with a value-body represented in value-expression . . . or not at all."[17] While Marx recognized capital's devastating effects on the subject in its "tendency to reduce individuals to bearers of value-forms," his analysis crucially recognized that capital finds its limits in the human subject.[18] Critical theory similarly recognizes that human beings "can never solely be bearers of [economic] functions."[19] The subject can never be swallowed whole, even its suffering is evidence of refusal. Subjection acts upon, imposes itself, attempts to subordinate the unruly subject. The autonomous subject is the primary grounding of any materialist analysis or emancipatory theory. As De Genova insists, grasping that which precedes and exceeds capitalist dynamics, the "genuinely ontological, transhistorical," in this case, the "sheer productive power and creative capacity of human life, the pure potentiality of its vital forces," allows a critique that is more penetrating to its object.[20] That is, it allows a ruthless critique of everything existing but does not limit the universe of imagination to that which is before us. An autonomous view of the subject prompts questions such as, What vital human trait, relation, or process does capitalism latch on to? And how does capital transform or rather deform and pervert human realization as such? Subjection is secondary; there is always a literal rub—the human subject chafes, bristles, suffers, resists, and refuses capital's yoke. These processes constitute one of the primary axes of the subject's formation within capitalism. Simply put, "the subject is a battlefield."[21]

After critical theory, any serious critic of neoliberalism has had to contend with subjectivity, the sense that the drive of capital more deeply penetrates the human subject—how humans seem to more willingly acquiesce to its demands for the subject—to behave as, feel, relate to others as value-seeking-valorization. Yet the processes by which capital penetrates the subject's formation are largely opaque, foreclosing an adequate analysis of the extent and specificity of capital's intensified domination of the subject, its deeper penetration into the human psyche and the simultaneous invisibilizing of this yoke in neoliberalism. These processes remain elusive because their crucial foundations transpire in motherhood and childhood, domains that are largely thought to be outside of "politics" proper by traditional and critical theory alike. Figuring social reproduction as the site of capital's most destructive methods of accumulation, I stake my central claim in this book: "Capital's tightening chokehold on the human subject is partly effected through the intricate takeover of the most intimate relation in social life (mother-child), the most important labors of social life (subject-making), and the most sensitive time period in human development and for the formation of subjectivity (childhood)."[22]

Under the guise of increasing the odds of a child's "success" in a precarious future or how to be a "good" and well-informed parent, capital orients mothers to shape children's cognitive, social, emotional, and psychological traits in specific and measurable ways that ultimately serve capital—rendering children as bearers of value. Capital's penetration into the most important social relation for the reproduction of human subjectivity has repercussions beyond mothers and children. Capital subsumes mothering and the mother-child relation in order to dominate us all. The terrain of subjectivity in capitalism is always a battleground, the problem today is that capital has new weapons and new targets.[23] Yet in spite of and because of capital's deepening grip on mothers, women's ambivalence, doubts, and desires to care for children in ways other than this newfangled role of mothering for capital also intensify, though in ways that do not announce themselves as such. This book tracks this terrain of struggle—life against capital.

Mothering for Capital is a theoretically robust and ethnographically rich account of how the drive takes over the elementary dynamics and relations of social reproduction and its concrete effects on subjectivity. It addresses neoliberalism's intractable political crises through a child value theory of maternal labor. Building upon a long legacy of Marxist feminist scholarship, I am interested in advancing a theory of social reproductive labors, specifically the labors of mothering, and how the premier product of that labor (namely the child) comes to be socially constructed as a repository—indeed, an embodiment—of value that can potentially generate greater value—with maternal intervention. By tethering mother's care to a child's value, I trace how capital intensifies its hold on subjectivity and extends and legitimates deepening forms of class, gender, and race oppression. There are two distinct yet entangled components of my interpretation of the child's relation to value and valorization (each with substantive nuances that are elaborated throughout the book) that map on to the political crises of neoliberalism. In the first sense, I identify the rising compulsions for mothers to intricately shape children as future bearers of labor power, which Cleaver emphasizes is not simply the "ability to work for capital" but also the "willingness" to do so.[24] That is to say, Cleaver emphasizes volition (which we may understand as particular relational, emotional, and psychological dispositions to management and domination) and ability (particular cognitive skills, abilities, and capacities) to labor for capital. In the second sense, I identify the binding of maternal labors to more than a nebulous sense of a child's future "success," but also to the child's precise monetary value in the future and in the present. Indeed, the obscene valuation of the child, once tucked away in economists' publications, is now an open secret. Each new skill and disposition that children must master by the age of five, ten, fifteen, is abstracted, normed, measured, and priced. For instance, in all the front-page hand-wringing over the trillions of dollars in future income purportedly lost to children due to school closures during the COVID-19 pandemic ("learning loss"), few seemed to notice how children's present day reading or math skills have come to be tightly bound to a precise market value. The child's future value hovers over the child's present as never before. This value is produced first and foremost we are told, by mothers. As mothers are relentlessly goaded to labor to increase their child's value, the value of their own embodied labors—which crucially includes that of their flesh, health, and experiences—are transmitted to and embodied by the child.

Hierarchies of race, gender, and class always subtend social reproduction in capitalism. In neoliberalism these hierarchies are consolidated and redoubled through the real subsumption of maternal labors—rebranded as the middle class project. Race is rebiologized and the value of flesh is reinscribed through a specific form of gendered oppression that is presented as upward class mobility and legitimized by its appearance as objective differences of individual abilities or talents, now reframed as "human capital" value. Thus, the middle class project is not only about ambition, aspiration, and achievement; it is intrinsically a project of capitalist social reproduction. In its specifically neoliberal form, furthermore, the middle class project is achieved by deliberately targeting mothers to constantly and ever more intensively orient their child's development in ways that are favorable and legible to capital—both in ensuring the commensurability of the child's capacities and dispositions as value and by submitting to and reproducing capital's domination of human subjectivity.

Mothering for Capital accounts for how capital manages to extend, intensify, and transform mothers' work of caring for children into labor for capital—labor whose form and content are dictated by capital's thrust to expropriate the creative capacities of the unruly subject and route them toward value. And there is arguably no more unruly subject than the child. While children are too slippery, too unruly, too irreverent for capture by such abstract and impersonal forces, mothers, trammeled by the responsibility of increasing the odds their child might "succeed" and, even more so, by the fear that they won't, are uniquely vulnerable. And children, however unruly and irreverent, are still vulnerable to their mothers' recognition and approval. And so capital's drive extends to children—the ultimate targets—through the emotional chains of motherly subjection.

Subjection, aimed at the psyche, taps into primal needs and desires for love and security, targeting the deepest vulnerabilities and fears. Mothers are the perfect hostages of subjection to capital. To mother within capitalism is to enter one of the most profoundly fraught emotional relations—given prime responsibility for another vulnerable life about which one feels so compassionately and tasked to ready children to make their way in a damaged world. It is important to emphasize that I make no claim here about any primordial feminized love but rather the emotional attachments that arise within anyone who carries the responsibility of caring for a largely helpless child. Capital enters through this vulnerability. Maternal love and care are filtered through the prism of value, and children are subordinated to capital through the maternal bond. Critical theory has long recognized the family as the forging ground of "primary politicization," where our "disposition to domination" is formed.[25] The family is not a dress rehearsal for politics; it is social relations where domination is exercised and reproduced. And this is what is so novel and dangerous about what appears as "intensive parenting": it radically alters the relationship of mother to child.

By infiltrating the primary bond between mother and child, capital is free to experiment with the developing child's subjectivity. Rather than attend to nurturing any of the nearly infinite qualities of their child that might help them flourish as autonomous, convivial beings, mothers are tasked with instituting children as subjects that embody all the right skills and dispositions to succeed in the future. It is no accident that the qualities mothers are tasked to cultivate in children—grit, focus, and resilience, for example—are also those that *Harvard Business Review* espouses in Emotional Intelligence, its newest book series for business managers.[26] These are all traits that economists have marked as valuable and easily abstracted, and indeed, they have now begun to be measured in schools. To reiterate, the problem here is not simply that mothers are incessantly goaded to invest in children's abilities (and they are, incessantly), but rather that mothers are tasked with cultivating qualities that are valuable to capital as laborers, what in neoliberalism is ideally a subject that is "simultaneously self-directed and manageable."[27] The other side of the coin is just as crucial if we are thinking in emancipatory ways, conversations with which this book is centrally occupied. That is, critical theory must contend with those virtually limitless human qualities and capacities that might help children and adults flourish as autonomous beings—those very qualities that in contemporary mothering are inhibited or left to lie fallow. In neoliberalism, the child becomes the site of capital's most audacious aspirations—to tame, flatten, and empty human life of all that is superfluous or dangerous to capital's drive for valorization—and to create a subject in its image, a human form of capital.

By studying capital's drive as it hijacks mothers' love, work, and care for children in neoliberalism, I have come to understand capital and its aspirations differently and stake one of the central claims of this book. Thus far, Marxist theory has understood capital's drive as seeking value, a drive that requires yet is utterly indifferent to life. I aver that capital's force on the human subject can't best be explained in terms of wresting more value from human life alone. Capital does not only behave "rationally." By studying capital as it subsumes the near-infinite reservoir of the developing human subject, I argue that the drive of capital seeks life for itself. If each thing, living and nonliving, "as far as it can by its own power, strives to persevere in its being," then capital's primary goal is not value but life, and always more of it and from it.[28] Capital aspires to continue its undead reign not by sheer coercion or compulsion, however invisible, but through subjects' own volition. It wants human subjects to see themselves and others on its terms, to be "good" subjects for capital, to renounce, sacrifice, and devote themselves to capital, to view its rule as a godlike, suprahuman order that represents the one and true human community, where serving is a moral and ethical good, pleasureful even. Capital's drive pushes forth to take over the unruly human psyche, its passions, secret wishes and fears, its dreams and nightmares of wake and sleep. Dominating the human subject is the means to this end. The drive's ultimate aspiration, I conclude from my study of mothering, is to create humans *for* capital. This is a heterodox analysis that foregrounds the autonomous human being—our collective struggles and aspirations to be free, rather than capital's drive to accumulate surplus value. Surplus value is not my primary preoccupation. My primary concern is the effects of this drive for surplus value on the human subject, and those effects are devastating. But they are not totalizing. This push against capital's forces of subjection—what we might call life against capital—is the ultimate struggle within capitalism.

Understanding how capital's drive operates on subjects intensifies the resolve to refuse and abolish this undead force imposed on us and strengthens determination to make life in spite of it. If capital aspires to create humans for capital, then the task that faces us is to fortify subjects for this struggle, to help construct humans *against* capital. But first we must recognize the drive. And this is the difficult part, as capital is inextricably a part of us, our own subjectivities forged within and against it. Nonetheless, analysis means to unknot, and so subject and object must be disentangled. That involves facing the subject—real mothers and children, their activities, and the material condition under which they live and labor. Just as crucially, it involves asking how mothers experience these conditions. What can maternal guilt, anxiety, ambivalence, fear, and uncertainty tell us about how mothers perceive and resist capital's undead force? Before we confront the subject, we must turn to the object—capital, in the ideological form with which it disguises itself to mothers and others in neoliberal society. It is disguised in the irresistible form of the middle class project. This is a world in which one endlessly sacrifices one's life to capital, lives by carrying as much as its undead weight as one can support, or to die. The American dream has morphed into a waking nightmare, its transmutation hiding in the spectacle of motherhood. Motherhood and childhood are key fronts in struggles against capital, yet they are obscured by the middle class project, whose cunning is representing capital's reign of value as the only world possible—and representing capital's dream as our own.

From American Dream to Middle Class Project

The middle class project is the ideological appearance in which this radical restructuring of social life presents itself as the only chance to thrive in the crisis-ridden context of neoliberalism. The problem is not only that the ideal of motherhood better reflects middle class norms and lifeways and is thus oppressive to and unattainable for poor and working class mothers. It is also that women who appear to be relatively privileged are targets of neoliberal governance and subject to new kinds of labor demands that then ensnare poor and working class women in reconfigured relations of race and class domination. This form of gendered oppression and exploitation signals a novel disciplinary project. Mothers and children become vehicles by which capital more deeply dominates human subjects by refashioning subjectivities and a moral order. Through mothers, capital seeks to orient all aspects of children's lives to capital—to get kids to eat healthy for capital, to sleep for capital, to play for capital, to exercise for capital, to be happy for capital: in other words, to *live* for capital, to become human for capital. In short, the stakes for virtually everyone are to be subordinated in new ways to the requirements of capital's reproduction.

The middle class project, the radical restructuring of social reproduction that routes maternal care toward shaping children as repositories of value, is a project whose reach is indisputably global. While there are of course different inflections of this parenting project across geography, I maintain that there are more similarities in maternal practices of women who identify as, aspire to, or are interpellated as middle class in the United States with any mother in Colombia, Germany, India, Lebanon, or Nigeria than between any of these women and poor mothers in their own locale. This is a global expression of the global fact of capitalism. Amid the cultural and historical variations, my focus throughout this book are the ethnographic particulars of interpellating mothers as investors in the US context.

Because the relations of the struggle unfold right before us yet remain disguised by the spectacle of mothering, *Mothering for Capital* defamiliarizes ubiquitous practices, discourse, and images that appear to be good for children, scientifically backed evidence and "expert" advice for producing their "success," arguing that they are instead ways that capital orients the development of subjectivity as value. We are surrounded by these maternal directives yet do not recognize their connections: from nutritional advice for pregnancy ("nine foods to boost your baby's brain development while pregnant") and reading and playing classical music to the fetus ("uterine environment rich in music and language"), toys for newborns labeled with their cognitive development benefits ("build new brain connections"), the real estate industry's targeting of parents-to-be with information about "good schools" defined by school rating companies and children's test scores, omnipresent exhortations about the benefits of reading to children and directives on how best to do so, advice on how to turn mealtimes into discussions of school learning, ads for apps to do "bedtime math" with children, workshops that teach parents breathing techniques to reduce children's stress, and school information backpacked to the home with the exact phrases to use when children stumble or fail to help develop their "grit" through adversity, "a growth mindset," and other "social and emotional" skills that experts tout as important for success, even all the moral panics associated with the lack of maternal labors and the gaps they ostensibly produce—the so-called achievement, parenting, and, most recently, mortality gaps.[29] Although these discourses and practices appear to be good for children, they represent ways through which the most important maternal labors—the shaping of human becoming—become subject to capital in unprecedented ways.

A mother's "time" (effacing maternal *labors* as such) produces the child's value. This is what that dangerous pairing of economics and the "psy" disciplines have normalized, albeit in colloquial fashion. Through this coupling, capital seizes those precious human processes (banally referred to as socialization) and tethers them to value. I demonstrate how economists marshal the enormous advances in the science of the subject (not only various branches of psychology but also increasingly neuroscience and epigenetics), and task the recognized child experts with identifying, abstracting, and measuring the cognitive, social, psychological, and emotional traits they deem valuable. Drawing on the psy disciplines' claims that young children's brains are more developmentally "plastic," economists argue that investments into ever younger stages of childhood yield the largest returns, so they shape fiscal policy to reflect that. The psy disciplines identify "early life," even the "time spent in utero," as a "critical" or "sensitive period" for human capital growth.[30] The anxious temporality that critics of contemporary motherhood have identified is the ticking time bomb of capital's investment in children's "neuroplasticity." The child is certainly the target of these interventions, but they are effected through the mother. The recent history of motherhood and childhood—from the rise of "intensive mothering" to the obsession with children's (cognitive and now "social-emotional") development—evolves in almost lock-step fashion with the notion of childhood as the biological stage and substrate from which to obtain the biggest return for investment. The obsession with mothers maximizing children's cognitive development is itself a consequence of how "intelligence" has become the "new sorting mechanism" of the postindustrial information economy.[31] Contrary to contemporary critics of motherhood and childhood, then, I argue that the problems and changes they diagnose represent capital's seizure of social reproduction. Every moment of a child's life is a potential point for a mother to intervene, invest, and "develop" specific abilities. That is, the most opportune time to transform life into labor for capital and, ultimately, to make humans for capital.

The middle class project is one of the key ideological threads that holds neoliberal capitalist society together and represents perhaps its last chance at capturing people within its ideology—that a good life is at all possible within its terrible miseries. Worse yet, that this miserable option *is* the good life. This is capital's dream—to be the only possible world that exists, to endlessly orient life to it, to replace human aspirations with its own.

Capital's takeover of the most precious and complex processes of social life—the way humans become human, an almost silent coup in which mothers seem to voluntarily participate, could be achieved only in the political economic context in which the hallowed American dream has already collapsed—in a word, neoliberalism. One of neoliberalism's hallmarks is the reconfigured relations of capital and labor, wherein despite or because of multiple crises, capital's hegemony is reinvigorated through intensified forms of class, race, and gendered domination and exploitation. Many of neoliberalism's political economic shifts directly affect the lived experience of that large swath of people in the United States who understand themselves or identify as "middle class." This includes the precarization of the middle class, the widening gulf of wealth between the bottom 90 percent and the top 10 percent, the rendering of ever-larger numbers of the population as waste or surplus, the "return" of inheritance, the redoubling of racialized forms of exploitation and subjugation, and the multiplication of crisis after crisis, from climate to housing to care. As capital's extraction of surplus value increases, wages stagnate or decline while the so-called cost of living and debt increase. By the fifth decade of neoliberal hegemony, scholars, politicians, and pundits from both left and right generally acknowledge that the US middle class is in danger, shrinking, disappearing, or sinking. Colloquially, virtually everyone understands that it is harder to "make it" and that even the middle class is "struggling." Even worse for the collective psyche of a nation accustomed, if not addicted, to continual growth is that for the first time, parents cannot expect their children to be in a better or even same position than themselves, even if they have and do all "the right stuff." Perhaps most tragic of all for the American psyche are the forecasts of downward mobility. In a nation perpetually and increasingly riven by conflict, political divide, uprisings, the stripping of rights, revanchist politics, rising fascism, rampant police killing of innocent Black and Brown people, and waning influence on the global stage, the "promise" of middle class prosperity to all that work (and study) hard has served as the most powerful absolution of all national sins. What, then, when the middle class is "disappearing?"

The processes that this book documents—capital's subsumption of maternal labors and its takeover of the production of subjectivity—supply one kind of answer to this vexing question. Neoliberalism's crises are partly buried in motherhood—that is, it appears that the aforementioned problems have been partly created by and can be solved by the work of mothers. Within these multiple crises, capital is unleashed to experiment with new forms of subjugation in motherhood. The middle class project's radical transformation of domestic life and politics itself could only cohere when considering the emotionally laden status of the middle class in the United States.

Who or what is the middle class? Does the middle class even exist? The considerable debates surrounding these questions, while interesting, do not directly inform my analysis. First and foremost, I consider the middle class an imaginary, an open signifier that hails a large chunk of the populace through its ideological work. It is in this sense that I use terms such as the "middle class project" or "figure of the middle class mother." As David Roediger argues in *The Sinking Middle Class*, the discourse of the middle class has come to define politics in a nation notoriously mute and hostile to the language of class, where the category becomes a bipartisan lodestar, repository of national and personal virtue, and where those who are in it must be protected from "sinking" at all costs.[32] It is no accident that people in the US overidentify as middle class, and even those with the most conventionally working class jobs understand themselves as such. The discourse of the middle class is a way "to NOT talk about class," a method to encourage people to understand themselves through an "individualized consumption oriented vision of social life."[33] However, the category is not only an ideological project. I also use the term "middle class" as an emic or real category to refer to how people identify themselves and others as such, and I take seriously subjects' claims of middle-classness as reflecting the lived experience of their material conditions and its contradictory location.[34] Both senses situate the middle class at the center of this book's puzzle—how capital subsumes mothers' love, care, and work and orients them to shaping children as value. This puzzle cannot be "solved" in the realm of theory or at the level of discourse, for the "middle class mother" is more than an ideological figure. The "middle class mother" is a powerful and capacious symbol that conscripts real women who are struggling to give their child a shot at this elusive, disappearing, and largely fictitious middle class comfort and security. And despite the scholarly focus, if not obsession, with the white middle class professional mother, the middle class project targets a much wider swath of mothers, regardless of the actual class, racialized, and other differences among them. Indeed, the middle class project is the disguise, the spectacle, the branding that captures these women.

The View from Everyday Life: Materialism and the Ethnographic Encounter

A materialist analysis is grounded in concrete experience—how ordinary people bear the weight of their subjection, how they navigate its confines, how they feel and understand it, how they resist in everyday life. Likewise, this account of capital's subsumption of reproduction is grounded in how actual women experience, understand, and feel the force of capital on their mothering and how they resist and escape its ordering of their love, labors, and relation to their child. I explore what the struggle to subordinate women's reproductive labors looks like on the ground, how it feels to take on these labors, how women apprehend the forces in which they are embedded, and the unique emotional and psychic conundrums of mothering for capital. Finally, I ask how these labors, in the Marxist sense as "a definite form of expressing their life, a definite mode of life," transform who women are as mothers, women, and human subjects.[35]

Grounding this study of capital's subsumption of reproduction in women's experiences is not simply about method or a reflex of my disciplinary training in anthropology. All methods to understand reality may be flawed, but ethnography is perhaps best suited to capture social life's inherent open-endedness, a method closest to understanding the world in the spirit of Marx's oft-quoted assertion that people "make history but they do not make it as they please; they do not make it under self-selected circumstances, but under circumstances already given and transmitted from the past."[36] In other words, ethnography, Marx's quote, and the first premise of the materialist method ("real individuals their activity, and the material conditions under which they live") embody an ontological-political stance that befits radical scholarship—ordinary people make and remake the world, and they can make it differently.[37] This stance insists that capital's drive to master the human subject will always be thwarted. Leaving aside cynical claims about scholarship's limited potential to effect social change, any thinker committed to human emancipation, consciously or not, writes with the understanding that the world is made, unmade, and remade, not from "pure" action (a questionable category) but through subjects' understanding of the world and their place in it—how humans apprehend their world—"*sensuous human activity, practice* . . . subjectively."[38] It is a practice of discipline and a sober optimism that holds St. Siouan's advice dear: "Keep your mind in hell and despair not."[39]

Women and the conditions under which they mother are the book's center of gravity. By studying women's everyday experiences of struggle, I was able to approach some of the key puzzles of neoliberal mothering: How does capital coerce mothers to take on such extraordinary labors that harm them and children? How do mothers come to understand capital's impositions as good or in the best interest of children—or do they? Do they take on the labors imposed by capital willingly, enthusiastically, and without struggle? Do mothers criticize, resist, refuse, or try to escape these impositions on their time and energies? (How) do they find time to be with children in ways that are contrary to capital's demands? Why do Marxists concerned with domination, labor, and subjectivity ignore mothering? Why are even most Marxist feminists uninterested in analyzing the material and experiential contexts of mothering and how its labors have dramatically changed? Why are those who study the everyday of motherhood, even those cataloging its current crisis-ridden context, so unable to connect what they describe with the way capitalism pumps value from human life?

With these questions, however inchoate, I embarked on this ethnographic project with a diverse group of twenty women who lived around me, in a neighborhood in New York City's borough of Queens. Queens is famous for being "the world's borough"; it is purportedly one of the most diverse geographic areas on the planet. Each neighborhood in this world's borough is unique in its particular history, mix, and dynamics of diversity. In my focal area, the majority of incoming residents move so that their children can access the area's "good schools." Like me, they were trying to be "good moms" amid a set of impossible demands and in the material and ideological context of New York City's educational scarcity. Yet these women are nothing like the caricatures of the helicopter or snowplow mothers in public culture, nor like the white, upper middle class professional women in most scholarly representations of intensive mothering. First, these women are middle class in the sense discussed here. They are neither rich nor poor, and a few might even be considered working class by sociological accounting. All but one or two of the women were first-generation middle class—born to parents with conventionally working class jobs and had working class childhoods. My participants were traveling the path of upward mobility into what is more or less understood to be that capacious category "middle class." They were either in the process of becoming or were already newly middle class. In the terms of this project, these women were engaged in the middle class project and its prime targets. They were taking on specific labors so that their children could have better chances of "success" (middle class futures) and felt that, as mothers, they could do more for their children (in terms of labor) than their mothers could do for them.[40]

To reveal the middle class project as the branding for a much broader restructuring of social reproduction than one seemingly limited to white professional women, I purposefully selected women to capture a wider array of perspectives than most scholarly portraits of "intensive mothering." Of my twenty interviewees, six are East Asian, two are Black, six are Brown, and six are white. Eight women had migrated to the US as adults (China, Croatia, Egypt, Israel, Mexico, Trinidad), nine women were born in the US or mostly raised here from parents who came to the US (from Albania, China, Greece, Guyana, Haiti, Italy, Japan, and Turkey), and three were second-generation or more and born in the US (two are white European and one is Afro-Caribbean). Although only two of my twenty participants had a parent (father) with a college education, 80 percent of the women had a bachelor's degree, and one had a postsecondary degree (law). Education had been their route to middle-classness, and so this was the only familiar route they knew to emphasize (rather than say, bequeathing money). At the time I interviewed them, five of the women were long-term stay-at-home mothers, two had recently quit their full-time jobs (one moving to a part-time job), one was on long-term medical leave, one had been recently laid off from her full-time job in finance, and the rest of the women were employed either full- or part-time. These positions were more in flux than static. Those currently employed included teacher, cashier, licensed practical nurse, retail sales, tarot reader, administrative assistant, former lawyer now restaurant co-owner. A methodology section provides more details on the ethnographic encounter (see the appendix).

These ordinary women's experiences ground this project. These women were neither activists nor organizers, nor were they political or politicized in any conventional sense of the term. Yet by carefully attending to their experiences, listening to their desires, doubts, inchoate fears, and hopes for their children, it became apparent that struggles against capital are animated even among beleaguered moms who may have never used the term "capitalism" in their lives. Their narratives were ones of struggles against an abstract force that they could not quite perceive nor articulate. Yet ambivalence, anger, guilt, uncertainty, confusion, anxiety, and existential doubt spill from their narratives. In our conversations, women unburdened themselves, however fleetingly, of the psychic weight of their struggles. In the unleashing of emotions, between the said and unsaid within their narratives, I also found desires—conscious or semiconscious—for other, more emancipatory ways to be a mother, impulses that are disavowed, repudiated, or steamrolled by being positioned as the "most decisive factor" in children's success. Locating desires for other ways to care for children, alternative forms of being and relating that preexist, escape, or are in opposition to capital's trampling disciplinary force poses a tricky analytical challenge. If the new labors prescribed for mothers are aimed to shape children for capital and are decidedly not for children's own good—as this book argues—then how are mothers convinced to take on these labors and the goal to which they are oriented: "success"? How did this relatively novel end come to be the primary goal of social reproduction, verily behind mothers' backs?

Making It, with the Right Mother

The declining material conditions of those who identify as "in the middle," "not poor and not rich," enables capital to successfully encroach on its most captive subjects—those tasked with ensuring children can find a way in its ruins. In other words, the emergence of the middle class project of orienting life to capital is precisely how the mother becomes a key figure of neoliberal capitalism and why it is so pressing to understand its transformations from her vantage point. Not only does it capture the desires and identifications of a large swath of women; the middle class project—as the only seeming possibility for one's child to obtain a decent life—can hijack the hopes and, more poignantly, the fears of those whose children must live amid its increasingly elusive futures. While the middle class mother and her successful child are at the center of the project as its aspirational positions, it can exist only because their negations—the poor mother and her surplus child—forever lurk nearby.

While the poor mother has receded in public culture as the principal spectacle of mothering and is not the primary subject of this book, she is ever-present as the specter in and edifice on which the middle class project is built. The project coheres only through the nightmare scenario of its negation. The scenario of a child becoming part of the future surplus population—delinquent, criminal, unemployment check collector—has in some sense long existed as a possibility for mothers who "don't care" or don't perform the requisite labors. However, the nightmare now menacingly hovers over what might have previously been understood to be good mothering. The nightmare is no mere phantasm of hysterical mothers. It signals the accepted knowledge of any mother who understands herself as "not rich and not poor"—that the baseline labors of a "good" or even "good enough" mother that can guarantee her child enters the middle class have shifted considerably. Maternal labors previously recognized for decades as "caring" about children's schooling (e.g., ensuring attendance, checking homework, showing up for conferences) are now considered the bare minimum. To perform only those labors paves the way for one's child to become the default worker of the neoliberal economy—threading together the low-wage jobs at Walmart, the Amazon factory, securing or delivering their goods for low wages, with few or no benefits, and little or no job security. The middle class project coheres in a context in which "working class" jobs have degraded, and the carceral system and the surplus population warehoused there massively expanded in tandem with it. Mothering is the only solution on offer, and mothers are coerced at every turn to take up intensified labors for child success. Instead of reckoning with this fact as a society—that this is verily the "promise" on offer for going to school and working hard, a reckoning that would gravely threaten the social order—the matter is instead made to appear as if it depends on "correct" mothering and the right mother.

Mothers and the Counterrevolution of Everyday Life

Mothering for Capital unravels how mothers are coerced to take on extended, intensified, and alienating labors through the manufacturing of a new "common sense" where a child's "making it" through neoliberalism's degraded political economic context can be ensured by having the right mother. We find a perfect crystallization of the middle class project in the Brookings Institution's Social Genome Project, a research and policy hub that models "factors that impede or promote success" and mobility—or, how one becomes middle class.[41] Brookings's authority cannot be understated. It is one of the most prestigious and influential think tanks on the global stage; its board of directors and staff are poised at elite levels of federal government and business.[42] The Social Genome Project represents the closest approximation of what capital and state would say if they were speaking directly to mothers and speaking to the public about mothers.

"Is the United States still an opportunity society? Can people achieve the American dream?" Amid increased calls for political economic and social restructuring on a revolutionary scale, even the centrist Brookings acknowledges that the American dream is "often just that—a dream." Elsewhere, they decry that the "contract" of the American dream—prosperity to those "willing to work and contribute"—is "collapsing."[43] Brookings's ersatz criticality legitimizes it to offer what looks like a solution: "How can we help more people reach the middle class?" The changes proposed appear to tinker with or reiterate the conventional "work hard and succeed" formula.

Looking carefully at the institution's formula for achieving mobility and success, it becomes apparent that its solution entails a radical—one might even say counterrevolutionary—project for restructuring social reproduction and everyday life. Yet because the Brookings directives are issued to mothers and children, they do not even register as political, much less as a shift in the nature and structure of power in capitalist social relations.

If the think tank can be thought of as a node of power that brings together the key ideological apparatuses within contemporary capitalist societies—knowledge, education, media, the state—to produce and disseminate its "information" as a "set of imperatives" in the Deleuzian sense, then Brookings does more than produce "nonpartisan research to improve policy," as it describes itself.[44] Its research reflects and inscribes the truths of the social order, sites where "common sense" and consent are manufactured. Their efforts in the Social Genome emblematize the transformations that this book tracks—capital and the state's enormous efforts to train, extract, and regulate a new set of maternal labors oriented to the value of children as the new normal of social reproduction. It behooves us to pay attention to Brookings's directives.

Brookings's edicts for securing middle-classness emerge from its so-called Social Genome Model, developed from "complex research on learning and earning behaviors" that it translates into "policy-relevant results." Its life cycle simulation predicts who will be middle class on the basis of the identification of five decisive benchmarks. The troubling confluence of the social and genetic in the moniker is manifest in the emphasis on birth. Birth is couched in terms of "family formation," and decisive circumstances for future success are being "born at normal birth weight to a non-poor married mother with at least a high school diploma," elsewhere described as being born to "adults who are ready to be parents," or a "non-poor, two-parent family." After birth, the model tracks a path of diminishing returns; the possibility of success and mobility recede with each successive stage. The next key stages are at age five, when a child must be "ready for school"; at age eleven, when a child should have mastered core academic and social skills; at age eighteen, when the child graduates from high school with decent grades and has avoided risky behaviors; and finally, at age thirty, by "obtaining a postsecondary degree or the equivalent income."[45]

The Social Genome is more than a formula for individual mothers; it is the transformation of the American dream into capital's dream—mothers devoted to fashioning children's life in terms of its exchange value as human capital. This middle class project is borne by the child, and doubly so by the mother. After all, it's not the child who is responsible for its own birth weight or its mother's marital status or level of education! And who expects children to "ready" themselves at age five? Who is responsible for ensuring a child has mastered academic and social skills at eleven? Who is to blame when a teen engages in risky behavior? Every discourse of the child is a proxy for a social mandate for mothers.

The most radical changes within neoliberalism have been decades in the making, yet they do not register as such because they transpire in and through mothers' and children's lives. The mother is hidden in plain sight in the restructuring of the political and libidinal economy of neoliberalism. Hidden are the transformations of maternal labors, a decades-long sequence of complex, exhaustive, and exhausting labors that begin when a child is born, or even before. Maternal labors are hidden in plain sight by scholarly and popular discourses of "intensive parenting" and "helicopter moms," which at once disguise and trivialize these labors *as* labor and euphemize the depth and breadth of the changes in motherhood and childhood. Worse yet, scholarship and popular culture obscure how these labors are made necessary and coerced by a host of state institutions, knowledge industries, and what Marx called the "silent compulsion of economic relations" of postindustrial capitalism.[46] Hidden deeper still is the renewed emphasis on genetics and a racialized value of life through which the afterlives of slavery persist in the present. Brookings represents an attempt to normalize the return of genetics wherein success requires a child to be born to a particular kind of mother, not only one who has made certain "choices," but one whose racialized embodied value includes her physical and mental health, which have made her "fit" to do the job. Most hidden is how mothers become captive to capital, so that we can all become captive subjects.

Disentangling Appearances from Reality: Framing the Restructuring of Reproduction

Mothering for Capital exposes the terrain of struggle within social reproduction, one that is alive, active, dynamic yet hidden. Disentangling what mothers authentically want for themselves and their children from capital's prescriptions is verily the most difficult analytic task I faced writing this book and the most challenging task for the reader. We cannot simply "look" at mothers and see capital encroaching on their practices and understandings of "good mothering." These processes are enshrouded in dissimulation. First of all, capital's prescriptions have become completely normalized and incorporated as parenting "best practices." Even more challenging is that we are all continually formed as subjects by capital's absurd regime of value, seeing ourselves and others through the economic character masks that we are compelled to don—we should all be "productive" and "successful" people! And so, the first half of the book does not focus on mothering but builds a conceptual framework to frame mothers' experiences in terms of how capital operates in the reproductive sphere. This task requires grounding in Marx's critique of capital: in its drive, laws of motion, mechanisms of rule, and methods of operation in the productive sphere. However, this project is not bound by orthodox Marxist frames limited to what Marx "really" meant or a faithful adherence to his categories. To paraphrase Fanon's oft-cited quote, Marxist analyses should always be slightly stretched when it comes to addressing the woman problem.[47] My work sees Marxism as an "open and experimental form of theory and practice" that is constantly transforming itself in response to shifting relations in various geographical and historical contexts.[48]

I incorporate traditions that go beyond where Marx could have conceivably gone—Marxist feminism's concerns with women's subordination in the reproductive sphere; Black feminist insights on how motherhood is critical to the creation of value and a site of deepening racial subjugation; critical theory's concerns with the domination of subjectivity; psychoanalytic theory's articulations of the subject and the complexity of the young human's emotional and mental life; and finally, critical childhood studies conceptualizations of children as subjects that shape their own and others' trajectories, but far from "just as they please," as per Marx's famous dictum about the way humans intervene in the world. Together, these traditions enable us to "see" capital's varied arsenal of power, including its "silent" modes of economic compulsion, to defamiliarize its abstractions, revert its inversions, and reveal the social relations of struggle through which capital tethers maternal labors of subject making to children's value.

As the elementary dynamics of social reproduction become subject to capital's forces of abstraction, compulsion, and homogenization in unprecedented ways, these methods appear as good parenting or as ultimately good for children's future success. The first crucial step in analyzing neoliberalism's battleground of social reproduction begins with defamiliarizing human capital theory. This warped abstraction of individual abilities and ingenuity and its expression as a monetary value emerged in the mid-twentieth century and is now ubiquitous in business, politics, and childhood. Theorizing human capital theory as a machine, in Marx's sense as a technological innovation that insidiously transforms the work and worker on whom they are meant to "improve," enables analysis of how the hegemony of mothering for capital is manufactured in public culture. I model this process as a series of concentric circles where each circle directs the activities of the next consecutive circle within its sphere of influence, with mothers and then children at the center as the ultimate objects of intervention.

Economists represent capital and are at the outer edge of this model, directing the two vast power-knowledge networks that reorganize social reproduction—the economic-psychological complex and the neoliberal education complex. The "econo-psy complex" is my term for a conjunction of economics with various fields of the "psy" sciences—developmental, behavioral, and cognitive psychology and neuroscience. Together they define for the public what is best for children and parents (i.e., mothers) in terms of what is best for capital. The term extends the more familiar "psy complex" on how psychological theories function as forms of power and normalization within state apparatuses and modes of administering various fields of everyday life. I add and purposefully foreground "economics" to signal how it guides the development of the psy complex and its reach throughout the social body.[49] While the econo-psy complex establishes its hegemony in public culture, it also has a direct bridge to mothers through the other complex it directs, the neoliberal education complex, of which schools are the central element.[50]

Schools are key to the regulation of maternal labors, continuously deployed to intricately discipline mothers. It is true that some of the facets I identify as mothering for capital have been markers of middle class domestic life and have been pushed on to poor mothers since at least the 1980s (e.g., encouraging reading to children). Yet there are many distinctive aspects of these labors in the past two decades or so that are entangled with schools as the site of formal subjection to the restructuring of mothering. First, maternal labors are directly coerced and legitimated not by random parenting experts but by a state apparatus with which nearly all mothers have direct contact. The state via schools extends, intensifies, and intricately regulates mothers' labors through both the "silent compulsion" of the market that children will formally enter and the ideological architecture of the middle class project. Historically, the state regulates poor mothers through punitive and repressive tactics. These methods are inherently backed by violence or its threat. And the state can and does take children from poor mothers, and especially poor Black mothers, with obscene regularity.[51] By contrast, mothers in the middle are regulated by bribes, inducements, encouragements, and persuasion of what is "best" for children—forms of subjection that do not appear as such.[52] Within schools, mothers are compelled to expand and intensify their labors to include a new set of labors geared toward fine-tuning children's subjectivities. There, they are explicitly taught which cognitive, social, psychological, and emotional qualities are valuable to capital and how to develop these capacities in children.

These labors are well defined and professionalized, and they entail inordinate time and work to learn let alone perform, to say nothing of the conflict with children they engender. Perhaps most unparalleled is how schools have become sites where children (and by proxy maternal labors) are subject to continual abstraction and measurement; their progress normed and tracked. Together, these elements represent a radical reorganization of social reproduction, a project that aims to flatten subjectivity into a form measurable as value in order to dominate the human subject. These are capital's aspirations. But this is not, of course, what capital gets. This is a terrain of struggle that a robust materialist framework makes visible. There are many dimensions to this struggle, and this book tracks them in its series of chapters.

The Structure of the Argument: Outline of the Chapters

Chapter 1, "Premises of a Materialist Analysis of Mothering" provides an alternative starting point to counter the vast scholarship on mothering. This chapter poses a response to what we might call uncritical theory, which cannot account for capital's restless and destructive drive in reproduction, its difference making, and its profound effects on subjects. I outline the driving assumptions of this work by proposing eight premises of a materialist analysis of mothering. Developed with insights from multiple traditions, including Marxism, Marxist feminism, Black studies, Black feminism, childhood studies, critical theory, and psychoanalysis, this framework is designed to enable analysis of moving struggles against capital as they play out within mothering. In this complex terrain, I center the production of subjectivity as a starting point for an open-ended analysis of mothering aimed at emancipation.

Chapter 2, "The Human Capital Theory Machine," considers neoliberalism's strange yet ubiquitous fetish, human capital, as capital's warped synonym for labor power. I demonstrate how this fetish reaches its most frenetic character around the child, for the child is where the "capacity for labor" exists in a unique form as pure potentiality. I introduce the neoliberal child in its double character as both priceless and differentially valued, where sentimental invocations of the child's pricelessness conceal the violent reality of the child's incessant valuation. I propose that human capital theory can be fruitfully understood as a machine—something made by humans that then confronts them as a mighty and alien power to which they must subordinate their activities. And like all machines within capitalism, human capital theory is a weapon of class, race, and gender domination. Built upon the constitutive violence of abstraction of the human in enslavement, this machine is profoundly racialized, and it operates to produce, compound, and deepen racialized valuations of the human, albeit in a seemingly meritocratic and legitimate register. What makes human capital theory unlike any other capitalist machine is that it is unleashed in reproduction. What happens when it is installed in the quotidian practices of mothering? The answer requires theoretical openness as no single tradition can adequately address it. Black studies on fungibility and the afterlives of slavery, Marxist theories of abstraction and subsumption, Wynter's notions of sociogenesis and racialized templates of value and non-value, and Foucault's insights into human capital theory and subjectivity in neoliberalism together illuminate how capital enlists mothers to develop capacities that can be abstracted as value and orients the child's becoming toward value. Instead of nurturing what is universally and particularly vital about each child, mothering becomes labor for capital, taken over by a machine to produce humans *for* capital.

Chapter 3, "Maternal Time, Child 'Value,'" is a critique of the political economy of motherhood, scrutinizing human capital economists' initial turn to motherhood in the 1970s through to its enduring focus on maternal time as their obfuscation for labor. I develop a child value theory of maternal labor to situate the changes in neoliberal motherhood within economists' singular focus on maternal time as the most important variable in increasing a child's human capital value. Countering a vast feminist literature on intensive mothering that emphasizes the "expert" control of mothers, I provide an alternate genealogy that discerns economists as the architects of the increase, intensification, and transformation within mothering for capital. Scrutinizing human capital theory from the perspective of its maternal science underlines the essentially racialized hierarchy of life at its center. This racializing logic is animated and proliferated throughout the social body in directives for social reproduction that are disguised as "best practices" for children and are understood to be racially neutral. Through a critique of maternal science, I substantiate my claim that the drive of capital seeks to dominate life for capital, an account that clarifies many seemingly disparate transformations in neoliberalism, in motherhood and childhood, in the realm of subjectivity, and in the shifting relations of class, gender, and race domination.

In Chapter 4, "Schooling Moms," I examine schools' offers to "support" mothers as so-called partner teachers in the form they have recently taken as literal "workshops" that teach mothers how to take on the labors of professional teachers, including conventional labors of instructing academic subjects and monitoring children's progress, as well as the recent addition of a set of affective and psychological labors to fine-tune children's subjective states. Despite their benign guise, these efforts represent unprecedented methods to extend and intensify a mother's working day, govern maternal labors of subject making, and reform the mother-child relationship into a managerial one. Reading schools' advice, suggestions, and workshops for parents as capital's wish list for childhood subjectivity, the family, and domestic life illuminates perhaps most clearly capital's aspirations for the "total subsumption of society."[53] Mothers are tasked with crafting capital's ideal subject, one that is perfectly modulated—psychologically, socially, and emotionally—to viewing life as endless work in order to increase one's value. The strategy of schooling mothers in this way radically alters the relationship of mother to child, positioning capital between them. The love and care that children receive are filtered through the prism of value. The family itself is thus reconfigured as a site of a permanent project of devotion to capital, with the home serving as shrine.

Chapter 5, "Emotional Chains of Motherly Subjection," explores how mothers take on capital's delegated labors of shaping manageable and self-managed child subjects and what the double subjection of mothers and children looks like on the ground. These look like deceptively benign scenes, such as a mother helping her child overcome her fear of taking a test, another calming her child through his anxiety about being left back, and several struggling to get children to focus on work and manage themselves. As the forces of economic compulsion hold women captive and orient their subject-making labors toward capital, we see women trying to find some wiggle room and the psychic and emotional tolls this exacts on them. As capital's discipline is naturalized and disguised through the vessel of mothers' care, the family becomes the site for the exercise and reproduction of distinct forms of neoliberal domination. I argue that the nature of subjection is transformed as capital disfigures the love within a child's prime relation and encroaches into the deepest recesses of the psyche. At every turn, I emphasize women's ambivalence. Their narratives contain glimpses of forms of being and relating with children that capital supplants, and we see most lucidly how children's unruly and insistent will to be free from the yokes of subjection is a source of continuous new energy in struggles against capital.

Chapter 6, "Spatial Labors," extends these themes by focusing on a complex set of maternal labors associated with accessing good schooling, understood as one of the most important labors to ensure children's success. I focus on a peculiar assemblage of institutions that compels these spatial labors and constructs the abstraction of "good schools." These processes are trapped in a circuit in which race as a material force with life and death consequences is exacerbated while at the same time obscured, critical aspects of contemporary forms of neoliberal race making. From the abstraction of children's value through testing, the construction of school quality based on children's test scores, and the valuation of property based on school quality—already-existing forms of racialized value are smuggled in, redoubled, invisibilized, and legitimized as a neutral and objective value. The emphasis in Chapters 5 and 6 is how capital and state, through the econo-psy and neoliberal education complexes, coerce the labors in question and route them to reproduce class, race, and gender domination, all while appearing to be women simply "choosing" to parent in ways that reproduce inequalities of class, race, and gender.

Chapter 7 explores how women manage the conflict between the compulsory ideals and their critiques and perceptions of alternatives, one I find apt to characterize as a perpetual "schizophrenic maternal state," the core psychic condition of neoliberal motherhood. I read psychoanalysts' and feminists' long-recognized state of maternal ambivalence through a materialist lens. As women practically accept the labors that capital and state prescribe, they also critically perceive the illusory nature of the abstractions and ideological fictions governing their lives. Within the rich interview material, one bears witness to women coming to terms with the weighty burdens of capital and how it depletes them and makes them mother inauthentically, as well as flashes of alternative and emancipatory desires, ones they have little time to ponder in the hustle of everyday mothering, and even less "choice" to enact. However partial these critiques may be, or however fleetingly they hold on to such insights, they are decisive points in my analysis.

The conclusion, "Mothering Against Capital," brings the flashes of insight from women's partial critiques, refusals, and alternative and emancipatory desires, however inchoate, into conversation with utopian strands in critical theory and elsewhere to suggest ways that all of us, not simply mothers, can be engaged in forms of caring, relating, and being with children and one another that might nourish ourselves to be subjects against capital.

Ultimately, *Mothering for Capital* seeks to uncover the concealed tragedies within mothering in neoliberalism. The tragedies are multifold. Women's already substantial obligatory work is increased and transformed into labor that further alienates women from their mothering, their children, their own selves, and others. The labors of neoliberal mothering inflict psychic pain on children, and women themselves endure almost continual psychic trauma that they must disavow to keep going. Most tragically, the work and desire to love, care, and nurture children become usurped and hijacked by capital, routed to perpetuate the very capitalist totality that maims them, children, and us all. Mothers (much more than children) become subjects of and to capital—their relations to children, their free time, their social lives, and their vitality dimmed and oriented to capital.

While outlining capital's destructive effects on mothers, children, and us all, this is ultimately an optimistic book because it is attuned to the activities and feelings that are against or outside of capital's reach. Although mothers may not precisely identify the source of what they struggle against, they perceive capital's force against their lives and that of their children. And in spite of, or because of, capital's deepening grip, women's desires to care for children in ways that diverge from this newfangled role of mothering for capital also intensify, although in ways that do not announce themselves as such. Most cogently, they understand that the stakes are life itself, one worthy of the name. And it is children that incessantly remind them, with anguished cries and ferocious wills so indomitable that even the force siphoned from the totality of our collective energies cannot stamp out. At its core, the book asks questions that it cannot answer: What, then, is for children's own good, and to what ends should love and work of care for children, ourselves, and others, be for?

1

Premises of a Materialist Analysis of Mothering

MOTHERS MAKE THE DIFFERENCE for children's future success. This is the resounding consensus in a vast social science literature on the family and class in neoliberalism. Where there is disagreement, it is in the moral valence of the proposition. Some consider the major role of mothers to be a good thing and offer advice on how to best enact or enhance it. Others are neutral and simply assert its facticity as they locate mediating mechanisms and mitigating factors. Still others denounce its importance as unfair and seek to reform mothers or institutions so that mothers' roles are less decisive. What sounds like a chorus is a cacophony of abstractions, distortions, and half-truths. This book is an extended argument with these positions. Rather than "mothers make the difference," I argue that "mothers are *made* to make the difference." There are vast ontological, epistemological, and political differences between the two positions that mirror the distinctions between traditional theory and critical theory.[1]

This chapter articulates the premises that guide a critical analysis where the ideals and imperatives of capital are the objects of critique. Mothers are *made* to make the difference signals a wide-angle lens that looks away from mothers to see mothering anew. This position locates the function of maternal "difference making" within the way mothers are entrapped in restructured circuits of class, race, and gender domination within reproduction. The focus on how "mothers make the difference" legitimizes social inequalities as if they are an inevitable by-product of maternal care and familial reproduction. That lens inevitably conceals the mechanisms of power in capitalist society and reproduces its abstractions and ideologies. Redirecting the lens to the particular combination of forces of power in capitalist society pierces the mystifications that entrap us in capitalism's permanent catastrophe and centers the social relations of struggle that are concealed by conventional understandings of motherhood. The standpoints of emancipation and an anticapitalist politics are inseparable from the conceptual framework of my work. I refer to this framework as materialist to gesture toward its grounding in both mothers' lives and in Marxist theory that stretches beyond its conventional limits to include Marxist feminism, Black studies, Black feminism, and critical theory. A materialist framework employs these perspectives to analyze mothers as "real individuals, their activity, and the material conditions under which they live, both those which they find already existing and those produced by their activity."[2] What makes this account "materialist" instead of simply "critical" is that the analysis is a critique of ideological illusions and abstractions, the empirical realities that get enshrouded in them, and how they come to shape mothers, their labors, struggles, and relations with their children and the world. As such, materialism is a stance that perceives capitalism as a mode of production that encompasses much more than the "economic," and most profoundly the social and the political. It is a lens that is specifically formulated to understand the unprecedented manner in which the requirements of capital's reproduction dominate social life, including and especially mothering. There are eight premises that guide this materialist analysis of mothering within capitalism.

PREMISE 1

In capitalism, value is the dominant force in society, a force that crucially depends on human life yet ravages life in its

insatiable drive to accumulate. One must therefore grasp capital's power from the standpoint of human emancipation.

We might call the drive of capital its soul, "unconscious," motor—the "thing" that makes capitalism such a dynamic and destructive force in human history, that makes it move, so to speak.[3] At base, most understand that capital has a thrust that seeks surplus value or what appears as profit—a motion that pushes money to generate a larger sum of money as if by magic and whose directionality can be deceptively simplified in the formula M-C-M′.[4] Marx's most powerful insights into capitalism (and his resolve to abolish it!) revolve around this drive. On the one hand, Marx demystified the drive by showing how its force is a product of human practice, generating surplus value by abstracting human labor. On the other hand, Marx demonstrated that the thrust for surplus value encapsulated in M-C-M′ contains a power that is also independent of human actions and motivations, wherein capital is able to reproduce itself as an "autonomous power" with a "will and soul" of its own.[5] Capital's pervasive power is at once everywhere and nowhere, amorphous and changing forms, disguised and lurking in plain sight. Marxism is the only tradition that has been specifically developed to home in on this unprecedented world-engulfing power and how it structures and disfigures social relations and life itself. Its theoretical insights are therefore indispensable.

A materialist account begins with the premise that what is unique about capitalism as a social formation is that its drive to produce value exerts an inexorable power to which all (not just those in the "workforce") are subject in order to survive. Capital's relentless thrust to increase value (encapsulated by the formula M-C-M′) amasses a power harnessed from living humans that it then turns against them as it ceaselessly seeks expansion on an ever-expanding scale. It is when describing the magnitude of the drive's power and its effects on the subject that Marx used his most colorful language—its "werewolf-like hunger," that "vampire-like, lives only by sucking living labour and lives the more, the more labour it sucks," a "serpent of their [workers'] agonies" and as an "animated monster which begins to 'work,' as if its body were possessed by love."[6] It is no accident that the majority of such vivid images appear in *Capital*'s most "ethnographic" chapter—the chapter on "the working day." Marx reached for supernatural metaphor to represent the damage that capital's insatiable drive unleashed on factory workers with the adoption of large-scale machinery. Machines enable the drive to dominate the human subject more effectively, rendering the person "a cog," a "living appendage of the machine."[7] The drive to accumulate value spurs innovation and increases productivity, as is often noted, but this is not to ease human labor but to intensify it, not to satisfy human needs but to satisfy capital's needs for expansion.

Once capitalism as a mode of production prevails in a society, its unappeasable thrust for expansion comes to subordinate human needs. The drive's movement to accumulate value becomes the dominant power in society. Marxist theory elaborates the peculiar combination of forces of power within capitalist society—violence, ideology, and the force of the "process of economic compulsion" that entrap capitalists and workers alike, an "impersonal" rather than intersubjective form of domination that is mystified in its reproduction.[8] The latter, understood with terms such "impersonal domination" or "impersonal compulsions," captures Marx's emphasis on how "individuals are ruled by abstractions" that "arise from and exert palpable force within lived relations."[9] Marxist perspectives thus turn the "freedom" assumed by traditional theories on their head: Freedom in capitalist society is the freedom to be subjected to the law of value or to perish. In other words, violence *always* undergirds the softer or "mute" force of compulsion. If this idea ever seemed overly theoretical or far removed from everyday life, far-fetched or exaggerated, the resounding call to keep businesses open by risking and sacrificing human life for "the economy" during the COVID-19 pandemic would quickly disabuse one of this notion. Capitalism is "a social formation in which the process of production has mastery over man."[10] Humans are for the first time in the species' histories, "ruled by abstractions," with value as the preeminent abstraction.[11]

Since Marx, critical theory has understood that the drive of capital subjects and animates human actions to the ends of its own forward motion. Yet no increase of productivity can satisfy the drive.

The nature of a drive is to continually operate on its object. In this case, the object is the human subject—the source of the seemingly magical transformation in M-C-M′. The key task for critical theory is to track how "lynx-eyed capital" seeks to incorporate ever more of human affairs under the rule of value.[12] In the productive sphere, the drive seeks expansion by innovating, intensifying, and extending work. Quenchless, it does not cease there. It moves into reproduction to pervert a broader set of human affairs and, finally, into human subjectivity—shaping human consciousness and its psychic, emotional, and relational currents. The drive's ceaseless "hunger" for value forever wants more from the human subject, as the abstraction of human labor is the only source of its movement and all new and additional value.

Materialist accounts are radical in the sense articulated by Marx—"grasping the root of the matter," that is, *any* matter and social relation that debases humans and obstructs their emancipation.[13] Capital's rule of value is inherently destructive to human and nonhuman life. It is a social formation whose totality is "negative," structured by a "universal principle" or progressive "rationality of the *domination of nature*, the control of both external nature and man's inner nature."[14] While it may be technically possible to divorce Marxist analyses from anticapitalist politics, doing so makes scholarship not more objective but rather irresponsible in the face of capital's destruction and degradation of life. Marxist perspectives make no such pretenses to neutrality or false objectivity, maintaining that capitalism is a social formation irredeemably crisis ridden, antithetical to the flourishing of human possibilities, and a key obstacle to human emancipation. Life is valued only insofar as it concerns capital's narrow calculus of value and its iron law of accumulation. Capitalism's insatiable drive consumes and depletes life for its pursuit of value—life is utterly disposable when its utility for capital expires. Marxist analyses are thus implicitly or explicitly communist, if "we call communism the *real* movement which abolishes the present state of things."[15] The materialist analysis of mothering proposed here emphasizes the ethical and political stance that scholarship must take in the face of capitalism's destructiveness, its domination and maiming of subjects, its extraction and utter disregard for life. Mothers and children are dominated, exploited, and maimed in ways that are crucial to capitalist reproduction, yet they are not largely understood.

PREMISE 2

Because mothering involves labor that produces children as laborers crucial to the reproduction of capitalism, it is doubly subject to capital's systemic domination of value, and so the way capital structures mothering must be the primary object of critique.

Capitalism is not the "background" or the "context" within which women mother, but the dominant force structuring society, including and especially mothering. Humans are ruled by the abstraction of value, their existence determined and negated by value, their only means of survival depending on how their labor will be measured by this abstraction, an abstraction that grounds the exchange of fictive equivalents that contains within it the central political antagonism of capitalist society. Mothers are doubly subjected to this power because they are *also* responsibilized with how children will fare within capital's rule of value. A materialist analysis of mothering fixes capitalism in the foreground of the analysis or risks obfuscating the historically specific dynamics of mothering under current capitalist conditions and confusing them with the transhistorical facts of mothering as a feature of human procreative reproduction. Mothers are no more "free" from capitalist imperatives than anyone else; in fact, I argue that they are less so. A materialist analysis of mothering sets out to establish precisely *how* the imperatives of capital accumulation and the movement of value direct and define the labors, social relations, and everyday subjective experiences of mothering at particular times and places.[16]

How capital structures mothering is fundamentally an open-ended question that does not presume that everything is organized by value and nothing escapes its logic. Rather, value dominates and constrains various aspects of the social world. It is not bound exclusively to "the economy" and subsumes the dynamics of other spheres, including the relations and activities within the seemingly private sphere of the family. Marxist feminist perspectives insist that the family is indispensable for, and irredeemably "shaped by the imperative of endless accumulation."[17] As the producers of laborers, mothers are at the center of capital's reproduction, and they are at the very center of its key contradiction—the antagonism between the reproduction of life qua life and the reproduction of capital. Marxist feminism verily begins the analysis of "the woman question" from within this contradiction, locating the conditions of women's oppression in the social reproduction imperative in capitalist societies to produce laborers. Marxist feminism emerged to develop Marx's distinction between productive and reproductive labor within the unitary whole and the constant flux of the capitalist totality, and to extend his recognition that the "perpetuation of the worker, is the absolute necessary condition of capitalist production."[18] While the resurgence of Marxist feminist work since the early 2010s has generated multiple meanings, emphases, and debates about reproductive labor, it generally refers to the work, largely unpaid or low paid and performed by women, that generates and maintains or *reproduces* the lives of laborers or future laborers and consequently is essential for the social reproduction of capitalist relations.[19] Reproducing laborers or labor power—"the capacity and willingness to work"—is crucial because labor power is what Marx understood as the "peculiar commodity"; it is the only one that can produce more value or surplus value (from which capitalists derive profit as well as the capital that they reinvest to expand production) because its cost (the wage) is less than the sum of new value that it generates through productive activity.[20] The historical and social fact of capital's dependence on women's reproductive labors "induce[s] capital and its state to control and regulate female reproduction and which impels them to reinforce a male-dominant social order."[21] As such, issues with which feminism and women's liberation have been concerned cannot be understood through patriarchy narrowly conceived, nor a "dual system" of patriarchy plus capitalism. Rather, Marxist feminism conceives a "unitary system" in which patriarchy is irreducibly entangled with the dynamics of capital accumulation.[22] The devaluing of women's reproductive work vis-à-vis productive work is a crucial aspect of women's subordination in capitalism.[23]

A materialist analysis grasps how the ever-shifting dynamics of capital accumulation structure the relations and activities of mothering in particular times and places. There are no fixed answers because capital works unevenly. Indeterminateness entails exploring the different ways mothers are situated in the relations of production and reproduction. Regardless of their location within these spheres, all women are thrust into a specific set of social relations in which they must mother. These relations are presupposed by dispossession, the violent and continual processes that ensure that the masses of people are dependent on selling their labor power in exchange for money to purchase what they need to live, resources that have been transformed into private property. The condition of "being 'free' to work yet barred from reaping the full value of our labor" is one of capitalism's fundamental contradictions.[24] The imperative to accumulate value means that some members of the family must take their labor power to the market, and some must (also) prepare children for a future as labor. Yet this imperative and its underlying violence are concealed and disguised, often taking the guise of "good parenting" or doing what is best for one's child. The rub is that this is both fiction and fact, fictive in its assumption that living under the domination of this imperative is the only world possible.

The social reproductive imperatives of mothering with capitalism operate as direct and indirect forms of compulsion and domination that alienate mothers from the work of caring for children, their child, themselves, and others. The way these imperatives operate as such are not readily apparent to mothers. They appear instead as the specter of the child's survival—or in the hegemonic parlance of the day, their "chances for success"—haunting mothers insofar as their care for a child is oriented toward this end, willingly or not, consciously or not. Neither are capital's social reproductive imperatives apparent in scholarly frames that conceal, naturalize, or take for granted capitalism's forms of power and how they operate through various ideological conceptions, reified appearances and abstractions (generally, freedom, equality, fairness, and more specifically, good parenting, best for the child), forms of compulsion, and violence. Irrespective of women's willingness or consciousness, these are the relations in which they mother. Grasping this moves the analysis away from a narrow focus on mother's "choices" to instead interrogate the relations that structure mothers' "choices," how mothers manage, experience, understand, and live these contradictions and how they sustain or, alternatively, subvert them. Disregarding capitalism misrepresents women's struggles in a way that blames mothers for inequality and pits them against one another, places false hopes in reformist solutions, and legitimates the destructive forces of capital on mother's and children's lives. From the critical perspectives from which this book derives its premises, there is no tinkering, adjusting, or reforming capitalism's crisis-ridden tendencies; that is its systemic feature.

PREMISE 3

Mothering is as a thoroughly racialized project, a site where mothers themselves are racialized and their labors are routed to produce racial subjects, racialized spaces and populations, and the racialized value of life itself.

Race and racism are constituent features of capitalism, and no feature of capitalism—synchronic or diachronic—can be properly understood without recourse to frameworks that are attuned to how capital accumulation mobilizes this socially constructed difference and how it structures every aspect of life from birth to death. Race is at base a hierarchy of human value, the most violent split in social relations, the key organizing principle and "ethico-political signifier" of the modern era.[25] It is produced and reproduced at various sites and scales of social life, and all value within capitalism is inherently racialized value, hence the term "racial capitalism." The curious circuits of value within which capital accumulates crucially involves the differential valuing of humans through race. These processes are often ignored in accounts where race is understood to be either separate or to "intersect" with class rather than irrevocably bound together in the violent processes of accumulation.

Within capitalism, motherhood is thus a thoroughly racialized project, a site where mothers themselves are racialized and their labors are routed to produce racial subjects, as well as the racialized value of spaces and populations and the racialized value of life itself. Motherhood is saturated with the embodied and lived practices of racialized hierarchy and inequalities, and it is inevitably implicated in the social reproduction of these racialized relations. Premise 3 develops this insight to understand how motherhood is more than an ordinary site of race making, but a dynamic and critical one. Mothering has a special function within capitalism as the site of creating labor power and subjects—both of which are profoundly racialized. Further, race and motherhood have their own separate and intertwined tragic histories within capitalism.

While slavery's foundational role to capitalism's modes of valuation and accumulation has increasingly been acknowledged through the resurgence of the racial capitalism frame, women—or more precisely, mothers—do not as often appear in these narratives as critical to the creation of value and capital.[26] Yet a key insight of one of Black feminism's interpretive veins is that the regulation of women's reproductive activities is central to "multiple systems of oppression."[27] Enslaved women's flesh was marked as the "prime commodity of exchange," and enslaved women's reproductive labors produced the material conditions of slavery and its social and symbolic relations.[28] These socio-symbolic relations inaugurate racial, gendered, and class relations of domination and fictive distinctions between public and private that animate, subtend, and enable capital accumulation and form the structural conditions of everyday life.

Beginning with "the womb" or "the belly" is not simply a correction to the omission of enslaved women in the annals of history.[29] Rather, it is an analytic move that allows one to grasp how the foundations of racial and gendered violence of our social order were instated through the maternal and how they persist in present practices even when they do not appear to do so. This frame serves as a weapon with which to pierce through the varied ideological cloaks through which the "racial calculus and a political arithmetic" of the afterlives of slavery persist in (and generate) the "skewed life chances, limited access to health and education, premature death, incarceration, and impoverishment" that imperil Black lives.[30] The present, structured by the afterlife of slavery, including its "reproductive afterlife," ensures that motherhood is racially saturated to its core, with the value, ideals, and reproductive labors of white mothers always already in relation to the subordinated reproductive labors of Black women and other women of color.[31]

The way that mothering, as the production of human subjects and as labor power, is racialized and routed to produce racial value is continually morphing. This premise allows for the tracking of these processes in an era when institutions and practices do not appear to be racialized and in which subjects themselves may be of any race, even antiracist. Critical race theories are apt for grasping the way that mothers are systematically recruited to produce the deathly apparatus of race in its peculiar neoliberal figurations. Drawing on Gilmore's oft-cited definition of racism as "the state sanctioned and/or extra-legal production of and exploitation of group-differentiated vulnerabilities to premature death, *in distinct yet interconnected political geographies*," Melamed emphasizes how the last clause sets the task of critical scholarship: tracing the dialectic that separates and connects the "valued and the devalued."[32] Exploring mothering with critical race theories makes visible how women's labors are routed to reproduce labor power by simultaneously reinscribing the deathly apparatus of race. The open-ended question is mapping how this does so, not in some staid comparative exercise or to demonstrate endless variations within the circuit, but to understand the terrain of struggle and the cracks, possibilities, and existing forms of resistance within it for the purposes of liberation.

PREMISE 4

The key contradiction of mothering in capitalism is that the work of caring for children as autonomous beings is in antagonistic relation to the imperative to produce children as

laborers, a moving struggle illuminated through the Marxian rubric of subsumption.

A materialist analysis of mothering begins with the premise that the work of caring for a child as an autonomous being is in an antagonistic relation with the work of reproducing laborers. This premise frames the stakes of struggle as life itself, beyond the limited sense of the biological capacity of an organism to maintain its living status to the more expansive sense of cultivating a life worth living. Thinking about reproductive labor with insights from Marx's twofold conception of labor as living labor and abstract labor can further illuminate our understanding of domination within capitalist society. For Marx, the antagonism between living labor and abstract labor is the key to the analysis of capitalist production; he even referred to it as "the whole secret of the critical conception."[33] In terms of use-value, Marx elaborated a conception of labor that goes beyond considerations of value within capitalism—where labor is the "living form-giving fire, it is the transitoriness of things, their temporality, as their formation by living time."[34] One need not conceive of labor as the most essential thing about being human to appreciate its transhistorical significance as "practical activity" by which humans engage with the external world, activity that expresses reality and helps "create it anew," thereby re-creating human subjectivity.[35] Nevertheless, emphasizing human creative capacity for world (re)making allows for a more penetrating critique of that which exists but not limited to that which is before us. An expansive view of labor allows questions such as, Which vital human trait, relation, or process has capitalism latched on to? And how does capital transform or rather deform and pervert this universally human activity?

A broad-based Marxist view on labor is doubly important in terms of mothering, because mothering is not just work in the sense of caring, and the often drudging, repetitive, necessary range of activities of feeding, cleaning, or simply "looking after" a child. Mothering is also creative, among the most cooperative and complex tasks in which humans can engage, at once intuitive and improvisational as well as learned through experience with and from others, and the means by which humans sustain and reproduce human social life. Bringing the Marxist corpus on labor—in its ontological or human sense and in the way that capital degrades that work and those performing it—to the analysis of childcare opens up new vistas on mothering as a crucial node of struggle within capitalist society. The potentially transformative possibilities of the work that produces human subjects should hold particular significance for critical theory—for the collective and convivial qualities of the human subject can be encouraged precisely in this work, qualities that are instead relentlessly stamped out in capitalism's antisocial sociality.

Capital's relentless drive to valorize value is not neutral with respect to the processes of reproducing biological and social life; it is hostile to them. Capital has one interest in the child—as labor power—the value it can potentially produce, or in today's parlance, the child's "human capital." Capital subsumes, orients, and usurps mothers' work to shape children as labor that will valorize value. Elaborating on Marxist feminist insights on reproductive labors, Sue Ferguson maintains that such labors are always in a "necessary but contradictory relation" to capital accumulation. She distills this contradiction as that between "life making" and "profit making"—or, because the latter prioritizes money and things over people, the "dead" products of labor already completed in the past over living labor, and, because the actual acts of laboring within capitalism are so hazardous to health, as life making versus "death making."[36] Reproductive labors thus sit at the intersection of multiple contradictions—between producing life and labor power, necessary to the functioning of capital yet potentially antagonistic to it, and from the point of view of capital—the contradiction of needing living labor yet depleting labor of life. Some Marxist feminists emphasize reproductive labor's "life-making" or "life's work" aspects, while others object to the use of "virtuous" terms for work that contributes to the reproduction of capitalism as a totality "with all its attendant social misery."[37] I see these terms as, rather than a debate to be resolved, capturing the key antagonism of mothering in capitalist society—the tension between making life worthy of the name and the necessity of producing laborers that are key to reproducing capitalism and its crisis-ridden nature. Indeed, this antagonism is mothering's constitutive contradiction and point of struggle, one that is always morphing. With this tension at the forefront, Marxist feminism can be one of the most potentially incisive tools in the critique of capitalism. For within mothering, the struggle of life against capital can be theorized most clearly and its ultimate stakes made apparent.

Premise 4 directs the focal point of analysis to how capital's drive for value subsumes the work of caring for children as autonomous subjects that can flourish and create other worlds and instead regulates, debases, and orients that work to capital. Like all labor within capitalism, mothering is subject to the dictates of capital, processes usefully approached with Marx's subsumption thesis, the historical tendency for capital to assume greater control over labor as it historically develops through social and technological means (division of labor, science and technology, scale). Marx characterized these processes as political and irreducibly defined by struggle: "The worker's subjection as worker to the supervision and therefore to the command of capital or the capitalist. Capital becomes command over labour."[38] Marx distinguished the formal and real subsumption of labor, wherein the formal implies integrating the labor process within the rule of value without changing it, and real subsumption implies that the form and content of the work are dominated by value.[39] The activity, purpose, social relations of its production, and subjective orientation of the laborer to the activity are subordinated to the rule value. As capital assumes greater command over the labor process, Marx recognized an increasing tendency for capital to absorb humans' vitality and creativity that are outcomes of cooperation—the "social individual," "social brain," "general intellect," that is, the quintessentially human aspects of the human.[40] The subsumption of labor reduces the subject to "a pure abstraction" as she "steps to the side of the production process instead of being its chief actor."[41] In this process, all humans' various productive capacities are reduced to dead labor or fixed capital, "fixed capital being man himself"—that is, human life (living labor) in an objectified and alienated form (abstract labor).[42]

Subsumption, the "metamorphosis of human making into capitalist labor," elucidates the irreducible struggle between the work of caring for children as autonomous beings and working to shape children as laborers for capital, and disentangles the two as the latter has been verily distorted to appear as the former.[43] The subsumption thesis has long been an inspiration for autonomous Marxist accounts of how capital's relentless drive for value escapes the productive sphere and "penetrates everywhere" so that "all of society lives as a function of the factory and the factory extends its domination over all of society"—a social factory.[44] Autonomous Marxist feminism develops these insights to demonstrate how women's lives, activities, and relations as wives and mothers, seemingly separate or outside of work—especially within that private "haven" of the home and family—are oriented to and ultimately structured by value.[45] This perspective (one largely ignored by orthodox Marxist perspectives) sharpens political analyses by analyzing how the work of mothering is unfree labor, disciplined, even if indirectly, by relations of production. Capital rules both waged and unwaged laborers, but the exploitation of the latter is hidden by the absence of a wage.[46] By revealing how the capital relation subsumes reproductive labors, autonomous Marxist feminists reveal the "variety of the trenches" from which counterattacks on capital arise.[47] To disregard how mothers' care is work is to "mystify it as a natural resource" and capitulate to the masculinist and bourgeois logic whereby work is only that which gets remunerated; it re-reifies the wage.[48] Worse yet is the implication for politics, allowing the working day to be defined by capital.[49]

Although developed in the context of technological development of factory work, the subsumption thesis clarifies capital's "appropriative logic" on constantly evolving forms of gender "exploitation, expropriation, and domination."[50] Yet there is not widespread thinking about reproduction through the subsumption analytic because for traditional Marxist feminism, concepts derived for productive labor cannot apply to reproduction because the market does not directly mediate such labors.[51] For example, Gonzalez and Neton argue that reproductive labors are not under the compulsion of "abstract market domination" in the way that productive labors necessarily are, and there is no "mechanism or way to objectively quantify, enforce, or equalize rationally the time and energy spent in these activities or to whom they are allocated."[52] I emphatically disagree with this position. First, much is made in terms of direct and indirect control of reproductive labors, as if indirect power were somehow categorically less relevant or effective than direct power. In fact, I argue that mothers are doubly captive by capital's law of value.

Maternal labors within capitalism have always been under the command of capital in some form or another because, to ensure a child will be able to do more than merely survive within capitalist social relations, mothers must—they have no choice—orient their children to their inevitable future as laborers. Because capitalism is a ceaselessly morphing system, mothering within capitalism is therefore under constant new pressures to perform new kinds of labor in order to (re)produce new kinds of future workers. How mothers do this is an open-ended question, and a materialist account examines how those parameters change as capital continually makes more demands for labor and also appreciates the variable and creative ways mothers work within these confines. It entails historicizing how certain maternal practices have been imposed, distorted, and disciplined by capital's shifting relations of production and requirements for the reproduction of labor power. The goal here is not to generate a more accurate accounting of exploitation and surplus value; instead, it concerns our collective capacities to shape social life.

Contra the orthodox Marxist feminist view, this book illustrates the various complex ways that the work of caring for children is indeed under the compulsion of the market—which is to say under the command of capital. Children are subject to relentless "objective" measurements from birth (see Chapters 3–5). Mothers are held directly responsible for these measurements and are goaded to improve them. Where once it may have been scandalous to point out parents' influence on children's educational performance, this book documents how capital and the state, through the econo-psy and neoliberal education complexes, increasingly coerce mothers to extend and intensify their labors to improve children's performance.

Parents with children in school are inundated with objective measurements of their child's performance, and enormous efforts to continually improve it, a measure that is persistently linked to their future employability and success. This discourse is so penetrating and normalized, that it becomes background noise. It is common sense in the most hegemonic inflection of the term. Parents increasingly take on labors of increasing children's value for capital as defined by schools (which are oriented to employment within capitalism) because children's chances for a decent life depends on the value their labor (tied to their education) will fetch in the market.

Amid debates within Marxist feminism about whether reproductive labors are "productive" (produce surplus value), the political stakes are often obscured. A materialist analysis insists that the activities involved in mothering are labor not merely to claim recognition, respect, or even remuneration but to develop an understanding of how capital dominates subjects. When the founders of the International Wages for Housework Campaign averred that "the role of housewife, behind whose social isolation is *hidden social labor*, must be destroyed," they did not reject motherhood and taking care of children tout court; they rejected mothering and taking care of children within capitalist social relations and imperatives.[53] Mothers are at war with capital, even if they do not know it. Autonomist Marxist feminism emphasizes women's role in struggles against capital. Indeed, this struggle might fruitfully be conceived as one of capital's many Achilles' heels. While capital absolutely requires living laborers for its sustenance, life does not require capital. It is only in the historically specific context of capital's ascendancy that most of humanity is dispossessed and can access the means of subsistence and its reproduction only through the wage, that capital finds a "virtually fathomless surplus population."[54] Capital can disregard women's work producing labor power because "it will find labor available when needed," and so "conceals its dependence" upon this work.[55] While capital can "conceal its dependence" on women's reproductive labor, capital could not function as we know it if paid for labor's reproduction—reproduction in the more limited biological sense and in the fully social sense of a human socialized in the habits, values, and modes of being in capitalism. The subsumption thesis provokes crucial yet rarely asked questions about mothering. How do capitalist social relations and reproductive imperatives disfigure the work of caring for children? What kind of work are mothers being compelled to do *for* capital that is inimical to children's flourishing? And how can we—those whose horizon is human emancipation—collectively create and valorize ways of caring for children that allows them to flourish as autonomous human subjects? These questions, difficult, if not impossible, to answer, are among the most important to ask in the struggle against capital.

PREMISE 5

Because mothering's constitutive struggle revolves around shaping the human subject, a materialist analysis requires a robust framework of subjectivity within a psychosocial nexus.

If critical theory is preeminently concerned with emancipation and human happiness, then it requires "reflection on the contradictions that hinder it" or "the contradictions of the subject."[56] While subjectivity is a crucial site of struggle, the methods by which capital penetrates the subject's formation are largely opaque or represented in rather facile ways because few Marxist accounts are psychoanalytically attuned and grounded in everyday life.[57] And more so, because the foundations of these processes transpire in motherhood and childhood, domains that are naturalized, idealized, and largely thought to be outside of politics proper by Marxists and non-Marxists alike. While caring for children involves various types of work—feeding, cleaning, cooking, and so forth—the most important work, from a human point of view and from capital's, involves shaping human subjectivity. The fifth premise of a materialist analysis of mothering highlights that one of its constitutive struggles turns on the formation of subjectivity.

This struggle emerges because the primary and universal task of reproduction from a human point of view—caring for children so that they can flourish as autonomous beings—is antagonistic to the capitalist imperative to shape children as subjects willing and able to work for capital. The empirically, onto-epistemologically, and politically prior task entails protecting children from various harms, nurturing various capacities that allow children to realize themselves as subjects (recognizable as part of a particular communities), and allowing them to flourish as humans in the manifold ways that are the birthright of being human. This work, even at its most basic—protecting children from various harms—is fundamentally at odds with the primary task of reproduction from capital's perspective—the production of labor power, or what I call humans *for* capital. This term evokes Marx's insights on how capital compels subjects to act as personifications of their categorical role within capitalism, or their "economic character masks" (*Charaktermasken*).[58] And so, emancipatory frameworks must account for the forming and deforming of subjects, and the possibility of creating subjects and society anew. The tragedy of mothering is that capital routes the work of nurturing children to flourish toward labors that create bearers of capital—people who personify these categories all the time. The work of shaping children as subjects is where Marxist theory can illuminate what is most fundamental, distinct, most dreadful, yet potentially revolutionary about mothering. The work of mothering can hardly be said to be automatically emancipatory or revolutionary. Yet without prescribing emancipatory or revolutionary subjectivities, critical theoretical frames posit some horizon to highlight their tension with capital's logic, drive, and systematic deforming of subjects and social relations.

Realizing this fundamental contradiction does not predefine the analytic task. In fact, teasing out the production of human persons from the production of laborers is a critical task facing analysts of mothering. To rephrase the problematic, one must ask, Is this good for producing humans as autonomous subjects? Or is this good for producing laborers for capital? This begs the question of the opposition between them, a question that is difficult to answer for several reasons. Chief among them is that within capitalism, the world confronts subjects in its inverted and perverted categories so that it verily *appears* that what is good for a laboring subject (for capital) is good for humans. As Lefebvre cautioned—within capitalism, appearance and reality "intertwine," with appearances "grafting themselves onto reality, encompassing it, replacing it" and where the appearances and "theories and abstractions which express these appearances—seem the only reality."[59] While Lefebvre cut through the pseudoreality that envelops us with Marx's notion of alienation, concepts from psychoanalytically attuned critical theory can further disentangle the two to make reality available for criticism and transformation. Ultimately, it inspires the question that, though not completely answerable, nevertheless needs to be asked: If capitalism inherently truncates the possibilities for human flourishing, then which sorts of subject-making endeavors might broaden the purview of being and becoming human?

To think in emancipatory ways about the subject entails understanding the ways we are determined by forces other than ourselves. Indeed, the term "subject" rather than "individual" highlights its constitution at the psychosocial nexus where both the psychological and the social are inseparable and dialectically related.[60] Jared Sexton refers to this as the subject's "heteronomy," or the "distinct but related sources of social determination and unconscious determination."[61] This opens up analysis to a long and revived tradition of critical theory engaging with psychoanalytic articulations of the unconscious, an alliance that politicizes psychoanalytic theory and deepens materialist thought and practice.[62] To engage the problematic of subject making without an understanding of the complexity of the unconscious, the role of drives, fantasy, and desire and how they function in experience and social life would be telling half of the story as it were. One might go so far as to say that one cannot have a materialist theory of the subject without an understanding of the unconscious.[63] Engaging with the unconscious resituates the "individual" in a social context and more resolutely disrupts the individual-society dichotomy that characterizes some materialist thought. Further, the unconscious jettisons the conception of the rational individual that often limits the relevance of materialist theory and practice from addressing pressing historical and political questions. For instance, Wilhelm Reich's invaluable insights about fascism were possible because he refused the frame of "ignorance or illusion on the part of the masses" and instead brought desire into the account, more specifically, a "perversion of desire" in which, "under a certain set of conditions, they wanted fascism."[64] Materialist engagements with the unconscious highlight how the unconscious is formed through our primary social bonds and so subject making (and the possibilities for remaking) is fundamentally conflicted, fraught with ambivalence, somewhat opaque, dynamic, and thus always open-ended.

A concern with subject making inevitably brings one to the mother-child relation, for there is no more profound temporal period of subject making than this bond. While children absolutely participate in their own self-making, and we may posit that they are born both dependent and autonomous subjects (which are not inherently contradictory), initially at least, subject making is primarily the result of the work of other adults, chiefly mothers. It would not be hyperbolic to say that mothering is one of the most important sites, if not *the* most important, of subject making in social life. Psychoanalytic theory has been verily built on theorizing the psyche's foundation as formed through the mother-child bond while insisting on its irreducible ambivalence.[65] Within an object relations view of the psyche, such as Melanie Klein's, the drives are the "internal organizing force" of the psyche.[66] The drives, which is to say, the unconscious, are formed by social codes. For Jean Laplanche, the universal and "fundamental anthropological situation" is that the unconscious is formed in childhood through a child's primary object relations.[67] Critical theory's abiding concern with the unconscious is because the unconscious is an object of domination (what Adorno called domination of inner nature) within capitalism. Alternatively, the unconscious serves as an important source of resisting domination for Klein, Adorno, and Lacan, the latter of whom sees the drives as serving as a "kernel of rebelliousness."[68] Drives, it is important to maintain, are fully mediated by the social. They "acquire aim and force in the complex interchanges of early life": "We are held, caressed, cooed at, coddled . . . Later we are encouraged, corralled, admonished, disciplined . . . In is in these experiences that drives are not elicited but formed—we learn what it is to love, to master, to aggress."[69] If this—inarguably the most important and formative relations and experiences of the psyche and hence the subject—is being captured and deformed by capital, then a conceptual arsenal that can account for how this occurs is absolutely necessary.

Mothering—as work and labor, as bundles of emotional and psychic activities, and as relation to child—also constructs the mother as subject. Recognizing this makes available a vast body of maternal theory to materialist analysis to address the problematic of subject making. Maternal theory is organized by Adrienne Rich's distinction between motherhood and mothering, as well as the relation between motherhood as institution and ideology and mothering as experience.[70] While motherhood studies are largely concerned with how normative femininities sustain women's oppression, they are rarely framed by materialist theory. Yet such studies can be productively incorporated into materialist studies by connecting how hegemonic femininities and ideologies of motherhood are literally put to work. Through materialist frameworks, phenomena that appear as cultural norms of parenting or innovative (even "countercultural") parenting techniques can instead be analyzed in terms of how such methods transform mothering into shaping subjects *for* capital. Studies of mothering as experience can likewise enrich materialist accounts by illuminating the complex ways subjects incorporate and refuse the imposition of capitalist logics. The perspective of mothering as experience brings the intractable unconscious to the fore. And if, as Jacqueline Rose avers, society displaces its deepest conflicts and contradictions onto mothers, mothering is also a place where analysts can discover and dislodge those contradictions.[71] This opens up new avenues for critiques of political economy and emancipatory politics. Mothering is not only a site where capitalist relations are reproduced but one from which each day begins anew, where emancipatory possibilities can be rehearsed, prefigured, and lived.

PREMISE 6

The state constitutes and regulates the family through race, class, and gendered regimes of domination, tasking mothers with producing subjectivities for capital.

A materialist account of mothering recognizes that, contrary to many feminist perspectives, the state is not the horizon of hope for mothers and will not resolve the so-called crisis of care within capitalism. For liberal feminist accounts, the state is a neutral instrument that is largely independent of capital and is democratically responsive to "the people." In fact, much feminist scholarship in its most critical vein calls for state intervention to tame the "excesses" of capitalist accumulation, a site on which to apply pressure to resolve the crises of care through expansion of state programs or the welfare state itself. Marxist feminists have long argued that the state can only ameliorate or paper over any crisis of care insofar as those reforms, policies, or programs "don't interfere with the imperative of accumulation."[72] Materialist conceptions of the state and its relation to families and mothering radically differ from traditional social scientific accounts. Where there are many Marxist perspectives on the state, they are united in the understanding that the state is not outside of capital but is the specific political form of bourgeois social relations.[73] Disagreements about the state's dependence on capital concern the matter of degree, not its apparent separation from capital, or the autonomy of the political from the economic—these perspectives reflect another perversion of capitalist society.[74] As the state represents the reified social relations of capitalist society, it serves capital accumulation even in its neutral or "democratic" guises—securing, directing, and managing the conditions of social reproduction and legitimizing its forms of domination through its political-legal apparatuses and ideological and repressive functions.

Within neoliberalism, the state is redeployed as the "core agency" that establishes the infrastructure of rule for capital, a "Centaur-state" that "reserves liberalism and its benefits for those at the top while it enforces punitive paternalism upon those at the bottom."[75] The apparatuses of the capitalist state—police, military, the law, the courts, prisons, schools, and indeed, the family—likewise facilitate capital's varied forms of domination and exploitation, partly through the making of subjects. The state's production of subjectivity occurs through these apparatuses and ranges from directly repressive and punitive measures like criminalizing protest to indirect hegemonic measures of shaping opinion, making the order of things seem more or less natural or inevitable and alternatives disagreeable or even unthinkable.

A materialist account of mothering begins with the premise that the state, for which manufacturing subjects is a premier concern, constitutes and regulates the family for this purpose. This premise guides exploration of how the state does so and to what effect, questions that are difficult to consider because the family, perhaps as much as or more so than motherhood, is saturated in sentimentalism. The family's cloying mawkishness reflects and obscures its political importance as a moral project for neoliberal governance.[76] Until quite recently, this sentimentality quelled radical perspectives on the relationship of the family to the state, recently revived under the banner of "family abolitionism." This strand of critique emerges from Marx and Engels notorious call: "Abolition of the family! Even the most radical flare up at this infamous proposal of the Communists."[77] The resurgence of this tradition, aware of the hysterical reactions it provokes, unflinchingly lays out how the family is a fully public institution functioning as capital's elementary social and economic unit.[78] It is in the apparent fact of the family's "privateness" that its crucial function is predicated—its "managerial regime of social reproduction."[79] Marxist feminists writing in the 1970s perceived the state's power as encroaching into the family and regulating women, in service of capital accumulation. The Committee for Wages for Domestic Work in Padua articulated this relationship as the state being "the *boss of* women and the controller-guarantor of the reproduction of labor-power."[80] While acknowledging that shaping subjects for capital occurs in diffuse locales throughout social life, materialist analyses of motherhood begin with the premise that this production "remains concentrated" in the family.[81] Premise 6 brings together critical perspectives on the family, the state, and subjectivity, as the crucial maelstrom of capitalist domination in neoliberal society.

Many conceptual resources on the state's constitution, enforcement, and regulation of the family, while not framed in Marxist or materialist terms, deepen and extend insights into the relationship between the state and the family. For whatever reason, Marxist feminism has been unable to rip off either the veil of sentimentality from the family or the shroud of neutrality that envelops the state. Yet it would be difficult for even the most naive optimism for the family or the state to persist after accounting for the histories of the state's alternate denial and imposition of the family form onto racially subjugated people. The state's violence toward Black, Brown, and Indigenous families reveals the state in its naked form as the guarantor of capitalist domination through its continual reproduction of race and gender inequalities. Strands within Black feminism demonstrate how the family is fundamental to the operation of the state; indeed, the family "animates its power."[82] By exploring how the state subjects Black women's reproductive labors to "scrutiny and biopolitical surveillance," Black feminism further exposes the mythical fiction of the family as separate or private sphere.[83] Ideologies and discourses that mark white motherhood as virtuous or normal and cast Black maternity as pathological and excessive are crucial to the state's regulation of the family.[84] Black feminism provide a lens for viewing the state as a punitive regime for racially subordinated women. These projects include the reproductive control of who can be a mother in the first place: the legally sanctioned kidnapping of enslaved, Indigenous, and undocumented women's children; the sterilization of Puerto Rican women; and the Supreme Court's 2022 overturning of *Roe v. Wade*.[85] For racially subordinated mothers, every legal apparatus of the state and its "surveillant assemblage" of child services, welfare system, health services, border enforcement, and the school lurk with the ever-present threat of taking away children.[86] The state tasks the family with creating subjects for capital, and the state threatens to bring any family suspected of not performing this function into the fold by breaking the bond it deems sacrosanct within idealized conditions of white bourgeois motherhood.

Indeed, the same institutions that might be viewed as doing "good" by supporting families deemed worthy—schools, hospitals, social work, and family courts—punish those deemed unruly. Critical perspectives on the state acknowledge that the state provides no "free gifts" to families; these things are accompanied by the state's repressive and regulatory functions.[87] Even when providing relief or support, the state serves a disciplinary function to ensure the perpetuation of the family and its role in social reproduction of a privatized, individualized, constricted form of sociality for accessing care and the production of hierarchical relations and subordinated subjects for capital. Because the state's regulation of the family is so mystified, and because families are themselves so sentimentalized and naturalized, it can be difficult to perceive how the state's disciplinary apparatus is fully operative even, or especially, within the so-called private sphere of the idealized family of middle class heterosexually paired couple devoted to their respective vocations of work and children. Viewing the state's historically punitive and paternalistic regulation of racialized and working class families as the norm rather than the exception makes visible its less spectacular forms of power that sustain the family as the manager of social reproduction. This is an urgent task, as the family has taken on an outsize role and responsibility for capital and the state in neoliberalism.

Within neoliberalism, the state increases its muscle as the "boss of women" through the institution of the school in both the punitive and the more diffuse disciplinary sense. In terms of punishing children and families of the poor and racially minoritized, it is important to note that the school is the site of first contact with the police for many poor young people of color, and it is the site from which many mothers are reported to be delinquent. In terms of the state's more diffuse disciplinary and regulatory functions via the school, success in school is now, more than ever, made to depend on maternal labors, labors that are coerced by ideologies of motherhood that proliferate in schools. Within the neoliberal era, "intensive mothering" is the ideal form of motherhood, with its characteristic suite of labors to support a child's education as the only pathway to future "success." What is most unprecedented about the state's increased control of the family through the school is the proliferation of methods to measure the child. That is, the state, as the "boss of women," can coerce, regulate, and manage maternal labor through the endless evaluation and relentless datafication of children's performance in school. Particularly troubling in this respect is emergence of so-called social-emotional learning in schools, which attempts to measure and instill particular subjective traits that are attractive to capital (see Chapters 4 and 5). The state enlists mothers to labor in particular ways to create the ideal laboring subject for capital. While there is a robust literature on the state's interventions into the family that is inspired by Donzelot's *The Policing of Families*, the analysis is fundamentally sharpened when the state is understood to regulate and discipline the family *for* capital.[88]

PREMISE 7

To mother is to inhabit a variable set of largely irresolvable relations of class, gender, and race domination and points of struggle that encapsulate capitalism's antisocial sociality.

To mother is to inhabit a variable set of largely irresolvable relations of class, gender, and race domination and points of struggle that encapsulate capitalism's antisocial sociality, the inherent violence of living within a system whose dominant thrust is hostile to life. To care for a child within capitalism's monopolizing of care within the family necessarily involves being uncaring or denying others—even if only implicitly, indirectly, or involuntarily—the possibility of flourishing, even within the impoverished terms and limited possibilities of the capitalist ideal. The variable ways that mothers are enmeshed within contradictions of care and uncare are not simply apparent, nor immediately read off of mothers' various identities and locations within intersecting systems of inequality. Mothers do not have to be "racist" or "classist" or to have internalized "misogyny" to reproduce these hierarchies while mothering, nor are these processes similar across time and space. Beyond banal observations that mothers occupy different locations within production and reproduction due to their class, race, and gender, a materialist account explores the variable ways mothers are situated within these contradictions and implicated in the key struggles of our time.

These contradictions are both inescapable and irresolvable within the terms of the capitalist order, and no mother can "rise above" them with individual choices. For within capitalism, mothering takes place within individual families that are ideologically and practically pitted against the other. That is, within a context of scarcity, helping one's child obtain a good that is not available to all means competing with and, if successful, denying that good to others. This contradiction of care and uncare in which mothers are enmeshed is most visible in the oft-discussed "care chains" where mothers exploit the labor of other women, many of them also mothers, to take care of their children.[89] Indeed, the image of white, professional, middle class mothers employing women of color as private nannies has become the paradigmatic scenario of this contradiction. While not diminishing the cruelties and superexploitation that women in this situation often face, often compounded by their precarious legal and economic status and the isolation of their workplace, this scenario's obviousness masks the fact that virtually all mothers inhabit this contradiction. This is not a universal or necessary feature of mothering but mothering within the terms of a capitalist order. That is, scarcity is a socially organized and socially imposed condition, as well as an ideological fiction imposed by capital and state, a condition that can and should be transformed by solidarity and collective struggle against capital. Thus, either by misrecognition, accommodation, complicity, or resignation, mothering within capitalism places one in an antisocial relation with other mothers. And so even a working class, racially minoritized mother, while clearly in a wholly different circumstance in terms of the paradigmatic domestic worker scenario, whether she jostles to get her child in one of the very few seats in a "gifted" program in her school system, or whether she drops off her child to be cared for at a day care by a woman in even worse working conditions than her own, will still be implicated in this contradiction of care and uncare. These processes can be difficult to perceive because they occur indirectly and because they often proceed in an apparently aracial or racially neutral register.

Mothering within capitalism is irreducibly defined by these struggles that are more or less concealed. This perspective on antagonism and struggle does not naively presume that there is only and ever open and conscious conflict. Nor does this perspective assume that struggles are predefined. Such struggles include but are not limited to the most obvious ones involving the gendered division of household labors, maternal leave policies, and day-care affordability. Marxist feminism reconceptualizes class struggle by including women's reproductive labors as one of its terrains.[90] Indeed, Briggs argues that the most important class struggles of this moment—protecting housing, schooling, health care, racial justice, and the environment from the ravages of capital—can all be thought of as reproductive politics, struggles where women and children are central.[91] These struggles are determined by developments within capitalism because they are verily struggles between capital and labor that arise from the most elementary fact of capitalism—all individuals are subordinated and subjected by capital because they are compelled to participate in its relations as laborers without access to the means of subsistence and reproduction. These relations of domination are articulated, experienced, and signified in other registers, such as gender and race, because capital emerged and developed by exploiting these already-existing differences. Thus, subjects often endure and experience these "strategies of exclusion and abjection" most painfully in terms of race and gender because those differences close them out of their needs for housing, health, dignity, and so on.[92] These contradictions are inevitable because capital "continually reproduces ways of knowing and feeling that conceal the exploitative human relations that the accumulation of profit requires."[93] To mother is to immediately enter capitalism's irresolvable relations of class, gender, and race domination in amplified form.

The most concealed relation of class domination in which mothers are enmeshed is the one that places mothers in tension to and in an antagonistic relation with their child. Within capitalism and neoliberalism especially, mothers' relation to children is analogous to managers who must work to squeeze the most out of labor and betray the class to which they belong in exchange for salary, benefits, and promises, while they are still themselves controlled as much as their subordinates.[94] Mothers too must betray their primary loyalties to their child. In exchange, they receive the tacit agreement that their child will benefit in the future. For this fictive promise, they are coaxed to be "good" parents—that is, to produce "good" children, which is to say children "good" for capital. Yet these mothers face an opponent as formidable as the laborers that managers encounter—incorrigible children—whose desire to be loved by their mothers is matched by their will to be free from any yoke of power, including that amorphous power of capital that seeks to contain and regulate them. This represents the terrain of struggle to tame the child that is, by birth and by right, a bad child, for capital.

PREMISE 8

Maternal labors are only a vector for the ultimate object of capital control—children, who must labor for capital throughout their childhoods, and whose emancipation is intimately bound to any authentic liberatory project.

Children are autonomous subjects in their own right whose humanity is so routinely denied that critical thought rarely registers clearly apprehensible facts that face us: Children are penultimate objects of capital and state intervention. What they do in school is indeed work, work that is consistently denied as work, work that is not paid, work that is forced upon them, work that they routinely despise, work that they (and others) are told is for their own good, work that is ultimately labor for capital. Children's emancipation from forced labor of schooling and children's liberation more broadly is necessarily bound with any project of human emancipation. As such, any framework positing the abolition of capitalism and the incorrigibility and autonomy of the human subject, including a materialist account of mothering and Marxist feminism more broadly, must be grounded in critical childhood studies and child liberation frameworks to grasp the relationship between reproductive labors and the domination of subjectivity. Key insights from childhood studies—concerning how children are not only objects of intervention but also subjects in their own right that transform the processes to which they are subject; the very question of who is verily understood to be a child; childhood as biocultural state with various cultural and historical figurations; childhood as a site for naturalizing, legitimating, and elaborating difference making and inequalities; assorted approaches for accessing children's unique (and often impenetrable for adults) experiences—facilitate these analytic and political goals.

The child is a conceptual abyss in traditional social scientific accounts of mothering, blank slates onto which mothers input their (dis)advantages and their forms of capital. Scandalously, children rarely appear either in Marxist feminist accounts of social reproduction or even mothering, perhaps peering around the corner as objects of drudging and endless labor or lurking in the shadow of their own future as laborers. Within broader Marxist work, children are also absent, making an appearance only as the aberration of child labor in historical studies and in the various sites around the world where children labor for money—including in the West (as in migrant youth who even in 2023 legally labored in factories).[95] This is seen as an outrage because children are not being allowed to be children when they work for money, whereas ostensibly they are allowed to be children in school, implying that they are blissfully free from the compulsions of capital. The absence of a wage, much like that of the "housewife," conceals what is considered labor for capital. Even within Marxist sociology of education and in its touchstone texts, children's labor is effaced by the gloss of "socialization" to their future as laborers.[96] The fact that critical scholars specializing in the analysis of labor within capitalism do not consider what children do in schools labor is a profoundly embarrassing twist for Marxism. The few important resources that assert this perspective come from autonomous Marxist feminist and anarchist child liberation frameworks.[97] Indeed, my ethnographic work with children in schools affirms that children understand what they do in schools as labor—forced labor, unwaged labor, drudging and alienated labor.[98] To add insult to the injury of routinely denying or rendering their labor in school invisible, what children are forced to do in schools is presented as "good." Real-life children and a grounding in critical childhood studies can help disentangle what capital wants from children as future laborers and what might be best for children on the basis of their own emancipatory desires and demands. In my study of ten- and eleven-year-olds in school, the kids articulated their demand as "More free time!" "Free time all the time!" and "No work for a whooooole year!"[99] While this book is not based on children's experiences, my empirical work with children and my everyday relations with real-life kids have indelibly stamped my analysis of mothering.

While they do not consider what children do in schools as work or labor, Sue Ferguson and Cindi Katz are among the few Marxist feminists who bring the insights of critical childhood studies into their work on social reproduction, understanding the core contradictions of childhood (and motherhood) in reference to the continually shifting terrain of capitalism. For Ferguson, it is the constant negotiation between the instrumental focus of producing children into capitalist laborers and subjects, and children's playful relation to the world as "agents of their own transformation."[100] Katz centers the erosion of childhood in the contradiction between children's work and play, and the "complex non-innocent integrations and connections" between the two figures of the child as accumulation and the child as waste.[101] Both foreground children's agency and the necessarily open-ended potential of childhood, while not underestimating the "ether of contemporary childhood" that subjects their lives to relentless schedules, surveillance, and outcomes for an inescapable "fate as capitalists present and future laborers."[102]

Child liberation frameworks insist that children's unique needs and contributions are bound up with and necessary to any project of human emancipation, and these perspectives are crucial in materialist accounts of mothering. While I have sketched a few concerns about children, their nature and needs, and the uniqueness of their perspectives in the foregoing premises, I conclude by gesturing toward children's alterity, their sometimes incommensurable (with adults) demands and desires, and the stubbornness of the child-adult boundary and the way it doggedly delimits the expansiveness of radical thought. It is precisely children's alterity that make their inclusion in any emancipatory project such an urgent necessity. Any genuinely radical elaboration of how we might want to live perceives that the work of revolution is always necessarily unfinished and will always need nourishing from a beyond. Children are a reservoir of imagination from the beyond. Materialist accounts of mothering should engage with thinkers who are bold enough to formulate their emancipatory visions with children *as* children: Critics like Madeline Lane-McKinley and Sophie Lewis, who refuse notions of children as property and call for the abolition of family and the adult-child border in the name of the child.[103] Thinkers like Walter Benjamin, whose optimism in the face of capitalism's ruins partly depended on his understanding of children's revolutionary consciousness, one that bourgeois socialization and schooling continually suppresses but cannot extinguish.[104] Thinkers like Toni Cade Bambara, whose child characters didn't wait for a revolution because they were *already* free.[105] Better yet, a materialist account of mothering should do as mothers do because children demand it—that is, listen to actual kids and their explicit and implicit revolutionary desires to be free.

2

The Human Capital Theory Machine

Making Human Capital

> I see human capital as really doing just the opposite, if I can be blunt: as freeing up individuals.
>
> —*Gary Becker*

"THE WEALTH OF societies in which the capitalist mode of production prevails appears as 'an immense collection of *human capital*'; the *individual* appears as its elementary form. Our investigation therefore begins with the analysis of the *individual bearer of human capital*."[1] We might begin an investigation of neoliberal capitalism, like Marx began his of industrial capitalism, with its fetish object—human capital, that mysterious measure of the potential lifetime value of an individual based on their health, abilities, ingenuity, education, and skills. With this measure, the human being in toto is abstracted and expressed in monetary terms that can be rendered equivalent to specific quantities of any other commodity, be it yards of linen, coats, tea, coffee, corn, gold, or iron.[2] A composite measure of the sum total of the human capital of all individuals is ubiquitous in business and global politics, a seemingly neutral indicator of a corporation's or a nation's worth, and its presumptive status and hegemony vis-à-vis its competitors. Human capital represents both the individual and the collective, and its increase is seen to benefit both—the individual as earnings and the collective as economic growth. Since the mid-twentieth-century rediscovery of the concept, human capital theory has become the governing principle of social life—a premiere concern of states and capitalist firms, with nongovernmental and philanthropic organizations evangelizing investment in it. For instance, the World Bank's Human Capital Project developed a "human capital index" of different nations that predicts the human capital that a child born today will embody when at age eighteen, in order to promote policies that ensure all children can "enter the job market as healthy, skilled, and productive adults."[3] It is a sign of the peculiarity of these times that a concept denoting the human subject's market worth can so comfortably proceed as an unremarkable way to talk about nations, populations, and most oddly, children. Indeed, it is around children and childhood that the fetish of human capital reaches its highest proportions.

With human capital theory's ascendance and eventual hegemony on the world economic stage, critics of neoliberalism diagnose some of its most vexing political problems within subjectivity—how humans seem to more willingly acquiesce to its imperative to "enhance the self's future value."[4] Foucault first mapped the intricate connections between human capital theory and the transformation of neoliberalism's dominant form of subjectivity. *Homo economicus*, once a "partner of exchange," is now an entrepreneur. Foucault's description of this subject is well recognized—"an entrepreneur of himself, being for himself his own capital, being for himself his own producer, being for himself the source of his earnings."[5] The most prominent innovation of this theory, he argued, is that it inaugurates a new form of power—a power seemingly without coercion, one where subjects are "freed"—to *subject* themselves. Reading Foucault's analysis through Marx, I argue that human capital theory's key innovation is that it provides capital's unique form of power—the "silent compulsion of economic relations"—with tentacles to intricately govern social reproduction.[6] This is not simply about the subject entrepreneurializing their "everyday conduct," as conventionally narrated. To grasp human capital theory's catastrophic repercussions for human social relations and subjectivity, we must situate it as a form of capital—as *dead labor* whose massive, zombie-like force to accumulate by pumping out life—that now courses through the subject from within. And this is where mothers are absolutely critical.

"Capitalist production has seized the vital forces of the people at their very roots," Marx asserts.[7] Figuring human capital theory as *capitalist reproduction*, this chapter insists that capital's disfiguring of our vital forces has been woefully underestimated. By unleashing capital's drive in motherhood and childhood, human capital theory seizes the most profound and sensitive social process of human development, blocking, stunting, hollowing, and distorting the movement of life toward the undead. I invoke Marx's poetics to make these repercussions resound in light of the utter defamiliarization of "human capital" and its conventional language of critique.[8] And further, to crack the edifice of the spectacle of motherhood and the intense fetishization of childhood, where these repercussions lay hidden and disguised. Within the nexus of the mother-child relation, capital has relatively free rein to burrow into the subject. Human capital theory literally puts mothers to work "investing" in the child's present and future value. Value—dead labor—courses through motherhood and binds to its animating force of love and care, malnourishing children and depleting mothers. Through the stealthy takeover of social reproduction, human capital theory operates to realize capital's most audacious aspirations—to flatten and empty the human subject of all that is superfluous and irreducible to capital, to inhibit all that is dangerous or willfully resistant to its "insatiable appetite" for labor, to fashion a subject in its image, one that constantly seeks the valorization of their own value. In short, to make humans capital.

Human capital theory entraps mothers in reconfigured relations of gendered exploitation and domination as it pumps value out of their labors of "investing" in children. Even less apparent is how human capital theory reorganizes reproduction so that mothers' *embodied* value is bequeathed to children. Human capital economists have always included maternal experiences, biology, genes, and health in their equations of the potential value mothers transmit to children. Every single one of these embodied aspects of maternal value is profoundly racialized. Yet critical appraisals of human capital theory have bafflingly overlooked how this peculiar measure, human capital, inexorably carries the violence of race. This chapter reads human capital theory's repositioning of the mother through Black feminism to demonstrate how human capital theory redoubles the material and symbolic aspects of race in its incessant valuation of the human. The body is the locus of race, and by making the mother everything, human capital theory brings birth, bodies, and genes firmly back into the equation of one's worth. Yet race now appears, or, as it were, *disappears*, in a guise of objective and racially neutral exchange value. The obscene moniker of "human capital" is no mere rhetorical excess, and the fact that it does not chafe our ears means new strategies of defamiliarization are necessary. Resituating human capital theory in the context of its emergence in chattel slavery reveals how it is indelibly marked and a technique of racial domination. As it extends its reach into and becomes hegemonic within reproduction, human capital theory enacts and extends its racial regime of violence, and reproduction becomes a crucial vehicle through which the afterlives of slavery are revivified in the present, their spectacular violence and anti-Blackness disappeared in the mother.

As it pumps value out of mothers' bodies and labors, human capital theory inaugurates a perverted notion of freedom—capital's vision of freedom. In this formulation, humans are suspended in capital's power, formed as subjects in its image, and free to act within its delimited range. Human capital theory is a machine that proliferates capital's power throughout the social and ceaselessly whirs to realize capital's fantasies for subject and society—the reduction and abstraction of the human to pure exchange value, the realization of "freedom" to achieve the perfect conditions to buy and sell labor power, a temporality of a human present devoted to its future accumulation, and most profoundly, its intricate forming, or more accurately, *deforming*, of the processes of human becoming that represent the domination of human subjectivity. Human capital theory's revolutionary repercussions in reproduction are akin to those of machines in production, squeezing value through the reproduction and exploitation of human differences, tethering the rhythms and intimate relations of human life outside of work to the automaton of capital. Capital's poisoning of life at its "very roots" is concealed in the spectacle of the priceless child.

The Priceless Child Versus the Differentially Valued Child in Neoliberal Racial Capitalism

The child, too, like the commodity and as commodity, is a bundle of contradictions—most apparently in our culture's endless sentimental paeans to the pricelessness of the child and in the drudging reality of the child's valuation.[9] Marx began his analysis of the two-sidedness of the commodity by first noting its transhistorical character as a thing-in-itself—as use-value. This strategy signals its ontological, practical, and political primacy as such—the thing exists outside capitalism, whose irreducible concrete sensuousness escapes its abstractions. And so is the autonomous child—born with an indomitable will and life force, always already an intersubjective being in a vast network of social relations that span the globe, inheritor of the wisdom and folly of the species, and primed to make their way into and transform a subset of this massive collective undertaking we call culture. It can be said with no false sentimentality that the child confronts us with the mysteries and peculiarities of the species and life itself. Each and every child is inviolable and each and every child—and adult for that matter—deserves the bounties of the earth and the species, and none of its unnecessary tragedies.[10] We can adapt Ruth Wilson Gilmore's oft-quoted maxim "Where life is precious, life is precious" to say, where life is precious, the child is precious. What is the use-value of the child? The child has no "use" for anything or anyone but its own self and as such should have no price either: the child is priceless. The inviolable nature of human autonomy applies to children and extends to humans throughout the life cycle. Yet stressing the child's pricelessness demonstrates how badly society fails even in its own inverted terms, where only children are afforded even the veneer of being outside the market's value calipers.

Ritual incantations of the child's pricelessness enable and mystify the other side of pricelessness—the absurd reality of the child's exchange value. Endless efforts to measure children's value, the price of their potential lifetime earnings and contribution to the economy looming over their heads, the ticking time bomb of the declining returns on investment in children as they age—all these cues nag and gnaw at sanctimonious notions of children's pricelessness. Still, the priceless child figure looms so large that it conceals the violence of abstraction to which children are continually subject—their irreducible uniqueness and heterogeneity, that is, their preciousness, flattened into infinitesimal measures of various isolated cognitive abilities and, more recently, the curious quantification of specific "social and emotional" qualities, which are presumed to lead to "success." The priceless child further conceals that the "priced" child also has two sides. For investment involves discernment—what or who is worthy of investment? The invisible hand seems to determine matters here too. Some children yield bigger returns and befit a strategy of "accumulation," Cindi Katz asserts, while others are disinvested, seen as "waste."[11] Not only are children incessantly measured and rendered into value theoretically exchangeable with specific quantities of yarn, coats, or iron; some children are worth more yarn, coats, or iron, and some are worth less.

The "priceless" child, then, is no mere ideal but a mystification that inverts the image of children's domination as it stands before us. The vast majority of children in this world are deprived, abused, exploited, and robbed of any semblance of childhood. Even relatively privileged children of advanced economies are conscripted to work learning a set of knowledge under the more or less harsh conditions of schooling. Yet few understand schools as a site of forced labor. Instead, schooling appears as good or neutral and necessary, something that children should enjoy or at least endure. The incredible efforts to intensify children's labors to build up their storehouse of potential value, and to standardize, measure, and norm their labors of learning are not considered forms of violence subjecting children to the forces of abstraction that ultimately reduce them to a price. Capital does place a precise value on children's various skills, abilities, and dispositions, same as it does labor power. And this *differential* value has always been figured in and through race. And so, while Gilmore emphasizes that "life is precious," she maintains that racism is life made less precious. This dramatically concerns children. Yet children's subordination as differentially valued racialized subjects remains stubbornly invisible within critical theories. How can the double character of the child, as simultaneously "priceless" and differentially valued, appear without contradiction? Reading human capital theory with Marxist theory on productivity elucidates capital's vicious attempts to subordinate the human subject in childhood.

The Machine of Human Capital Theory

The fetish of human capital coheres around the child because human capital is nothing but capital's warped synonym for labor power. Labor power, in Marx's terms, is the "capacity for labor" and is the sole "special commodity" in the capitalist mode of production because it is the *only* one with the "peculiar property of being a source of value," and capital "always seeks to enhance" this peculiar property.[12] From capital's point of view, childhood is where labor power is made, and most crucially, where it can be made better—a unique stage of life in which the human can best be shaped as an ideal subject that is willing and able to work for capital to generate as much value in the future as possible. The child, in the midst of developing its various properties and capacities, is capitalism's most precious commodity, for in this stage labor power exists as pure potentiality. As the latest psychological research continually emphasizes the plasticity of the child's developing brain, economists have increasingly emphasized that childhood is the critical time period for investment in the child's future value.[13] The earlier one invests in the child, the more pronounced is the augmentation of its human capital. Early investment is strategic because more capital is created with seemingly fewer resources (maternal labors are largely invisible or undervalued). In this way, greater productivity can be achieved in reproduction.

Economists' principal concern is productivity. To wit, human capital theory was explicitly articulated as a research program in the mid-twentieth century as economists associated with what is now known as the Chicago school, Jacob Mincer (1958), Theodore Schultz (1961), and Gary Becker (1962, 1964), asked how to make humans—as a form of capital—more productive.[14] The theory is founded on the Mincer equation, which examined income as a function of schooling.[15] This "schooling model" was soon extrapolated to the population level—to ask how societies can invest in their population to grow capital. The model's scope includes the human qualities that yield the highest returns, accruing to the individual as income, for the economy as growth, for the capitalist as surplus value or what appears as profit. The human aspect of human capital marks the fact that it is "embodied"; it cannot be separated from the person, unlike other forms of capital. The concept tries to account for how qualitative differences in laboring subjects (e.g., health, cognitive skills, education, training) produce quantitative differences in value (e.g., income, capital, economic growth). It is an attempt to harness particular qualities of living labor to intensify work and increase (relative) surplus value that appears as profit, that is, to make labor more productive.

Where "productivity" may seem like a gain for the individual, Marxist theory has incontrovertibly demonstrated that capital's efforts to make labor more productive through whatever means it has at its disposable (technological, scientific, managerial) have never been about reducing the amount or onerousness of labor, to "free" labor as it were. Freeing humans from more drudgery, or speeding them up so that there is more free time, is certainly a theoretical and practical possibility of technological development. Indeed, this is the utopian substance of the ancient Greek poetry that Marx cites in his discussion of machines. Antipater of Thessalonica dreamed that the waterwheel would "spare the hand" of the women who toil at the mill to "softly sleep" and "rest from work and enjoy the gifts that the goddess sends us."[16] Yet this possibility has never been pursued in capitalism—in fact, the very reverse.[17] Productivity is another unremunerated way to intensify and pump more surplus value from labor, to increase the rate of exploitation.[18] Further, productivity is a method to more firmly place workers under capital's command. This is how Marx, and the earliest industrial laborers on whom they were imposed, viewed machines: as further shifting the balance to capital in war against labor. As human capital theory is fundamentally about productivity, it is worth quoting Marx on capital's central obsession at length, with my emphases:

> Within the capitalist system, all methods for raising the social productivity of labour are put into effect at the cost of the individual worker; that all means for the development of production undergo a dialectical inversion so that they become means of domination and exploitation of the producers; they *distort* the worker into a fragment of a man, they *degrade* him to the level of an appendage of a machine, they *destroy* the actual content of his labour by turning it into a torment, they *alienate* from him the intellectual potentialities of the labour process in the same proportion as science is incorporated in it as an independent power, they *deform* the conditions under which he works, *subject* him during the labour process to a despotism the more hateful for its meanness, transform life-time into working-time . . . beneath the juggernaut of capital.[19]

What is ultimately at stake in technological advancement or so-called productivity is the domination of the human subject to the automaton of capital.

Because human capital theory is a scientific-technological intervention to raise labor's productivity, I find it apt to consider it a machine. While this may seem an awkward formulation because a machine is not a concrete object, machines can involve material objects yet still be in essence immaterial. For instance, Taylorism, or any form of "scientific management," would not be reduced to its physical objects like conveyor belts. The machine in its Marxist sense concerns the organization and application of technological knowledge to command labor and the labor process. In Marx's read, technological advances in production do not spring ex nihilo from capitalists' ingenuity and innovative spirit but are introduced to subordinate unruly labor. Human capital theory similarly emerged as an essentially reactionary force to discipline labor and quell liberatory movements. The 1960s were a period of capital's multipronged counterattack on labor's successes in stabilizing the forty-hour workday and negotiating higher wages for rising productivity in the 1940s and 1950s.[20] Just as critically, human capital theory developed in a historical moment of protracted struggle for women's liberation, as well as Black struggle, uprising, and rebellion (1960s and early 1970s). Human capital theory was never intended as an academic model of reality but a weapon to discipline labor, women, and racialized Others, and a method to instantiate a social order where the market allows "natural" hierarchies to flourish.

Abstraction and the Capital That Is Human

Human capital theory appears to be economists' attempt to view human labor qualitatively rather than an undifferentiated mass of labor power—humans embodying various assets, resources, skills, and experiences. Yet it is economists' more capacious attempt (vis-à-vis their predecessors) to quantify the qualitative aspects of living labor and render the complex properties of the human subject more homogeneous and exchangeable. The concept presupposes a host of social processes and techniques of abstraction whereby human value can be measured as another form of capital. That is, it is a perverted yet quotidian way to refer to human subjects that depends on abstract labor, the category Marx derived as the social substance of value homogenized from concrete labor. Sensuous living subjects recede from view, and what advances instead are bundles of knowledge, skills, and dispositions that happen to be embodied in living beings—humans as capital.[21] Marx's untangled the warped form of abstract labor from the living substance that it mystifies, a strategy that pierces the antagonism at the heart of human capital theory.

Marx's notion of labor power is "the aggregate of those mental and physical capabilities," which assumes its empty generic form as abstract labor within capitalism—a pure undifferentiated abstraction of labor time is the substance of value in its various forms within capitalism.[22] Abstract labor enables the equivalence of all things, so that they differ "only in a purely quantitative way," placing the concept at the center of Marx's theory of value.[23] Marx described how commodities are able to appear in the form of exchange value emptied of their substance in concrete living labor: "There is nothing left of them in each case but the same phantom-like objectivity; they are merely congealed qualities of homogeneous human labor, i.e. of human labour-power."[24] Labor itself is able to appear as exchange value in a similar process of emptying the human subject of its concrete living aspects. Grasping the social relations and material processes that create the reified forms of value—abstractions—in capitalist society is at the heart of the Marxist project. And above all, unraveling the mysteries of how human labor in capitalism takes the peculiar form of value and how this process dominates humans in ways they cannot perceive.

The abstraction of labor's exchange value from its living substance allows the valorization process and constructs the unique form of domination through impersonal forces in capitalist society: "Individuals are now ruled by abstractions, whereas earlier they depended on one another. The abstraction, or idea, however, is nothing more than the theoretical expression of those material relations which are their lord and master."[25] Marxist articulations of "real abstraction" theorize the forms of power within capitalist society, where capital's categories and motion—products of human activity and social relations—come to dominate humans not through illusions, false consciousness, or interpersonal domination but as real forces of compulsions that operate on subjects, albeit "behind the[ir] backs."[26] Abstraction not only shifts the form of capital's domination of subjects; those abstractions coerce subjects to reproduce those forms themselves.[27] Labor power, abstracted from all its living qualities, can appear on the market and fully exchangeable for a wage. The presupposition of exchange value makes the sale of labor power possible: "As the objective basis of the whole of the system of production, already in itself implies *compulsion over the individual* . . . hence that the *whole negation of his natural existence* is already implied; that he is therefore *entirely determined by society*."[28] The abstraction of the wage, Marx reminds us, places us in the "Eden of the innate rights of man" where everyone contracts as presumptively "free agents."[29] The violence, force, and compulsions that brought about the appearance of the conditions of this "equal exchange" are hidden.

The force of human capital theory in social life is illuminated by Marx's conception of living labor's antagonism with the abstraction of labor power that brings to the fore the antagonism between capital and labor. Living labor, "irreducibly affiliated with heterogeneity" "cannot but remain a kind of inimical alterity within the constraints of abstraction, homogenization, and objectification."[30] Value emerges through this struggle to "fix" this unruly form, which then reacts back on social relations as a force of impersonal compulsion.[31] In human capital theory, capital finds a technology to realize its drive of reducing human life to exchange value, to render the commodity labor power into a complete abstraction, and to have a living form of capital to claim its own.

Human capital theory's domination of subjects and social relations is further illuminated with Marx's "fragment on machines" passage of the *Grundrisse*. Here Marx poetically summarized capital's drive to absorb, deplete, and route human vitality and creativity toward its own reproduction. In a passage that captures the dialectical inversion of how "all methods" to boost productivity are turned against humans (cited earlier), Marx explains how machines, representing the development of science and technology (a product of human "general intellect"), come to absorb the "general intellect" that laborers cultivate in their free time and higher activities only to reduce and objectify human activity to fixed capital or dead labor.[32] When Marxist scholars take up the notion of human capital, it is often regarded as a tool to measure the value of the "general intellect" as "fixed capital" in capital's "regime" or "war" of measure imposed on labor.[33] In an analysis of "human capital" from the perspective of the machines fragment, Jason Read argues that Marx tries to articulate a future he could "barely envision, a future that has become our present: the real subsumption of society by capital . . . the incorporation of all subjective potential, the capacity to communicate, to feel, to create, to think, into productive powers for capital"[34] Human capital theory unleashes "the ravages generated by social abstraction" far outside the sphere of production, onto subjectivity and social relations, a process theorized as "capital's colonization of what others will name 'life,' 'being,' 'society,' 'culture,'" or "total subsumption."[35]

Marxism's accounts of capital's inexorable drive to pump labor from human life for its accumulation of value, its abstraction of living labor into the peculiar form of value, its monstrous tendency to subsume all human affairs have one goal—to explain human unfreedom within capitalism. Yet this account of the "*mastery* of human life by production" must be pushed forward to ask why this mastery has "pervasively assumed the form of *racial* domination."[36] Understanding racial domination necessarily entails revisiting the origins of capital in enslavement. The horrors of capital's genesis reveal the crucial role of violence and racial subjugation to capital accumulation, and how this fundamentally involves capital's seizing the means of reproduction. Insights from Black feminism expose how human capital theory is a mode of power, governance, and subjugation that resurrects and revivifies capital's aspirations of total domination of the human subject.

Reproducing Humans as Capital

Human capital theory's capacious attempts to reduce and abstract the human subject into the value-form appear unremarkably, a specialized, if ubiquitous, measure within employment and education. Yet the foundations of sorting, ranking, quantifying, commodifying, and assigning human life a differential valuation vis-à-vis other human life are to be found in the very origins of capital itself in chattel slavery.[37] Indeed, the earliest critiques of the concept of human capital were directed at its name, which so brazenly echoes the language of enslaved labor. The theory's hegemony and ubiquity seem to have wiped away this association. As Gary Becker, one of the theory's founders and its most energetic cheerleader, remarked: "I think economists have forgotten about this now. It's no longer brought up very much. And politicians have forgotten about it now."[38] Heeding scholarly interventions to reframe capitalism's foundations within enslavement to construct a theory of reproductive labor that is able to account for its racialized legacies in the present, this chapter seeks to remind readers that the term "human capital" was never figurative. We might consider, with Jennifer Morgan, that the decisive moment of modernity was the "possible commodification of all bodies" where they could be assigned a stable monetary value, a moment that had the "rawest and most devastating articulation" for the enslaved.[39] Human capital, like every measure of life as a form of value in modernity, is marked by the centuries-long world-catastrophic events of slavery, mobilizing race and anti-Blackness in the present. Capital is "capable of converting anything it touches into a monetary equivalent," and it is indelibly haunted by "the specter of slavery, the slave auction block, the slave trader's ledger book, the specter, quite precisely of another wounded, suffering human body."[40] Fungibility, anti-Blackness, and race as death-making apparatus are at the very heart of capital.[41] The total abstraction of the human subject inherent in human capital relies on the very same material and symbolic structures set in motion by slavery. Human capital, a technology to reduce the human to capital, must then be considered a transmuted and evasive form through which the "afterlife of slavery" haunts the present.[42]

Whenever and wherever human capital theory is mobilized, it inextricably summons slavery's "racial calculus and political arithmetic."[43] Though absent in conventional accounts of the origins of capitalism's modes of valuation, as well as the material, social, and symbolic relations of domination that subtend our present, enslaved women's reproductive labors were critical in their creation.[44] The contemporary presence of enslavement's violent and "obscene abstractions" is concealed within seemingly ordinary processes such as finance, trade, kinship, and even ethics, which require a "methodology of relatedness" to make them visible.[45] These insights illuminate the ways that capitalism's foundational racial and gendered violence and domination persist in mothering and childhood today, even when they do not appear to be so.

The quotidian and incessant valuations of children are irreducibly processes of abstraction set in motion by enslavement. Anti-Blackness and racial hierarchy are thus built into human capital theory and revivified whenever valuations or "investments" into the human are made. Black studies' elaborations of fungibility—the equivalence or exchangeability of qualitatively different things—broaden the analytical possibilities offered by Marxist discussions of abstraction, particularly how we might think about the way human capital theory continually extends its force in reproduction.[46] While measuring the value one acquires through education and training (social or "acquired" traits), the concept of human capital always incorporates biogenetic ("innate") forms.[47] Chief among these is intelligence, a measure human capital theory conceives as straddling both genetic and acquired traits. The history of the concept of intelligence in modernity (i.e., IQ) is fully shot through with the history of white supremacy and racial subjugation. Although the recurrent revivals of arguments concerning the purportedly inherent racial differences in IQ are often associated with the fringes of the so-called right and do not seem to require serious engagement, the concept of human capital quietly smuggles this inherently racialized measure in a neutral guise. Insights from Black studies prompt a reframing of every scene of investing in the child as a scene of subjection, one that reanimates and proliferates racial hierarchy because every aspect of human capital is fully racialized.

From its foundation in enslaved humans as exchange value to its emergence as a theory to reinstate hierarchies of class, gender, and race, to its reliance on measuring the fully racialized notion of IQ, to the way it smuggles in the valuation of bodies and genes, and finally, its reliance on women's reproductive labors and its transference of the mother's embodied value to the child, racial hierarchy is at the center of human capital theory. This racialized tool is global, assigning all the world's people and populations a potential monetary value, and it imbues race with its characteristic neoliberal form—a seemingly neutral quantitative measure by which human subjects are understood and governed in the economic sphere.

Mothers and the Machine: Reproducing Humans for Capital

What happens when capital—that undead substance congealed from the living human subject only to be turned against it—is unleashed on the most sensitive time period of human development and the most formative relation between parent and child, when the interactions, care, and work for a child are oriented toward its accumulation? Thus far, critical theory has not considered such a question. It necessitates an account of subjectivation that links Marxist and Black feminist insights with Foucault. Foucault is hardly known as a theorist of motherhood. Yet his analysis of human capital inadvertently gives us a framework with which to grasp the alarming repercussions of capital's targeting of its most vulnerable and valuable objects—mothers and children.

Foucault places the concept of human capital at the center of neoliberalism's key transformations in *The Birth of Biopolitics*, his lectures outlining the emergence of a new form of state power to administer life. Modern governmentality, he figured, is a mode of power in which economics establishes the government's "truth telling" and economists become liberalism's "sole thinkers."[48] For Foucault, human capital theory provides an avenue to extend bourgeois economic rationality to new domains and is responsible for constructing neoliberalism's unique form of subjectivity. Foucault contends that human capital economists aimed to fill the "vacuum" of classical economic theory's incomplete abstraction of labor.[49] Human capital economists recognized that laborers naturally differ and that they could intervene to develop desirable traits that generate a larger return, glossed now as the "capital" that they both possess and embody. This seemingly simple innovation imbues capital with almost limitless possibilities for governing human subjects for productivity. That is, capital can create subjects with qualities it finds attractive by identifying those qualities valuable because people are "free" to invest in themselves and self-appreciate. Since all behaviors and experiences potentially appreciate or depreciate their value, it becomes possible to govern or "act on the way subjects govern themselves, by inciting them to adopt conducts *deemed* valorizing."[50] As income accrues to abilities that are inseparable from the person, the subject becomes the object on which to act rationally in all realms. As Feher put it adroitly, "my human capital is me."[51]

In the intervening fifty years since Foucault gave his lecture, human capital theory has so thoroughly pervaded social life that the answer is self-evident to his question "What does it mean to form human capital, and so to form these abilities machines which will produce income, which will be remunerated by income?" "It means, of course, making what are called educational investments."[52] Capital has long relied on schools to shape working subjects, ever since children ceased to be deemed acceptable as paid laborers. Critics of capitalist schooling point out that schooling imparts knowledge and skills aimed at laboring for capital, as well as specific dispositions to laboring for capital—bodily habitus, adapting to specific temporal rhythms, and obedience to authority.[53] In a foundational lecture delivered many times, Becker emphasized how "good habits," such as the "virtues of punctuality and honesty," are also investments in human capital.[54] Schools are fundamentally involved with creating such subjects for capital. Yet Foucault pushed his analysis beyond traditional concerns with schooling to the intimate domain of the home, where the bleaker repercussions for subjectivity occur.

Mothers and children appear as actors, however briefly, in Foucault's discussion of the repercussions of economists' concern with subjectivity and the emergence and dominance of biopolitics in neoliberalism. Investments in human capital go beyond "simple schooling and professional training" and include the "time parents devote to their children," and even the "simple time" a mother spends "when [a child] is still in the cradle."[55] While hewing closely to the early literature, Foucault pushes beyond its pretenses of neutral mathematical calculations of maternal time allocation to arrive at a dystopian image of domestic life under the tyranny of human capital calculations: "We thus arrive at a whole environmental analysis, as the Americans say, of the child's life which it will be possible to calculate, and to a certain extent quantify, or at any rate measure, in terms of the possibilities of investment in human capital. What in the child's family life will produce human capital? What type of stimuli, form of life, and relationship with parents, adults, and others can be crystallized into human capital."[56] This is perhaps Foucault's most prophetic tangent in his far-reaching lectures on neoliberalism's transformations. If afforded an opportunity to develop his insights concerning the repercussions for mothers and children, perhaps Foucault would have revised the defining trait of

Homo economicus. For "the child" is not capable of being an entrepreneur "for himself." Nor could schools effectively institute such a subject. Rather, this coup is achieved by positioning the mother as "an entrepreneur of [her child] . . . being for [her child] the source of [their future] earnings." The issues that Foucault gestured toward as a possible dystopian possibility and bracketed off for a later discussion—human capital's subsumption of the minutia and intimacies of mothers' and children's everyday lives, their "forms of stimuli, forms of life, relationships"—are now firmly normalized as "good mothering." In the half century since Foucault sounded this warning, childhood reproduction is precisely the arena in which capital has made the most gains in its drive to hollow out human vitality. Capital's intensified domination of subjectivity occurs in plain sight. Yet critics see only good mothers, bad mothers, suffering mothers.

Turning to motherhood and childhood with multiple critical traditions allows us to grasp the invidious force with which human capital invades the porous process of human becoming. Reproduction in neoliberalism substantiates and extends Marx's critique of capital's domination of the human subject, Black feminism's insights into the violence undergirding abstractions and the extension of its logic to seemingly ordinary social relations and symbolic structures, and Foucault's account of how subjectivity is formed within structures of power—capital's power. Human capital theory enables capital to seize reproduction. Where Marx made clear how capital systemically steals human ingenuity as it develops and turns into a force against humans, human capital theory functions in ways we are only beginning to fathom in reproduction. If all maternal experiences, knowledge, and relationship with the child is devoted to investing in that child's "capital," then free time no longer exists—not for mothers and not even for babies. By conscripting mothers to "invest," the machine of human capital theory subverts and deforms the manifold open-ended processes of human becoming into a singular tunnel of becoming value for capital. When Feher avers that human capital "erodes the distinction between reproduction and production," he emphatically meant that reproduction *becomes* production.[57] We are no longer laboring for capital, but living for capital.

Human capital theory silently whirs to harness life at the "very roots" and binds it to the motion of value, so that our vital forces become a productive force *for* capital, wedding life to machine. Machines, to return to Marx, are dead labor that suck more life or living labor from humans. When the machine is installed within the subject, it becomes a subject formed against its own life.

Becoming Racialized Value or Non-value

Sylvia Wynter's articulation of how subjects are initiated as such is an analytic through which we can appreciate how human capital theory coheres on subjects and just as crucially, how it becomes a key vehicle through which the afterlives of slavery are revivified, even as it dissimulates its derivation from race and appears racially neutral. Wynter—and Fanon, from whom she expanded the concept of sociogeny (literally "birthed by society")—figures humans as hybrid beings, as much social-symbolic as biological. She signifies our hybridity in couplets such as bios and mythoi, skin and masks, "inner eyes which with we look through our physical eyes."[58] Every society, she proposed, initiates its members into "a master script containing its truths," "sociogenic codes of symbolic life and death" that define why and how subjects are valued or devalued.[59] Wynter illuminates how profoundly race structures society and psyche by demonstrating how race is inherently a template of value or non-value. Race incontrovertibly defines the reigning conception of the human in modernity, built in the rubble of slavery, colonialism, and capitalism. It saturates our symbolic systems and is the central kernel of modernity's knowledge, values, relationships. We are initiated into the hierarchies of humanness, nourished or as it were malnourished, in and through the symbolic structures of race, the master signifier of capitalist society.

Human capital theory is currently the reigning material and symbolic code of value in neoliberal society. It provides the explanatory framework of the present order, defining who is valued, who is not, and how one obtains more value. Subjects are initiated into this symbolic system in processes that begin in childhood. Human capital theory's continual ranking of a child's value from birth—as part genetic endowment from parents, and part potential to be developed by mother via her time, education, and her own genetic endowments—marks mothers as key to the reproduction of that pernicious abstraction of value. Value becomes the mask and "inner and outer eyes" through which subjects see the world. It hijacks and institutes the general and perhaps universal desire of mothers within any value system, to institute their children as "valued" members of their social order. To do so in neoliberalism involves an entire "project" where mothers are induced to devote their lives increasing the exchange value of their child. Human capital theory seizes human becoming and routes it toward the valorization of value. Further, human capital becomes a vehicle through which mothers' own embodied value is transmitted. Whether genetic or acquired, this embodied value is inherently delimited and determined by race. Through the targeting of mother and child, the racialized technology of human capital reinscribes racial hierarchy to produce differently valued subjects for capital. Children are always already-racialized subjects and childhood is an important site of race making, although these processes are often obscured by seemingly universal constructions concerning childhood.[60] For instance, the notion of innocence that coheres so strongly to childhood and to which adults are so invested is routinely denied to children of color.[61] Similarly, the hegemonic figure of the universal child and its scale of development at the center of psychology appears applicable to all children, yet is built upon the normative white child masquerading as universal.[62] Human capital theory redoubles race and normalizes the most grotesque hierarchies of the human because it applies, increases, and intensifies an array of seemingly ordinary and objective measures (scores, rankings, exams, grades, credentials) of human ability and capacity. There is a seeming circularity to these operations, which are about how they are reciprocal and self-reinforcing. Chattel slavery, and the centuries of racial domination in its wake, established hierarchies of value by which human life could be sorted, ranked, measured, and commodified. It made such quantifications and valorizations ubiquitous and routine, and it lent racial domination the semblance of something objective, natural, and universal. The incessant assessment and evaluation of children in schools today enables the quantification of their worth as "human capital." These measures are neither neutral or objective attributes. They are based on a tangle of traits that are always already saturated with racial (as well as class and gender) hierarchy. Through these measures, inherited social inequalities get recoded as intrinsic differences of inherent (quasi-biological) value and appear to reconfirm the seemingly natural hierarchies of race as biology. These measures meld onto the child, the innocent priceless figure through which a seemingly objective racial valuation of human life is concretized.

While disavowing race, with its innocent exhortations for mothers to make the most of their children's seemingly infinite potential, human capital theory *compounds* the racialized value of children's lives. It coerces mothers into the continual investment in their children as capital and unleashes capital into the love and care for a child. All societies encourage the development of a finite set of the nearly infinite human capacities and discourage others in a more or less collective yet contested processes. In neoliberalism, capital usurps and stealthily distorts this collective human endeavor through human capital theory. Instead of nurturing what is universally and particularly vital about each human, human capital theory enlists mothers to suppress the development of those vital forces that would refuse their subordination of life to capital. In its drive to subordinate life to value, human capital's ground zero is the slave. Enslavement inaugurated the human as capital and depended so crucially on women's reproductive labors. The machine of human capital similarly subordinates women's reproductive labors to make humans capital. It subordinates mothers and children to its unique temporality—its future in the present—so that a child's being and becoming is pulled into the cycle of capital's becoming. This machine is dependent on, animates, and proliferates anti-Blackness, however much it also mutes and legitimizes it. Its aspirations and repercussions for children's lives are laundered by the everyday language of mobility and prosperity, education, child development, and most profoundly, care and love for one's child. Ultimately human capital can cohere in subjects because it poses as theoretically and practically open to all, with the right mother.

3

Maternal Time, Child "Value"

A Critique of the Political Economy of Motherhood

> The most important price in the production of children during the early years of each child is the price of the mother's time.
>
> —*Theodore Schultz, Economics of the Family*

IT SEEMS THAT time itself haunts mothers: never enough time, never good enough time, the opportune time always slipping away. No mother has to read the *Journal of Human Capital* to have understood that "investing" her time in a child's upbringing is supposedly "the strongest predictor" of her child's future success. Economists, child development experts, and education experts endlessly underscore the importance of maternal time. Its irreplaceability is emphasized in public culture—including the National Institutes of Health and pamphlets in pediatricians' offices; DC-based think tanks that offer to shape work-family and educational policy; the dedicated parenting sections of publications such as *The New York Times*, *The Atlantic*, *The Wall Street Journal*, and even *The Economist*; and the US Department of Education's and school systems' near-daily missives to parents. It is not simply the amount of time; it is also the "quality" of that time and, most crucially, the experts insist, *when* in a child's life mothers give that time. Mothers must synchronize their efforts with the arc of the child's development. Any interference with the timing of the ideal arc, experts warn, spells loss, even irredeemable disaster.

The only thing more irreversible than losing the opportune time to invest in the child seems to be death itself. In fact, in the United States, from the first weeks that the COVID-19 pandemic began to ravage city after city, the media mourned the loss of children's learning more that the loss of life that remains collectively unmourned. "Disastrous test scores," "intractable obstacles," children to be "punished throughout their lifetime" and bound to "suffer a lifelong drop in [future] income."[1] Commentators bemoaned how this loss is irrecoverable for children and for "the nation," with economists estimating between a 0.6 percent and 2.9 percent drop in the country's gross domestic product "for the remainder of the 21st century."[2] Trillions irretrievably lost in the abyss of the gap. For, like everything else in the pandemic, the losses (and gains) are not borne evenly but exacerbate existing vulnerabilities and inequalities. Politicians, experts, and pundits sounded the alarm that the pandemic widened the so-called gaps that are the perpetual outrage of US society—the wealth gap, the racial gap, the achievement gap, and most recently, the mortality gap. A widely publicized study by economists in 2023 found a life gap of eight and a half years between those with a college education and those without one.[3] Major media outlets blasted the findings: "Americans without college degrees live shorter lives"; "Without a college degree, life is staggeringly shorter" and "Americans without college degrees die younger."[4] And here, we circle back to mothers. For ever since these gaps have been identified and made the object of knowledge, anxious hand-wringing, and intervention, all causal arrows begin at mothers. It is from mothers, we have been told for over half a century, that all the gaps that bedevil society emerge. The resounding chorus—whether experts in the pulpit or parishioners in the pews—is that mothers' time makes the difference.

A vast feminist literature on time-intensive mothering emphasizes the control of mothers by "experts" such as child development professionals.[5] Yet few critics trace the dominance of expert-backed styles of parenting to human capital economists' initial forays into the family in the 1970s. In contrast, I situate the transformations that register as "intensive parenting" as manifestations of economists' singular focus on maternal time as the key variable of human capital investment, and thus a child's future "success." I pursue an analysis akin to Marx's scathing critique of the field of political economy that has analyzed "value [human capital] and its magnitude," but "has never once asked . . . why the measurement of [maternal] labour by its duration is expressed in the magnitude of the value of the product [the child]."[6] In this spirit, the object of my critique is not the child's human capital value, but why maternal "labor takes the form it does and with which political consequences."[7]

This chapter is an extended critique of the political economy of motherhood, discerning economists as the architects of capital's subsumption of reproduction that increases, intensifies, and transforms maternal work into labor, crystalizing into a child's value. The central object of scrutiny is economists' equations concerning maternal time. Economists couch their concerns with mothers in terms of time investment, or simply time. And not simply time loafing around; economists demand "quality time." "Maternal time" is their obfuscation for labor, a category that they and others routinely deny to mothers (see Premise 3). The work of shaping children into labor power is indeed labor *for* capital. When economists speak, they do so not on children's behalf, but on capital's behalf—they are pronouncing capital's directives for children's becoming. On capital's behalf, economists demand an extension of mothers' working day, beyond even its natural limit of rest and regeneration (more time), and they demand to intensify and regulate maternal labors ("quality time"). In Marxist terms, they want to extend and subsume mothers' working day of reproducing labor power. We are squarely in the terrain of struggle. Yet it does not appear as such because "mother" appears as a universal category outside of class; because mothering is denied the status of work; because mothers' supposed "labors of love" are perverted into a prolonged process of preparing children for the competitive demands of the market, where they will fetch a price.

Economists, I underscore, are not simply another set of parenting "experts"; they are liberalism's "sole thinkers" whose "truth telling" represents the interests of capital and delimit the possibilities of freedom for its continued accumulation.[8] Economists do not hide that they speak for capital—they plainly say so themselves. What requires exposition is how economists' delimiting of human possibilities for capital comes to define the universe of parenting and what is best for the child, established as more or less accepted as true and, further still, rarely questioned. Indeed, a curious, if generally unremarked-upon, feature of the contemporary era is that economists hold center stage in parenting culture. They author bestselling books, publish op-eds, and are centrally featured in discussions about parenting in influential venues, and journalists call on them and translate their findings to the public. This is not simply a case of "economization," where parenting is considered one more domain where economists' logic prevails. The frame of "economization" is profoundly depoliticizing because it suggests that the matter simply involves a neutral cost-benefit calculation, a rather technical means to the end of doing what is best for children.[9] It does not appear as a decades-long profound hollowing and perversion of how we understand what is good for children and what is good for us collectively. What disappears from the economization mode of analysis are the operations of a political rationality that governs subjects. Economists' deceptively neutral technical language, coupled with their inversion of our collective understanding of what is good for children, dissimulates how capital's fury invades and transmogrifies one of the most important political processes within social life—the construction of persons in the anthropological sense. Economists' obsession with mothers and children ultimately concerns the hollowing of human freedom and our collective future horizons.

This chapter critically apprehends economists' equations concerning the relationship between maternal time and child success, scrutinizing the field's abstractions of those two concepts and the variables that alter their relation. I first analyze how maternal science establishes its hegemony as it circulates throughout the public sphere. I then examine the foundations of maternal science in human capital theory's initial turn to mothers in the mid-1970s, reading its formal articulations from a Marxist perspective as centrally involving the subordination of labor. With this reframing, I interrogate current maternal science research, finding its logic and assumptions relatively stable, albeit with its methodology and variables refined and its reach considerably expanded. With this hegemony, I illustrate how maternal science proliferates a racialized hierarchy of human life throughout the social body with its notion of maternal quality, via economists' policy recommendations and directives to parents during the pandemic. Viewing economists' directives for mothers, capital appears not as the rational yet destructive force in human life that Marxist theory conventionally narrates, but as an irrational undead force that dominate the social relations of reproduction.

The Family Firm Goes Public

A critique of the political economy of motherhood cannot be confined to economists' obscure publications, conference proceedings, and think tank position papers. It must target the ways that economists' "truth telling" circulates unremarkably in the public sphere and becomes the "common sense" and "best practices" of parenting culture. In their highly visible public profile as dependable, objective, and rational parenting and child experts, economists pitch themselves as parents' wise yet practical best friend, one who can help organize the chaos of contemporary parenting in a way that helps parents raise successful children while maximizing their own freedom. The highest-profile economist-cum-childcare expert is Emily Oster, whose best-selling parenting book series is marketed as "data-driven" advice to "empower parents." In *The Family Firm*, Oster guides parents to craft a "big picture approach" and "overall structure for your household firm." Sounding a personal note, she claims to help parents "work your way through your own" dilemmas—from deciding whether a mother should go (back) to work to figuring out how to prioritize children's extracurricular activities. Oster announces that hers is a "business book" and insists that such an approach "is best suited to this new age of parenting."[10] In their quest to differentiate themselves from other childcare experts, economists gain legitimacy by reminding the public that they are scientists, patiently laying out their methodology, their analysis of data, and its significance in lay language. They invite disagreement—on their terms. That is, their assumptions, categories, and ultimate goals are opaque and thus unassailable. At every turn, mothers' labors are invisibilized and euphemized as "decisions." Oster claims her approach helps save "time—and pain" in the end. And at every turn, the data are mustered to make decisions about child "outcomes"—performance on tasks that can be measured and normed, that is, school grades. Economists have defined school performance to be the decisive goal toward which all our conduct is oriented. The public somehow tacitly consents to these terms of order.

A close look at a rare occasion when an economists' fundamental assumptions were challenged is instructive. This was a disciplinary spat between economists and sociologists over maternal time that spilled out into the public, when a group of sociologists set out to test economists' apparently indisputable thesis concerning maternal time investment. The sociologists concluded the following: "Overall the amount of maternal time with children ages 3 to 11 did not matter across key domains" of "offspring's behavior, emotions, or academics."[11] The study was taken up in a variety of news outlets, with high-profile cultural commentators declaring a victory against time-intensive parenting. "Spending time with children doesn't change anything" declared the journalist, cultural commentator, and blogger Matthew Yglesias in *Vox*—the news site he cofounded.[12] The feminist journalist and blogger Jessica Valenti took it up in *The Guardian* with the headline "Don't Stress Out. Our Kids Are Just Fine When Their Mothers Work Late."[13]

So-called superstar economist Justin Wolfers coolly stepped into the debate to defend human capital economists' fundamental variable in *The New York Times*: "Yes, your time as a parent does make a difference."[14] He debunked what he characterized as the "latest salvo in the mommy wars" by claiming that it was based on inaccurate time measures and translated technical debates about time measurements for the public.[15] He faulted the enthusiastic media reception of the study (naming nine prominent outlets that reported on the piece) and shamed the cheerleaders for relying on wishful thinking. As a tired parent himself, one "who doesn't get enough time to work out, who hasn't seen a grown-up movie for months, and who wishes date night were an actual night rather than an idea," Wolfer sympathized with why one might "seize on studies suggesting we should take more time for ourselves." Yet he warned parents not to base their decisions on selfish desires, fantasy, or "misleading research": "Far better that we make our parenting choices informed by the broader set of more reliable studies, which [a developmental psychologist] summarized for me as suggesting that when parents spend *high-quality time* with their children, their children are more likely to succeed."[16] A child's success is the trump card, and the one who possesses that card is the arbiter of truth in the anxious world of neoliberal parenting. In this instance of public pedagogy, economists and psychologists joined to teach parents and others what good parents do and what bad parents should do differently. Good parents spend time—lots of time and, most importantly, quality time—with children. Good parents make choices informed by science. Good parents are exhausted. Good parents sacrifice. Good parents make decisions for long-term goals—successful children on their way to successful adulthoods.

The econo-psy complex works in plain sight to compel mothers to dedicate their life to laboring for capital. Labor oriented toward appreciating children's value for capital appears as wise choices and sacrifice in order to care for children. Perceiving these demands as such is challenging because parental directives are framed by an obfuscation (time), guided by an abstraction (human capital), and couched in terms of love, moral duty, and sacrifice—then complex and contested goals are simplified into certitudes (successful children, best for children). "Economics is the formula of an inverted and bewitched world," and so any critical apprehension of mothering must refuse its perversion of our central categories for thinking about childcare; including "maternal time investment," "human capital," and perhaps most crucially, "successful" children (and adults for that matter).[17] The ensuing discussion reverts these inversions when such terms are used.

The Limitless Value of Maternal Time

Mothers' care for children is work. While a seemingly uncontroversial claim, many begrudgingly add a proviso that suggests hesitation or suspicion. "Yes, it is labor, but it is a labor of love! Don't you love your child?" liberals and conservatives alike seem to say. It is on the point concerning the function of this work that liberal feminists (to say nothing of others) dismiss Marxist feminism for arguing that women's reproductive laborers are crucial for capital accumulation. Yet economists themselves say so plainly, all the time. While the perspective that mother's care for children is labor for capital should be a seemingly unproblematic claim for the left, provisos abound here as well. "Yes, it is labor, but it has little bearing on class struggle!" orthodox Marxists say. "Yes, it is labor, but it is not subordinated to the dictates of capital" some Marxist feminists say. All these provisos invisibilize, intentionally or not, the radical repercussions and political possibilities opened up by framing maternal work as labor.

For economists, women's reproductive labors are absolutely crucial for capital; they are the key variable in the "quantity" and "quality" of the labor supply. This is the basic assumption around which they orient their concerns with women and the family. "The scarce resource that matters most," Theodore Schultz writes in his introduction to human capital theory's first full-length edited volume on the family, *Economics of the Family: Marriage, Children, and Human Capital*, is "the economic value of the time of women."[18] The guiding question of maternal science's foundational text is how time allocation (then the discipline's new conceptual tool) and other factors, such as women's income, their embodied human capital, and other "disequilibria" (changes in economic value of education, improvements in contraceptive techniques, rise in income), affect women's decisions about the quantity ("fertility" or "the supply of labor") and quality of children as "forms of human capital."[19] Economists establish good or "most effective" mothers (by which they mean "most effective mothers for capital") through the process by which the mother transmits the value of her time (duration and quality of labor) and, crucially, her own embodied value to the "quality" of the child as future labor.

Becker's touchtone text *Human Capital* considered women to be economic agents insofar as how a "housewife" allocates her time in choosing and altering consumer goods in household production.[20] A decade later, the concern shifted to women's production of "heterogeneous stock of human capital"—children. If we consider the threats to traditional gender and family norms in the decade between the two texts (1964–1974), this focal turn is unsurprising. That is, human capital theory functions as a counterrevolutionary tool that disciplines women into gender and family norms in light of their unruliness and rejection of their reproductive roles. Although I focus on economists' concern with women's role in reproducing "quality" children, "quantity" is an eternally submerged concern that surfaces whenever the birth rate hovers near or drops below the so-called replacement level of 2.1 children per woman. These recurrent panics about women's rejection of child-rearing (one in which we are currently in the midst) reveal the utter necessity of manufacturing women's childbearing potential as natural and ideal role. This constructs women's reproduction as a "free" raw material that allows labor power to "appear continuously in the market . . . by procreation."[21]

Surveying recent articulations of human capital economists' maternal science highlights the urgency of framing it as labor subordination in the sphere of reproduction—mothers must be brought to heel. If we think with Marx, it should come as no surprise that economists hold maternal time to be the most precious variable. Time is after all the preeminent abstraction through which the value of labor is abstracted and expressed. We appear to and do, in many ways, sell our time. Time is the measure of how we sell our bodies, and time cannot be detached from bodies. Marx approaches his discussion of the working day with the deceptively simple, "But what is a working day?"[22] Deceptive because the answer is inherently variable—it depends on struggle. And thus Marx proceeds with his most detailed historical and ethnographic analysis of workers' militant struggles—that over *time*, to achieve the so-called normal working day.

Autonomous Marxist feminists' response to "what is a working day?" is perhaps their most important contribution to Marxist theory—the labors of reproducing labor power are part of the working day and must be considered an essential part of the struggle against capital. This is best expressed in one of the Wages for Housework movement's manifestoes, *Counter-Planning from the Kitchen*: "OUR STRUGGLE FOR THE WAGE [for housework] OPENS UP FOR THE WAGED AND THE UNWAGED ALIKE THE QUESTION OF THE REAL LENGTH OF THE WORKING DAY."[23] The wage demand is not about proper remuneration but reveals how capital invades the home and disciplines subjects for value accumulation. This political intervention reveals that the home is not a "haven" from capital and subjects are no more "free" from capital's rule there than they are at work. Their demand is a weapon in class struggle that reroutes and recaptures the domestic from capital to—in their unflinching words—"destroy" this work and capital itself.[24]

Like all other commodities, the price of labor power is the value of the material that goes into producing it (the means of production or in the case of reproduction, the means of subsistence) and the labor time needed to produce it.[25] Unlike all other commodities, the labor time of the commodity labor power is completely free when mothers provide it. This is the chief reason economists are fixated on maternal time "investments." Furthermore, unlike income-based investments in the child's human capital (economists' second major variable with an impact on child success), time investments have more elastic limits. It is possible to extend this work across mothers' unwaged time. And beyond that, it is possible to continuously intensify maternal labor through scientific and technological means. As Marx made clear, "lynx-eyed capital" searches beyond the working day, which has social, moral, legal, and natural limits, however elastic, to target labor's productivity, which has no foreseen limits.[26] Thus, the *intensity* of maternal time or its "quality" becomes the major point of intervention. This can be accomplished by professionalizing mothers and more tightly managing their labors. It is important to note that both professionalizing and managing mothers is less a matter of direct control and more a matter of intensifying and internalizing the disciplinary pressures operating on mothers. Coerced forms of self-discipline are nevertheless forms of submission and compliance, and indeed, indirect forms of power can be much more effective. The next chapter tracks the multiple apparatuses that are increasingly involved with direct, formalized, and concerted efforts to extend, intensify, and manage maternal labors in ways that augment children's value.

In the fifty years since human capital theorists established maternal time as the most valuable input for child development, women's reproductive labors—as reproducers of the labor supply or future labor power—remain in economists' direct field of vision. Yet their chief concern with mothers is now expressed in terms of the value they add to the child—euphemized in multiple ways as "later life outcomes," "future capacities," "future success," and so on. In his introduction to *Economics of the Family*, Schultz definitively declared: "The most important price in the production of children during the early years of each child is the price of the mother's time."[27] Current research expresses the fetish of maternal time as "one of the most valuable inputs for child development."[28] Half a century later, the language is strikingly similar in the hundreds of papers published annually that center maternal time allocation; for example, "the most important output of a household [woman] is the number and 'quality' of children it produces."[29] The field continually refines its abstraction of mother and child "quality." To wit, it enlists the psy sciences to quantify children's cognitive, social, emotional development, and likelihood of criminality. Early in human capital theory's development, economists began isolating various maternal traits—physical and mental health, age, educational level—to predict how they affect a mother's time or labor investment. Various traits of mothers have been further disaggregated, abstracted as variables, measured, made object of investigation and points of intervention. Advances in the field refine the relationship between maternal time allocation and children's performance on IQ or cognitive skills tests as putative measures of their development, intelligence, skills, and abilities, as proxies for current or future educational performance, and future lifetime of earnings and national economic productivity. Economists also refine how maternal time is mediated by other factors such as women's marital status, formal childcare such as day care, paternal time, and budget constraints.

Economists assume that mothers, like all others, are rational actors who would choose to maximize their "expected lifetime utility, optimally choosing her labor supply, childcare inputs, and the number of hours to spend with her child."[30] They analyze the effects of various public policy scenarios on women's time and how certain changes can tip the scales in either direction of the so-called trade-off that "households" must face in terms of maternal employment. On one side of the maternal equation is the "income effect"—the positive effects of the dollar amount that mother's income has on child development in terms of the array of commodities potentially purchased to provide comfort and economic stability. While an additional thousand dollars "improves cognitive development by about three percent of a standard deviation," an annual increase of one hundred hours at work (away from child) "decreases child development by about three percent of a standard deviation."[31] Economists posit that after a certain base level, additional income (goods purchased with commodities) does not accrue additional cognitive gains to the child. However, maternal time investments have no such boundaries. For economists, maternal time is an elastic unit whose upper limits can be stretched toward a fantasy of unfettered human capital growth. Maternal time's lower limit is just as fantastical—a nightmare scenario of criminality, delinquency, and every conceivable behavioral problem and psychopathology.

LOW-QUALITY MATERNAL TIME

In the public sphere, economists' intricate equations and specialized terminology are translated into common sense through the syntax of the moral panic. Witness the recent alarm that mothers were not meeting their quantity of labor time nor their labor "quality" requirements in the discourse of so-called distracted parenting. Virtually unheard of before 2015 and in full frenzy by 2018, the term refers to a phenomenon by which mothers purportedly neglect their children's emotional, psychological, and cognitive needs because they are focused on their own electronic devices. "It's the curse of 2022: Distracted parenting," bellowed one headline.[32] Articles and op-eds list a litany of detrimental effects on children: developmental delays in cognition, behavioral issues, psychopathologies (anxiety and depression), even brain damage. A BBC feature "Why Can't Our Children Talk?" made connections to children's educational performance: "Teachers all over the country report that children are arriving at school unable to communicate properly. They have limited vocabulary, no eye contact, don't know nursery rhymes or stories, may not even know their own address—why?"[33] The accompanied image answered: a sign posted outside a school pickup zone depicted a maternal figure with a cell phone to its ear struck by a bold red *X*, "Greet your child with a smile, not a mobile."[34] Experts warn that distracted mothers place their children on a destructive track: "Children who start school with reduced language skills may never recover. A child's vocabulary size at age two predicts their academic achievement right up to age 16. Children arriving at school with limited language skills are twice as likely to be unemployed."[35]

With its language of furtive misbehavior, distracted parenting discourse portrays mothers as idle workers shirking their duties behind managers' backs. *The Atlantic*'s "The Dangers of Distracted Parenting" framed the phenomenon as a double contradiction: despite women's increased participation in the workforce, mothers are spending more time with children, yet their engagement is "increasingly low quality."[36] The American Academy of Pediatrics accordingly coined a slogan—"laps not apps"—and parenting magazines offer advice for "tech addicted parents."[37] The articles and op-eds refer to studies by developmental psychologists detailing how mothers (the subjects are always mothers despite the gender-neutral term "parenting") behave in experimental and naturalistic settings. Many pieces include anecdotal observations of mothers tuning out their children to depict the issue as one of public concern. In *The Atlantic*: "Anyone who's been mowed down by a smartphone-impaired stroller operator can attest to the ubiquity of the phenomenon."[38] In *The New York Times*: "Yes. I saw that guy in the coffee shop who was so fixated on his tablet that he ignored his child's shining eyes. Don't be that guy. Yes. I saw that woman walking down the street with her little kid while her whole being was invested in her phone call. Don't be her, either."[39] With their looming imagery of damaged brains, neglected children, safety hazards, and public disorder, the econo-psy complex deputizes the public to regulate maternal labors on behalf of capital. All hands must be on deck for capital's quality assurance of its most precious source of value, even and especially during a state of emergency.

MATERNAL TIME DURING THE COVID-19 PANDEMIC

From the early days of the pandemic, a flood of media articles acknowledged the difficult position of mothers who, while experiencing this unprecedented period along with everyone else, had also lost their paid jobs, gained a job of managing children's schooling, or both. While seemingly sympathetic, the media's representations of and prescriptions to mothers during the COVID-19 pandemic became a site to coerce, expropriate, and control women's maternal labors, albeit in drastically uneven ways. Media portrayals of pandemic mothering seemed to adhere to a formula: Acknowledge mothers' difficulties in a seemingly sympathetic way; then deepen, displace, and negate them with a more pressing concern—the economy, children's learning, or both; and finally, saddle mothers with more labor.

As quickly as the virus spread, mothers were interpellated into a pandemic iteration of what the neoliberal education complex calls the "partner teacher" or the child's "first and most important teacher" (see Chapter 4). This maternal figure was depicted as the frustrated, anxious, yet sacrificially suffering subject downloading apps, straightening children's posture, and making sure children were "on task" throughout the virtual school day (three things my child's school explicitly coaxed parents to do during virtual schooling).

Schools throughout the US relied on mothers to help children with the transition to online learning and to manage children's efforts throughout the day.

Education experts continually sounded the alarm that despite rising death tolls and hospitalizations—time was of the essence in the ticking time bomb of decreasing returns on children's development. Not any old person's time but maternal time. Mothers' difficulties and their various chaotic scenarios were acknowledged only to emphasize that children were not learning. Educational experts sounded ominous warnings that were dutifully reported in the media: "Parental engagement has long been seen as critical to student achievement, as much as class size, curriculum and teacher quality. That has never been truer than now."[40] Students without "close" supervision would be even "worse" in terms of being "behind." The article closed with two mothers who seemingly had everything worked out to remind women that, with effort, anything is possible. Amid unprecedented fear and confusion, the media manipulated mothers' guilt and offered a salve of recognition to coerce additional and intensified labors. Mothers were expected to sacrifice for their children's education and futures, and they were rewarded much like congratulatory clapping for health care workers—symbolic recognition without any proposals for institutionalized action to ameliorate conditions. In a curious formulation, parenting, child, and education experts proposed "solutions" to mothers' exhaustion through methods that entailed more work. For example, experts advised mothers to create a visual schedule with a detailed list of things to keep children "on track" and "focused" on learning.[41] In "How to Get Your Kids to Treat You as a Teacher," *The New York Times* recommended creating a school area, with schedule and timer.[42] The media's window into mothers' plights during the pandemic was a relief valve to quell mothers' anguish by mere recognition. As New York City's chancellor of schools said to parents at the height of the city's death toll, "We see you, we hear you," before immediately asking mothers for more work.[43]

The displacement of the pandemic's unprecedented tragedies into economic damage is fully realized in the moral panic surrounding "learning loss." The phrase entered the lexicon along with new virus variants and vaccines, but unlike them, it has not been forgotten in collective memory. Economists and consultants from the World Bank and international organizations such as the Organisation for Economic Co-operation and Development estimate that $700 billion is needed to fix the nearly $1 trillion in learning loss caused by the pandemic.[44] A widely publicized study by the global management firm McKinsey was subtitled "The Hurt Could Last a Lifetime"; it predicted children's future lifetime earning losses across three possible scenarios, each with the catchphrase "loss of learning leads to loss of earning."[45] Consulting firms and venture capitalists investing in educational technology quickly jumped in to position themselves as experts with solutions.[46] In early June 2020, after three months of remote learning, *The New York Times* was stoking fear that, by September, some students would be "losing the equivalent of a year's worth of academic gains."[47] Much of the reporting focused on the disparities within this so-called loss, making clear that only the children of the wealthy, with their private teachers, tutors, and schools, would remain unscathed.[48] The moral panic triggered mothers' anxieties and guilt (the two most common affective states of neoliberal mothering) to coerce additional labors from already-beleaguered mothers charged with managing children's schooling. How else could mothers respond when seeing their child's potential lifetime earnings slashed in graph after graph?

Initially, the media ignored that the challenges of remote schooling were gendered. For instance, one month into online schooling in April 2020, *The New York Times* reported: "It Was Just Too Much: How Remote Learning Is Breaking *Parents*."[49] In the summer of 2020, the paper's article "In the COVID-19 Economy, You Can Have a Kid or a Job, but You Can't Have Both" wondered how New York City's shaky reopening plans for the fall, with students in school only one out of every three weeks, would affect "parents."[50] After a series of academic research explicitly situated parents' struggles during the pandemic as a women's issue and linked it to the ongoing crisis of care, the media began to take note.[51] In the fall of 2020, the NPR article "Stuck-at-Home Moms: The Pandemic's Devastating Toll on Women" reported that four times as many women as men had left the work force in September, pushing women back to 1988 workforce levels.[52] Women "are seeing the fabric of their lives unravel," and "they don't really have choices." NPR reported that "economists are worried" because the problem is bigger than individual women's personal and professional lives, for women's job loss would have devastating effects on "the economy's potential growth rate." The piece detailed mothers' "buildup of rage" and a "collective cry of anguish and an anger that is spilling out" onto various social media platforms, only to displace them with more important concerns—children or the economy, as befits the maternal sacrificial subject.

The pandemic starkly revealed the truth of the capitalist order—"in the trade-off between *economic* health and *workers'* health, capitalism sides with the former, which is another way of saying that capitalism sides with death over life."[53] Parenting, education, and child experts as well as the media added fuel to maternal anxieties of generalized neoliberal precarity. The only solution on offer is an inexhaustible set of additional maternal labors. Mothers are put to work at any cost. Moral panics concerning maternal time perform important ideological work, defining for mothers and the public what good and bad mothers are like and what they must do. Behind the distracted mother, behind the working mother whose child suffers needless learning losses, the good mother stands enshrined—the mother who sacrifices personally and professionally to devote herself wholesale to child and economy.

Maternal "Quality," the Transmission of Value, and Race

At its core, maternal science concerns evaluation and measurement of the ways mothers transmit value to their children, and these calculations inexorably produce distinctions between maternal quality. In colloquial terms, they produce good and bad mothers for the public. In their research, human capital economists identify and measure key traits that makes mothers "low" or "high" quality in terms of maternal "inputs" into children. The field outlines two circuits through which value flows from mother to child. First, the value transmitted through duration and quality of maternal time as a euphemism for labor, and second, mothers' own embodied value as genetic inheritance. Human capital economists are clear that both circuits define maternal quality, which is a matter of both "innate" and "acquired" characteristics. This is also the case with their key variable of concern—the supposed intelligence or IQ of both mothers and children (see Chapter 2). The scientific production of maternal quality is the thread that unites the field. The equations that produce the quality distinctions between mothers, calculated through genetic and social traits, serve important functions in the political and libidinal economy of neoliberalism—they are *racialized* technologies that explain, or explain away, the enduring force of race in society.

Arleen Leibowitz's "Home Investments in Children" is the field-defining text, included in the foundational volume *Economics of the Family*.[54] The chapter contains the first elaborate equation linking parental investments with children's future income (fig. 3.1).[55] The equation reveals the premium economists attach to parental "genetic endowments," coded as "parents' IQ." For Leibowitz, parental IQ is causally related to children's "ability" (IQ), while parents' IQ and education together influence the quality and quantity of the time that they invest in their children, as well as the quality and quantity of goods invested. Consequently, this means that maternal time investments are not equal—differentials in maternal IQs and education levels are understood to transmit different magnitudes of value. From this perspective, a mother with a higher IQ and education level adds more value per unit of time than one with a lower IQ and educational level. Thus, Leibowitz maintains that every variable is partly determined by genetics: "parents genetic endowments and their education [together] determine the quality and quantity of time inputs into the child."[56]

Each and every variable and causal arrow within this equation is connected to intelligence, an embodied substance that is presumed to be inherited and heritable. Further, this embodied substance is abstracted and measured, a quantity used to rank humans on a hierarchy of quality. From the start, then, maternal investment equations

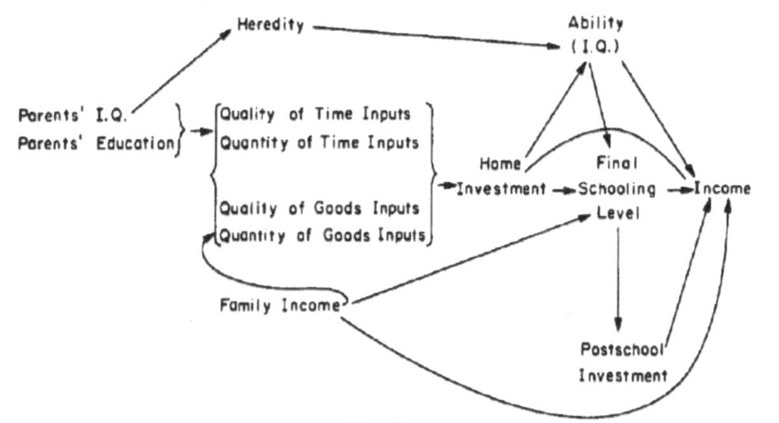

Fig. 1

FIGURE 3.1. IQ, heredity and human capital in early maternal science, from Leibowitz's "Home Investments in Children"

are a profoundly racializing technology, tethered to the material and symbolic postulates of chattel slavery, in which human beings were differentiated as property of varying quality and therefore as capital of varying quantity. This is also evident in the exposition of the argument, which begins with the now-familiar specter of the so-called achievement gap that haunts public narratives on race in the US, a paradox that Leibowitz purports that only economists can address: "By the time children enter first grade, significant differences in verbal and mathematical competence exist among them. These differences reflect variations in 1) inherent ability and 2) the amounts of human capital acquired before children reach the age of 6."[57] Discourse on the so-called achievement gap is an important way in which subjects are hailed into racial common sense regarding a seemingly naturalized hierarchy of human value. The public pedagogy about the gap does not simply provide information about the existence and persistence of racial disparities as a vexing problem in society. More profoundly, it implicitly explains why and how racialized inequalities are generated and persist. In a society where structural analyses are systematically obfuscated, racialized inequalities are understood to emerge because of individual differences in biology or genetics. Economists' maternal science proliferates race and anti-Blackness throughout the body politic in their construction of one of the most vexing issues in US society. They ring the alarm of the racial gap, and then blame mothers for it. Instead of addressing the disparities marked by the gap, human capital theory in fact amplifies them. In this way, human capital theory produces the curious arc of race in neoliberalism. Reinscribed as a mark of a natural (genetic) hierarchy of humans, racialized inequalities of life and death are laundered and legitimated, made to seem like an inevitable result of individual mothers' different bodies and capacities.

A hierarchy of maternal "quality" is amplified and refined in economists' current work.[58] Brilli's work is representative in regard to the way it distinguishes maternal quality by mothers' educational level, whereby the time of "high-educated mothers is more productive than low-educated mothers and that of nonparental care."[59] The work posits that a 10 percent increase in a "high-educated mother's" time (2.5 hours) leads to an 18 percent difference in a child's cognitive ability, compared to the 10 percent of a "low-educated" mother (formal childcare makes for a 7 percent increase and informal childcare for a 5 percent increase).[60] In economists' terms, "high-educated" mothers or mothers with "high human capital" face a bigger "trade-off" when they work, as their labor has a weaker "substitutability" with market-based childcare.[61] In lay terms, good mothers' kids have more to lose if their mothers work and more to gain if their mothers stay home. Within the field, this "trade-off" or "substitutability" is widely understood as the reason mothers with higher educational attainment are more likely to leave their paid jobs to take care of children. Indeed, "substitutability" very nearly introduces the implicit distinction between "skilled" and "unskilled" labors within motherhood. The labors of mothers with lower education attainment, lower IQ, or lower income are interchangeable (more easily substituted) with comparably "unskilled" childcare workers. Crudely expressed, maternal science suggests that low-educated women should work outside the home and send their young children to day care, while high-educated women should stay home and take care of their young children.

Economists' distinctions of maternal quality bring to the fore the multiple ways that race is deeply embedded in human capital theory. Two problematic categorical constructions, themselves interrelated, entangle race with biology, genetics, and inheritance to reinforce a naturalized hierarchy of human value. First, maternal quality, the most important vector of investment in children's human capital, is crucially a matter of genetics. Second, the significance accorded to IQ in the measuring of human capital value, or, in the case of children, a panoply of tests measuring cognitive ability. While contested, the hegemonic conception of intelligence is figured as a combination of genetic and acquired traits. And since its inception, the "intelligence quotient" has been thoroughly constructed through a white supremacist and anti-Black calculus. Maternal science might then be considered an elaborate body of knowledge dedicated to studying the transmission of intelligence, the almost-mystical substance at the center of even the most colloquial understandings of meritocracy. Its explicit function as a racialized technology is further evinced when considering its emergence and development in the late 1960s and early 1970s, a historical moment of women's struggles for liberation and Black struggle, uprising, and rebellion. The "war on poverty," the Moynihan Report, and the Kerner Commission were all constructed as weapons against gains in both movements, infamously producing the categorization of Black mothers as the source of children's delinquency and lower academic performance, and unleashing a generation of social scientific interventions into Black women's mothering.[62] This hegemonic construction of Black mothers is continually reproduced in scientific and seemingly objective form in economists' equations of maternal investments, however veiled.

Economists' emphasis on genetics is intricately linked with the state's maternal policies, as well as its baldly eugenicist reproductive control of women of color. Indeed, a "forgotten chapter" of neoliberalism's history is economists' close linkages and intellectual traffic with eugenicist ideas of an "intelligence hierarchy."[63] Intelligence, figured as the key variable in a "natural" meritocracy within the population, is key because of how well it suits the postindustrial "knowledge economy" and its "symbolic analysts" and "brain workers."[64] Within the development apparatus, economists deploy human capital to delay and reduce women's fertility in the Global South, where the discourse of educating, empowering, or "investing in girls" directly links the expansions of education with fertility reductions.[65] The anxious campaigns to reduce teenage pregnancy in the US also rhyme with these efforts. For instance, Brookings's "Futures of the Middle Class Initiative" includes efforts to delay poor and working class women's pregnancies.[66] Human capital economists are similarly inclined to use language that evokes social Darwinism's "survival of the fittest" principle when discussing maternal quality. The Parenting Gap, one of the Brookings Institution's hallmark press-friendly reports, contains a bar graph comparing how children succeed in each life stage "by quality of their parents," with bars representing children of "weakest," "average," and "strongest parents."[67] The chart asserts that success indicators are "unambiguous": "Children of the strongest parents succeed in each life stage at much higher rates than children of the weakest parents." Below the chart, they pose a counterfactual: "If the weakest parents were turned into average parents." One of the three scenarios pertains to reducing fertility of the "weakest": "6% fewer of their children would have a child by 19." The position paper was favorably cited and circulated throughout the country's leading newspapers and weeklies, including *The Economist*, where it ran with the flippant headline "Choose Your Parents Wisely."

Economists' goal of increasing the population's human capital through reproductive interventions again calls forth Foucault's lectures on biopolitics. Here, Foucault set forth various dark scenarios that might come to pass when governing the social through human capital theory. Two involved future scenarios in which genetic technologies would be used to manipulate traits (strategizing unions to eradicate disease or to ensure the high-human-capital genetic makeup of a child and encouraging or discouraging the fertility of populations).[68] He raised and then quickly dismissed fears that human capital theory could be used in a way that would produce "racist effects."[69] Yet the production of maternal and child "quality" has come to be the dominant form of governing life in contemporary neoliberalism, as its eugenicist reasoning guides state calculations of who should (not) be born based on human capital value. In their role as society's singular "truth tellers," economists' maternal quality informs public policies—from welfare regulations, investments in childcare and educational infrastructure, and maternal leave. Perhaps most astonishing about human capital theory's maternal science is how its eugenicist logics and aspirations remain so stubbornly opaque.

RACIALIZED MATERNAL QUALITY DURING THE COVID-19 PANDEMIC

The state of emergency brought on by the COVID-19 pandemic is often analogized as an x-ray that revealed core social structures that are often invisible during so-called normal life. Similarly, the racialized core of maternal quality was revealed in the prescriptions to mothers from economists and from education and child experts during the chaos brought on by school shutdowns. The media's intense coverage of pandemic mothering colloquialized economists' notions of maternal quality, and especially "substitutability." Within media representations of pandemic mothering, two obverse maternal figures emerged. Good pandemic mothers materialized as professional, middle class women who sacrificed careers to devote themselves to their role as partner teachers. Bad pandemic mothers appeared as poor and working class women whose children had to be saved by the state from disastrous learning loss and the abyss of an expanding achievement gap. These maternal figures were easily welded to well-worn racialized tropes that explicitly or implicitly blame Black, Brown, and working class mothers for enduring inequalities and throw into sharp relief how contemporary motherhood is a vehicle through which the racialized violence of neoliberalism is reproduced and recoded as legitimate effects of naturally occurring individualized differences.

Within the reportage of pandemic mothering, white, professional, middle class women looked like perfect sacrificial subjects, willingly choosing to suffer more for their children and society. Each piece treated them as proper subjects, written by subjects such as themselves, centering their particular personal, emotional, and professional struggles and perspectives.[70] Experts were brought in to give their voices legitimacy, to slightly rephrase their concerns, to resolve issues that were particular to their social and economic circumstances. This is not to belittle their concerns but to demonstrate how this was not typical of most mothers' circumstances. Working class Black and Brown mothers' struggles were rarely centered—mothers in communities where hospitalization rates were nearly triple that of white communities, who were wary of sending their children back to school, who had to physically report to work, and who were not able to supervise their children's online schooling. These mothers mostly appeared through their troubling absence or conjured through statistics—as mothers of children who did not have a proper device for virtual schooling or otherwise were not reporting to school, had not paid internet bills, and whose homes were without supervision or so toxic that schools had to be reopened as a refuge on their children's behalf.[71] Most often, they were reported on as the mothers of children falling further behind. Rather than subjects with voices worthy of being heard and whose plights mattered, experts anguished over the educational status of their children. For instance, one *New York Times* piece led with a photograph and description of a Black mother's considerable labors in support of her children's learning.[72] Yet the article quickly invalidated her efforts with experts' numerical projections of the amount of "learning loss" and the widening of the so-called achievement gap. Maternal quality was racialized as it was centered as the cause of the widening gap for "parents who are working outside the home or who are not tech-savvy, and are unable to assist with online schooling."[73]

The pervasive panic of pandemic "learning loss," indelibly attached to uncritical notions of the achievement gap, was another discursive site where racialized notions of maternal quality were reproduced. Here, the media reintroduced scenes of domestic chaos of Black and Brown working class families that are eerily similar to 1970s culture of poverty portraits of "pathologically disorganized" Black households that were the purported cause for Black students' educational disparities. A *New York Times* piece on how remote learning would affect "nonwhite" students chose to emphasize home environments "lacking the support that remote learning requires, such as computer access, quiet study space, and help from parents and tutors."[74] While most homes were thrown in chaos during the pandemic, the article described the home of a single mother with school-issued technology and weak internet connectivity. The disarray of professional, middle class households was not juxtaposed to or offered as cause of the challenges of learning during a pandemic, let alone "learning loss." A *New York Times* piece that centered mothers' struggles with remote schooling featured only one working class mother and took as much space describing her household with well-worn racialized signals instead of describing her specific experience or perspective: her husband who "still goes to work" at McDonalds, her seven children, her lack of technology, her status as a student at a community college, and her dependence on the stimulus check to purchase technology necessary for school.[75] Rather than centering scholars that have been studying the pervasive structures of white supremacy in schools for decades, media coverage of the growing gap associated with learning loss repeatedly shored up racialized figures of maternal quality as the root cause of social disparities.

The representation of Black mothers as objects of intervention was readily apparent in protracted battles over in-person versus remote learning, conversations often folded into those about "learning loss." Politicians, pundits, and journalists continually claimed that schools were reopening *for* Black families in their worry over the widening of the so-called gap.[76] The media and experts constructed Black mothers as not up to the task of "partner teacher" and advised them to send their children to school in the face of a deadly virus that was nowhere near being controlled. This is precisely how economists' conceptions of maternal quality and substitutability translate into everyday policy and practice. They reproduce the violent notion that the state knows what is best and could provide better care for Black children than their own families, thus constructing Black, Brown, and more generally, working class mothers as necessitating regulation. This was apparent in the way the media continually spoke *for* Black mothers in regard to their choices about remote schooling. Black families were voting with their feet by disproportionately keeping kids at home when given a choice.[77] Black parents asserted that they were doing so for the health and safety of their children, families, and communities in light of the pandemic's devastating toll on Black communities.[78] Further, Black families also expressed the wish to shield their children from the daily onslaught of racial microaggressions during this uniquely difficult time.[79] The stark difference in parent perspectives was evident in a University of Michigan study that showed Black parents' top concerns were racism and COVID-19, neither of which made white parents' top ten.[80] Yet despite clear articulations of their concerns for children's physical and mental wellbeing, loudly echoed by various public health officials, pundits confidently spoke over Black mothers' concerns about what was best for their children by marshaling economists' projections of "learning loss."[81] Another *New York Times* piece acknowledged that the majority of Black parents preferred remote learning, yet it focused entirely on the minority position, using a Black mother's experience to ventriloquize the dominant perspective on schooling: pro-reopening, anti–teachers' union, anti–public schooling, and schools as a "safe haven" for Black children above and beyond their families.[82] While Asian parents chose remote schooling at higher rates than any other group, no journalist, pundit, psychologist, economist, or educator purported to know what was best for Asian parents' children.

Representations of good and bad pandemic mothers recoded and made intelligible racialized constructions of maternal quality, normalizing the racial hierarchy of deservingness and desirability through which rights have been historically distributed to mothers.[83] Like all good and bad maternal figures, pandemic mothers functioned as disciplinary tools to enlist, expropriate, and police all women's maternal labors, albeit in drastically uneven ways. The good pandemic mother consolidates capital and the state's specific delineation of motherhood in the middle class project—endless intensified labors in the project of creating human subjects for capital in ways that deepen class, gendered, and racialized modes of domination. The bad pandemic mother reproduces and launders the racialized violence of neoliberal capitalism and, like all bad mothers, draws our attention and mobilizes our fears into labor for capital.

Capital Against Life

Economists' maternal science allows for a unique perspective on capital's political transformations in neoliberalism, partly wrought through its stealthy interventions into the everyday of mothers and children. The econo-psy complex manufactures the hegemony of mothering for capital through its enormous efforts to isolate, measure, and abstract various maternal traits in terms of the value they transmit to children, as well as the enormous efforts to intervene, extend, intensify, and professionalize maternal labors in order to generate more human capital value in children. Mothering is distorted into an enterprise where the pros and cons about what's best for children are ultimately weighed in terms of children's future earnings and value to capital, and where life itself is devoted to value accumulation. Yet why is this relentless drive to accumulate value *increasingly* fixated on mothers and children? Capital requires labor power, and mothers, with schools and other caregivers, have provided this all along. Mothers have taken care of children, socialized them with the language, values, and habits to be culturally recognizable persons. They have woken their children up on school days and ensured that children are fed, washed, clothed, and coaxed to do well in school. Why is this no longer enough? What changes necessitate the transformations of domestic life I mark as mothering for capital?

Critics and theorists of neoliberalism writing on the family recognize that the family is a vehicle through which social life is governed and reorganized.[84] For Melinda Cooper, the family is where neoliberalism's key moral projects are enacted—the family as the key economic unit responsible for individual and social welfare ("family responsibility").[85] For Lisa Adkins, the family, via finance capital, is transformed into a site of "investment that funds itself via private debt."[86] However, these feminist critics and others largely ignore the massive efforts to extend, intensify, and regulate maternal labors. For instance, focusing on the way finance capital reconstitutes motherhood as an entrepreneurial venture, Adkins maintains that the post-Fordist family is less about the reproduction of labor power than it was before. It is true that debt ties families to circuits of global capital in new ways and ushers more women into the wage imperative.[87] However, like other feminist critics, including Marxist feminists, Adkins emphasizes commodities (goods and services) purchased within the family through income or debt in the reproduction of the child, at the expense of maternal labors. Analytic frames that focus on the accumulation of value and its movement through different forms (money, commodities) lose sight of the proverbial ball and chain—capital's domination of human *being*.

The real subsumption of maternal labors is the truly novel phenomenon of the neoliberal family. Capital's intensifying dominion over the human is at stake in the intricate regulation and management of maternal labors. Yet it is continually ignored, trivialized, or euphemized, even in accounts of neoliberal transformations of gender, the sexual contract, and the family. Women's reproductive labors are subsumed to construct a subject that is psychologically, socially, and emotionally modulated for labor, one who would consider their life in terms of their value in "the economy." The factorylike conditions of most public schooling are no longer sufficient for this task. This intricately modulated human for capital subject requires the focused and intensified labors of mothers, who are also presumably more invested in the "quality" of the product (fig. 3.2).

The reproduction of this subject requires intricate control of maternal time. Indeed, economists are obsessed with maternal time because capital disciplines and subordinates labor through time. Cindi Katz extends Marx's insights on time to argue that intensive parenting is a site where state and capital together discipline women and keep them all-consumed in "productive time," which leaves no room for "disposable time."[88] Marx figured the latter as idle time and time for higher activity, "itself the greatest productive power" that leads to the "full development of the individual," one that "transform[s] its possessor into *a different subject*."[89] Various Marxist theorists elaborate the importance of disposable time in such a register. Raoul Vaneigem conceived it as "unitary" time—privileged moments that escape capital's productivity; moments of pleasure and creativity.[90] Key in this regard is the autonomous Marxist concept of *autovalorizzazione*—self-valorizing or self-making activities

	FORDIST	NEOLIBERAL
Desired subject	Labor for capital	Human for capital
Primary site and model of reproduction	Schools as factory	Nuclear family home as atelier appended to human capital machine
Primary agent of reproduction	Teacher	Mother as investor and "partner-teacher"

FIGURE 3.2. Fordist and neoliberal modes of social reproduction

through which radical subjectivities develop and flourish—which crucially depends on free time.[91] *Autovalorizzazione* is not reducible to activities that are reactive or resistant to capital; it is crucially those activities outside of capital's frame, ways of being and relating developed as people pursue their own needs and interests. As capital seeks "by its inherent nature, towards the appropriation of labour throughout the whole 24 hours in the day," such ways of being are necessarily *against* capital.[92]

Autonomous Marxist feminists who emphasize capital's control of maternal labors and the importance of wresting this work back from capital are especially relevant here.[93] Efforts to control maternal labor represent capital's aspirations to subordinate life. This subordination takes the form not only of "class struggle" in the conventional sense but also of the struggle to intervene in the social, emotional, cognitive, and psychic development of the child. Do all these efforts result in more human capital value in the child, and hence more (future) value for capital? While one could argue and demonstrate that they do, my primary preoccupations are not pursuing debates internal to Marxism and Marxist feminism about the status of reproductive labors as (un)productive or as value or valueless, nor with children's future earnings or "success" as hegemonically defined, nor with national or global economic productivity. I am concerned with how capital transforms and perverts the daily rhythms and social relations of everyday life, how labor becomes the site of our collective subjection, how fealty and devotion to capital are increasingly required to live in a way that is more than survive.

If drives are insatiable and require only the continual exercise of their force, then mothers provide capital with the biological life of labor *and* the infinite reservoir of developing human possibilities. For mothers, this translates to the impossible expectation to do it all, wholesale devotion and endless labors to produce children with traits deemed valuable to capital. This complex and largely hidden terrain of capital's war against life must be recognized to be refused at every turn. Becoming human, who we are and who we can and might be, is the center of the struggle against capital, which we may appropriately understand as the struggle for life against the undead.

4

Schooling Moms

In the Workshop of Subjectivity

> What in the child's family life will produce human capital? What type of stimuli, form of life, and relationship with parents, adults, and others can be crystallized into human capital?
>
> —*Michel Foucault*

"WELCOME PARENTS AND caregivers!" the educational technology company greeted me. The company had promised to help me develop my child's skills that "colleges and employers are looking for as they recruit." The principal of my child's middle school (six through eighth grade) directed parents to this website in a message informing us that the school, like many others throughout the New York City public school system, was using this company's instrument to measure and develop "eight domains of students social-emotional wellness."[1] Parents were encouraged to learn more about the skills via a two-hour workshop offered by the school and through the company's website, both of which offered guided activities and resources for developing each skill in children. "Self-management," "goal-directed behavior," and "optimistic thinking" are among the skills identified as promising "success." These should be unsurprising for any analyst of neoliberal subjectivity, or anyone in business, management, or so-called leadership. Indeed, Harvard Business Review Press recently launched an "emotional intelligence" book series whose titles are uncoincidentally enough, virtually identical to those parents are asked to develop ("focus," "energy and motivation," "positivity and growth").[2]

The ed tech company's parent portal explained each skill in child-friendly language. Self-management was introduced like so: "Both children and adults need to learn how to control their emotions so that they can get the job done." It went on: "Often when talking about managing emotions, we focus on how to calm down when we are angry, upset, or scared . . . but we also need to be able to energize ourselves when we are tired, bored, or just don't feel like working hard. Sometimes we need to calm down and focus; other times we need to 'psych ourselves up' to get the energy to tackle our schoolwork, our chores, or our jobs. Being able to 'psych ourselves up' is a lifelong skill that helps us be successful." For each skill, the company offers parents age-appropriate activities to "engage in with your family." To build the skill of self-management with my child who was in middle school at the time, I was advised to encourage her to make a playlist of "energizing or inspiring" songs to "increase energy level and motivation" for her schoolwork and another for "calming down and relaxing when responsibilities are complete."

Such "engagement" efforts go beyond informing parents to adopt recommended actions. They target and transform the mother-child relationship, and the subjectivities of both. "Self-management," like many of the other "social and emotional skills" that schools ask parents to develop, is ultimately about regimenting and modulating the subject for neoliberal modes of labor. Indeed, contemporary forms of work across the employment hierarchy rely as much on psychological dispositions as they do on skills—willingness, dedication, commitment, attitude, and personal investment have never been as important.[3] This requires a whole project of subjectification—one's emotions, sense of self, relationship to time, how one relates to others—that would best begin in childhood. For children are inarguably out of synch with this restrictive and repressive homogeneity, and the longer they might be allowed to inhabit their unruly and boisterous physicality, the more difficult their eventual governing for production would be. And since its institutionalization, schooling has been the site for repressing and modulating children's physicality and psyche for work. Most observers of schooling are aware that this project has been steadily extending to earlier grades—even kindergarteners should be "career ready." Yet few critics appreciate how schools are now involved in intricately modulating subjectivity for value production. Fewer still recognize how mothers have been recruited into this elaborate project. This is necessary because the psychological and emotional homogeneity required for today's forms of work is a far more complex project than that which can be accomplished in the factorylike conditions of schooling. Who might take up this project with more zeal than the mother, continuously warned that her child will be left behind, unsuccessful, and with no opportunities in the future?

And so while children go to school, mothers are positioned as "partner teachers," which is to say *students* who are extensively encouraged and taught how to transform domestic life to ensure children's future success in the workplace. On the surface, such efforts may appear as innocuous or even good. Education experts have long positioned themselves as the bridge between the worlds of schools and work. The neoliberal education complex offers a better bridge to work—the home, helping parents adopt behaviors, attitudes, and ways of being to give their child an edge or an equal opportunity for success in a competitive world. This chapter frames schools' recent concerted efforts to engage mothers as more intricate and invasive methods of governing children's subjectivities. As interventions into the intimate relation between mother and child, these methods potentially reach deeper into psyche and are more effective than those used in schools. They are designed for mothers to deliver as gentle forms of encouragement and coaxing, and intricately bound to her love and care. From a child's point of view, these methods are implicitly bound with their obverse—the fear and anxiety that this love and care might be withdrawn. Despite their benign appearance, then, "engagement" interventions target children through emotional chains of motherly subjection. Mothers are themselves subjected to the project of crafting children as subjects whose social and emotional dispositions to being in time is oriented to capital, beings whose most intimate needs and bonds are refracted through capital.

I reframe significantly expanded efforts understood as "parent engagement" as capital's attempts to seize the means of social reproduction. Capital steadily obtains incredible reach to transform the intimate texture of domestic life through the state apparatus of the school. Historically, schools have been concerned with altering the maternal practices of poor, working class, and especially Black and Brown women through deficit-based models of "parent involvement." While schools still rely on such programs in practice, "parent engagement" marks the neoliberal shift to the ideological architecture of the middle class project. Schools target mothers who see themselves as middle class and are understood to be "good" mothers who want to improve their mothering so that their children can be middle class, at the same time subjecting and interpellating poor and working class mothers to these new standards of mothering. That is the crux and success of "the middle class project." In this way, schools forge a new relationship between mothers and capital and mothers and children, regardless of individual mothers' means, opportunities, or realistic expectations. Parent engagement is a totalizing project, one requiring the devotion of domestic life to capital.

Drawing on an archive of materials encouraging specific maternal labors to which I and other mothers were subjected through my child's public school, I read parent engagement directives as representing capital's intricately specified demands for domestic life and human subjectivity. This extensive archive is composed of a seemingly endless set of communiqués that includes information in flyers backpacked home and emailed, workshops on offer, resources, and recommended activities. The mother who is engaged or a partner teacher is no vague interpellation open to individual mothers' interpretation. The new elaborate curriculum under the aegis of "parent engagement" and "support" of mothers as partner teachers, specifically the form they have recently taken as literal "workshops," teaches mothers how to professionalize their labors. These labors include teachers' traditional labors of instructing in academic subjects and monitoring children's progress, as well as a recently transformed set of affective and psychological labors to fine-tune children's subjective states to capital.

The term "schooling mothers" captures the multiple dimensions of transforming mothering in neoliberalism and the larger sociopolitical transformations to which they are essential constitutive features. At the most basic level, schooling captures how so-called experts increasingly regulate the institution of motherhood. Mothers themselves must learn an intricate and specialized set of knowledge, skills, and dispositions that are specified by "expert" scientists—developmental, cognitive, and behavioral psychologists, neuroscientists, with economists behind them—as well as educators. Second, schooling captures how efforts to regulate motherhood are increasingly concerned with developing a very specific and circumscribed set of child's cognitive and intellectual capacities, knowledge and skills conventionally associated with schooling, which supplants other forms of development and nurturing. Third, schooling points to how the institution of the school comes to dominate mothers' relationship to children and the home, its rhythms, activities, and purpose. The middle class project establishes schools as capital's communication system to parents, where it explicitly defines, legitimates, and announces which human qualities, habits, and ways of being are valuable for the world of work. As such, no mother can escape schools' regulatory reach, even if they do not send their children to school. Last, "schooling" moms evokes the more colloquial meaning of the term in hip-hop slang. In the most scathing of its multiple senses, "to school" means to "own" another. If you are "schooled," you are not taught a subject but put in your place. You become a subject to and for another—in this case, a subject for capital.

Mothers, positioned as the greatest source of investment in children's value, become a prime target of neoliberal governance, a vehicle through which a relatively new experiment of valuation is enacted to harness social reproduction to value. Capital's "lynx-eyed" methods in reproduction are as ferocious as they are in production: usurping, extending, regulating, and transforming mothers' work and care into labor for capital; reproducing racialized ideologies of good and bad mothers; compelling mothers to produce value in human life that is inherently racialized; employing the regulatory force of the state to coax or punish women. The gravitation force of the child's future value in the present has profound repercussions for the domination of subjectivity. The regulation and intensification of maternal labors—more hours, new tasks, more skills, and so on—supplant other vital tasks (including and especially free time), converting mothers to a "living appendage to the machine" of human capital, to rephrase Marx.[4] In reproduction, capital behaves like an irrational force that craves fealty from the human subject on which it depends, that jealously desires life all for its own. Schooling mothers thrusts society toward the state of "total subsumption," where "true community is increasingly replaced by capital as community."[5] In the minutiae of the routinized and seemingly mundane efforts to support mothers, the logic behind the frantic obsession of motherhood in neoliberalism is revealed. Mothers create a family where their love and labors (both idealized as naturalized, pure, selfless devotion to an Other) function as a synecdoche for human relations to capital, instantiating a community *devoted* to capital where "the economy" becomes a sacred domain.

The Partner Teacher: Mother's Sacrifice, the State's "Gift"

As the COVID-19 virus tore through New York City in the spring of 2020, the chancellor of schools addressed the families of its 1.1 million public school students to announce a revision to grading policies. He celebrated families' "resilience and resolve": "You have been there for your children in every way you can to support their learning despite not knowing where the next meal will be coming from, illness or loss in your family."[6] He thanked parents for their "essential, invaluable new roles to keep your children's education going and become *indispensable partners* to teachers." In the same breath—or tweet, as it were—he directed parents to "resources" for them to develop their skills in this new role—Parent University, the school system's website to "educate and empower families as *partners*" through an array of free courses such as "Supporting K–2 Literacy at Home: Fluency" and "Social Emotional Learning: Cultivating It at Home."[7]

The chancellor relied on a formula employed by school systems throughout the US, as well as in the media, to address mothers during the pandemic's disruption of "business as usual." The formula acknowledges mothers' additional labors, yet establishes them as an indispensable necessity, so crucial as to require persistence despite sacrifices to mothers' mental health and careers (the chancellor went so far as to intimate that mothers should keep supporting children's schooling among the "illness or loss" of family members). This formula belies an implicit imperative that maternal labors supporting children's schooling must be the top priority of any woman. Fundamental to this imperative is that these labors are framed not as labors for capital, and not even as labor at all, but as sacrifices. These sacrifices are, after all, a gift to women's own children. "You're not serving us," schools (on behalf of capital and state) seem to say. "We are doing this to help *you* fulfill *your* vocation as a mother. At the end of the (working) day, it is *your* child and their future at stake."

The particular role of mother as partner teacher to the school predates the pandemic, although it is relatively recent. In 2010, the US secretary of education proclaimed to the Mom Congress, a policy organization of mothers, "I want all parents to be *real partners* in education with their children's teachers, from *cradle to career*."[8] Mom as full partner in education, partner teacher, a child's first or most important teacher—any woman with a school-age child in the United States hears herself addressed by such terms. The hails of "partner" are always attached to offers of "support" and "resources." One discerns a request, or more appropriately an *urging*, in all the congratulatory praises to mothers for being "partners." It is always an urging for more work, yet it is couched in the symbolic terms of the gift. Prescriptions to work are benevolent "gifts" to mothers in exchange for their lifelong gift of "investment" in their children.

"They say it is love. We say it is unwaged work!" the Wages for Housework campaign declared.[9] These autonomous Marxist feminists considered the work of preparing children for school, and the work children do in school, as labor for capital. They recognized that the school was not a gift from the state to mothers and children but was mothers' and children's free gift of future workers for capital—a site for the production of labor power. This perspective is deceptively more difficult to think with that it seems. For we are enveloped in the pseudoreality of the appearances of love, sacrifice, what is good for children. Child experts' requests for maternal sacrifices, gifts, and acts of love for children must first be reframed as labor for capital.

With the premise that the work that so-called experts coerce from mothers is labor for capital, I ask why the demand assumes the guise of a gift at all. Mothers are amenable to increasing labor demands, especially if they are understood to help a child a succeed because "things are different now." Therefore, the guise of the gift cannot simply be about the extension and intensification of maternal labors. The language of gratitude, recognition, and gift conceals that the middle class project is not about a mother's sacrifice *for* her child, but about a mother's sacrifice *of* her child. It distorts the fact that the middle class project forges new relations between mothers and children and reconstitutes the family as a site of devotion to capital. It misleads mothers and others to think that good mothering and bad mothering are distinct and separate entities—that the home of the former is private, and the activities and relations within it are voluntary and free from the interventions of the state, whereas the home of the bad mother is public by necessity, so that the state can intervene to fill in the mother's lack. The guise of the gift subtends the spectacle of good and bad mothers. It disappears the way that capital and state harness and channel the labor of the good mother to produce the bad mother.

In Moynihan's Shadow: From Involvement to Engagement

Conventionally, mothers have been objects of state scrutiny and regulation when they have been deemed to be lacking qualities of "good" mothers. In the past half century, and even farther back, politicians, policymakers, pundits, and scholars have been keenly interested in poor mothers, single mothers, welfare mothers, absent mothers.

Save for the selfish career mother, vilified maternal figures have tended to be racially coded as Black or Brown. The goal was to make them more like the ideal mother—stay-at-home mothers, involved mothers, sacrificial mothers, figures racialized as white. In contrast, the new project of schooling mothers targets women who are already understood and interpellated as good mothers, mothers who are doing the right thing and want to do *more* to ensure the success of their child. Efforts to school moms thus appear to be completely voluntary pursuits by mothers who want to be "engaged," even and especially when women are suffering to keep afloat.

The partner teacher is the maternal role of parent engagement—the more recent hegemonic model adopted by schools in which intervention into families is poised as a "shared responsibility." In the everyday of parenting, this means that my interlocutors and I were subject to slew of communiqués from schools that held us equally responsible for everything children are learning. In the guise of support, these were interventions into domestic life that significantly differ from conventional practices long associated with middle class "parent involvement"—volunteering for bake sales, attending parent-teacher association meetings, and organizing fundraisers. All those still exist and are more or less valued by schools. Engagement fundamentally differs; it is a professionalization of mothers represented as a set of gifts bequeathed by the state's school system for children's benefit. Parent engagement is the most recent iteration of hegemonic educational discourses thought to foster "home-school connections" and "building trust or healthy relationships between school and home."[10] Enshrined in and required by federal, state, and local educational policies, every programmatic statement within official educational discourse frames "engagement" as critical for student success. And virtually all educational research touts it as "one of the strongest predictors of children's school success."[11]

Partnership or "shared responsibility" is the center of "parent engagement" and marks the "research informed shift in terminology" from "parent involvement."[12] The discourse of family involvement emerged from War on Poverty programs to address the so-called achievement gap facing Black students.[13] The Moynihan Report, as

The Negro Family: The Case for National Action (1965) is commonly known, directed attention to Black mothers and the "disorganized" Black family as the center, vector, and root cause of both intergenerational poverty and educational achievement. The report's influence within educational is monumental; every form of post–civil rights educational politics, policy, and practice that targets the so-called gap—from Head Start to the foundations of "urban education" to an entire apparatus of practices based on "cultural difference"—bears its influence. It was immediately bolstered by and translated into education policy and practice by the Elementary and Secondary Education Act (1965), which generated Head Start programs and "family involvement" components to any school with a majority of students in poverty (Title I schools). Officially justified as a way to have service programs reflect people's needs by involving or "empowering" them, parent involvement programs have been criticized for their middle class or "normative" understandings of families and their participation, and their pathologization of "nondominant" families, features that continue to be smuggled into "neodeficit discourses."[14]

Parent involvement models incontrovertibly reproduce class and race inequities in schools, and they are based on domestic practices that conform more to white, middle class norms. "Engagement" is already perched to reproduce these functions and its normative assumptions about children, mothers, and families. Yet there are other functions to engagement beyond unfairly privileging normative families to reproduce already-existing inequalities. I frame the engaged partner teacher as a racial technology that, while extracting maternal labors to produce subjects for capital, functions as a mode of governance that regulates women in profoundly uneven ways. "Good" middle class mothers are coaxed and congratulated through the symbolic structure of the gift, while poor and working class, especially Black and Brown, mothers are disciplined in ever more violent ways. Although it does so in subtler ways than its predecessor "involvement," engagement draws on the specter of the Black mother, too. And the current reach and frenzy of the spectacle of the "engaged" middle class mother is shaping up as having as profound an impact as that of the "deficient" poor mother. The

Moynihan Report operated as a "public documentary" about race in the post–civil rights public sphere, one of the most important "genealogical nodes in successive and hegemonic discourses about minority communities."[15] It constructed an official portrait of the imagined Black mother who, with deficient attention, care, and labor for her child's education, could be trained by school agents to be a better mother. It would not be an exaggeration to say that this figure lurks within all school policies addressing the family.[16] Such programs function as a key site through which to maintain the historical surveilling and policing of Black, Brown, and other poor mothers. As critical work examining social work and child welfare increasingly points out, the paradigmatic forms of expert control of mothering—through discourses of "what's best for children"—are the state's removal of Native children from homes and into boarding schools and unremitting threats of child removal by Child Protective Services, the majority of cases of which involve poor and racially minoritized families.[17]

I am not arguing that schools' efforts to extend and intensify maternal labors are equivalent to the state's brutal tactics of policing and disciplining minoritized working class and poor mothers. I am arguing that these seemingly separate phenomena are intimately entangled and constituted through one another. As Maurizio Lazzarato insists, the governing of subjectivity is the "soft" face of neoliberalism's double-sided power, the public face that conceals its violent underside.[18] Further, the violent histories of regulating poor and racially minoritized women help us discern how current efforts to school mothers are part of an arsenal of state power, a mode of governance that is difficult to perceive in less spectacular manifestations. The fraught history of the state's interventions into motherhood prompts reconsideration of seemingly racially neutral parent engagement discourse alongside the racially charged parent involvement discourse that targeted poor and working class Black and Brown mothers' supposed lack of care or, in more liberal guises, lack of resources and means. Situating "engagement" within the conglomeration of racializing discourses and practices from which it descends generates a different standpoint of critique. The engaged mother that seamlessly and effortlessly takes up the new role offered by the school can be revealed as a figure that regulates and perpetuates the ideal family form for capital, one whose raced and classed obverse becomes increasingly policed and subject to punishment. Juxtaposing the two maternal figures exposes parent engagement as a site of the subjection of all women that unevenly disciplines them. The middle class project does not only implicate the white, middle class mothers in devaluing the working class and poor, especially the Black and Brown, but it similarly enlists the poor and working class "good" moms against the "bad ones."

This critical frame homes in on continuities and breaks in the state's repressive and regulatory interventions. How do the state's modes of regulation shift as the targets change? And why this enormous investment and shift in educational policy to target mothers that are presumably "good mothers"? After all, the major criticism of half a century worth of scholarship centered the purported "match" between educational policy and white, middle class domesticity, as well as its oppressive imposition on other families. If middle class mothers are ideally involved, then efforts to engage them signal that their labors do not spring ex nihilo from their desires, style, or class habitus. Analyses that painstakingly establish a natural "match" or "mismatch" between schools and middle class homes ignore how middle class mothers, in the emic sense of mothers in the middle, are subject to the state's forces of compulsion and shifting demands, subjects who must continually learn new skills that reflect the latest expert advice of the econo-psy and neoliberal education complexes. In other words, capital and the state intricately produce maternal and child subjects to reflect neoliberalism's shifting regimes of valuation and extraction. Against the scholarly consensus that engagement reflects actually existing middle class family norms, I maintain that these similarities reflect the subsumption of maternal labors—efforts that have profound effects on women's labor, social relations, psychic and emotional well-being and subjectivities. I read engagement materials in these terms and trace how their "soft" regulation works with and through the repressive regulation and devaluation of Black and Brown working class mothers.

Workshopping Motherhood

"How does [school name] support parents?" my child's school PTA asked in the orienting document sent home on the first day of elementary school in 2019, as it had every previous year. The document pointed to a range of conventional channels of communication such as report cards, biannual parent-teacher conferences, and school rules and calendar. There were recent additions required of New York City public schools and other systems, including "parent engagement" resources such as a back-to-school evening, weekly teacher time dedicated to parent communication, and finally "workshops for parents." I would go on to receive notices for over a dozen workshops organized by the school in one academic year and for dozens more workshops within the local district. True to form, I also received weekly newsletters serving as "homework" workshops "designed to keep the school-home connection growing," and these came on what became Teachers and Parent Tuesdays. Workshops are a new feature of the middle class project, and they are a phenomenon that is sweeping school systems across the country. *Education Week*, one of the largest education news organizations, anointed this shift in a feature article, declaring, "It's parents that are learning the skills their children need to master."[19]

Workshops, endless resources, even the question "How does our school support parents?"—these seem like warm, welcoming invitations into a child's school. Indeed, schools' fostering of a school-home connection is widely posited as one of the key variables of a good school, one that parents seek in their quest for the elusive good school (see Chapter 6).[20] Yet the PTA's inaugurating question represents a tactical inversion that represents and interpellates parents as the primary educators of children; schools are mere auxiliaries. Workshops are both symbolic marker and site at which the state transfers responsibilities of educating children from state to families. These workshops perform three categorical functions that map on to three different types of workshop. The first workshop type appears to be simply informational, reporting on the ever-changing school policies and practices. Yet they have a psychoaffective function—

they instill a particular worldview, drum up fears and anxieties about the future and the role of the parent-child relation vis-à-vis the economy. In this way, I refer to the first as the interpellational-ideological workshop: Mothers are socialized into their new maternal role as partner teacher. The second category teaches parents which psychosocial and affective states of the child are valuable for success in the future and how to instill them. The third type explicitly trains parents in how to transform ordinary family leisure activities and time into productive school activities. In practice, these categories bleed into one another and together represent the three chief functions of the schooled mom—anxiously yet sacrificially shaping her child for capital.

Workshop 1: Econ for Moms 101

In the first type of workshop, parents learn about schools' evolving standards, curricula, policies, and practices. At first glance, these workshops appear utterly benign, if not banal. Individually, each workshop is an occasion to communicate to parents about what is happening in their child's school. If we recall Deleuze's intervention to consider the act of informing as a "set of imperatives," then these workshops seem less like neutral sessions and more like the state's command to take up the hegemonic family form.

These workshops are a form of job training that represent the professionalization of motherhood. As a "job" like the rest of them, mothers are beholden to bosses and managers, the experts who may enact changes at their whim and to whom mothers must immediately comply by modifying their labors. Every shift in school practice becomes an opportunity to train or "engage" mothers. If the school changes from one corporate math program to another, they communicate and find ways to "empower" parents about it. While school personnel are (when belonging to a union) recognized and compensated for the labor of keeping up to date with constantly evolving policies and practices, and students are recognized for being under their demands and the increased stress of high-stakes schooling, mothers too are expected to learn this new information in order to shepherd their child through schooling successfully. Yet this considerable set of maternal labors is largely invisible in accounts of reproductive labor.

When critically considered together, workshops' true function is revealed—they are pulpits to promulgate the middle class project while hailing mothers as primarily responsible for children's future success; in them, love for children means ceaseless work to augment their value and involves an ideological inversion by which subjects should be grateful for opportunities to serve the economy. My community school district organized two workshops informing parents about new science and social studies standards implemented by the State of New York. In these sessions, parents could "learn about the skills and concepts students are expected to master from kindergarten to eighth grade." Both events followed the typical format of the workshops I observed: Educators present the new school policy, practice, or standard; discuss its importance and rationale; explain how students will be assessed; and lead a Q&A segment. Each workshop provides parents with a collection of expert literature and additional resources for "further learning" at home. At the science and social studies workshops I attended, the new standards' importance and rationale were characterized as reflecting new skills required in the competitive knowledge economy of the future. The need for the "Next Generation Learning Standards in Science" were justified as such: "Never before has our world been so complex and scientific literacy is critical to making sense of it all. Science is also at the heart of America's ability to continue innovating, leading, and creating jobs for the future. That's why all students—regardless of whether they pursue college or STEM careers—should have access to a high-quality K-12 science education."[21] Even a mundane communiqué about slightly revised learning standards is an opportunity to instill a moral and social order where "the economy" is prioritized. While the economy is presented as an exogenous and unruly force to which humans must endlessly adapt to survive, this is conveyed with much fanfare and celebration. The document suggests it is the state's gift to children to help them participate in this "complex" economy and a gift to parents for whom the ultimate responsibility of ensuring their child's success lies. Where educational scholars have always recognized workforce training as the hegemonic rationale for schooling among other more humanistic and democratic rationales, within the workshops there is only one (happy) rationale—schools' complete instrumentalization and subservience to the economy.

With every new school practice comes a new way to measure the child's performance in it, a method to educate mothers to understand this measurement, and resources for mothers to boost their child's performance. And so informational workshops emphasize the measurement of one's child against a specific norm and against other children putatively figured as competitors. In New York City, at the four periodic points throughout the year when a child's reading level is measured, parents are given tools to understand what this means in terms of "specific reading behaviors, skills, and strategies" measured by accuracy, fluency, and comprehension. When my child was measured to be at "Level R," I was given information on "specific ways to work with your child" to move them forward to "Instructional Level S." I often wondered why schools might imagine I would want to be informed on the particulars of each measurement. The answer, I realized, was that each measurement functions as part of a larger sum of the child's total human capital and the larger project to which I should be ostensibly devoted, the expansion of this sum total. Every bit of knowledge, skill, and more recently social-emotional disposition (see the following section) that is presented as necessary or important for children's future is broken down, mapped, and normed; its growth is tracked; and the effectiveness of methods for speeding the progress of that process are measured as well. For the teacher, these measurements appear as standards and benchmarks. For the mother, these measurements appear as sites of infinite capitalization potential.

Informational workshops are deeply affective sessions that target mothers' psyche and emotions. Attending or even simply being informed about the existence of a workshop, one intuits the anxiety, fear, competition, and scarcity that animate them. Women don't just don masks of chief investors in children but are subject to these affective manipulations and inhabit these affective states. Every workshop offers an explicit or implicit carrot-cum-stick: "Your child's future is at stake, and only your investment can secure them a viable future." Mothers receiving the carrot should be grateful to be offered such opportunities. In a context of vast inequalities that are visible on local and global scales, workshops ensure that mothers understand that only their sacrifices can make the difference.

Workshop 2: The Social-Emotional Profile of Human Capital

The second type of workshop is the most novel in terms of the maternal labors it institutes. These workshops train mothers to develop and regulate specific social and emotional states of children deemed valuable for school and career success. Since Foucault, the extension of the market's rule of value onto subjectivity—the production of *Homo economicus* as entrepreneur of the self—is considered one of the key political transformations of neoliberal society. Schools have more or less taken part in this project of producing subjects that see themselves as a commodity, a "special commodity" whose value can be enhanced with investment.[22] Yet social-emotional learning (SEL) in schools is astounding in its prescriptive reach within the subject. With heavy investments by venture capital firms and philanthropists, and rapid adoption within global governing bodies such as the World Bank and the World Economic Forum, social-emotional learning has rapidly proliferated into educational discourse globally. The SEL project reflects "the increasing governmental mobilization of scientific knowledge about the body, its feelings, and how to enumerate and value them."[23] Capital, through the econo-psy complex, explicitly and intricately defines desired psychological traits for subjects. Schools, through the neoliberal education complex, train mothers to instill and develop these subjectivities in children. Despite the positive language and innocent and cartoonish imagery contained within SEL educational technologies, these tools are forms of "psycho-compulsion and behavioral modification."[24] Good mothers should put these psycho-compulsion theories into practice, developing desirable traits in children, ensuring their success as well their ultimate happiness.

New York City school districts, like many throughout the US, mandate that schools incorporate SEL into the curriculum. New York schools have adopted SEL practices in various ways: "mood meters" that students use to identify their feelings, breathing exercises, writing activities ("write about a time you practiced a new skill and got better . . . how did you feel?"), "dopamine dances," "kindness challenges," and more. To accommodate the city's policy, my child's elementary school, like many others throughout the US, adopted the Yale School of Medicine's RULER (Recognizing, Understanding, Labeling, Expressing, and Regulating feelings) approach.[25] Yale's program was designed with parent engagement as an essential component. Classrooms initiated the program with a classroom charter, and a "homework" workshop was distributed to parents. Parents were asked to allow time for children to lead a "Family Charter activity" to create a "positive emotional climate at home: research shows that when we feel emotionally connected and respected, we are more successful learners." The twenty-minute activity directed children to interview family members about the feelings they'd like to experience at home, including their own, to write them down, and to repeat these wishes as mantra: "Put your whole heart into it." For parents wishing to go further, Yale included a list of "feelings" vocabulary that would "increase both oral and written literacy by understanding character development . . . a basic 21st century skill." This in turn was followed by another workshop that included a reflection on the activity and a preview of "what comes next in RULER both in school and for your family."

Parents are further compelled to participate in SEL efforts through the force of metrics. My child's school principal sent parents a formal email informing us about a new instrument ("screener") to measure students' social-emotional learning, the Devereaux Student Strengths Assessment. This instrument relied on teachers rating children's performance in "eight domains of student social-emotional wellness: personal responsibility, optimistic thinking, goal-directed behavior, social awareness, decision-making, relationship skills, self-awareness, and self-management." Administrators informed parents that children would be assessed again in the spring to measure growth in these domains. They assured parents that results would not be "used on report cards, will not have any impact on grades, and will not be used to make any diagnostic or evaluative decisions." While putatively informal and voluntary, the specter of the metrics nevertheless compelled parents. The same message directed us to the parent component of the corporation's website that contained age-appropriate parenting tips and activities for each of the eight desired subjective traits. For "personal responsibility," parents are taught to "encourage before they correct" children, with an instructive scenario that demonstrates the skill's relevance in the market. This was construed as beneficial for parents' own psychological health, even in moral terms: "Likely all of us have known a co-worker who did shoddy work and relied on others (like us!) to review and correct their work. These individuals may lack Personal Responsibility and take advantage of others. That certainly isn't who we want our children to become. So rather than correcting their work, encourage children to keep trying. Be positive and supportive. If your child becomes frustrated, give them some gentle guidance, but don't solve the problem for them. Encourage before you correct. They will feel proud and more confident if they learn how to solve it themselves."[26] Traits like "personal responsibility" are intricately linked to human capital buzzwords such as "growth mentality" and "grit." They are by-products of the econo-psy complex—traits identified by experts as valuable in the workplace and immediately adopted by the neoliberal education complex. Social-emotional learning workshops are one vector through which such subjective traits enter social reproduction. Mothers themselves are targets of these projects and made subject to similar techniques. For instance, my child's school invited parents to a "life hacks" workshop to help us reflect on "values, passions, [and] strengths" to "reveal your best self." There were many workshops to shape maternal subjects, such as one for "self-care" and another to enhance my (presumably maternal) productivity and "accomplish life goals for greater success and happiness."

Critics of social-emotional learning have argued that such programs "perpetuate a harmful hegemonic positivity" that does not allow space for negative affects and difficult feelings, thus perpetuating a "paranoid-schizoid mentality" that accords with neoliberalism's "happiness imperative."[27] Most egregious in this regard are workshops to manage children's negative emotions, which are more prevalent that those promoting positive emotions. It is no coincidence that events to manage children's stress were offered at the same time that test preparation shifted to high gear in New York City. Many of the mothers in my research who had children in testing grades (third and above) actively worried about the stress placed on their children (see Chapter 5). The neoliberal education complex imposes the toxic conditions of high-stakes schooling onto children yet conceals its role in producing and exacerbating children's stress, anxiety, depression, and more severe disorders. Rather than reorganizing schooling to prevent these unnecessary negative effects, schools implement SEL programs to neutralize students' negative emotions and convert them into positive affects. The labors of mitigating the harms inflicted on children are also imposed on mothers. Parents are coerced to join efforts to convert children's negative emotions ("pulling through the discomfort") to produce "productive, happy, and calm" children. Acknowledging how "testing can bring on stress and anxiety for children—and parents too," my child's school organized a "testing anxiety" workshop. We were informed of the different types of anxiety, then given strategies to "figure out what is affecting your child" and a slew of SEL activities to convert stress into calm. Closer to the state examinations, parents received a notice outlining activities to begin "during the weeks leading up to the TEST." The detailed instructions for the night before and the morning of the test resembled what I imagine would be a professional athlete's regimen on game day. Parents were instructed that their priority is "to make your child comfortable and confident about the test." To achieve this purpose, we were supplied with a suggested bedtime, breakfast menus, relaxation techniques, and positive affirmations. Mothers, perhaps more than most, are burdened with the "happiness imperative." Schools enlist mothers to manage children's negative emotions that neoliberal schooling produce, labors that require managing their own emotions as well. For as my child's school warned on their tips to testing success: "Remain positive! Staying calm will help your child stay calm."

The focus on positivity extends beyond traits conventionally thought to be conductive to concentration, academic performance, and productivity in general. On a workshop before Thanksgiving break, when the nation ostensibly expresses gratitude for stolen land, parents were assigned homework to harness children's kindness: "We are continuing to explore caring, kindness, and gratitude. As the school becomes more immersed in social-emotional learning (SEL) we want families to become familiar with and be engaged in the work too. Next week, we will send home an activity that your child will lead, based on what she has been doing in school." The home workshop included an excerpt from *The Kindness Advantage: Cultivating Compassionate and Connected Children* that had been reprinted in *Psychology Today*.[28] The book, article, and parent homework emphasized how kindness is intricately connected to "future success," "self-esteem," and "good mental and physical health." It was an offer no mother could refuse: "And don't we all want that for our children, our families, and our community?" Parents were offered methods to be a "kindness role model," to make kindness a "part of the daily conversation," to "say something" any time we "catch" children exhibiting it. The workshop concluded by emphasizing the vital role of mothers and the declining returns of maternal investment: "By starting young we can help them create kindness habits that will last a lifetime."[29] This introduces anxiety about the loss of the opportune time and emphasizes that mothers must be entrepreneurs for children, because by the time children can be entrepreneurs of their selves, it will be too late.

Social-emotional learning in schools and homes represents what Ben Williamson calls "the governmentality of psychological concepts," "the increasing governmental mobilization of scientific knowledge about the body, its feelings, and how to enumerate and value them."[30] This biopolitical governance of children sets mothers to work to develop subjects willing to work for capital, despite the physical and psychological harm and distress of working within such social relations. This is not only behavioral modification; it is subjectivity modification on a grand scale. Social-emotional learning is a technology through which psychologists and economists, with child and educational experts, craft an ideal subject amenable to working within capitalist social relations, one that is mindful, calm, and happy to do so, and also would view fashioning their selves to be those ways as growth. Coaxed through the forces of economic compulsion, mothers are enlisted in this project of neoliberal governance, bestowing on capital the "free gifts" of their labor and their own and children's subjectivity.

Workshop 3: The New "Family Time"

The third category of parent engagement workshops teaches parents to transform ordinary family leisure activities into productive school activities. The maternal labors encouraged do not simply represent a quantitative increase in the conventional work supervising children's homework and the occasional provision of help for special projects or exams. This third type of workshop signals the qualitatively new role of mothering for capital, in which she leads a household dedicated to augmenting her child's human capital and whose time is completely colonized by this project. Virtually every new learning standard and educational program (from literacy to science to the aforementioned social-emotional learning) is accompanied by a slew of suggested ways to support children to "make a HUGE difference." The template for enlisting these labors within the workshop takes a simple format: describe the new practice, why it matters, and how "you" (mother) can help.[31]

What is most striking about these offers to help children succeed is how these labor impositions are represented not as labor at all, but as ways to transform intimate family interactions into a new ideal of domesticity. "Make reading a part of your family time!" a flyer exhorted. "Family time is so important. Why not make reading part of this valuable time with your kids? Here are some tips for integrating reading into our daily family activities." Dinnertime is an opportunity to ask about children's writing, "an opportunity for children to rehearse. Say, 'Tell me that story,' and 'How will that essay go, what are your main points?'" Even bedtime becomes an occasion to ensure children's success. I was encouraged to install the Bedtime Math application on my phone to "make math a fun part of kids' everyday lives, as beloved as the bedtime story." The beloved bedtime story itself has been debased into an extended school activity to "build fluency, vocabulary, and comprehension skills." Parents are plowed with appropriate questions for various literacy skills while also warned to not overly critique or "turn them into tests." Maternal labors are intricately managed and intensified, these workshops suggest, not only to help children succeed in school but because such activities are intimate and fun!

The continual labors of learning involved with being informed of schools' constantly shifting demands, the managing of children's negative emotions resulting from increased pressures and work, the instilling of positive affective states required of the neoliberal child subject, and the colonization of family time by the dictates of school production—workshops are sites where the neoliberal character masks of the partner teacher or investing mother and human for capital child are inaugurated. Although most mothers do not attend these workshops, they still reach all mothers in some way. Their mere presence looms over mothers and radiates into the home. The chorus of their messages is continually echoed in packets sent home with children, in multiple weekly emails, in the physical space of schools, in schools' social media accounts that parents are encouraged to engage, in media reporting on education, in apps that parents are compelled to download onto their phones—mothers can scarcely escape their interpellating force. Workshops are one mode by which the human capital machine enters and suffuses the home to transform mothers' mode of being and relating with children. We might posit a general idea of mothering as the work of caring for children that fosters their well-being in the present and equips them to a future of open possibilities. Workshops offer a new ideal of mothering, a happy state that results from making family time productive and at the same time fun. This ideal is foisted upon mothers by capital's forces of economic compulsion and backed by the power of the state, powers that are always coercive regardless of whether their demands exist as threats, looming punishments, or gifts and promises of rewards.

Capitalism rules through time, by organizing time, by subsuming time to the dictates of capital accumulation.[32] The time of production is an endlessly repetitive temporality, what the philosopher Walter Benjamin called "homogenous, empty time."[33] Children in capitalist societies must learn to adapt to this "restrictive temporal normativity."[34] Within reproduction, capital tethers women's care to the temporal regime of its cycle of valorization. This is a temporality in which the present is subordinated to a perpetual repetitive future of capital's cycle of accumulation on an ever-expanding scale, M-C-M′—an endlessly changing same. Capital's future pulls the child's being in the present and the child's becoming into its cycle of becoming. Family time workshops demonstrate that capital and the state want nothing less than a complete takeover of maternal time, every waking moment of a mother's time directed to investing in her child. Such demands are so compelling because they work through human capital's particular mode of valuation, coercing mothers to labor through the punishments and rewards of the child's future. This is how capital's forces of compulsion enter reproduction—mothers must ensure that children are able to survive and thrive in a precarious world as future labor (see Premise 2).

Human capital theory tethers mothers to capital's dispersed reproductive factory, where they are organs augmenting children's value and instilling within children the will and desire to see themselves as a form of capital. Capital's relentless expropriation of humans' creative capacities within neoliberalism crucially depends on shaping subjects who views themselves as bundles of potentially appreciating or depreciating capital, subjects nurtured and cared for through the prism of value. Maternal labors are essential for this large-scale project of remaking subjects: They manage and augment the labors of the school, keep abreast of its changing policies, and clean up the emotional and psychic wreckage of these toxic conditions as best they can. More decisively, they can potentially shape subjects who are singularly devoted to working for capital, who view the sacrifice as a moral honor and even a joy.

Schooling Mom and the Holy Family

As political theorists ignore the family as a site of "real" politics, capital and the state quietly experiment with new modes of governance within it. Mothers are a linchpin of neoliberalism's reconfigured power relations and intensified regimes of extracting surplus value from subjects. Mothers help construct subjects oriented to their own value, ones who manage their own selves for this purpose and, most critically, help instantiate a social order in which "the economy" takes on an almost mystical sacred form. By taking up their newfangled prescribed role for capital, mothers help transform the family into a laboring-cum-devotional unit to it—capital's "holy family."

First, mothers are tasked with laboring to produce subjects perpetually investing in their own selves as capital, subjects cognitively, socially, emotionally, and psychically prepared to work intensely and intently for capital. This links mothers more directly into circuits producing future surplus value that will be wrested from their child's labor. The human capital investment strategy is key to neoliberalism's modes of capital accumulation—through speculation; through the innovations of knowledge, tech, and creative industries; through service economies in which what is for sale are subjective aspects of the human such as personalities, emotions, and affects—all these modes verily depend on a subject intricately modulated by and oriented to capital.

Second, the subsumption of maternal labors profoundly alters the subjectivities of mother and child. The drive to assume greater control of mothers and children represents the "irrational" side of capital's drive. Understanding capital's drive requires a critique of political economy as well as, in the register of psychoanalytically informed critical theories, of libidinal economy, or what Tomšič articulates as its "unconscious."[35] While the conception of libidinal economy is conventionally formulated to understand how social forces adhere to individual psychic life, it proves useful to understand capital's reach on the human subject where it does not make sense from a political economic frame alone. Why all these enormous efforts to school mothers? Why not further extend, intensify, and regulate children's and teachers' working day in schools? Does practicing math or a narrow set of reading skills really increase children's human capital value; does it contribute to the economy and the gross national product? Do the architects and managers of schooling mothers really believe that children will be more able and willing to work for capital if mothers engage in such labors? As I argue, human capital theory is an instantiation of capital's drive, a machine installed within the human subject that seeks control of its personality, emotions, relations, desires, its inner life. This drive is fundamentally irrational—it is domination for domination's sake. This insatiable and irrational desire is revealed in capital's aspirations for mothers and children and the relation between them. The neoliberal family serves as a model for social relations as a whole—where the family unit can be devoted, in a quasi-religious sense, to capital.

Marxist theory has long pointed out how the nuclear family is crucial for the reproduction of capitalism—absorbing its crises and producing its subjects. More recently, Melinda Cooper convincingly demonstrates how neoliberal policies (punitive, pedagogical, and regulatory policies) perpetuate a reconfigured family form in which families represent the ideal relations of "self-sufficiency" in the neoliberal order.[36] In a broader, more anthropological frame that connects psyche with society and culture, the family is crucial for instantiating the neoliberal cosmogony (from the Greek *kosmos*, or "universe," and *gonos*, or "offspring"), where "we tell the world, or at least ourselves, who we are."[37] The family within neoliberalism manifests and symbolizes the model of human psychic, emotional, social, and spiritual relations to capital. A mother's relation to the child is, inarguably, one of the most important social relations in society for the subject's formation. As psychoanalytic theory emphatically maintains, it provides the model for all other relations. Motherhood is also an idealized site where labors are naturalized and rendered invisible as love, duty, and sacrifice, a site with no conceivable limits to this sacrifice, one where sacrifice supposedly leads to her own satisfaction, fulfillment, and delight. Within the mundane discourse of schooling moms, prescriptions for mothers on how to best love their child are equated with what is best for capital, verily transformed into prescriptions to mothers to sacrifice for capital. Capital prescribes relations within families that are a synecdoche of neoliberalism's reconfigured relations between families and the state and families to capital. These relations are characterized by commitment and gratitude—mothers should be delighted to be engaged in these pursuits, should feel lucky that their children are given "the chance" to participate in the community of capital, should ensure their children eat, rest, play, learn, and live as offerings to capital.

Capital is "motivated by the economic fantasy of total subsumption of life-day under workday and life-force under labour-force."[38] Neoliberal capital unleashes the drive into reproduction to plunder the relation of mother and child and dominate human becoming, one of the many "free gifts" that capital appropriates from life. Yet this plunder should appear in inverted form, as if subjects freely and happily grant this gift of life and are grateful for the opportunity to do so. One might justifiably speculate whether there will be anything left to plunder if there is no free time, if all of subjectivity is one staid replication of capital's demands, if the unruly life and death drives are replaced by a parasitic, undead force? Yet this type of speculation replicates capital's fantasy of total subsumption. Capital's perverted fantasies for the subject can never match its aspirations. The subjective powers of life always precede and exceed capital's capacity to subordinate them, the eruptive force of life is primary. Capital exists only secondarily by consuming the vitality of living humans. Nevertheless, capital's unrelenting quest to subject and subordinate ever more of the subject is one of the key struggles of our time. Recognizing this, a materialist analysis proceeds with how actual flesh-and-blood subjects—in this case mothers, navigate this nightmare—how their lives, labors, relations, struggles, and anguishes are structured by it, and how they make the world in spite of it. A materialist account of mothering seeks cracks, potentials, and spaces to intervene. The perspective from everyday life reveals that while they may not precisely identify it, mothers partially perceive and refuse the intrusion of capital into their mothering—not simply their labors but also their own hopes and aspirations for their children's lives beyond labor, as actual human persons. Understanding capital's ambitions for mothers, children, and us all should clarify and strengthen our collective determination to refuse this undead force imposed on life becoming.

5

Emotional Chains of Motherly Subjection

Making the Manageable Self-Managed Child

> The rule of capital through the wage compels every able-bodied person, under the laws of the division of labor to function in ways that are if not immediately, then ultimately profitable to the expansion and extension of the rule of capital. That, fundamentally, is the meaning of school. *Where children are concerned, their labor appears to be the learning for their own benefit.*
>
> —*Mariarosa Dalla Costa,* Women and the Subversion

REFLECTING ON THE enormous pressures that young children currently face in schools, forty-six-year-old Gloria recounted her recent efforts managing her ten-year-old daughter's test anxiety and resistance and trying to get her to take the test with a positive attitude. The difficulty of this work was compounded by the fact that Jamila had been doing remote schooling for the previous year because of the COVID-19 pandemic.

> Jamila was nervous about taking it. I had her go in to take the test, she was so nervous, and she was like [defiantly] "But why?! I hate it!" And I was like, "Well, first of all, it's a practice test, it doesn't

> count for anything, and it's good practice. Secondly, you decided not to go back into school and I think it would be good for you to go back to go into your school." That's what I told her because that's what I believe, you know? So she went in, she was so nervous the day before. And I was like, "Why are you so nervous? It's just a practice test." And she was like, "Just the word! State test mommy! And you said for the ELA [English language arts] test I had to work on X, Y, Z." See, she's very literal. So I said, "Just because I said you have to work on a certain skill doesn't mean you didn't do a good job! You did a *great* job! But this is just something you want to work on harder, you know? We would want to strengthen this part." But she takes that as like, she's very literal, and I said, "You did a great job! It's just, we could *Always. Do. Better.*" A lot of our kids are just taught to get 100s, and let's get in the 90s, but you want to do the best you can. There's this whole growth mindset thing that I'm trying to teach her.[1]

Although her own work, anguish, and pressure recede from view in the narrative, Gloria recounted a set of intricate labors whereby she delicately balanced a host of simultaneous and conflicting tasks to shape her child's subjectivity. She encouraged the child to do her best in school while not forcing her; asserted her parental authority to instill a sense of ownership of her schooling; nurtured confidence to impart an ethos of self-management; and, finally, cultivated comfort to express negative feelings, only to swallow them for the sake of a larger goal of success. These labors of guiding children through their own labors and anxieties of schooling, coaching them to accept them as obstacles that they must overcome and face them as challenges that lead to "growth," and helping to construct them as emotionally managed, productive, and motivated selves is the work of mothering for capital. This radical restructuring of reproduction happens in and through the seemingly mundane daily interactions between mothers and children in everyday life. In practice, shaping children into human for capital subjects involves prioritizing and developing qualities that are currently deemed valuable or can be rendered as value over other qualities or experiences. Mothering should be devoted to creating a subject whose dominant characteristic is the unique neoliberal amalgam of being what Kathi Weeks terms "simultaneously self-directed and manageable," a curious form of subjectivity that "poses an ongoing puzzle for the capitalist."[2]

Constructing the manageable yet self-managed subject, one who even sees their own value for the economy as a moral and ethical good, involves painstakingly intricate labors. Within the productive sphere, this is virtually the job description and mission of management. In the reproductive sphere as well, shaping a child subject involves many different types of managerial work. Mothers must marshal their own emotions and personality and apply a complex set of knowledge and skills onto to an individual child, their evolving concerns, characteristics, and temperament. Emotional or affective labor, the work to manage or create a particular feeling in another subject, cognitive and communicational labor—these, too, are part of neoliberal mothering.[3] The well-recognized turn toward "immaterial labor" in postindustrial economies means that most jobs involve affective, communicative, and cognitive labor, from so-called manual to professionalized jobs. Marxist and critical theories have long considered both family and school as the sites where children are subjected into the dominant order, socialized to accept obedience and hierarchy, if not despotism, and thus become capitalist subjects.[4] Yet even as Bowles and Gintis recognized fifty years ago, "The aim of [school] discipline is no longer mere compliance . . . Discipline is still the theme, but the variations more often center the 'internalization of behavioral norms' and equipping the child with a built-in supervisor than on mere obedience to external authority and material sanctions."[5] Bowles and Gintis did not emphasize compliance but the correspondence of discipline to the capitalist workplace. Where the factory's more despotic structure requires a certain type of worker passivity and obedience (Marx described worker's activity as "determined and regulated on all sides by the movement of the machinery"), the postindustrial economy of the US and other advanced economies depends on the internal discipline of the self-regulated, self-managed, self-aware, self-supervising subject, even of so-called unskilled laborers.[6] Because they involve command over workers' "personality and subjectivity," such jobs heighten the antagonisms in capitalist work.[7] Within mothering, the antagonisms are exaggerated, though taking different form, because they involve a double subjection—the struggle to exert command over two subjectivities, one of which is unruly and whose will to be free from coercion is still quite acute.

This chapter explores the multifaceted terrain of struggle involved in the double subjection of neoliberal social reproduction, from mothers' point of view. The previous chapters argue that capital subsumes maternal labors to produce new subjectivities of mother and child, the mother as chief investor in a child's value and the child as living value for capital. Value comes to dominate the mother's relationship to child and the home, its rhythms, activities, and purpose and in the sense of becoming subjects for capital. Yet capital dominates not blank slates, objects that happen to be mothers, but women whose desires for themselves and their children exceed and oppose capital's drive. It is true that all the women in my research, in some form or another, took on at least some portion of the suite of subject-making labors prescribed by capital and state through the econo-psy and neoliberal education complexes, labors deemed necessary to help their children survive-cum-succeed. Approaching mothering in terms of subjection means that the labors equated with good mothering are coerced, the result of an irreducible struggle, the manifestation of a complicated by-product of mothers' adoption, acquiescence, as well as refusal. To get from the surface to this underlying layer means asking how mothers understand these labors, how they feel about them, and how they may both desire and resent them. Within the stream of words, emotions, stories, and complaints in their narratives, I try to discern how the force of capital appears, or disappears, from their view. How do women understand the key political transformations in which they are centrally involved?

Critical theory's intermittent interest in the family is precisely because it is the forging ground of what Robyn Marasco calls "primary politicization"—one's "basic orientation to authority" and "disposition to domination."[8] The family is not a dress rehearsal for the peculiar forms that domination takes in neoliberalism—its intensified forms that reach the psyche, its invisibility, its enacting by subjects on their selves. The family is *the* site for the exercise and reproduction of neoliberal domination. As psychoanalytic object relations theorists like Melanie Klein aver, mothers are children's primary Others.[9] The mother-child bond is the foundational substrate for the development of the individual's psyche and profoundly shapes all their other relations. Therein lies the tragedy of the family: Our collective subjection is partly produced within the intimate bonds—or more precisely the emotional chains—within the family.

As Gloria's narrative demonstrates, subjection does not arise from parent's autocratic rule—punishing and withholding love from children to secure demands—rule whose force is clear, direct, and immediately resisted or resented. Rather, children and mothers are subjected to capital's drive through love and sincere efforts to care. Capital's drive hijacks mothers' love, transforms it, routes it toward the middle class project of devoting life to capital. Capital's subordination of the human subject is a complex process that can never said to be total. Outside of the workplace, industrial capital chiefly delegated this task to the state and its schooling. Within neoliberalism's heightened demands for the subject, the antagonisms are amplified and so mothers are called on board. Capital's delegated authority becomes maternal authority, where it is strategically naturalized, disguised and invisibilized. Mothers' subjection of children, imbued with sincere desire for children's own good and optimally delivered through gentle coaxing, is more effective than any attempt to subject children through impersonal relations. In this way, maternal labors perform a different function. The central struggle within neoliberal social reproduction is not strictly about labor (mothers' or children's) but involves creating subjects within a "community of capital," subjects that freely, willingly, happily devote their life to capital.

Capital encroaches into the deepest recesses of the psyche by disfiguring the love within a child's prime relation. The maternal relation, while imbued with the sincere desire to do right by children in the present and future, is continually distorted by capital to imagine those presents and futures solely within its rule of value. Capital's rule through the wage, even in its future form, compels mothers, however gently or otherwise, to see their own and their children's labors to be, as Dalla Costa notes in the epigraph that opens this chapter, *for their own benefit*.[10] And children, for their part, have a deep desire, however conflicted and ambivalent, to be that which their mothers desire. By hijacking maternal authority and love, capital orients children not to their mothers, but to capital behind them.

Although capital perverts the maternal role, labors, and bond with the child, mothers' doubts and ambiguities about their labors and the subjectivation of their children, as well as women's sheer exhaustion, deepen the cracks and fissures in the reproduction of these subject forms. Incorrigible children often create the cracks as they continually refuse, negotiate, and attempt to shirk the labors involved in their subjection. Social reproduction thus remains a dynamic terrain of struggle with a vast potential for subversion. The unruly child is the point where capital meets its fiercest opponent. Recognizing children's antagonism toward their mothers' delegated subjection and defamiliarizing ourselves from maternal labors performed for their benefit can be a strategy to deepen those cracks.

The Subsumption of Motherhood: From Fantasy to Bedtime

Mothers and children are prime targets of capital's ceaseless drive to valorize value because their potential is seemingly endless—every waking moment of a child's life from birth could be a point for mothers to intervene to "develop" and "invest" in their abilities, as per Foucault's abilities machines (see Chapter 2). Neoliberalism's good mother is perhaps more impossible than other maternal ideals. It is seductive nonetheless, functioning as a fantasy around which women imagine they might be able to realize, only if circumstances allowed. My participants imagined warm and fuzzy domestic scenarios in which they could perform the labors of the "good mother" as they envisioned they were meant to; not in an anxious frenzy as part of a "fourth shift" of work, but leisurely and with the pleasure and patience with which a good mother would perform them.[11] As profoundly as it alters their labors, capital infiltrates women's understanding of themselves as mothers at the psychic level, transforming what they imagine to be the ideal life.

My interlocutor Juliet revealed a domestic fantasy that allowed her a better chance to perform the impossible labors of the new maternal ideal. Juliet, born and raised in Queens to Haitian immigrant parents, is a former lawyer now business partner with her fiancée, with three daughters (one ten-year-old and nine-year-old twins). At the time of the interview, Juliet was forty-eight and in the midst of multiple dramatic life changes. She was planning to move the following fall from New York City to be with her new husband in suburban Pennsylvania, a place she thought would allow her to be a good mother for her three daughters. As she discussed her reasons for the move, she fantasized about the new life she would be starting:

> I'll take them to school in the morning, and the schools are nice there, they're all cute. I'll probably get more time with the teachers. I'll get more involved with the school at that point because I'll have time. And then while they're gone in school, from 8 to 3, 8 to 2:30, I'll be doing what I need to do. *And then there will be family time, to do homework together*. Kevin wants me to do that. He's a kind of guy that wants to be a provider. It's a little old-fashioned in that way, which is fine. I would [in the past] rebel at that. Like, I should be able to work! But part of me likes that at this point. I've worked all my life, you know? I've had to. I feel like I'm taking care of everyone all the time. It's nice when someone wants to take care of me and the girls.

Juliet's fantasies make invisible the various struggles of her frenetic life as a single mother and former corporate lawyer in the city, with continual strategizing to find good schools and meaningful and affordable extracurricular activities in a competitive rat race, the shuttling of herself and her kids from one part of the city to another. She pictures a suburban idyll where the schools are "nice" and "cute" and presumably easy to navigate so that even the act of transportation seems pleasurable. It takes time, a lot of time, to be a good mother for capital. And in Juliet's fantasy, time is in abundance, to communicate with teachers and be involved in school. Most notably is how Juliet punctuates her fantasy with "And then there will be family time." And at the center of the hearth, evoking the domestic bliss of a log crackling in the fireplace, she huddles with her children "to do homework together." Juliet's fantasy reveals how insidiously capital subsumes motherhood in neoliberalism, where the image of mother and children performing imposed labor in the hopes of bettering children's chances at a decent future can somehow appear as voluntary and ideal. Mothers' authentic desires to be good mothers, to work for their children's good, are so entangled with capital that we need sharp analytic tools to defamiliarize them, lest we remain mired in their ideological traps. Critical concepts can reveal the silent and indirect way compulsions of capitalist relations are imposed on mothers, the subtle ways mothers are made to desire them, and the profound ways they distort mothers and children's lives and make them unfree.

The focal labors of this chapter are indisputably reproductive labors that produce that "special commodity—labor power," and therefore are indispensable to the reproduction of capitalism and our collective immiseration. The lens of subsumption makes visible how capital transforms mothering's most important task—shaping children as subjects. Subsumption is best conceived as a moving struggle—historical, political, contestable, emerging, and contingent upon antagonistic social relations in everyday life—at the workplace, in public space, at school, and in the home. David Harvie's discussion of the subsumption of teachers' labor helps illustrate how capital transforms maternal labors into drudgery, into alienated labor for capital, and the specific kinds of subjectivities that are constructed.[12] For Harvie the focus is on how teachers' labors (re) produce humans qua humans or as labor power. He poses the question not to establish closure but to direct focus to the daily struggles within schools to transform teachers' and students' labors into labor that produce students as abstract labor, the substance of value. Teachers and students work is increasingly subject to control; imposed and regulated by external accrediting bodies and the state. "Increasingly forced to subsume their own interests to that of capital," teaching and learning become sensuousless activities and are increasingly "becoming-alienated."[13] Rendering the unruly labors of teaching and learning into commensurable quantifiable abstractions is a complex and profound struggle. The newly imposed teaching labors—whether they are "additional" labors or whether they replace or displace other labors—are designed to make students more easily measurable as value and to shape students into particular kinds of laboring subjects, manageable and self-managed. The impositions on teaching labors to create the educated person *for* capital exists alongside and often in opposition to other teaching labors, those labors that nurture and sustain students' learning and curiosity in the world, those labors that many teachers imagined they would be doing when drawn to the profession.

Capital's distortions of subject making are amplified when mothering is transformed into capitalist labor, because mothering and the familial are not understood to be domains of real work. When such subject-making labors occur in these domains, then, they are familiarized and verily *appear to be good mothering and for the child's own good*. Conceiving of this terrain as one of moving struggle helps disentangle subject-making labors for capital from the work of nurturing children as autonomous beings. I offer an example from my own experiences reading with my child to illustrate the concealed struggles involved in the subsumption of mothering, how capital seeps into everyday life, women's psyches and relations with the child, and women's and children's resistance to this force. I had begun reading books to my child when she was quite young, perhaps one and definitely by age two, an activity that petered out and ended abruptly when she was about eight or nine. Reading occurred randomly throughout the day, and it was also a firmly established part of an outstretched bedtime routine. When she was younger, pleas of "one more book" turned into three or four picture books and when she was older, "one more chapter" of novels. These were enjoyable experiences for both of us, a time to unwind, one of the few moments when my active child held still for a prolonged period, completely engaged in the universal human ritual of sharing stories. As a lifelong reader and enthusiast of children's literature, I loved exploring old favorites from when I was a kid and my time as an elementary school teacher, as well as the whole new world of children's literature that had opened up since those times. As an exhausted person, I genuinely cherished an activity where I could be sitting or lying down with my child. Of course I was familiar with the marching orders all around me—injunctions to *read with your child every day* are inescapable. From parent magazines to pamphlets in pediatricians' offices to early childcare centers to schools to libraries, the educational benefits are touted—reading skills, various other cognitive skills, test performance! Mothers are told, "Your child isn't just having fun, they're learning!"[14] The same anxious temporality that imbues learning in neoliberal schooling pervades maternal directives to read—"It is never too early to read to a child. Studies show that one should begin reading to a child as early as the last trimester of pregnancy."[15]

While I was not reading to my child in order for her to succeed in school and eventually the workforce, my activities likely contribute to these ends. For a long time, my kid was a voracious independent reader (until the simultaneous hit of the COVID-19 pandemic, and cellphone acquisition) and did well in school as measured by standardized test scores and report cards. My free maternal activities helped augment my kid's value within current relations of production, embodied skills that will eventually be exploited to create surplus value. Yet I would firmly not designate my reading with her as an example of capital's subsumption of mothering. For the problem, as it were, is not that I inadvertently contribute to capital accumulation in the future while I lay around having fun with my child (although I would make a political-ethical case that I ought to receive the value of my labors of shaping a laborer in a context where I must sell my labor to access the means of subsistence). The problem is that capital's incessant drive to valorize itself means that it is not enough to siphon value from already-existing free activities. Capital's inexorable need to expand penetrates and *distorts* free activities. Marx wrote about "real subsumption" as involving the transformation of the labor process so that it is organized around the logic of capital accumulation rather than, for instance, the freedom or pleasure or desire of the laborer or the quality of what is produced.

Reading to my child was a target in the same way that any free activity and any aspect of human social life is prospective game to discipline and from which to orient toward value. Subsumption is the point at which our activities become subject to the distorting force of capital, when we become less free. This is a point of struggle whose case is never closed. For even I, with my incipient critical perspective on these phenomena at the time, was not impervious to the endless communiqués from school and every other corner of the parenting and childcare universe. The good mother, the partner teacher, the chief investor does not just read to a child in any old way. There are specific and technical best practices that purportedly help develop children's reading, cognitive, and listening skills, vocabulary, and attention span (see Chapter 4). At every first day of school, and with every quarterly report card, parents of young children in New York City schools receive a "literacy tip sheet" for "3K–4K" (prekindergarten) or "K–2," sometimes printed on cardstock to encourage a prominent space on the fridge. The city's Department of Education has a downloadable and printable sheet or poster available in ten different languages. The guide includes such tips as stopping while reading to "ask: 'What was that story about?' or 'Did you like that character? Why?'"

One bedtime when my kid was about five, on the second or third picture book and with all the "best practices" dancing in my head, my looming sense of guilt about not adequately "developing" her reading and vocabulary skills reared its head. I thought, this activity need not be strictly pleasure, I can incorporate some business as well! I stopped in the middle of a page and asked her what she felt about what was happening, much like how I was recommended to do. She immediately threw a disapproving glance my way before insistently tapping on the page and impatiently declared, "*Read*, mama." And so I read. Her simple injunction taught me to never *school* our reading rituals ever again.

Such is capital's force to discipline the family that it invades ordinary intimate interactions between mother and child, even while tucked in bed and enjoying a good story well past bedtime. Yet every day, children and adults oppose these abstract homogenizing forces that are organizing their lives, even if they are not aware of what they are resisting or escaping. My schooled question was an effect of capital's disciplining my labor through the forces of economic compulsion—my child's future wage and notions of good mothering loomed before me, filtered through the econo-psy and neoliberal education complexes' dictates, orienting my labors and interactions and ideas about "what's best for my child"—toward her value for capital. "Read, mama" was my child's refusal of capital's unremitting drive to distort our beloved activity, our relation, and our free time.

Thinking through reproduction with the lens of subsumption attunes us to such struggles. It helps defamiliarize parenting practices to ask if and how capital organizes them into labors that consume and deplete mothers, that deform the bond between mother and child and the subjectivities of both—the points at which subjects become more unfree. Women's narratives about their struggles reveal moments where they somehow grasp capital's invisible compulsion and the damage it inflicts, even if they do not precisely identify their origins. Sometimes, women expressed alternative desires for their own and their children's presents and futures, moments where they imagined life outside capital's control.

Constructing the Manageable Self-Managed Subject

No mother can escape the compulsion to take on the new subject-making labors associated with the "successful" child. Irrespective of any formal participation in schools' direct efforts to train them (as in workshops described in Chapter 4), the econo-psy and neoliberal education complexes directly and indirectly decree the importance of children having the right "attitude," "outlook," or "mindset"—the self-managed manageable subject. Chapter 4, "Schooling Moms," showed how school districts throughout the US, including in New York City, respond to capital's dictates for subjectivity via mandates to incorporate so-called social-emotional learning. This slew of skills identified as important for "success" include a constant cultivation and investment in the self or a "growth mentality," the ability to withstand the pressures of continual investment in the project of schooling and competition of austerity, all wrapped within an "oppressive hegemonic positivity."[16] Maternal labors are targeted, I argue, because this subject form requires intricate psychological, social, and emotional modulation. While teachers must comply and incorporate "social-emotional learning" into their direct instructional efforts, however perfunctorily, incorporating mothers into this enterprise relies on seemingly voluntary methods of encouragement. Yet in the particular context of neoliberal austerity where mothers know their children will enter the labor force either scrambling to survive or scrambling up the elusive ladder of "success," mothers are not choosing a "style" of parenting, they are bound to an imperative—mother for capital.

How do mothers take up this imperative in everyday life? How could practices that hijack mothers' and children's lives for the valorization of value be transposed onto the intimate familial domain when mothers presumably love and want the best for their children? In a fictional dystopia, one might imagine capital's knowledge henchmen of economists, psychologists, and educators delivering specific socialization dictates to mothers that they immediately adopt under surveillance and fear of punishment, perhaps interacting more authentically with children only in furtive moments and whispers. The subjection of mothers looks quite different in everyday life. Women do not simply adopt the econo-psy complex's imperatives for socialization and jettison their own practices that have developed from their experiences with their children. Rather, mothers must constantly internally wrestle with the incompatibility of their emergent philosophies with the scientific expert-backed "philosophy" that purports to create successful, even *happy* children. Human capital theory is not as easily portable into the familial domain of socialization as the experts suggest. Every mother has had to contend with the damage that its ideology of continual "growth" and orientation to success wreaks on children while disregarding the damage this impossible position wreaks on them. Although women struggled against human capital theory, the silent forces of economic compulsion compelled them to integrate its demands into their own philosophies of parenting and childhood, however unevenly or uncomfortably. Women's narratives reveal how the imperatives for subject making take hold of mothers, how they get mixed up with mothers' own authentic desires in such a way that domination appears to be voluntary or does not appear at all.

Rebecca, a forty-six-year-old mother of two kids, Sara (age eleven) and David (age ten), tried to incorporate the econo-psy complex's most recent socialization injunctions into her own well-articulated philosophy of childhood. Rebecca had struck me as particularly chill about mothering when I saw her and her kids around the neighborhood, joyfully running or biking around parks and playgrounds, with their sweet pit bull often in tow. Rebecca was born in Israel, where she obtained a degree as an early childhood educator. She ran a licensed day care in her home that was, at the time of the interview, not serving any children. Her educational and professional experiences likely contributed to her particular philosophy of childhood. While all moms indeed had an implicit philosophy of childhood and parenting, Rebecca's was more explicitly articulated. The excerpt below begins with her using the term "philosophy" unprompted to describe her view that parenting is about letting children find their own unique path and guiding them along this path. Rebecca's struggles are instructive because her philosophy conflicted with parenting "best practices," and more so, because these practices were inflicting such harm and suffering on her ten-year-old. Rebecca considered her efforts managing her son's panic attacks about the pressure of contemporary schooling. Rebecca had to integrate her ethos of spiritual unfolding with the econo-psy complex's techniques of emotional regulation and self-management to guide her children through these pressures. She discusses labors of trying to find a balance, labors to clean up the emotional and psychic mess the school made of her son, and labors to orient him toward facing challenges and seeing them as opportunities for growth. Like Gloria, her own labors and emotional and psychic plight recede from view as she navigated more pressing and primary concerns, her child's impossible situation.

Maria: So yeah, you're so cool and laid back, and I was wondering if it's because . . .

Rebecca: Yes, my philosophy is this. Every kid has their own path, and

I'm just here to guide him. It's the only thing I can do.

MARIA: Would you say you learned this philosophy from like doing it, or is it something you learned even before you became a mom?

REBECCA: I think before I became a mom. It's that, we bring a soul to this world, and I can't control it. It's not my job. I can just care for it, and the space, and the kindness, and the self-esteem. But what they choose in life, that's not my problem. They have their own path. With Sara I can say it's easier because she's calm and she doesn't need extra. With my son, he needs extra. He's more sensitive. So he needs extra pushing, I think. But I think it's because of the ages. Sara is eleven. She has her moments, don't get me wrong. I think they are, well David is more, um, it's hard for him to focus, that's all I can say. You know, he's very smart, he just needs to focus. And here it's hard because here they push him to the limit. I have a problem with him and the tests. I almost didn't send him. It doesn't matter. I said to him, "Do the best that you can. If you don't want to do it, I want you to try. If you tell me, Eema [Hebrew for mother], I don't want to do it, I'll work with you. Please try one time, because it's the first time." And he's like, "Oh what if they're not going to let me go to the next grade." I'm like, "What?! There's no way! You're going to go to the next grade, I'm going to show you. Everything will be fine." I don't know what the fuck to say to them, but it's freaking me out! He was freaking out, he was like, "Eema, I can't breathe!" I was like, "Listen, do what you can do. And that's it." My thinking is, I don't want to *not* send him for the first time because I don't want every time he sees a test to get scared and say, "I'm not going to do it." And this is going to be a habit. No. First face the fear, and see that it's nothing. And then we work from there. And then after he was like, "It wasn't my expectation, it was so bad, it was six responses." And I was like, "Do two, that's it. Do the best you can. Do how much you can, but do it the *right* way. That's it!"

MARIA: Do you see, even if we opt out of the test, we're not opting out of months of torture that they've been torturing the kids with.

REBECCA: This is what I'm saying! This is, what the heck? My son isn't even learning anything! Anxiety, anxiety, anxiety! Sara was different. She didn't have anxiety, she can just go through. She can handle it. He is freaking out for a month already. And it's not his teacher [imposing pressure], he has a substitute. I spoke to the counselor and I was like, "Look, I'm not going to let him do the test. Leave this kid alone." And she talked to him to tell him not to worry. Who told him he's not going to get to fourth grade? Who the heck? I'm like, "You're going to go to fourth grade and fifth grade and nothing is going to happen and I'm going to show you."

MARIA: She cleared out her backpack this morning. Look what the fuck they've been doing the past few weeks [grabs and shakes nearby test prep worksheets]: Test prep, test prep, test prep!

REBECCA: YES, YES, YES! Everything! David is so frustrated! He keeps saying, "I'm not going to do good." And I'm like, "STOP!" [exhales deeply] For me it's so weird because he's stressed ridiculously, stress. He's not a stressed kid, he's very chilled out, peace and love, "I'm fine." He is very, very, very nervous now, very nervous. He can't sleep, and sometimes he's like "I can't breathe. What am I going to do, what's going to happen tomorrow?" I can tell him what to do because I do meditation, I do for them meditation at night.

MARIA: That's amazing because I see my daughter has so much stress.

REBECCA: Do the meditation, you can find it on YouTube. It's just a story, but it's in a different voice, and they tell you to breathe, and let go, just like that. And then they calm down. It's hard for them. So in the beginning of the mediation, I will sit with him. Listen with him and do it with him, until he calms down. It's ridiculous. Before he would put his head on the pillow and [snore]. And then he's like, "I can't sleep, I can't breathe." Anxiety in third grade?! Are you kidding me?!

Rebecca's anguish from seeing her child suffer because of schooling was not unfamiliar to me, nor would it be to any of the mothers in my research. In these situations, mothers put on a brave face, disavowed their feelings of rage and sadness, and momentarily put aside their doubts about the project of orienting children's lives to success. They soothed and guided children through negative feelings in ways that conform to the emotionally self-regulated subject dictated by the econo-psy complex's child experts.

To be sure, these subject-making labors have some parallels to the ways parents work with their children through other childhood agonies—from scraped knees to existential fears about death—the inevitable pains and difficulties of growing up. Yet the agonies of schooling are not inevitable facts of life, nor are they necessary for children's healthy development. We could argue that they are inimical to the child's flourishing as a human being. Rebecca's anger and frustration indicates she did not truly believe David's suffering was necessary or inevitable, or that it was "best" for him. When reporting what she told David, she used the voice and cadence she used with him—a soothing guided-through-meditation type of tone. When speaking to me, her voice was full of fiery outrage: "It's freaking me out!" and "anxiety in third grade?! Are you kidding me?!" She angrily rejected the high stakes and pressures of school pushing her child "to the limit" and the educational utility of doing so—"What the heck? My son isn't even learning anything!" Her outrage led her to the school counselor to complain about these pressures—"Who told him he's not going to go to fourth grade?" Who the heck?" I cannot say why Rebecca chose the route of sending her child to take the test rather than doing what she wanted to do and was ready to do ("I almost didn't send him" and her threat to the counselor: "Look, I'm not going to let him take this test. Leave him alone!"). I would propose that she could not explain why either. While keeping in mind that many parents who opt their children out of high-stakes testing are not oriented toward collective liberatory action (parents in conservative districts throughout the US have opted out of testing en masse), I am interested in the potential possibilities of channeling authentic parental anger into social justice for all children, not just their own. Part of the task requires sitting with Rebecca's feelings without offering resolutions and critiques that would paint her as not stridently resistant enough or as simply duped into laboring for capital. It requires facing the conundrum that most mothers face quite alone—accept the present right before them and a future that seems inevitable and manage to "fit" children as best as possible to it, or . . . The crux of the question is, what is the alternative?

Capitalist relations act as forces that compel mothers to distort their labors and interactions with their children. In the context in which women mothers and children will be adults, these are the relations that will likely prevail. In this respect, these methods verily appear and might even be justified as being for the child's own good. In most cases. I imagine some readers would disagree with Rebecca's ultimate decision to take on additional labors of helping David through his psychic and emotional turmoil rather than refusing the test. I also imagine many readers would agree that Gloria, in the opening vignette, managed and channeled her child's negative emotions into the desired outcome in the best possible way. She did not deliver an authoritarian edict for her child to comply and take the test. Rather, Gloria negotiated with her child in a way that rested on her assenting and taking a positive orientation toward the test. By negotiating, Gloria was also able to instill an orientation toward more complex goals and success—to make her child feel good about the particular goal, to see the good in it, and the good of continual "growth." While few mothers employed the specialized psycho-management language that Gloria used ("growth mindset") to describe their labors, they adopted similar management discourse. They did this either because they believed that it would help children succeed, because they thought it was the more effective way to manage children's resistance, or both. Mothers struggled to manage children while contending with their own ambivalent feelings about doing so. They labored for children's supposed good, yet they also contended with children resisting, scowling, crying, struggling, even throwing up. Children presented mothers with evidence that the conditions of contemporary schooling are harmful, if not absurd. Children prompted mothers to waver, question, and then justify their actions through the discourse through which human capital theory has melded into the various industries that purport to help subjects become their best selves—from health, wellness, and fitness to leisure, romance, and self-care. Such industries normalize the pursuit of continual growth not as a crude concern with employability but as becoming the best possible version of one's self, albeit a self that is considered a form of capital that must constantly appreciate—or risk *depreciating*. Human capital theory can infiltrate the intimate domain of reproduction because it targets subjects' nearly infinitely creative capacities and potential, and what mother would not want their child to reach their potential?

Capital so cunningly imposes the labors of constructing self-manageable child subjects that the fact that they are labors, imposed ones at that, often recedes from women's views, despite their exhaustion from performing them. Rebecca's labors, like Gloria's, were highly skilled, complex, tailored to the individual child and their limits, and entailed something more than the ordinary psychological insights of highly attuned individuals but a rudimentary knowledge of neoliberal management. Rebecca guided David to calm himself and face his fears, see them as a challenge—that is, opportunity for growth, admitting that he needs some "pushing": "Just try" and "Do the best you can. Do how much you can, but do it the *right* way." She goaded him, despite his pain, despite feeling that this was unnecessary and not in his best interest. These labors were oriented toward the long-term production of a self-managed, optimistic, and goal-oriented subject that is willing to swallow harm and take risks for so-called growth: "I don't want him every time he sees a test to get scared and say, I'm not going to do it. And this is going to be a habit. No, first face the fear, and see that it's nothing." Her nightly labors guiding him through meditation were also tailored toward this ("Sit with him. Listen with him and do it with him, until he calms down"). Rebecca managed David through the pains of high pressure by teaching him to manage his negative feelings, precisely the characteristics promulgated by the econo-psy and neoliberal education complexes. Neither Rebecca nor Gloria demanded compliance, certainly feasible options for both women, and likely less time-consuming and laborious. But neither woman was oriented toward the immediate goal at hand; rather, both were oriented toward the larger one of managing children to manage and regulate their own emotions in the long run.

These actions do not represent authentic emotional development, and they are injurious to both mothers and children. Yet even mothers who rejected high-pressure childhoods felt they had to contort their stance into an approach that emphasized so-called growth, even when children were suffering and they themselves were suffering from witnessing their child's anxieties. Yet they took on these labors, and they exhausted and depleted themselves psychologically and emotionally. The pressures of neoliberal schooling, which is to say, the economic compulsion and force of the future wage, which depends on the child's "value," disciplines women into inauthentic mothering. Their interactions and free time with children are transformed into capitalist labor.

One of the tragedies of mothering for capital is how subject-making labors deform the mother-child bond. Neoliberal schooling harms children in myriad ways. As many instances as there are of kids like Jamila's nerves and David's anxiety, there are more that don't express resistance in ways that register to analysts or even mothers. These are children who may have already received the message that you swallow, cover, or "manage" your difficult feelings. Or children who may have understood the very injustice that is being a child—adult authorities that rule your life simply do not understand the injustice, that tell you it is necessary, good, or that's how life goes and there are no alternatives. Virtually every day in school, children hear how important schooling is for their future, however hazy "the future" might be to children in the first place. To be sure, neoliberal schooling has not single-handedly ushered anxiety into childhood, nor has it single-handedly promoted an unhealthy and inauthentic emotional style vis-à-vis negative feelings. Childhood is imbued with positive and intensely negative emotions, including trauma and anxiety, even for psychologically healthy children. Adults often disavow this psychoanalytic truism, despite childhood memories that demand otherwise. Adults' expectations and insistence on "happy" childhoods leads them to discount children's negative feelings as they rush to resolve them rather than helping them work through them in ways that might lead to more authentic ethical and empathetic growth.[17] Even more troubling is how neoliberal schooling folds the unhealthy obsession with "happiness" into emotional regulation for augmenting children's value. Children's negative emotions, their nerves, panic, vomit, sweat, shakes, sighs, and sleeplessness represent those inextinguishable bits of subjectivity—their bodily declarations of resistance. Capital targets these emotional excesses for intervention.

Virtually all parents manage children's emotions to the best of their abilities and in ways that are highly variable at the social, cultural, and individual level, and also responsive to the daily life vicissitudes of its members. The women in my research all worked to ensure that their children were happy, and this work was rarely performed as labor, duty, or obligation. This ranged from taking bike rides, watching TV together, visiting kin and friends, going to a favored restaurant, or just hanging out. Yet, the econo-psy and neoliberal education complexes have made mothers anxious that idle or "free time" is a lost opportunity to develop a child's value. This exacts extraordinary psychic injuries and emotional difficulties on children that mothers must clean up and reroute toward the very thing that children resist—at the surface level, schooling, and deeper still, the rule of capital. Rather than work with children and others to help children flourish in life-affirming ways, parents are left to negotiate and emotionally manipulate their children into seeing these things as *for their own good*. The subsumption of maternal labors proceeds not through women's simple acquiescence to capital's command, but through mothers' defeated compromises made in the name of secure futures, futures where the prize is endless labor and devotion to capital.

Managing Homework, Managing Subjects

Monitoring children's homework has been traditionally understood as the labor marking parents as "involved" in children's schooling, and its absence is one of the defining characteristics of "deficiency" or lack in dominant educational discourse. Traditionally, those labors could be as simple and hands-off as uttering the declarative "Do your homework!" or the interrogative "Did you do your homework?" To this, children have answered in the affirmative irrespective of truth. At most, maternal labors entailed a glance and scribbling a signature if required. This was more or less all of my participants' own childhood experiences, information that they volunteered unprompted while reflecting on their considerable labors to manage children's homework in ways that shaped them as self-directed and goal-oriented subjects.

Women's labors and struggles to manage homework were considerable. This is due to a variety of interrelated reasons, if we accept the premise that what children do for schooling is indeed labor (as I argue we should; see Premise 8). First, children's labor associated with homework has increased in time and intensity, a trend that even touches children in kindergarten. Second, this mirrors the trends of the intensification of children's labors within schools. Third, in the context of other trends in neoliberal schooling such as the gutting of physical activities such as gym and even recess; the reduction or elimination of other nonacademic subjects such as art, drama, and music; and the increased pressure-cooker environment ushered in by neoliberal accountability policies; it is understandable that children, no fans of homework at any point, are increasingly resistant to taking on extended school labors. Last, schools' expectations for parent "involvement" in children's homework has increased so considerably that mothers are verily positioned as the child's "most important teacher" and their labors surrounding homework deemed the primary variable in a child's academic success or failure.

Despite educators' considerable critique of homework's utility for promoting learning or academic success, a critique that repeatedly makes its way to mainstream educational and parenting discourse, children's homework and the work of managing children's homework seems here to stay, at least for now. However, homework's utility in relation to children's learning as measured by objective instruments does not concern me. My main concerns are mothers and children's autonomy. Maternal labors of managing homework are a site for the double subjection of children and mothers, and a site to inaugurate the "holy family's" devotion to capital.

My participants have been taught and felt compelled to take on labors managing children's homework in a way that mirrors professional management. That is, managing homework functioned as "quality-control" of the product of labor as well as the laboring child. Homework was the opportunity to explicitly or implicitly instill the habits as well as psychosocial and emotional characteristics of neoliberal subjectivity: self-managing, self-disciplining, responsibility, time management, and most important of all, an orientation toward the larger goal of investing in one's value. The transformations of domesticity to revolve around investment in children have become so normalized that mothers' activities receded from mothers' view as *labor*. It was such that when I directly asked women if they helped with or managed homework, many reflexively answered that they did not, or that they "only" or "just" checked it. But when I asked about after-school routines, women revealed that behind their initial gloss were a whole slew of labors supervising, managing, and coaching children through homework.[18]

Rebecca's description of her children's after-school routine includes a series of labors—structuring their time and choices; steering them in various ways to do their homework, including withholding "free time"; supervising their labors; and coaching them to have a positive and productive affective state while performing their labors:

> After school, they come home, take a break and snack, apple or whatever they want to eat, and then they have choices. They can have fifteen minutes to veg, or they're going to do homework. I prefer they do homework. Sara does her homework herself. David does most of his homework by himself but sometimes I'm sitting with him, just to sit. It's not, just to calm him down, to relax and just focus, that's it. So he does his homework. And then they're free.

Despite this complex host of labors—time management, priority setting, supervising, coaching, and the considerable emotional labors of getting children to focus after a school day—Rebecca minimizes and makes invisible her time involvement and labors. She describes this work as just "sitting." Many jobs of course involve just sitting, but few would claim it's not work. This was so even for "stay-at-home" mothers who constantly felt disrespected as not working. Alejandra, a forty-year-old woman who moved to New York City from Mexico in her early twenties, was a stay-at-home mother whose interview was full of complaints about people who assumed she did "nothing" all day. Yet she, too, downplayed her labors to manage homework. While Alejandra acknowledged that she had to actively manage her five-year-old son's homework when I asked about the after-school routine, she underestimated the labors of managing her daughter's homework. Only when I probed further with concrete questions did Alejandra reveal a host of additional labors:

MARIA: Do you have to check the homework or . . .

ALEJANDRA: For Diana, not anymore. For Luca, I have to. For Luca, I just do it because sometimes he's just rushing. So he forgets to answer questions. It's not that I help him, I just have to just make sure he did it, or make sure he's not doing the same activity over and over again, you know the easier one. That's basically all I do. But for Diana, I just sign her notebook.

MARIA: I know some moms, they have to, not help but coach, like, come on, you can do it. Or else the kids will start, you know, playing with their pen. But Diana will . . .

ALEJANDRA: No, she *will* daydream, she will start telling me things. Normally they go to different rooms, because you know, she's like, "I can't concentrate because he's [her brother] talking too much." And sometimes she's talking to me like, "Mommy, guess what happened?!" And I'm in the kitchen and she's in the den and she's talking to me, and I'm like, "Di, finish your homework and then you tell me." Or I will go over there and she'll tell me the story and then she'll start writing again. Or she'll start telling me another story, or start telling me whatever. So yes, but overall, she's good. She'll sit down and finish her homework.

MARIA: Lately [my kid] has been annoying with the homework.

ALEJANDRA: Yes, like [imitates whining] "Why do we have to do it?"

MARIA: She asks me if its good and rips it when I tell her it's not. "Do you want me to lie? Look, I don't care but you asked."

ALEJANDRA: I'm just telling you what it is. I do, when I see she's doing it a little sloppy, I tell her to do it again. I do. "I know you know how to write nicer. I have seen it; you have to show an effort." But she's in a rush.

MARIA: With the spelling and stuff, she's a terrible speller. In a rush.

ALEJANDRA: See, I think she's a better writer than I am. You know, I'm not a good writer to begin with, not in English and not in Spanish. So when it comes to that, I am very self-conscious about what I'm telling her. That's why I check and I kind of read it, and I tell her to reread it herself to make sure it sounds OK to her. But I don't tell her because I'm not sure either, you know what I mean?

"Being there" is indeed labor, and it is indeed one of the essential labors of childcare. It is one of the reasons the work of caring for children is unique, for the labor cannot be sped up (although it can be made more efficient when you add more children). And as anyone who has done it knows, the labors of "just" checking a child's homework are infinitely more complex, as well as fraught. As Alejandra intimates, there are considerable labors involved in learning about the particulars of homework and the unique and sometimes frustratingly nonintuitive and precise ways that schools require them to be executed. Leaving aside these labors and the unfair presumption that parents are willing and able to perform them, what interests me is mothers' management of children's labor, and the way it becomes invisible as labor and naturalized as part of the maternal role. For Alejandra, the tedious work of going through her five-year-old's homework and checking his answers was visible. Yet the work of goading Diana to finish, rerouting her attention, and putting a cork in her effusive talk about her day and her inventive stories (talk that Alejandra was genuinely interested to hear), coaching her to defer her desires until after work was complete—that, too, is work. In the same way that Rebecca's activities of getting her son to "calm down, to relax and just focus" are also work. These labors of overseeing a child's labor rely on and employ the emotional bonds between mother and child to enlist children's labor. The labors also construct particular kinds of subjects.

While women often did not refer to these activities as labor, they often described them as having to be "on top of" their child, somewhat akin to how a manager might imagine their job. One woman described managing homework as such: "You have to be like 'Stop fooling around!' And now we have to go on to the next thing! You have to be on top of them." Chris, a white, forty-three-year-old, licensed practical nurse studying to be a registered nurse, discussed the necessity of being "on top of" her son by showing what happened when she assumed her managerial labors were no longer necessary.

MARIA: So yeah, so you ask moms about homework, it's not so much that they have to help but . . .

CHRIS: You have to make sure that they're doing it. Yeah, you have to be there. Yeah.

MARIA: So if you weren't there at all?

CHRIS: Yeah, he was doing fine in the beginning. He was doing his work, and then I'd let him do his stuff, whatever he wanted to do, video games, playing outside. There's technology out there so . . . I was OK with it, but now, I'm holding off with the technology because his teachers are sending me notes that he's not doing everything he's supposed to be doing, because I'm not watching him as much. So now, he can't play videogames, he has to do his homework. *So now I have to be on top of him as well.* Because it's a different age group. He's twelve, starting to you know, like girls, and you know, just not think about school. It just started this year and he's socializing, and he's like, "Mommy, I have Katelynn that likes me and this one that likes me." And I'm like, "You have to concentrate on school." So everything's a challenge.

The exhausting yet invisible labors of managing children become visible when something goes wrong. We might say that Chris's scenario is one that mothers fear—children slipping up and being called in by the school to reenlist their absentee maternal labors. While teachers were "sending me notes that he's not doing everything he's supposed to be doing," the accusation is that *she* was not doing everything she was supposed to be doing. Chris more or less accepted this accusation, she says, "because I'm not watching him as much."

Chris's explanation of how her management style differed from her husband's revealed her internal struggles and disenchantment with the goal of success. Chris's family dynamics were unique in that her husband also participated in the labors of managing homework.

This was partly because he often worked from home while she worked considerable hours and was finishing her nursing degree, and also because she deferred to her husband's expertise since he had completed a higher level of education than she had. However, her husband's ethos was more of a masculine-coded authoritarian overseer rather than the gentler maternal authority through which she managed her son.

MARIA: Are you more the manager, like do you have to say [to husband], help him, or is it more, organic?

CHRIS: Yeah, like he [husband] will come over and say, "Did he do his homework?" My husband is more assertive than I am. I'm more the pushover mom. "Mommy I'm tired, let me just rest for an hour," and I'll be like, "OK." But my husband is more like, [in a stern voice] "No, get up, do it now!" So I think it's a good kind of balance for him [laughs]. Because I think it's important that he listens and that he's not a slacker. I think it's also a part that we're all human. You get tired. I'm more the nursing type. Like, "Oh, you don't feel good? You're tired? Lie down." So, my husband, he sometimes thinks I'm too lenient, you know? But I think sometimes he's too assertive, and he doesn't understand that his nose is running, you know? He doesn't feel well. But the outcome? The job gets done.

In juxtaposing their managerial efforts, Chris reveals what she believes is a more authentic way to mother—being responsive and prioritizing her son's physical and mental health. She momentarily toyed with the idea that her husband had a point pushing her son more aggressively because she didn't want him to be "a slacker." But she immediately returned to her gut feeling: "I think it's also a part that we're all human. You get tired." In some indirect way, Chris recognized that coaxing kids to work means ignoring their humanity. Managing children's labor is labor for capital, labor that alienates mothers and children and disfigures their bond.

Teachers function as proxies for the neoliberal education and econo-psy complexes, and the specter of their disapproval disciplines and intensifies maternal labors. This disapproval similarly loomed over Eugenia. Eugenia, a thirty-six-year-old teacher and mother of two children who was born in New York City to parents from Greece, punctuated the necessity of her labors, which she also described as "being on top" of her nine-year-old daughter's homework. Strikingly, Eugenia found homework to be pointless and devoid of any educational benefit, and she assigned minimal amounts of homework for her elementary students. Yet she still dutifully performed the labors of managing homework, exhausting and frustrating herself in the process:

> Yes, I mean, I have to be like, "Come on just finish, come on!" Because every question, every something, she looks up like [mimes staring into space], and I just want it done. I don't want to keep going. So you have to *be on top*. I don't think I'll ever *not* be on top of her homework until high school. Parents who are like, "Your kid is in fifth grade, they should be doing it on their own." That's not true, they're not responsible or they're going to do it half-assed. I mean, one time, one week I didn't check and she didn't look at the back of the sheet. And she got an incomplete, and she was like, "I didn't know there was something on the back." Like the *one time*, you know what I mean? I don't necessarily check to see what she wrote but to see that it's done, and did she skip one or something. The math she always needs help with, I do have to go over it with her.

Other mothers echoed Eugenia's sentiment of "I just want it done," and they tried to get it done by encouraging focus and offering rewards of free time. Eugenia's more impatient prodding and overseeing rather than the more gentle "positive outlook" type of coaching gestures toward how exhausting and depleting it is to manage children after both mother and child have had a full day of work. Like other mothers, Eugenia also downplayed her own labors, especially anything suggesting that those labors helped children achieve. Eugenia euphemized them by saying she had to "go over [math] with her" when the child did not understand the material. In practice, this is effectively what teaching entails. While there was a psychological block to admitting these were labors, women were implicitly conscious of them as such. Their exhortations to children to finish was just as much to end their working day as to end children's. They too wanted free time from capital.

Free time is precisely what is supplanted when capital disciplines the home and makes it a site of labor for capital, free time to be with children in ways that are not oriented toward their value, "disposable time," time to be autonomous subjects. In the absence of these imposed labors, we might imagine Chris and her son having time to linger and discuss this new stage of his burgeoning adolescence and his interest and relationships with girls, Alejandra listening to her daughter rehearse the day's dramatic events, Rebecca allowing her son to blow off steam hooting in the backyard, Eugenia noticing her daughter examine her pencil or stare into space and wondering what she was thinking about—we can bet it wasn't schoolwork! This aspect of mothering—simply letting children *be*—is precisely what capital colonizes and routes toward value. When kids want to discuss the school day, it frequently revolves around the social—interactions, relations, feelings. Subsumption usurps mothers' time to attend to these aspects of kids' lives, to engage and respond in a thoughtful, open-ended manner. These are interactions that may indeed "teach" children, yet no parent considers them work in the same way. This work does not deplete mothers, nor does it alienate them from their children.

Consider my participant Cemre, a spirited thirty-four-year-old woman born in New York City to Turkish parents and a stay-at-home mother of three children (seven years, four years, and twenty months). She was perhaps the most outspoken and defiant about the pressures of schooling. She was equally adamant about teaching her kids life lessons she thought important for them as humans, or what she called "good people."

CEMRE: So this kid says to my kid one day, "I don't want to sit next to you, your food stinks." I was like, "Naim, this is exactly what you're going to say to this kid: 'Does your mother cook food for you every day, honey? All right, what are you eating? Let me see what you're eating! Everyday you're going to ask him what he's eating, you're going to show him the food you're eating. You're going to tell him to smell it. Does it smell good or does it smell bad? My mom makes an effort to make me this food every day.'" I told the principal, he was rolling. He was like, "I bet you I know who this is, and I bet you he eats chicken nuggets every day." And I said, "Look, there's nothing wrong with a parent giving their kid chicken nuggets because, you know, if that kid only eats chicken nuggets, then you gotta have her eat chicken nuggets rather than nothing! I get it." But I was like, "We got to teach our kids to respect one another, you know?" This is what the problem is with our world!

MARIA: You know, I would rather my kid get made fun of than be the dick.

CEMRE: I told myself the same thing! I was like, If you *ever* make fun of anyone for how they look, what they're eating, [what] their religion is, and in New Jersey, this is the problem, there's not a lot of diversity, so when I went to this racetrack, there were Hasidic Jews—you know, when they have those yarmulkes—and the white kids there were staring at them and laughing at them, and the fathers are there laughing along with them. And I'm like, these dads are like VPs and something, you can tell what they are. But unfortunately they had, I'm not judging them, but you could see . . . [They were] typical Americanized, the system is just like that, they have the money, the wives are getting their nails done and on the weekend, they're taking the kids. So, I was like, "I really don't think it's nice that you guys are laughing at them, I really don't, I don't see what's funny, what because they're different than you?"

MARIA: You said this to the dads? In front of the kids?

CEMRE: Yeah. You know they said, "We weren't laughing at them." I was like, "I clearly saw the kids. This is why our world is full of hatred because of parents like you guys who don't teach their kids to love one another."

MARIA: I can't believe you did that!

CEMRE: I really did.

MARIA: To a group of men.

CEMRE: Yes, there were three of them. But listen, if we don't speak up, and speak up in front of our kids, then our kids are going to be made fun of. And then they're not going to know that. My son is like, "Mom, there's a boy, he thinks he's the boss all the time." I'm like, "Look, Naim, there's always going to be kids out there who are not going to want to do what you want to do. They're not always going to want to play with you. You've got to learn to just get over those kind of kids." You know what I mean? Life is too short to be stressing about anyone else's kids. You have fun with yourself. This is why I always tell him [that] friends come and go. And I tell him [that] not every friend is always going to want the best for you."

Instead of spending her Saturday schooling her son and/or shuttling him to one of the many commercial after-school activities that are assumed to augment children's value, Cemre prioritized doing fun things. The mini–amusement park provided opportunities for authentic empathic growth, where she was able to foster respect and pride for his culture and for others. I do not claim that other women did not engage in these sorts of "life lessons" that shaped children outside of value. I am claiming that capital targets this time.

Consider Chaaya, a thirty-six-year-old, second-generation Indo-Guyanese woman who worked as an office manager at a local college. Perhaps because she had the youngest children (two boys, ages six and four) among my participants, her labors had not been as disciplined by capital. Her interview was full of examples where she shaped her kids as caring and empathetic humans. Here she recounted how she responded when her six-year-old told her about one of his classmate's troubles:

> There's this one kid in Ethan's class, I guess she's homesick. She cries every morning. And Ethan was like, "She misses her daddy. She's always crying for her daddy." And some of his classmates were asking the teacher, "Why is she always crying?" And I told Ethan, "Even if one of your friends is making fun of her, you don't. You ask her if she's OK or if she wants to talk." I'm trying to teach them not to be influenced by others. Because it's so hard growing up, you

> feel like you have to do what everyone else is doing. We felt that pressure growing up, I don't want them to fall into that habit. So I tell them, little as they are, "Don't judge people, be kind." Ethan is just like me. He can see someone on the street and just say hi. He will just wave out the window to people and I love that about him.

In such interactions, mothers shape children as collectively oriented subjects, they strengthen the bond with their children and forge that bond in loving and free ways rather than through chains of emotional subjugation.

Women's narratives reveal the hidden violence of managing children's labors and the way it deforms the mother-child bond to mirror capitalist social relations. This was most evident in the frequent fights that erupted in certain households over homework—whether it was a matter of doing it, when, for how long, the quality, and the attitude taken toward it. For example, even though I was relatively disinterested in homework, when my child asked for my feedback and I gave it honestly, my child erupted in anger, as I mentioned to Alejandra. Eugenia also described her daughter vehemently resisting advice that she herself had sought, which would then erupt into full-fledged arguments, tantrums, and bad feelings persisting for hours. In Chapter 6, I discuss Hannah's daily dramas of managing her children's homework after getting home from work in the evening, remarking, "It always, I would say 75 percent of the time, it escalated in a fight." In such tense encounters, women lost their cool, yelled at children, resorted to punishments rather than rewards, and took on more authoritarian styles than gentle forms of psychological-emotional coercion. These moments were breaking points where women felt pushed beyond their limits. I don't include detailed descriptions of these quarrels because I know too well how embarrassing these low points can be. I mention them to underline how capital coerces children's and mothers' labors, usurps the free activities of both, and disfigures their bond. Within the more belligerent encounters, compulsion and coercion became more visible while bringing women's ambivalence about these labors to the fore. The fact that women persisted performing these labors, virtually daily, underlines the strength of capitalist relations of economic compulsion, and the ideological inversion of what is good for capital into what is good for the child.

Between Mother and Child

Capital's subsumption of the family is so dangerous because subjection occurs through primary relations and is suffused through care and love. Penetrating subjectivity and the porous process of human becoming, capital stands between mother and child as never before. Backed into a corner, mothers direct their labors toward shaping children for capital to help them succeed in the future, despite their ambiguities and inner conflicts. Because these impulses represent mothers' sincere desires for children's good, they take on the semblance of authenticity and become the affective baseline through which they face the resistance of their children and negotiate with them.

Children's will to be free from these forces of subjection and control is a mighty force. Perhaps equally powerful is children's desire to be that which their mother desires. Attuned as they are to their mother's desires and its ambiguities, children negotiated within that space. Writing with children's interests in mind, Harriet Fraad discusses how psychoanalytic theory insists on children's considerable expenditure of emotional labor to live through the desire of their mothers, and the "emotional exploitation" children face within the family.[19] She poignantly expresses the reverberations for children's subjectivities: "Attention to the injuries of childhood reveals the family as a site of deep humiliation, teaching lessons of self-abnegation in the face of powerlessness. In its enforcement of emotional servitude, childhood is a training ground preparing individuals for the accumulating set of ideological and official subjections that together constitute the adult world of contemporary capitalism."[20] In many accounts of the family and especially of mothers, women—their authority, their labors, parenting styles—are portrayed as the agents of children's harm. Fraad's sympathy to children does not extend to mothers. I would argue that mothers are just as emotionally exploited as children. They are bad parents if they are unable or unwilling to devote themselves to specific maternal labors by the public, and school personnel who surveil the evidence and product of those labors. Children resent mothers as they coerce and convince them that their forced labors and emotional regulation are for their own good. This depletes women, makes them mother inauthentically, and contributes to the schizophrenic state of neoliberal motherhood that I explore in Chapter 7. Thrust into managing children's forced labor, mothers and children together struggled with and against their own and each other's ambivalent desires—their subjectivities taking shape through one another, and within and against capital's drive to command their life. In this multifaceted struggle, children's unruliness ensures that capture will never be total. Children resist capital's yoke in various ways that often takes a more obvious and visceral form (whining, refusing, crying, sweating, loafing, daydreaming). Women too resisted capital's rule within the family in various ways. These ways do not register as loudly as children's, yet they are there, partial, submerged, and ripe for more strident refusal.

6

Spatial Labors

The Racialized Production of School, Property, and Child "Value"

DISCUSSING HER MOVE from southern Brooklyn to northeastern Queens before the oldest of her three daughters (ages eleven, nine, and six) was to enter kindergarten, Hannah, a thirty-eight-year-old lifelong New Yorker whose parents came to the US from China in the mid-1970s, recalled her own comparably simpler childhood and underlined the intensified anxieties of parenting in the twenty-five years that had elapsed. "I remember when I went to school in Brooklyn, you just showed up on the first day of school with your marble notebook and a pencil. Now it's like, people think about it when these kids are in utero, 'Where are we going to put them in school?' So Drew [husband] actually started that conversation, and I was like, 'What do you mean? She's not even born yet!'" While Hannah highlighted the absurdity of thinking about relocating for schools while "kids are in utero," it is utterly commonplace for parents to begin worrying about the quality of schools that surround them when the child is quite young. Among the extended, intensified, and professionalized labors that mothers are compelled to perform in neoliberalism for a child's "success," finding what is understood to be a "good school" is widely understood, by experts and my interlocutors alike, to be one of the most important. Indeed, Hannah and most of my participants had begun to think about relocating for their children's schooling before the child was born, with some far-sighted couples making decisions about where to live before they even conceived. Certainly by the time their oldest child was nearing school age, the perceived necessity of living near a "good school" loomed larger as their inchoate thoughts matured into what was for many, the most complex and fraught cost-benefit analysis of their lives. They weighed "best schools" against considerations such as the price of housing, property taxes, transportation costs, and commute time to work. There were other costs associated with relocating for schools that were largely invisible, even to the women that shouldered them. These spatial labors, as I call them, are the work involved in studying different schools and school districts, additional time to access kin and/or a childcare support network, arranging for or the work of transporting children, complex negotiations with kin, the costs of the diminished possibilities for employment and enjoyment, and the psychological and emotional costs of being tied to a particular place whose main draw is its "good schools."

This chapter explores women's spatial labors associated with relocating for their child's schooling as part of their multilayered labors to increase their children's value and chances for "success." While centering women's narratives concerning their ongoing gendered labors and associated burdens revolving around relocating for a good school, I underline the material and ideological forces that compel women to perform them—that is, that make a "good school" a necessity for a child's future "success," and that depends on and naturalize those labors as sacrifices of good motherhood. The focus is how a peculiar assemblage of forces and institutions within the neoliberal education complex coerces the maternal labors associated with finding a "good school," constructs the abstraction of a "good school," makes the existence of a "good school" scarce, and coerces mothers' labors to access one, all while producing ongoing stress and anxiety. This assemblage of forces includes federal, state, and city bodies of governance whose continuous efforts to apply market-based logics of standardization, efficiency, and accountability to reduce teaching and learning to the acquisition of a discrete domain of knowledge and skills that can be abstracted, quantified, and measured at regular intervals and are assumed to be necessary for a child's future occupational success and for the economy itself. A new set of corporate actors has been incorporated into the neoliberal education complex as appendages that include real estate, testing, and tutoring companies, as well as nonprofit and for-profit school rating websites. These bodies work in tandem to abstract children's "value" according to their performance on seemingly objective scores on assessments, which they then fuse to measures of school quality and property values.

Women's spatial labors associated with accessing a good school, I argue, are routed to produce racialized subjects, populations, and spaces. I explore how these intimately connected processes—maternal labors oriented toward children's value through "good schools," incessant testing to measure children's value in schools, the construction of seemingly objective measures of school quality based on children's test scores, and the valuation of property based on school quality—smuggle in, redouble, and invisibilize already-existing forms of racialized value. Because this race making proceeds through *apparently aracial registers*, mothers of any race can be entangled in these processes. As such, I argue that maternal spatial labors are key sites of neoliberal race making, where the production of race as a life- and death-dealing force is deepened, yet its force is obscured behind seemingly objective and racially neutral measures of value—test scores, school quality, property values.

I trace how women's spatial labors oriented to increasing a child's value in a "good school" are already imbued with racialized value. These embodied labors partly produce the value or quality of the school, a measure that is intimately entangled with racialized populations of good and bad students. Furthermore, these labors contribute to the production of property values and reinscribe race onto space—augmenting the value of some spaces while diminishing the value of others. Recent work has expanded our understanding of the role of property in race making and how property mediates the relationship of race and capital accumulation.[1] Mothering and childhood are integral to these processes—sites where race, bodies, and space become fused and imbued with abstractions of value. That is, mothering is where race acquires its double-sided facticity in neoliberalism: in the material fact of its death dealing and its illusory appearance as objective measure of seemingly nonracial value. Ultimately, these labors are routed in ways that reproduce the material and symbolic order of race as the hierarchy of human value.

The Limited Critique of School Choice Literature

An extensive body of scholarship focuses on how mothers take advantage of "school choice" policies in neoliberalism, thereby exacerbating race and class inequalities. While illuminating the immediate causes and repercussions of school choice policies, such scholarship is limited in fundamental ways. By obscuring the force of economic compulsion of capitalist relations, such scholarship centers individual women's maternal practices and blames them for neoliberalism's heightened race and class inequalities. This ultimately enfeebles critique and obscures the social relations of domination in which mothers and children are locked.

In the past two decades, critical education scholars have demonstrated how school choice policies (a signature element of neoliberal educational reforms) have toppled policymakers' claims that choice dismantles educational disparities, showing how choice policies allow upper middle class families to navigate them in ways that exacerbate and entrench class and raced inequalities and patterns of residential and school segregation to reproduce class and racial inequalities of urban space, substituting an illusion for needed reforms.[2] In a related vein, decades of research within the sociology and anthropology of education maps the causal links between middle class mothers' school choice stratagems and securing children's educational and economic success.[3] While most research focuses on policies that expand local choice, another strand explores how families exercise school choice through housing and how relocating for schools exacerbates historically entrenched inequalities of race and class, which is the predominant process.[4] Scholars in this vein emphasize how good public schools, linked to both race and space, are exemplars of Cheryl Harris's notion of whiteness as property, with whites using every means to limit racially minoritized people's access to neighborhoods and schools.[5] Reviewing the volume *Choosing Homes, Choosing Schools*, Eve Ewing concludes that white anti-Blackness is the "overarching phenomenon" that structures both types of school choices.[6] Individual racism is indeed an operative force that reproduces segregation and racialized and class inequalities. This interpretive vein acknowledges preexisting articulations of race, class, and property, but the analytic priority (and political target) is placed on individual agents (mothers) who could or should choose otherwise in a context where choices that can contribute to racial justice are presumed to exist.

My goal is not to excuse such processes, or verify them, or add to the list of mechanisms by which maternal labors around school choice do or do not secure children's futures in highly differentiated classed and raced patterns. Rather, my concerns turn on a different argument about how maternal labors associated with school choice are locked into a set of social relations mediated by value abstractions of child, school, and property that reproduce class, gendered, and racial subjugation in uneven ways. School choice embeds women's reproductive labors into highly abstracted capital flows in which property and race are entangled and "come into being in mutually constitutive ways."[7] Women make "choices" in a context where capital and the racial state have historically and persistently (de)valued neighborhoods by spatializing race and racializing space through banks' lending and mortgage practices, the Federal Housing Authority's appraisals and redlining, federal and state routing of resources to white suburbs, and property taxes and school funding policies.[8] Housing, increasingly shaped by financialized capital flows, rerouted from suburban to urban space, essentially sells "white space" and allows the entrenched dynamics of racial domination within housing to appear as if they were racially neutral.[9]

It is true that mothers' spatial labors are implicated in widening forms of class, gendered, and racialized relations of domination. Yet as Werner Bonefeld emphasizes in his elaboration of the Marxist notion of economic compulsion, Marx's critique is of "the *entire* system of economic categories": "Capital as an economic thing does nothing. It does not accumulate great wealth, exploit, dominate, and maim. Rather, it is Man in his actual social relations who accumulates, exploits, dominates, maims, and struggles to make ends meet, and he does so by 'pursuing his aims' as a *personification of his own objective, capitalist conditions*."[10] Where social theory might be characterized as showing how the individual only acts as an embodiment of the social, critical theory might be said to show how individuals, who are always and irreducibly attached to what Marx called their "character mask," are coerced into reproducing the conditions of their domination.[11] Women are indeed making certain choices in which race and class are reproduced in predictable ways. Despite middle class women's relative privilege in performing certain labors vis-à-vis working class and poor mothers and likely more firmly securing their children's advantages vis-à-vis other people's children, these labors are not a "choice" in the conventional sense. Rather, they are coerced by the particular configuration of social relations of neoliberal racial capitalism. Critique must be oriented to the relations that structure women's choices and that have embedded them into the racialized production of property value, as well as the material and symbolic valuation of human lives based on race.

Abstracting Child Value

As Hannah affirmed in the opening vignette, the search for a "good school" begins early and earnestly as parents worry about children's futures. I employ scare quotes around "good schools" to defamiliarize this taken-for-granted term. We might imagine that to establish such a notion, parents (and others) would consider a variety of characteristics—the school's philosophy, curriculum, extracurricular or enrichment offerings, the state of the school building and surrounding space, ratio of teacher to students, programs for children who have particular interests or needs, and so on. Yet the notion of a "good school" is increasingly based on standardized test scores that supplant indicators that might be more meaningful. Equating standardized test scores with notions of school quality and the school ranking system that is based on these scores are direct results of the neoliberal reforms of schooling. George W. Bush's federal No Child Left Behind Act of 2001 and Obama's Race to the Top of 2009 sought to "improve" public schooling by establishing higher "standards," increase student "performance" on test scores, and hold teachers, administrators, districts, and cities "accountable" for student "progress." Critical education scholars convincingly demonstrate how these reforms evacuate curriculum not geared toward increasing student test scores and further pervert teaching and learning and the alienation of teachers and students, all while routing billions of dollars to companies that sell tests, score and report test results, develop and sell test preparation, and staff development materials to schools.[12]

Human capital theory informs the essence and thrust of these reforms. The force of the apparent facticity of test scores as a valid measure of children's abilities that determines the value of their future earnings and contributions to the economy cannot be underestimated. Human capital theory is the drumbeat behind the anxious hand-wringing that undergirds educational reforms since its ascendance, the same drumbeat that drives mothering for capital. Under the guise of concern for individual children's future economic position, even claiming the mantle of equity and justice, the state has ushered in neoliberal reforms to save "a nation at risk," as the Reagan era report that inaugurated the neoliberalization of the US education system was named. Neoliberal reforms, of which testing is the center, aim to increase children's value in the market. Children in schools are relentlessly subject to quantified measures of their value and methods of teaching that supposedly increase that value. It is a long-held truism in Marxist analyses of education that schooling is geared to producing labor for capital that entails a complex conflict-ridden process of instilling particular abilities and habits of mind and body (discipline). Yet equally integral is the conflict-ridden process of rendering students, from among their infinitely varying qualities, into a quantified and exchangeable abstraction of value. In schools, human capital theory is unleashed to intensify the human subject's abstraction and magnify the antagonism between concrete or living labor and abstract labor (see Chapter 2). Children are targets of this "global war of measure."[13]

If one of the key tenets of Marxist theory is that capital is the movement of "self-valorizing value" that depends on the law of abstraction governing society—where persons and things can be rendered equivalent, then reducing schooling to test taking and rendering students into test scores is key to neoliberal forms of accumulation and domination.[14] Capital rules children, too, by abstraction. In my ethnographic work in a kindergarten classroom, I revealed how children, from the moment they enter school at the age of four or five, are subjected to the alienating force of normative developmental standards.[15] Their initial forays into reading the printed word are structured by periodic testing and oriented toward their progress on hierarchical scale of "reading levels." Their sense of joy and conviviality are trampled upon as they are initiated into an order that compares and ranks them within a hierarchy of value. This value is racialized through and through: Decades of critical scholarship have incontrovertibly demonstrated how racism, white supremacy, and anti-Blackness are built into the instruments that measure students' abilities. Yet despite the perpetual critique of testing as a racializing apparatus, tests continue to appear as straightforward and objective measures of aptitude.

Rather than idyllic places nurturing children's curiosity, fostering their learning, and encouraging their becoming autonomous subjects, "good schools" are those that have successfully oriented children to abstractions of value. Within neoliberalism, school rankings, based on these abstractions, are widely disseminated in public culture. The proliferation of ratings is also a direct result of federal mandates (No Child Left Behind and Race to the Top) that states produce and make these metrics public so parents can make informed decisions in the educational marketplace—to facilitate school choice. The quantification of school ratings links school choice, accountability, and testing, the signature neoliberal reforms that govern education in market terms.[16] School systems, as well as various third parties such as for-profit companies and nongovernmental organizations calculate school quality ratings from publicly available data on student test scores. The colloquialism "good school" is now perceived as an objective measure, one that is easily available with a simple internet search. Real estate and school ratings websites are now part of the neoliberal education complex, maintaining the validity of these measures, publicizing them, and inciting maternal and public anxieties about the necessity of accessing "good schools."

Rating Schools, Ranking Bodies and Space

My participants were anxious about finding a good school and learned about schools' ratings through their social networks, or as something "everyone knows," and increasingly, their own or their partners' research on the internet. The majority of my participants moved into the research area of northeastern Queens because they had used such websites to find their current homes for the schools. As important and decisive as these tools were in their family's trajectory, the women did not remember, dwell, or reflect on them any more than a diner would reflect on the utensil used in their meal—it was a tool that vanished in the process of achieving an objective. They glossed the tool and portrayed the matter as one of simply looking. "So I started looking for apartments to rent near a good school," Chaaya said offhandedly. Similarly, Hannah said, "We looked into the grades [of schools]." Rehema only mentioned the web ("we looked it up online") after I asked how in fact she was "looking" for schools.

As a key resource to obtain information about school quality, I scrutinized school ratings websites and collected data on searches as if I, too, were looking for a good school in New York City. Using Google to search "best schools in [location]" takes one to the following sites: GreatsShools.org, InsideSchools.org, SchoolDigger.com, Niche.com, PublicSchoolsReview.com, and Zillow.com. Websites vie for parents' attention, selling homes and hope as they exploit parents' insecurities and instill anxiety associated with scarcity. Make "informed decisions about your child's future!" (InsideSchools), know the "worrisome signs" (GreatSchools). The sites have many commonalities: search engines and filters, ratings, map views, and linked profiles for individual schools with information such as demographics and detailed breakdown of test scores. For example, if one searches for a good school in Queens on a school rating website like SchoolDigger, one finds high- and low-rated schools clustering in specific geographic areas.[17] Many sites include links for homes to purchase or rent along with school profiles. On their end, real estate industry websites also promote links between homes and school quality. The largest national real estate websites—Zillow, Realtor, and Redfin—partner with GreatSchools, the most influential school rating site.[18] Zillow even redesigned its search function to enable searching for homes according to their GreatSchools rating. For example, one can search for homes via school ratings in New York City on Zillow and filter to display only homes within the catchment area of schools rated a 10. The partnership between school ratings companies and the real estate industry further converts school values into property values. A popular online resource for New York City real estate, Brick Underground, advised New Yorkers (even those without children) to be attuned to school ratings: "Make sure you buy a place that will be in demand by families when you sell!"[19]

In the guise of empowerment, school ratings websites and the real estate industry drive conversations about school scarcity and the datafication of schooling for the testing, tech, and global finance industries, capitalizing on both.[20] This infrastructure is dependent on the middle class project to exact the gendered labors of perpetually investing in children's human capital. Furthermore, the coupling of real estate and school ratings exacerbates the differences between "good" and "bad" schools through scarcity logic while reifying and compounding the racial inequity baked into test scores and exacerbating race and class segregation.[21] So strong are links between school ratings and race that fair housing advocates have raised concerns about the websites: "A school rating map mirrors a racial dot map," claimed the director of the Central New York Housing Authority.[22] When one maps the highly rated schools in New York

City, ratings are inversely correlated with the percentage of Black students, verifying the proxy status of race in value assessments. Education activists advocating for school integration are faced with propertied interests, which city officials are quick to defend. "You have to respect families," then mayor De Blasio replied when opposing a rezoning school proposal, "[who] have made massive life decisions and investments because of which school their kid will go to."[23] As Wall explains, such a rezoning would mean less access to coveted schools for those who effectively "paid" for them through their property value and would also likely lower those property values, and "no mayor wants to suffer the wrath of irate middle and upper-class parents and property owners."[24] Such comments understandably direct attention and ire to middle class families, especially mothers. This is the scapegoat face of the three-sided spectacle of middle class motherhood (see the introduction). A commitment to racial and social justice requires an analytic and political focus on how the state manufactures, and capital profits from, material and ideological structures of scarcity and uses it to recruit families. Capital and state via the econo-psy and neoliberal education complexes position mothers as the most important factor for children's success and coerce mothers to perform a slew of spatial labors. These labors generate value beyond their child's human capital and help create the value of the "good school" itself and the concomitant higher property values that surround it. Women's spatial labors and struggles, exacerbated in the hypercompetitive context of New York City are entangled with these modes of race making.

The Business and Anxiety of "Good Schools" in Unequal New York City

While anxieties about securing a "good school" are a widespread feature of parenting in the United States, especially among those engaged in the middle class project or contexts in which schools are drastically underfunded, the stakes of the competition are exacerbated in New York City, a central node of capital accumulation where schooling is defined by scarcity and competition to access its "good schools." Within the city, these forces converge with other contextual features to aggravate the anxieties and stakes of the "good school" search: a highly unequal school system superimposed over racially segregated and devalued neighborhoods; segregated, rapidly gentrifying, and expensive real estate markets with heavy investment from global finance capital; and a dizzying patchwork of geographically varying policies within its unified public school system. New Yorkers are constantly reminded that they live not in one, but in "two cities"—a discourse adopted by city officials themselves. There are daily reminders of disparities between so-called good and bad schools, the need to fix failing schools, schools not making the cut, an "incident" at a "bad school." If offered a choice between a "good school" (e.g., Public School 59 in Manhattan, where over 90 percent of students tested at proficiency level) or a "struggling" school (e.g., PS 194 in Manhattan where less than 13 percent did so), a "good school" makes sense. Yet these valuations are saturated with racial meaning in one of the most fiercely segregated school systems in the country.[25] PS 59 in the townhouse-filled neighborhood of Midtown East is nearly 60 percent white and 20 percent Asian, while PS 194 in Harlem is 72 percent Black and 25 percent Hispanic. A "good school" in New York must be understood in terms of a highly unequal and racialized school system that is attached to housing and acquires its differential value through long and enduring histories of racial domination.

Within the city's thirty-two community school districts, there are considerable differences in the suite of choices offered to parents and the prevalence of choice itself. So-called choice-rich districts, where up to 60 percent of kindergarteners attend a choice rather than a zoned school, tend to be in neighborhoods where gentrification has recently "increased dramatically."[26] In such gentrified and gentrifying neighborhoods, choice policies, along with actual and magnified perception of "good school" scarcity, and the dramatic rise in number of middle class families, has turned choice into a constantly escalating competition. A New York City parent verily called it an "arms race."[27] They document how parents' anxieties about school quality consumed so much time, energy, and emotions that school choice dominated parents' lives. "Mom gossip networks," pickup at school, even dog walking, became occasions to keep up with changes in real estate, schools, zoning changes, policy, and strategies. This motivated a suite of actions that, because of their considerable advantages (money, networks, know-how) resulted in opportunity hoarding for their kids.[28] Navigating this bureaucratic maze requires an incredible amount of labor, know-how, and an extensive social network through which such know-how flows, and the skill set of the educated upper middle class is perfectly suited to "gaming" this system.

Although the bulk of recent scholarship on New York City families' educational labors focus on school choice policies, it bears reiterating that the expansion of choice policy is a rather recent phenomenon, and that the majority (almost two-thirds) of elementary students in New York City attend their zoned school.[29] Whether or not families move into or choose to stay in an area where choice is operative, or whether they choose to relocate to an area where their child will attend a zoned school, the fact of the matter is that all parents must face a school system where a cloud of doom surrounds "bad schools" and anxiety surrounds accessing "good schools." This highly charged emotional backdrop incites the perceived necessity of spatial labors of searching and/or relocating for a good school.

The imperative to seek a "good school" was an obligation of motherhood that went without question—notions of school quality work together with notions of maternal quality. While I do not dismiss women's desire to be a "good" mother or their love for their children, neither is an unmediated, universal, and idealized feeling. These feelings are structured by a highly unequal educational system that is ideologically and practically linked to the reality and ideology of "good school" scarcity. Where neoliberalism dictates children's future as either "waste" or "success" is determined by education, mothers must struggle to access the means of subsistence for their children. They are under the force of economic compulsion. Marxist analyses of education have long established how schooling legitimizes capitalist inequalities through its sorting function.[30] Yet the school system has dramatically morphed in the neoliberal era. Widening inequalities and the growing precarity of the middle class ramp up competition. Disinvestments in schooling spawn an economic infrastructure of testing, tutoring, and coaching industries to solve parents' dilemma. For example, two of the many companies that market their services in my neighborhood are NYC Admissions Solutions, a company that offers a suite of family services, including one tailored for pre-K through fifth-grade placement that promises saving "time and aggravation," and Bee Tutored, a company that offers a range of academic services starting in kindergarten to "fuel your child's success" and increase chance of entry into the city's highly rated specialized public high schools. Whether or not they are willing or able to purchase such services, the mere existence of this sector of the neoliberal education complex and its incessant targeting of mothers interpellates them into the anxious structure of feeling and compels them to become attuned to information about school quality.

The Neighborhoods' Schools

Interested in how mothers' spatial labors are enmeshed in class, gendered, and racial relations of property valuation, I grounded my research in a group of neighborhoods where families both live and send their children to school—indeed, where recent residents relocated, at considerable cost, because of "good schools." Geographic mobility for schools defines this group of eight neighborhoods in a ten-square-mile area with a population of about 120,000 in northeastern Queens. The demographic profile (Asian, 45 percent; Black, 3 percent; Hispanic, 12 percent; white, 39 percent) differs significantly from that in the schools, as younger and newer residents (families with school-age children) tend to be nonwhite, and fleeing residents are older and white without school-age children.[31] The neighborhood demographics do not capture the diversity or dynamism of the area, with its large percentage of recent and first- and second-generation immigrants, who complicate the alignment of race, class, and migration history. The significant, steady growth of Asian residents and their educational, commercial, and residential place making is one of the most definitive characteristics of the area, one associated with white flight.[32] The increase in Asian families with children is directly linked—as both cause and effect—with the area's reputation for "good schools."

Many of the newer residents in this area move into the neighborhoods to engage in the middle class project—that is, as people entering or solidifying their status within that wide signifier of middle-classness by ensuring their children will be middle class. For fifteen of my twenty participants, the area's "good schools" were a major factor, if not the singular factor, for moving to this area in northeastern Queens. The area's zoned schools are its biggest attraction, known as some of the "best" in the city. Clara Hemphill, whose *NYC's Best Public Elementary Schools: A Parents' Guide* book is blurbed as having "done for NYC schools what Zagat did for restaurants" introduces District 26 schools (representing about two-thirds of my research area) like so:

> District 26 consistently has the top test scores in the city, and many parents move to the district just so they can send their children to its schools . . . We've listed some nice ones, but, honestly, you can't go wrong in the district. Every single school in District 26 has test scores that are well above the citywide average in both reading and math . . . Parents here take their children's education seriously, and many sign their children up for after-school enrichment and test prep at an early age in the hope that they'll gain admission to super-selective schools such as Hunter College High School or Stuyvesant High School in Manhattan.[33]

Women's considerable labors to ensure children's success shape the sense of placeness in northeastern Queens, from the material (rising rents and property values) to the perceived quality of the schools (based on test scores), and in the built environment of the local landscape, with its notable "academies" (test preparation centers) dotting commercial strips. These academies include facilities that range from slick boutique outfits, to corporate run chains, to ad hoc spaces questionably suitable for their purpose. These private testing and tutoring centers focus on the "gifted and talented" entrance exam, elementary school state tests in reading and math, and predominantly the Specialized High School Admissions Test, the entrance exam for the city's specialized high schools. Their ubiquitous presence in the neighborhoods is a constant reminder to mothers that they could be doing more for children's success, that their efforts could be geared to helping children get on the surest path to success in the city that doesn't require extraordinary wealth of private schooling—gifted and talented or other homogeneously grouped elementary classes in highly ranked elementary schools to feed into New York City's elite high schools, where entrance into selective universities is all but guaranteed.

Mothers' Ongoing Spatial Labors for the "Good School"

Women's narratives about moving for school underline the ongoing spatial labors with which this important gendered practice of middle class formation is associated. I chose three women to illustrate the argument not because their cases are in any sense unique or extraordinary, but because their nearly uninterrupted accounts are strategic in a narrative sense, allowing me to enact a politics of representation wherein respect for the human encounter within ethnographic research is primary. That is, I am not only interested in how women's social reproductive labor is embedded in processes of value's abstraction and movement and race making. I am also interested in women's primary concerns about their kids, home, kin, time, money, spatial mobility, and professional opportunities, as well as their emotional and psychic conundrums. I understand it as my ethical responsibility to demonstrate how women experience those spatial labors around "good schools" as they try to do right by their children.

Hannah, a thirty-eight-year-old mother of three daughters whom we met in the opening of the chapter, had a career in finance but quit when her oldest daughter was eight. Like other women, Hannah took over the interview and addressed issues I had told her I was interested in, as well as issues I did not realize were relevant, in a way that reveals how they were knotted in her life. At the top of Hannah's mind when we began talking was her frustration at the lack of participation in the PTA, where she played an active role, because the other moms were "too busy working to pay off their mortgages." Unprompted, Hannah veered the discussion to how her family was compelled to move because of the schools:

> Like, I know a lot of you are here because we have the best schools in the area, this is the best district by far, one of the best in the city. No one can say otherwise, right? I know we moved here for the schools. I grew up in Bensonhurst Brooklyn. My parents are still there. And logistically my parents were like, if you guys want help with your kids, you have to live here [Brooklyn]. Because when Drew and I first got married, we lived in Forest Hills [Queens]. I mean that was great, Forest Hills is so trendy, all the restaurants, all the bars, that's the place to live. So you know, when we got pregnant, my mom worked. I mean, typical immigrant, worked her entire life, my entire life, and she was like, "Look, I can retire, I'm OK with that, but you have to come here. I can help you with the kids, but you have to come here." So we moved. We found an apartment close to our parents in Brooklyn, and we lived there, and my parents helped with the kids, well Emma at the time, and Stella when she was born. So when, I don't know, I remember when I went to school in Brooklyn, you just showed up on the first day of school with your marble notebook and a pencil. Now it's like, people think about it when these kids are in utero, "Where are we going to put them in school?" So Drew actually started that conversation, and I was like, "What do you mean? She's not even born yet!"

Hannah continued discussing how the move for school would move her away from her mother who was caring for her children:

> So we started thinking about where we wanted to live and we started looking at where the best schools are. And where we lived, in Bensonhurst, not too far from where my parents lived and where I grew up. I was like, it's not a bad school, but I never really thought, oh

> this is where I want to raise my kids. But then, you know, when we looked into the grades [school ratings] more, it was like, well, this isn't the same district it used to be, like the population changed a lot and things have changed a lot. So we started looking, where are the best schools, and there's [northeastern Queens], and Drew had friends that moved there for the same reason, so that was a factor, right? And we almost didn't do [northeastern Queens] because my mom was like, "Well, I can't drive there every day, like, what am I?" I mean, my mom was always with my kids, I worked really long hours, and there was always the sense of . . . something is not right. And Drew was like, "Look, I really looked into it, I looked at all the rankings, I think we should move to [northeastern Queens]."

Even though her mom "always made it very clear: 'If you want us to watch your kids, you have to live in Brooklyn,'" Hannah's mother unexpectedly followed, staying at their new house from Sunday night to Friday afternoon: "'OK, I'm coming with you!' and that just became the new normal."

The move for schooling was entangled with another touchstone moment in Hannah's life—leaving her career in finance for full-time work as mom. Hannah, like other mothers, explained how the school assigned tons of difficult homework to keep up its rating, homework that required parental support. Hannah described how tensions increased when her oldest daughter entered second grade and her mother could no longer help with the challenging homework requirements, despite having run her own grocery store for the previous thirty years. Hannah described scenes of the daily frustrations of managing homework that are familiar to many mothers: "By the time I got home, like 7:30, it was hard because your kid is spent, they're done, I was done, and to sit there and do homework with them. It always, I would say 75 percent of the time it escalated in a fight. And the more we yelled, the worse it got." By November, everyone had reached a breaking point, including Hannah's mother: "My mom was like, 'You can't do this. Either find a tutor or a program, or you stay home or figure something out because Emma's miserable, you're miserable, and I'm miserable because I have to listen to this shit.'"

Taking seriously Hanna's labors *as* labor shows the expansive and diffuse nature of the labors involved in accessing "good schools." These labors are not complete once the choice and move are made—spatial (longer work commute), interactional (negotiating with kin), and affective (managing children's emotions) labors were ongoing. Women performed or managed them at considerable personal and professional costs, costs they continually downplayed or justified. Nine of the twenty women relied at some point solely on kin, primarily their own mothers, for childcare when working. All who did spoke at length about the psychic costs of this "free" labor—the unpayable debts, obligations, and kin work that moving often exacerbated. Grandmothers' care labors and mothers' indebted labors to them in return played an important, if unacknowledged, role in the middle class project for these first-generation middle class women. In fact, the availability of kin to bring children to and from school and take care of them during the non-overlapping hours of school and work was an important factor that allowed women to maintain careers. These labors and costs are invisible in accounts of parental "strategies" about school choice and in accounts of women's reproductive labors.

Feminist discussions of agency as privilege, choice, and "freedom" versus various forms of compulsion, while impossible to resolve, are instructive in exploring this tension among women engaged in the middle class project.[34] Women who are considered "middle class" are often portrayed as "choosing" to work or "choosing" to engage in the labors of intensive mothering, of which relocating for a "good school" is but one aspect. The labors are certainly more of a burden on and virtually impossible for working class or poor women to perform. Yet this doesn't negate the fact that middle class women are also captive to neoliberalism's economic forces of compulsion. Nor does it negate the disciplinary effect of these forces on women that are "free" to "choose" to engage in such labors. Cataloging or ranking women's relative privilege or implicitly positing that certain women's "freedom" to choose produces the gendered, raced, and classed inequalities and forms of domination in neoliberalism are all analytic moves that obfuscate the most critical aspects of the problem.

First, they discount women's labors. Furthermore, such analyses ignore women's contradictory locations in reproduction and how gender domination and exploitation functions in the wider universe of patriarchal racial capitalism. More so, these frames reproduce impoverished reigning notions of freedom, and the inability of analysts to step outside the confines of concepts bound to the capitalist mode of production. Freedom for mothers, it appears, is the freedom to engage in the struggle to ensure that children will be able to commune with the market on more sure footing, or not.

Reframing the issue of choice to that of economic compulsion reveals women's struggles and dispenses with frames that obfuscate gendered, class, and race domination. Indeed, women who would be considered middle class are very limited in their "choices." Consider Rehema, a thirty-five-year-old single mother of an eight-year-old daughter. She had come to New York from Cairo ten years earlier, after she got married, having completed her degree and licensure in pharmacy in Egypt. She had divorced four years earlier and was struggling to make ends meet since she had to start, in her words, "at exactly zero: zero money, zero credit, zero job." She was juggling working, taking care of her daughter, and studying for the US licensure exam. Rehema also moved to northeastern Queens because of school ratings. Her circumstances underline the ongoing spatial labors and sacrifices some women endure for children's schooling. For our interview, Rehema invited me over to her home, an apartment renting for $2,200 per month. When I asked how she chose the home, her narrative unfolded to show the various processes in which relocating for school is implicated:

REHEMA: Schools! That's the main, main reason! We were in Rego Park [Queens], and then we were looking for schools because the schools over there are not that good.

MARIA: So how did you find out this is where the good schools are?

REHEMA: We looked it up online and PS [school] has the highest grades, it's rated, from all over New York. Educationally compared to there, and the community over there, he [the father] didn't want her there, and me too. I saw them [students] when we used to live there. I used to see them when they leave school, and I'm like, no. Because we wanted a community that was better for Laila to be there. Like over there, it was not the best community. The neighborhood was nice, but not to go to school with, you know what I mean? So her dad kept looking, and we knew that this was the best neighborhood for schools. That was our main point, why we moved here. And even when I wanted to move to New Jersey, when I had my internship, he was like, "No, I'm not taking her out of school which is rated one of the highest schools all over New York." [Shrugged] It has the highest ratings.

MARIA: I remember you telling me you wanted to move there [New Jersey] when I first met you, was it Weehawken?

REHEMA: Yes! I was looking at a school, my friend's son school, and he compared the two schools, and it was nothing to be compared. He sent me the numbers. Yes! He showed me the numbers, this school rates this number and this one is this number. There's nothing to be compared and I'm not taking Laila out of this school.

Rehema was, in a sense, locked into the neighborhood for its "good school." Her ex-husband threatened legal action if she moved Laila out of state because the schools did not measure up. During the time in question, Rehema was doing a paid internship as part of her licensure. The wage of $18 per hour was hardly enough to cover the transportation costs (daily tolls alone from New York to New Jersey are about $25), the cost of the after-school program, and someone to pick up Laila and watch her for the one- to-two-hour gap, an elderly Egyptian woman who integrated Arabic lessons into her childcare. The situation was increasingly difficult for Laila who was adjusting to her mother's long work and commuting hours, nearly impossible financially, and so physically and emotionally exhausting that Rehema had her mother come in from Egypt to mitigate the emotional, financial, and care issues. When her mother's thirty-day visa expired, the unsustainability of her former circumstances reappeared. She left the job after fulfilling the required hours for licensure and found a job closer to home with shorter hours in a medical office (making $14 per hour). She had to bring her mom back again to afford the initial fees for a new after-school program that had longer and more flexible hours than the school's program. Importantly, the program provided homework help, which neither her mother nor the babysitter could do, and which Rehema was too exhausted to fight with her daughter about when she got home.

Similar to Hannah and other women, the ongoing work associated with moving for a "good school" (despite fathers' desires and insistence) was Rehema's. This unpaid work also reverberated outward to other women—in both cases, grandmothers. For Rehema the situation would be disastrous without her mother as a safety net. She was immobilized by the school, paid considerable professional costs, and sacrificed her personal well-being, accessibility to what she considered more vibrant parts of the city, and her spatial autonomy. This calls forth feminist geographers' claims that urban planning is implicated in the reproduction of gendered inequalities that emerge through care work.[35] For my participants, the design of the city—the time to traverse the geographic spread of work (centered in Manhattan) and the most affordable place to live that guaranteed a "good school" via poorly connected public transport or expensive railroad meant something had to give. The difference, invisible in familial and scholarly calculations, was made up by women's labor, time, careers, and psychological well-being.

Thirty-four-year-old Cemre is one of the women who emphasized how burdensome—financially and in terms of labor—relocating for "good schools" can be. A mother of three children (seven years, four years, and twenty months), Cemre moved to northeastern Queens when her oldest was three years old so that he could attend a nursery or pre-K school and then kindergarten in one of its best schools. When I first asked Cemre about the move to Queens, she, like Hannah and Rehema, streamed into a long response that weaved through a set of personal and financial negotiations, labors, and sacrifices:

So we were living in Forest Hills before, then once I had my son, we moved because of the good schools. That's the only reason. Look online, everybody knows this . . . He was going to [a nursery school with Christian affiliation], even though I'm Muslim, he went to nursery and I was bringing him back and forth. And when I had my daughter, it was very hard for me to commute from Forest Hills to take him to school for two and a half hours, because they didn't have full-day nursery there at the time. But it was a struggle to get my husband to move here, because my sisters live here. He thought it was just like, it was an ego thing, like I don't want to live next to your sisters. When we moved to [northeastern Queens], my rent in my old house—[it] was a three bedroom—I went from paying $1,300 to $2,250. For my husband to accept that, it took a whole lot of begging, OK? Because my husband is cheap as fuck, and he doesn't believe in the schools, because he wasn't born and raised here. He was born and raised in Turkey, went to school in Turkey, he came here for college, didn't even freakin' finish college. Some kids are not meant for college and he's one of them.

What is remarkable is that two years after this initial move to access a good school, Cemre once again moved *out* of northeastern Queens and to New Jersey, also because of schooling, although for very different reasons. In the following excerpt, I was trying to piece together Cemre's geographic mobility since childhood, asking if she was raised in the area. This sparked a series of painful childhood memories and sharing with me how those experiences incited her second recent move. She explained that she moved to New Jersey so that her son would not be left back at the end of the year in the New York City school system. By moving in the middle of the school year to a state with an earlier cutoff date for grade entry, her son would be entering kindergarten rather than getting left back. This laborious effort involved a rapid real estate decision, packing the families' belongings, moving in the middle of the winter with an infant—all while deceiving her husband about the motives. All Cemre's efforts were oriented toward the educational benefit and emotional well-being of her child. Here she details these exhausting and exhaustive geographic labors:

> I went to school in Rego Park, which is so much more ghetto. I was held back in the second grade, because my reading was horrible and my mom was an immigrant who didn't know any better. That's why I tell myself, "Look, I'm not going to let my kid go through this." I wouldn't want my kid to get held back, because that held back feeling? It makes you feel so much worse than someone telling you you're too young to go to first grade. When we moved, I called the Board of Ed in New Jersey and I knew for a fact that he was going to go back to kindergarten. My husband doesn't know this; he thinks we moved because of his job. But the fact is I knew my son was going to go back to kindergarten and he was going to have that advantage of being the oldest. He thinks I moved because I felt bad for him, bullshit! I don't feel bad for him! What the hell do I feel bad for him for? You commute, Maria! Do you feel bad for yourself that you're commuting three days? No one feels bad for us! I was on the subway with crazy psychotic people yelling and staring at me because I'm a Muslim or whatever [Cemre wears a hijab]. And I was pregnant taking the subway, it took me an hour and twenty minutes to commute during rush hour, he didn't feel bad for me! I don't feel bad for him!

The particular constellation of spatial labors surrounding these multiple moves to access a good school for her son included: researching school quality, researching district regulations regarding age requirements, searching for real estate surrounding appropriate schools, intervening in and challenging school practices and policies, and the numerous hours of work to pack up a family's belongings with three young children, including an infant, in tow. While these practices are markers of middle class parenting, it bears emphasizing that for Cemre and many of my participants, they index a specific trajectory within the middle class project—class mobility through geographic mobility for good schools. Growing up without the social and cultural capital of the middle class makes this more laborious. However, Cemre understood these class categories and her mobility as a movement from "immigrant [working class]" to "American [middle class]." This substitution of immigrant or American for working class or middle class in her narrative also appeared in the descriptions of her multiple labors negotiating with, and then deceiving her husband about, her moves for her child's schooling ("Because my husband . . . doesn't believe in the schools, because he wasn't born and raised here . . ."). The misalignment of Cemre and her partner's parenting goals was unique among my participants. Fathers, including those separated or divorced from mothers, generally placed as high a priority on educational success as mothers, in rare cases even more so. While mothers performed the bulk of all tasks, managerial and rote, in either scenario, not having a partner with similar goals added to the weightiness of these labors. While hesitating to call these negotiations "emotional labor," whatever we call this work should be taken into account as hidden costs that affect women in profound ways. In Cemre's case, doing the best she could for her child meant friction with her husband, as well as guilt and regret for pressuring her son to succeed at the level expected by the good school to which she sacrificed so much to send him.

Despite her struggles to access a "good school," Cemre's narrative also revealed a critical perspective about the construct. Cemre launched into her critique when explaining more about her son's difficulties in school and her reasons for moving to New Jersey:

> He was always the youngest and I knew for a fact that my son was going to struggle. No teacher in [previous New York City public school], it's a 10 out of 10 [in rating system]. Listen I don't care! If my son is not a 10 in a 10 school, then to me, the school being a 10 doesn't mean anything! A good school to me would be a teacher saying, "Look Cemre, your kid, he's great in this subject but he needs help in this subject, and I'm going to help him." But that's not how it is. There they focus on the tops [top scoring students]. "Who is going to keep our scores up?" And then they forget about all the kids who need help. And the kids who need it are the kids who are claimed to be defiant or the kids who are claimed to be . . . Like, when he was in kindergarten, the teacher was crazy, she was going through a lot in her personal life. Very sweet lady, I like her personally but going back now, I'm like, why did I let my son go

> through this "red card, green card" [behavioral system used in the early years]? Who the hell does that to a four-year-old? He was four and a half at the time! And they want them reading! This! That! I told my son about the math test, "I don't care what you get." And he was like, "Yes you do!" I'm like, "I get mad if you don't get what you deserve because you rushed through it. Where are you going? Who are you trying to prove that you're done?" And I tell him, "Look, if you don't understand something, this is what I need to know or your teacher needs to know so you can learn it and not learning from your mistakes is not going to get you anywhere."

We continued our conversation:

MARIA: It's like, isn't that the point of the test?

CEMRE: And again. This (claps) is (claps) the (claps) problem (claps). How do you think they want to keep the Blue Ribbon [national award recognizing "best schools"]? How do you think they want to keep those scores? It's not because they truly want to help. You know what I mean? It's because they put so much pressure on these kids, more homework, more this, more that. I got to say, there's so much less homework in New Jersey, so much less. He gets one page of math, and that's it. And he does it by himself. And do you know that there is no proven fact that homework helps the child? None, it's like .8 or some shit like that.

MARIA: I love that you have stats!

CEMRE: I'm serious! Because my sisters don't believe me! They think I'm like, this mother who's like blah, I don't care. But I'm so different. First of all, I'm very Montessori. I feel like the child will learn on their own. I wish I could send all my kids. I wish I could afford it. I wish there were public Montessori schools, I really do. And I wish, and this is the only thing I wish, I understand that you know, the area is like, the price is like this much because of the schools, I get it. I wish that the schools were really worth us paying this much. You know what I mean? You get what I'm saying?

MARIA: Yes! Please, please go on! This is exactly what I'm trying to get at, so like this stupid house is probably like $800,000 now. I know it's a piece of shit and it should cost like $250[,000].

CEMRE: You know what I mean? It's because it's close to [public school].

MARIA: Now you're saying, the house is this much because of the school. But in actuality, the school ain't all that.

CEMRE: That's exactly what I'm trying to get to.

Cemre articulated her critique of the good school most explicitly among my participants because this so-called good school was not working for her child. She realized that the "good school" construct was an abstraction of other students' test scores that did not necessarily have any bearing on the quality of education her child received. In fact, she found the high pressures and the teaching to the test (and the focus on high-achievers) inimical to her child's progress. She also perceived that the inflated financial cost of the real estate—which she was willing to shoulder, we can recall—was a fiction. In the end this fiction wasn't worth it, and so she moved to a place where the schools were better, in her estimation, and homes cost less. Of course, she made up the difference with her labors and shouldered other costs such as being isolated from kin and friends in this new neighborhood.

Other mothers too implicitly recognized that they were paying quite a high price for an illusion. For instance, my participant Gloria also struggled to finance her home and recounted various personal and professional struggles to move to this area of northeastern Queens for schools. Her daughters were in New York City's coveted "gifted and talented" program in one of the local schools. Gloria explained how seriously parents of children in those programs take schooling. So much so that three of her daughters' classmates moved out of the city when the city announced it would be phasing out the gifted program in 2021.[36] She explained the reasoning of parents' emphasis on success. "It's the reason why a lot of people move to this area Maria. They're very like, 'education, that's why we're here.' You know? But it's not necessarily a bad thing either, right? It could be, it's good too because that's why our schools are good, you know? But at the same time, people take it so seriously." Gloria perceived that schools were rated high not because the quality of education received there. Rather, the high ratings were the result of her own and other women's labors oriented toward children's educational success. This had parallels to the experiences of my participant Lianna, a forty-five-year-old mother of four children (ages sixteen, twelve, nine, and seven) who was born in Brooklyn to parents born in China. When talking about her exhaustive search for a home when she was pregnant with her first child, she emphasized that she was guided by and finally settled on her home in northeastern Queens because of "value," which she then realized is not a result of the quality of the schools per se but is the congealed value of other parents' labors:

> I looked around at other areas in Nassau [a county of Long Island], and we looked at the value of the house. What kind of schools are you getting? What are you getting in terms of amenities? What's around in the area, and stuff like that, the taxes. And at the time, this was a very diverse area; diverse meaning everyone lives here. Now it's a little different. It's not diverse anymore. So now flip it, we're [Asians] not the minority, right? So for me, because I'm Asian, I've always been like, "Well, you know, if my kids are going to be around other kids who are going to be like, achievers, you know school's going to be really important to them because it's really important to their parents, well, OK!"

Like Cemre and Gloria, Lianna developed her critique of the illusory nature of the good school through everyday life. Yet at the very same time, albeit for different reasons, they still held on to the construct of the good school as reflecting some objective truth. This dual mode of critical perception of the illusory nature of the abstractions and ideological fictions governing their lives coupled with their practical acceptance is one manifestation of the psychic structure of neoliberal motherhood that I call schizophrenic maternal states, explored in Chapter 7.

Hannah's, Rehema's, and Cemre's ongoing labors and sacrifices for "good schools" illustrate themes that ran across the women's lives, points that would be left by the wayside if their labors were narrowly framed in terms of children's educational success or upward mobility within a frozen class structure. Sociological scholarship focusing on how middle class mothers secure their children's educational success portrays women's labor as freely available and costless resource. This frame analytically euphemizes the broader material and discursive forces that coerce women's labors. The political implications of such work are that enlightened subjects can choose to stop accruing advantages or that schooling should be reformed so that the way it sorts students is "fair." From the Marxist feminist and racial capitalist perspectives in which this research is grounded, mapping the unevenness and interconnections of oppressions directs attention to how state and capital manufacture scarcity to reproduce ongoing violence of class, raced, and gendered forms of domination. The gendered forms of subjugation involved in the seemingly ordinary processes of accessing "good schools" are a requisite aspect of neoliberal mothering. Within these processes, relations of racialized subjugation are reproduced and reconfigured while remaining opaque.

Routing Women's Labors to Produce Racialized Value

The neoliberal educational complex coerces and channels women's spatial labors to redouble and legitimize the material and symbolic order of race, disguised as seemingly objective measure of value of persons and populations. The material and symbolic redoubling of race is intertwined and each reinforces the other, and both registers operate in the continual assessing and ranking of children and in school ratings websites. The prominence of racial demographics depicted on school ratings websites for each school's profile is the most blatant way racial logics are summoned, presumably listed for parents interested in "diversity." More troubling is how websites exacerbate racialized associations of "good" and "bad" schools. The datafication of school ratings reproduce and proliferate anti-Blackness in veiled and circuitous ways that recruits subjects into its racialized hierarchy, subjects who might otherwise refuse explicit racism. The ratings themselves, the way the metrics are anchored spatially onto maps, even the architecture of the sites (the way links collate seemingly objective evidence from various sources) make these sites authoritative. And the neutral veneer of the metric and the market conceal and reinforce links between "achievement" and racism. School ratings confirm the hierarchies of humanness, via the validity of an army of neuroscientists, psychologists, statisticians, and policymakers. Good and bad schools, populated by good or bad children, are simply indisputable *facts*, objective value measurements.

I recall an insight that my child, then eight years old, told me about how her friend, who was soon moving to another neighborhood, "kept bragging that her new school is a 10 out of 10," and that the school they were both attending at the time was only a "7 out of 10." She reportedly told the friend, "Well, you're actually saying something bad about *yourself*, because *you're* in this school." The child perceived the most basic and often forgotten fact about this massive datafication of school ratings—school quality measures the value of the children within it. While she could not (yet) know of the racialized connotations of this value, this differential valuation is precisely what legitimizes the treatment of Black and Brown children as "waste"—subject to policing and the punitive behavioral systems, warehoused in dilapidated buildings, and subject to teachers' low expectations and the most dehumanizing educational processes.

School ratings websites conceal how race inequalities are built into the data on which they are based and so feed into the production of these disparities. This process is akin to how search engines reinforce racism.[37] Ratings websites harden and reinscribe racial logics, fusing racialized bodies and spaces to a hard, fast, absolute value, all while appearing racially neutral. While it is the same racial calculus (white value and Black non-value), the equation appears objective and legitimate. In their earnest search for "good schools," parents validate this technical apparatus and its violent rationality. The reproduction of a racialized hierarchy of humanness does not depend on overtly racist white mothers or the hypocritical liberal racism of "nice white parents" who received deserved scorn in the eponymous *New York Times* podcast, in the same way that the racial disparities in police murder of Black civilians do not depend on a few "bad cops."[38] Black mothers and Brown mothers in my research also relocated to the area for children's schooling, rearranged their lives, took on financial and personal debts, were forced out of or into jobs because they were trying to do right by their kids in the way they understood was best. After all, they themselves became middle class through educational success. Yet their efforts are entangled in processes that reproduce anti-Blackness and white supremacy.

The racialized processes that constitute NYC's hypersegregated schools and neighborhoods further dispossess working class Black and Brown communities. Economists neutralize dispossession by referring to the way school rankings are incorporated into real estate value as "school capitalization." Thousands of such studies have been published in the past two decades. One review found school quality "capitalized into property values in 8 countries" with house values rising "between 1%—4% for a one standard deviation increase in test scores."[39] A study examining data from 1988 to 2003 in New York City found an increase of about 3 percent.[40] Another study in New York City found school quality "consistently and strongly capitalized" by as much as 7.7 percent.[41] Locals in northeastern Queens (home renters, buyers, and realtors) gauge the increase in property values around the "good schools" to be even higher, especially around the area's "best" schools. In their elaborate abstractions and modeling, economists reify the racist basis of school ratings, and erase how mothers' spatial labors generate value that is incorporated into school ratings. Yet one does not have to accept their premises to see that economists are also implicitly claiming that maternal labors partly form school quality and property value. Property partly derives its valuation from mothers' congealed spatial labors, their other reproductive labors oriented toward children's success, as well as mothers' own embodied value (the sum of their educational and professional experiences and the racialized value of those labors, see Chapter 3). In sum, women's labors are incorporated into children's test scores, translated into school ratings, and transformed into property value.

Women's spatial labors increase the value of property and reinscribe the material and symbolic order of racial hierarchy. Nathan Connolly argues that race does "double duty through real estate."[42] It increases white wealth by devaluing and dispossessing Black communities, while dispossession then serves as self-evident fact to legitimate theories of Black inferiority. The framework of racial capitalism is pertinent here: Value creation is always relational regarding race, as is the racialization of space. Valuing one place means devaluing another. The lived experiences and meanings of race are deeply woven with space, and more concretely, property. This entanglement is driven by racial capitalism, the racial state, and resistance to them; an entanglement that is perpetually morphing: from theft and genocide that transforms land into property, to the enslaved who tilled it, to racial apartheid by law and then terror, to rational choices in the market. Current imbrications of property and race involve mothering in the middle class project. The state's rerouting of resources to the testing industry, with its ties to global finance and the tech and real estate industries, produces the scarcity of "good schools." This scarcity coerces mothers to make up for it through their spatial labors and sacrifices.

Reproducing Racialized Value of Life Itself

It is more urgent to grasp the production of racialized value through mothering in the symbolic register rather than in the financial sense of property value. This entails thinking about evaluation as measuring the value of life itself. My thinking about the differential valuation of life is informed by Sylvia Wynter's theorization of race's foundational role in conceptions of the human and how subjects are instituted and realize themselves within symbolic templates of value and non-value.[43] Indeed, evaluating students is an inherently bizarre practice that is both dependent on racialized ways of knowing and initiates students into racialized notions of value and non-value.[44] Rendering human life in standardized, quantifiable, and exchangeable commodity logics is "rooted in and reflects a racialist humanism that persists in producing and valuing whiteness over the lives of people of color."[45] The racial ontology of the human—white supremacy and anti-Blackness, is always at work when schools evaluate students.[46] It is built into the curriculum, into practices of belonging, discipline, and the resulting testing data on which school ratings are based. The systematic devaluing of Black life within schooling produces racial humanness in the ever-lurking specter that haunts the US educational system—the so-called achievement gap. Subjects are hailed into the deathly apparatus of race in the neoliberal era by confronting the stark chromatics in the empirical fact of the gap.[47] The neoliberal education complex proliferates school ratings in public, redoubles their mapping onto an already-racialized urban landscape, and capitalizes ratings into property values that rely on and reproduce race to ultimately reproduce the racialized value of life itself. In short, neoliberal schooling recruits mothers of any race into the middle class project, which inextricably involves the devaluing of Black and Brown lives.

Mothers, squeezed by the rapacious tentacles of capital into their contradictory location in reproduction, facilitate capital accumulation through racialized and gendered difference making. Capital and state, through the neoliberal educational complex, harness mothers' labors in ways that produce material, social, and psychic harm; debase women's work and relations to their children; channel their labors to dispossess the working class and poor; and reinscribe white supremacy and anti-Blackness. My analysis underlines the apparently racial neutrality by which mothers of any race are recruited into this violent race making, redoubled in its insidious surface neutrality. Abstractions of value rule our lives; they work behind our backs, outside of consciousness; they invade school and home; they dominate children's lives from the moment they are born, subjecting them to dehumanizing and alienating labors of learning that produce the ranking of their worth as humans at every turn. Yet mothers and children perceive, if only in flashes of insight, the absurdity of value, its basis in their labors, their bodies, their ingenuity. They do not, however, perceive that value tyrannizes them, that value itself must be abolished.

7

Schizophrenic Maternal States

A Materialist Analysis of Maternal Ambivalence

"ARE ANY OF them bad moms?" my then nine-year-old asked me in one of her rare questions about my research. She was uninterested in my explanation that I was concerned with ideas about good and bad moms and how they affect what moms do and feel. She insisted, "No, like really." When I replied, "There are no bad mothers," she chuckled and ended the conversation with a sarcastic "Right." That children are attuned to an almost formal dichotomizing of mothers into bad and good speaks to the potency of this organizing framework and ultimately to how condemnation is so easily and readily applicable to mothers. Although they did not use the bald category themselves, "bad moms" repeatedly appeared in my conversations with women about their own mothering. The bad moms appearing in my participants' narratives were rarely the familiar ones who purportedly neglect children but instead were those who did too much—the scapegoat of the neoliberal mothering spectacle. These bad moms served as figures against which to define their own mothering and to resolve some of the psychic anguish and emotional conundrums of neoliberal mothering. I construct a set of "bad mom talk" to map out a terrain of women's ambivalence about the key contradictions that cohere around maternal labors in neoliberalism: experts' claims of their necessity for children's success coupled with recent backlash discourse that such labors are excessive, frivolous, and potentially detrimental to child and society; the gaps between ideal quantity and quality of labors and mothers' willingness or ability to perform them; and finally, the clash between conflicting ideals and women's critiques and perceptions of alternatives.

A rich dialogue about labor lay beneath the surface of women's bad mom talk. Here women discussed, debated, and made visible the often invisibilized labors of mothering and a way for them to work out their understandings and ambivalent attachments to the radical restructuring of social reproduction in neoliberalism. Women worked through feelings about these labors in a context where anything other than happiness or "emotional togetherness" implicitly defines one as a bad mom.[1] They voiced ambivalent attachments and emotional struggles that are not allowed to announce themselves as such, with the limited resources and lack of possible resolutions at their disposal. As such, women's bad mom talk reveals the ideological, experiential, and affective structures of neoliberal motherhood for that vast stratum of women targeted by the middle class project.

Women's emotional and psychic struggles emerge from both the intensified labors of motherhood in neoliberalism and the negative affects that arise from their inability or unwillingness to perform them, from the *gap* between the ideals of motherhood and their real mothering. Ideologies of motherhood structure the everyday emotional, psychic, affective frames of experience. They are internalized as negative feelings—a mix of anxiety, exhaustion, guilt, second-guessing of one's self, constantly measuring one's self up against others and the ideal, feeling one is not doing enough, gnawing uncertainty, and feelings of being devalued. Yet these negative feelings often propel women's critiques of maternal ideologies and offer women glimpses of the forces and relations of power in which they are embedded. Women's feelings are conflicted in part because they coexist with their own alternative intellectual, ethical, or political assessments of what it means to do right by their children, as well as the joys and satisfactions that mothering entails, however limited.

This assemblage of diverging feelings and uneasy attachments to hegemonic ideals makes up a large part of what I am calling the schizophrenic maternal state characteristic of neoliberal motherhood. I do not use the term "schizophrenic" in the clinical sense of an individual pathology, but to denote the collective pathology that coheres to mothering in neoliberal capitalism where women partially glimpse the economic compulsions and ideologies beyond their control, the damages to self and child that mothering in capitalism entails, and the possibilities of more authentic mothering yet the seeming impossibility of realizing them—the inexorable push that they must keep on. This schizophrenic maternal state emerges as a response to the conflicting ideologies and intensified demands with which it associated, the gap between ideal and real, the chasm between what women are allowed to express and what they actually feel, and finally, women's actual feelings which are themselves fraught and contradictory. This persistent and pervasive schizophrenia is manifest as the fragmented state of neoliberal maternal subjectivity.

Inhabiting this schizophrenic maternal state is torturous but rarely announces itself as such—neither to others nor to oneself. If the historian's task is to "read what was never written," then the ethnographer's task is to "hear what was never said."[2] I found the intense feelings and psychic conundrums within bad mom talk; lurking behind humor and defense mechanisms, around the bend from deflections and justifications, and through the conscious steering or unconscious flow of topics. Bad mom talk, I aver, bubbled forth as a way to process and mitigate the tensions of this schizophrenic psychic state. It makes visible the links between material conditions and psychic and emotional life, revealing how women internalize and interrogate the forces to which they are subjected, and the inherent incompleteness of both processes. It was a site for the making and forming of maternal subjectivities.

In this chapter, I focus on how maternal subjectivities are formed among this particular group of women, situated as they are in place and time, and through their classed, raced, and gendered positionalities. What are the affective conundrums of trying to juggle the impossible demands of mothering for capital, demands that often conflict with their own ideals of good mothering, generated from practice and relation to the actual children before them? How do ideologies of neoliberal motherhood channel women's affective intensities in particular directions? How do they link and/or sever women from one another in (re)productive ways? And finally, what are the political stakes of these affective structures—how do they bind women to the unsustainable conditions of mothering within neoliberal capitalism? None of the women accepted neoliberal maternal ideologies hook, line, and sinker. Bad mom talk functioned as a site for normalizing the extraordinary labors that mothers have taken on in neoliberalism by scapegoating those who were over the top. Just as importantly, it was a site to externalize these ideologies and discuss maternal labors conditions, revealing partial recognitions, critiques, and visions for other possible ways to be mother and child.

The Bad Mom, Neoliberal Redux

Women's bad mom talk has the form of appearance of what is conventionally referred to as the "mommy wars," the antagonism and divisive dialogue between women regarding parenting practices, approaches, and philosophy.[3] While originally referring to the supposed tension between mothers who work outside the home and mothers who do not, the "mommy wars" currently revolve around and take their most heated form in the terms of the scapegoat spectacle of intensive mothering.[4] And wars they are. In her book *Mothers*, the feminist theorist Jacqueline Rose argues that mothers are the object of socially licensed cruelty and aggression and provoke a sadism that should not be underestimated.[5] Bad mothers are a historically potent trope, and the neglectful mother is the most recognizable. Yet at mid-century, the psy sciences constructed a powerful taxonomy of bad mothers who either did too little or too much, a taxonomy that "lingers culturally" despite being disproved.[6] Within neoliberalism, the bad mom continues to be defined by the same causal relationship; maternal labors, whether excessive or insufficient, produce various child pathologies. The bad mother is an "elastic category within a broader taxonomy of neoliberal family figures," one that is able to accommodate a host of characters, reinvented and recycled, according to the political exigencies of the moment.[7] In the late neoliberal tableau of bad mothers, one stands tall as the center of scorn—the middle class mother who does too much; the excess of her maternal labors her distinguish mark—the scapegoat by all her various monikers (bulldozer, helicopter, snowplow). As "props of neoliberalism," mothers are held accountable for society's inequities, injustices, and failures to live up to its promises.[8] If one were to survey the "mommy wars" without situating them within the intensified forms of class, race, and gender domination that are reproduced through neoliberal mothering, one might reasonably conclude that "mommy wars" are the trivial pursuit of catty insecure women justifying their lifestyle choices among a wealth of competing expert advice. Yet Rose's claim that mothers function as a focal "diversionary tactic . . . [that] deflects what might be far more disruptive forms of social critique" prompts us to look behind this frenzied discourse.[9]

"Frenzied" is perhaps an understated adjective for describing the recent culture wars surrounding neoliberal motherhood. In one camp, public institutions and experts exhort mothers that their children can succeed only if they invest extraordinary time and energies into their children. In the other camp, there is an extreme backlash against women who practice so-called intensive mothering. From helicopter moms hovering to tiger moms growling to snowplow mothers clearing all obstacles in their child's path, the figure of the middle class mother has become the object of ridicule and contempt for over a decade, reaching a hysterical pitch until the COVID-19 pandemic necessitated its temporary halt so that mothers would fill in the gaps of remote schooling.[10] During this time, *The New York Times*, *The Atlantic*, *The Wall Street Journal*, and countless online outfits pumped out vitriolic content on the excessive labors of intensive mothers. The gendered, classed, heterosexualized, and racialized figure of the white or Asian middle class mother is portrayed as a selfish, upwardly mobile class striver, playdate strategist, or hysterical woman with such idle pursuits; she invents things to worry about like additives in organic Goldfish crackers. The scapegoat mother's hypocrisy is an object of scorn from left and right.

The scorn heaped at mothers who practice "intensive parenting" or "overparenting" is ultimately judged on the basis of two effects. The first draws its sustenance from the dominant sociological paradigm on parenting and class exemplified by the "Lareau tradition," in which such mothers are portrayed as generating unfair advantages to their children and thus themselves producing the increased inequalities of life endemic to neoliberal capitalist class relations (see the introduction and Chapter 1). The media directs the collective gaze to ridiculing the labors of the most privileged of the middle class to divert attention away from their mooring in changing material conditions. Anyone engaging in the middle class project—that is, even poor or working class parents trying to help children become middle class—becomes morally and ethically suspect. A *New York Times* article explicitly linked the phenomenon to rising levels of inequality, opening with a Texas working class immigrant family angling to get their child out of diapers and into a good preschool. They were then blamed for exacerbating inequalities of neoliberalism: "Those who can afford to helicopter are probably making things even more unequal for the next generation. As with the Texan couple, this doesn't always match up to their beliefs."[11] The second reason for scorn is the purported effects intensive mothers have on the subjectivities of children and their future adult selves. Mothers' excessive efforts create a generation of helpless, overprotected, and burned-out children who become effete adult millennials who cannot handle simple tasks. Various parenting websites, even WebMD, have published pieces such as "10 Warning Signs You Might Be a Helicopter Parent" and "Are You a Helicopter Parent: 7 Signs You Shouldn't Ignore." NPR referred to the phenomenon as "The Overparenting Crisis in School and Home" in 2018, and in 2019 *The Atlantic* announced, "Intensive Parenting is Now the New Norm in America." While *The Atlantic*'s "The Overprotected Kid" mourned the loss of dangerous play and linked it to "increased levels of psychopathology," *The Wall Street Journal*'s "The Overprotected American Child" blamed "overzealous" parents "as a factor fueling the surge" of anxiety disorders among children.[12] With all this heat on excessive mothers who produce children with psychopathologies and mounting class inequalities, are they to do less? The title of a *New York Times* editorial answers baldly—"The bad news about helicopter parenting: it works."[13] In other words, it ensures children's future success. The "choice" is then handed to mothers.

This schizophrenic public discourse is a crucial aspect of the middle class project, one where neoliberal America finds its ideological coherence. At one and the same time, the middle class project legitimizes the intensifying forces of economic compulsion within neoliberalism—coercing mothers to endlessly labor and devote their own and children's lives to capital as the only way to ensure a decent life in the face of the "sinking middle class" while also blaming mothers who do so as producing America's economic decline with their pathological children, "disappearing" middle class slots, and widening inequalities of class to boot.[14] Society buries its deepest social and political contradictions in motherhood—where hopes for the future are hung and blame is pinned when those projects fail.[15] In neoliberalism, capitalism's last hope idealized in the American dream is hung on mothers, and the frustrations of its hopeless reality are displaced on them, too.

Women must mother in this schizophrenic space of highly charged and contradictory demands. Mothers wonder whether they are doing too much or not enough; they deny the intensity of their labors while also seeking recognition of their value; they want to be good mothers as articulated by all the experts, but they also repudiate this category that has been increasingly problematized and subject to ridicule. All identities are "determined by diverse and divergent aims," and inhabiting them is always a fraught pursuit.[16] Yet the stakes, emotional investments, and labors of becoming intelligible as a good mother are amplified. This is partly because the role of mother is first and foremost defined by its primary relation to the child as living human with needs and desires to which mothers are accountable. And the very acts of caring for dependent helpless children activates a unique powerful affective force that, because of its imputed association with the biological or natural and essentially feminine, is rarely delineated in ethnographic accounts. Wilson and Yochim are an exception in trying to account for this sentiment, describing it as an "undeniable pull" that mothers feel for their children, an "unshakeable affective force that is nonetheless historical and subject to assemblages of power (not simply patriarchy): it gets channeled, worked over, and exploited in myriad ways."[17] The key conundrum of motherhood lies in how this powerful affective force binding women and children is channeled—being a good mom in a manner that is socially recognized as such may very well violate women's authentic thinking and experiences with children.

Authenticity, Ambivalence, and Disavowal

Caring for children generates knowledge. It is an intellectual activity that the philosopher Sara Ruddick calls "maternal thinking"—"the intellectual capacities she develops, the judgments she makes, the metaphysical attitudes she assumes, the values she affirms."[18] Of interest is Ruddick's formulation of the way that ideologies of mothering conflict with or, in Adrienne Rich's terms, *steal* or *withhold* more authentic ways to care for and be with children.[19] Ruddick's notion of inauthenticity underlines how maternal labors involve "a repudiation of one's own perceptions and values," as they are directed to worlds that mothers did not make and may oppose—a "willingness to *travailler pour l'armée* [to work for the army] to accept the uses to which others put one's children."[20] This devastating phrase captures a central dilemma of being a mother within capitalism—the extraordinary labors of caring for children to make their way in the damaged world of capitalism, a present and future of perpetual insecurity and work for capital. Mothers are thus torn in two directions, pulled by their own experiences and judgments that generate knowledge contrary to and potentially dangerous to the social order and pulled another way by the forces of economic compulsion and ideologies designed to silence this knowledge, work it over, reroute and transform it.

If maternal thinking—knowledge built through everyday life experience—often opposes the "ideals" of motherhood or, said another way, shows that those ideals are wrong, how are mothers then supposed to carry the weight of inflicting what Adorno called the "wrong life" on children?[21] Bad feelings are bound to cohere to such an impossible situation with such high emotional stakes. Yet mothers must disavow them. Despite being "the only thing which seems to me to be eternal and natural in motherhood," ambivalence is impermissible.[22] Feminist affect, psychoanalytic, and maternal theorists have had to contend with maternal ambivalence, the dynamic coexistence of positive and negative affects associated with motherhood, in a context in which it is seen as pathological.[23] While ambivalence has been thought to characterize many, if not all, love relationships ever since Freud and then Melanie Klein situated it at the center of psychic and emotional life, the recurring importance of the concept within the maternal experience speaks to the extent to which motherhood is idealized as a site of pure, natural, positive affect.[24] Indeed, in the ideal spectacle, mothers inhabit or otherwise perform labors with emotional ease and agility. This affective duty is a "condition of one's political visibility" as a mother.[25] Yet despite a rich tapestry of explorations of maternal ambivalence in film, art, literature, pop culture, and feminist scholarship, the admission of negative feelings is still seen as taboo. Public expressions of negative maternal feelings are met with hostility and moral judgment, revealing the deep cultural unease of disrupting motherhood's "infrastructure of happiness."[26] Mothers are integral to neoliberal postfeminism—where happiness and positivity are the only intelligible emotional states.[27] When ambivalence is expressed, it must be somehow mitigated or accompanied by maneuvers such as humor that indicate women's ultimate commitment to good mothering and its promise of happiness. In everyday life and public culture, maternal ambivalence must be buried. Bad mom talk is one of the few places it was unearthed.

Extracurricular Labors and Rate Busting

Bad moms emerged at many turns in my conversations with women as they narrated their everyday struggles. At times, bad moms appeared in abstract or generic form. At other times, they appeared in concrete named form as sisters, neighbors, friends, or specific women with whom they interacted only as "colleague mother," such as other parents in the child's school. Women reconstructed bad mom figures in public culture and applied that to moms in their midst to partially resolve the emotional and psychic conundrums wrought by contradictory and excessive labor demands, a way to defend themselves from the sense of guilt that always lurks about them for not measuring up to the ideal, and ultimately a way to critique the labor conditions of reproduction.

Morgan, a married, thirty-six-year-old white woman with two sons, age nine and thirteen, wielded bad mom figures while reflecting on her experiences. As a teenager, she had moved to New York City to work as a nanny for a family to "escape" the Utah suburb where she grew up. In the following passage, Morgan sympathizes with the impossible situation of moms working outside the home and reframes the mommy war binary in terms of moms who do too much versus those who don't. We were discussing the homework routine when I complained about the amount of homework as one of the sources of our fatigue and overwork. Morgan steered the conversation to the additional labors demanded by the neoliberal education complex in the form of extracurricular activities. These activities, which she called "overscheduling," were among the more contentious issues around which women explicitly or implicitly defined bad mothers. In this excerpt, Morgan creates no less than three bad mom figures: one generalized, one unnamed, and one named, all overscheduling their children with extracurricular activities. Her portrayal of them as self-serving may function to protect herself from feelings of inadequacy in comparison. Yet alongside this defensive mechanism lurks what is essentially a labor critique, characterizing these women as rate-busters, those laborers that exceed the agreed-upon limits of productivity to outdo their colleagues and please the bosses, thereby increasing the labor expectations of all:

MORGAN: You see, I've never had a problem with the homework. I'm wondering, well, in junior high I'm wondering where it all is. I'm like [feigns looking around]. I hear other parents say, "Oh my gosh, there's so much homework." But first of all, I'm not big on overscheduling, I think kids need down time. Do I still feel immense pressure that I have not provided them enough? Absolutely.

MARIA: Do you?!

MORGAN: Yeah.

MARIA: That's another thing I'm trying to get at, where do moms get this? Like, I feel like, every mom is, we're all kind of resisting this overschedule and kill your kid, but at the same time, we're second-guessing ourselves.

MORGAN: I don't second-guess myself. I literally, I think I have, I'm going to say I think, even though I *know*, I have some kind of chronic fatigue issue that reoccurs, and you can literally see my cold sore. I can't take on more, I know my threshold.

MARIA: Well, that's awesome that your body actually tells you.

MORGAN: No, but my threshold is much lower than everyone else's threshold. So that's where it gets at me, because I watch these people do and do and do and do. And I'm like, that would put me in a corner rocking myself [rocks herself while laughing]. So I feel bad that I'm not trying harder, but at the same time I physically can't. I can't.

MARIA: I hear you! I think, you think that other mothers can handle it? I think maybe some are losing their shit?

MORGAN: I think a fair amount of them are. Absolutely. Especially if you're working. Mm-hmm. And we all lie about it too, that's what's hilarious, we do! [In breathy, feminine voice:] "Oh, we can't tonight. Joey has piano. Oh, we blah blah, we're so great." And inside they're like, like, it just creates all this turmoil but no one talks about that part, right? Like one of my friends is like, "Oh, Theo has aikido twice a week." Twice a week! I'm like, how are you paying for that? I've looked into karate, it's crazy! And twice a week? And that's not his only gig? Like what are you doing? He's got gymnastics. It's, like, seriously! It makes me tired to think about it. See, I think that's mean to your kids.

The first bad mom figure that Morgan mentions is a generalized mass of women who "do and do and do and do," exhausting themselves and others in the process. Morgan constructs intensive mothers as rate-busters who are part of the source of her particular problems—women who raise the bar of good mom labors to the point that she is unable or refuses to engage—as well as her ensuing guilt. When she first brought up the "overscheduled child," she countered it with her maternal thinking—"I think kids need down time." Yet despite her own intuitions, she admits that she still feels "immense pressure" that she has not "provided them enough." Morgan was compelled to apologize for her own body telling her it is too much ("lower threshold"), because of the loud chorus of voices "so that's where it gets at me." The women who "do and do and do and do," the women who make a priority of children's value and future success ("Oh, we can't tonight. Joey has piano") and falsely maintain a facade of competent tranquility, whose lives are dictated by "aikido twice a week" are the Others who signal her lack. While still feeling tormented by their standard, Morgan unequivocally declares that bad moms degrade the labor conditions of *all* mothers. They are constructed as maternal rate-busters, raising the ceiling of productivity and the source of the "immense pressure" and exhaustion. Morgan discusses how her chronic fatigue prevents her from performing those labors or she would be "in a corner rocking herself." Yet she maintains it still "gets" at her, making her feel bad that she is not "trying harder." Despite her assessment that other mothers are overworked, her authentic maternal thinking that kids should have free time, and her own body's signaling that mothers need free time as well, Morgan still feels like she is doing the wrong thing. This itself causes so much psychic turmoil, compounded by the resounding silencing and hiding of all the anguish ("we all lie about it too" and "no one talks about that part").

The caricature of the intensive mother within public culture directs women's ire and frustrations with the intensified labors of neoliberal motherhood onto other mothers. Yet there is more to bad mom talk than simply adopting misogynistic narratives of an updated mommy war. Women were finding ways to protect themselves in a context of increasing labor demands while also claiming dignity in a context where their own maternal labors are the subject of public scrutiny. However, by disidentifying themselves with intensive motherhood, they put themselves in a bind, for they then must underestimate their own labors while still worrying if they are doing enough. Mothers are pitted against one another by neoliberal scarcity as well as by contradictory ideologies of mothering. Despite the battle lines, Morgan's critique of labor conditions contains glimpses of a politics beyond it—she maintains a larger "we" of mothers that are harmed by its pressures; a critique of neoliberal childhood and motherhood. Morgan's critique of motherhood—its excessive labors and psychic conundrums—emerged from reflecting on her labors and position within relations of reproduction. The forces of economic compulsion and ideological penetration are not "visible." In everyday life, mothers encounter and are in relation to other mothers whose own desires, identifications, and activities materialize maternal ideals, however imperfectly. Bad mom talk allows women to glimpse, however partially and imperfectly, the relations of reproduction. Discussing everyday life allowed women opportunities to begin making these relations visible and, in such light, allowed more authentic critiques to emerge.

Despite its larger function in society to misrecognize the relations of capitalist reproduction and avert more thoroughgoing critiques, the scapegoat spectacle of the intensive mother and her overscheduled or overprotected children serves as a bulwark against neoliberalism's encroaching demands. Another one of my participants, Juliet, launched into her critique of mothering through this figure. Juliet is a forty-eight-year-old woman who is raising her three daughters (a ten-year-old and nine-year-old twins) with the help of her parents, who came to the US from Haiti in the early 1970s. She had recently quit her job as a corporate lawyer and was a business partner with her new fiancée. Reflecting on her maternal labors, Juliet articulated a resistance to overschedule her children through the bad mom figure, her interpretation of the parent advice industry, and her own childhood memories:

> I cannot be that mom who's going to have my kids involved in fifteen different activities. It's just not, I'm not even stressing that. I

> read all these studies about how these kids, completely burnt out, with every minute of after school being pushed. Besides being good at your grades, you have to be good at sports, you got to be a team player. You never get to be a kid, run around. You know when I was a kid, yeah, we had a priority on education, played piano on and off for a little bit, but our summers were free. We would read books, hang out with each other. And I feel like that made me a better, less stressed-out person. And these kids are so stressed out. So I always said to myself, "I'm not going to do that."

Juliet distanced herself from "that mom" who stresses and in turn stresses her own children. She conjured her own relatively easygoing childhood free from these worries, implicitly using her mom as the counterpoint for today's overscheduling mother. Childhood memories loomed large and served multiple functions in women's narratives about mothering. But childhood memories, as we have understood since Freud, are malleable and constructed, "almost like works of fiction."[28] Memories are selected, he tells us, because they are adaptable to represent certain fantasies and are activated by a point of contact with a repressed desire. For as we will see, Juliet's portrait of her mother as lax and easygoing is more complicated than the one she recalls here. Yet the more interesting point about childhood memories is not how they measure up to the past, but how they function in the present and what they express. In this vein, Juliet's expression of a childhood free from stress and worry and with an abundance of free time is as much a fantasy about such a life for her daughters as it was for her to be a mother free from the coaxing and coaching them through such childhoods. Women's reconstruction of childhood memories served a similar function to that of real and fictional bad mother figures—as tools to externalize and critique neoliberal motherhood and childhood.[29] Juliet explicitly articulates what other mothers expressed through their childhood memories—current expectations and practices of intensive parenting are deleterious to mothers and children both. Like other women, Juliet had to wade through and critically analyze a tangle of conflicting literature about parenting, interpret it through her childhood memories and the living curriculum of her children's present experiences, to come to a critique of mothering for capital, which "professionalizes" motherhood, robs children of childhoods, and steals from women more authentic ways to mother.

Epistemically Adrift and Existentially Uncertain

Critiquing the contemporary conditions of neoliberal motherhood and refusing some of its intensified labors did not protect women from their associated stress. Despite their own authentic assessment of what is right for their children, uncertainties persistently lingered and gnawed. This is due in no small part to the constantly growing and often conflicting expert advice that they must dutifully sift through, analyze, and interpret as appropriate for their children and their particular situation and ability to adhere to it, compounded by the resentment of mothers in the public sphere. Mothers are "epistemically adrift," a term that refers to how those living with mental illness are unable to flourish because there are "too many interdisciplinary disagreements" about the nature and existence of mental illness.[30] My use of this term is not a call for a decisive authority to settle ideal parenting once and for all, but to call attention to the negative feelings—stress, uncertainty, and guilt—that arise from navigating this tangle of expert knowledge amid the drumming beat of diminishing opportunities for decent futures. This inauthentic curriculum is a coercive force in women's everyday lives, and in the particular geographic area of my research, women were continually faced with a chorus of other mothers who were its agents, exacerbating the toxic affective mix and bringing it to the fore.

In my interview with Samantha, the mention of the "moms in this area" was the proverbial dam that released pent-up stress and frustration that women continually contain beneath a calm exterior. Samantha, a forty-six-year-old white woman with three children—a thirteen-year-old daughter and ten-year-old twins—is one of the moms with whom I became familiar through our encounters at various educational events and leisure spaces (playgrounds and libraries) in the neighborhood. She seemed to me to be one of those moms who took everything in stride. She moved back to the area in northeastern Queens where she had grown up for her children's schooling after quitting her job in marketing. In this excerpt, she discusses her oldest child applying to high school in the next academic year, which in New York City involves an anxiety-inducing process of applications, uncertainty, and in the area of my research, the expectation to at least attempt to get into one of New York City's specialized high schools (and the concomitant competition in doing so). Samantha's critique of how other mothers in the neighborhood also coerce the extension and intensification of maternal labors reveals the extraordinary stress, uncertainty, and guilt that form the affective structure of neoliberal mothering:

> Everyone in this area just assumes you're going to go to a specialized high school, or Catholic, or, I don't know. It just seems like everyone you talk to is like, "Oh! You know the bus for Bronx Science [one of the specialized high schools] stops right here!" You know, it all seems ideal. Even my friend, I was talking to my friend and she has an eighth grader, and she's telling me all the procedures on testing. She's saying you can take the specialized test, and then the Catholic test, which is a totally different kind of test prep and um, [nervous laugh] she's kinda stressing me out! And I was telling her, "Of course it's great to be exposed to other parts of the city and I'm all for it, but you're fourteen years old when you're starting high school, fourteen, fifteen, it's a big, big thing to commute and get up at 6:30. It's like a full-time job!" And she was like, "If she was to *get into* a specialized school why, *why* would you not jump on it?" And I'm like, it's just the concept of, she probably could get into it. Regardless, it's, I don't know, I feel like that's young. I don't know. And people think this is fine. But then you talk to people and they're like "Weeell, it's you know, they don't get any sleep, they do homework on the bus." And it's like, you have your whole life to be stressed out and have a forty-hour-a-week job—why start it at fifteen? I guess it's just the mentality of what you value. Everyone values education here, but you got to have a balance. To expose a child at fourteen, fifteen into a schedule of waking up

> and getting home at five and doing work, and I don't think you'll have any social life because you're like traveling and sleeping and eating. It's too young, it really is. I mean, college is one thing, college you go away . . .

I remarked, "I don't think I worked that hard in college," and Samantha continued:

> It's mind-blowing, it really is. They get up and they sleep only four hours, and I'm like, how are they even functioning? Kids are so stressed out and they're depressed because of this constant struggle to get above everyone. You know, it's just the area, everyone is just competing for the same seats, they're competing. You have a large pool of really good, gifted children who are extremely smart and they're competing for a limited number of seats so . . . There's only so many seats and there's so many children.

Samantha then contrasted the overcrowded schools in the neighborhood (most classrooms were at the maximum capacity of thirty-two children) with that of nearby suburbs with twenty children in a classroom. "Do you realize what an extra twelve kids is to a teacher? It's unbelievable! And we just take it [crowded schools] for granted!"

Samantha's critique of the neoliberal education complex and its concentrated demands on mothers and children, with competition and scarcity exacerbated in New York, emerged through bad mom talk. Similar to other women's narratives, Samantha's bad moms were a vehicle for displacing her ire—they were rate-busters intensifying maternal labors and damaging children, although she does also mention the structural conditions that coerce mothers to perform them ("there's only so many seats and there's so many children"). Samantha also drew attention to the distinctions between appearance and reality in a manner parallel to Morgan—"then you talk to people and they're like 'Weeeeell, you know . . .'" Perhaps this is one reason that it was difficult for her to sustain her systemic critique and shifted back to mothers. It was not just that other mothers are there, in the flesh, facing her, questioning her, goading her to perform more labor. They also act with an aura of certainty about their choices. Samantha, like Morgan, felt other women's partial truth telling was deceptive. The hegemonic happiness infrastructure performs its double ideological function: It tells women they should feel unequivocally satisfied despite the deeply unsatisfying conditions of their mothering and prevents women from together discussing their shared and unique conditions of laboring. Bad mom talk thus provided a valve to release the pent-up tensions about labor conditions and their relations with other mothers, mediated as they are by the spectacle of motherhood. So many of my conversations with women were like this. I would ask what I thought would be a rather straightforward question, prompting the release of these toxic affects. It was as if their truth were waiting to explode through the facade along with years of pent-up emotions and frustrations. These conversations seemed therapeutic for mothers—they left our conversations somewhat lighter, often telling me after how good it felt to get things off their chests. Engaging in group processing in more systematic ways may be an essential part of healing justice that forges solidarities between women organizing against neoliberal motherhood.[31]

Samantha repeatedly resisted the effects of mothering for capital in the interview. In the following excerpt, the ire was directed to a neighborhood parent, although the bad mom here took the rare persona of a father:

> That's the whole thing, my daughter is really good in art and of course the teachers are like, "There are great art schools in Manhattan." And we're like, you can do that on the side, but still, how do you get into Manhattan? Well, I know how: You take public transportation but it's still an hour and a half. But no one realizes it. The neighbor next door got into Bard [a selective high school], which is in Long Island City [in western Queens], and you figure, well, it's Queens. And I just saw her, and I was like, "How's it going? I haven't seen you." And she's like, "Well, it's going good but it takes me a long time to get there, an hour and a half!" And now I see the dad drives her, and I'm like, that's not even an option! Like, you can't

> drive a child to high school, that's a full-time job! And the father does it! And I'm like, it's not elementary, this is high school! When we were young, we didn't want anyone to drive us! Now everyone gets driven everywhere—they love it! It's just a different way of life. Now, no one lets their child out of their sight. It's just people run to pick up their kids. It's just, I'm all for giving kids independence, they've got to have a sense of . . . Everyone I notice around here is so super-overprotective of their kids.

Samantha struggled to articulate the actual target of her critique: Was it mothers overprotecting children by "holding the umbrella over their head to walk to school," as she said at another point? Or was it mothers pushing children too hard to labor, as she averred previously? Or overprotective mothers coddling children and stunting adulthood? Her reflections confront her with a contradiction: "I just think, a lot of people baby their kids too much. You got to let go, maybe. But then again, but then they let them go all the way wherever to go to high school and it's a whole other scenario." Samantha struggles to articulate the problem because the contradictions of neoliberal motherhood renders women "epistemically adrift" and because its ideals chafed against her intuitions and experiences about what is right for her children.[32] Other mothers serve not only as agents of compulsion but also as extensions and subjects of that authentic curriculum.

Cemre, the thirty-four-year-old woman with three children (seven years, four years, and twenty months) from Chapter 6 points to her sisters as agents enforcing neoliberal mothering, and the fact that their accusations of being a bad mom coerced her to adopt practices that went against her intellectual judgment and eventually caused harm to her child:

> CEMRE: I *do* feel bad for my son because he, I really saw him struggling, and I put so much pressure on him, because my sister is putting so much pressure on me, "Oh you really need to nyah nyah yada yada." I even got him *evaluated*—he has nothing wrong with him! But it's all this pressure! But again, the

society expecting so much from our kids, like at three and a half because of the cutoff date, you're capable of going to pre-K, and you're, and it's a long day, and these kids need to learn this, that. No he doesn't. Actually he needs to pick his nose. These kids, my son went at three and a half, because he's November [birthday], and it starts September, that's too young!

MARIA: When I was in kindergarten, it was two hours and we were playing and singing songs!

CEMRE: That's what I'm saying, but now they're trying to get them to read! This, that! Especially with this Asian mentality. They're so into the school, that they always want their kids to do this, and get good grades.

Cemre's narrative crystallizes the multiple and opposing pressures on mothers who are expected to shepherd children through high-pressure, high-stakes childhoods, as well as the psychic burden this places on women who see the damaging effects on their children. Cemre names multiple forces that coerced her to push her child: specifically named individuals, a racialized group of "Asian" parents, and later in the conversation (see the excerpt in Chapter 5) agents of the school and the assemblage of standards, timetables, and progress reports. Like other women, Cemre began with forces personified by intimate others in her circle who pressured her to repudiate her own curriculum. She names her sisters twice: once when mentioning how one sister put "so much pressure" on her that she sought an evaluation for special education services for her child and later, both sisters countering her stance on homework. She said, "My sisters don't believe me, they think I'm like, this mother who's like blaaaah." Yet she adamantly claims she doesn't care and is unique, putting forth her own philosophy of childhood—to just let kids be kids. Although Cemre is outspoken and adamant about her own intuitions that children just need to be kids, she *still* questioned herself and repeatedly went against her better judgment. And thus she sat with a host of negative feelings—the nagging uncertainties of her way being the best path, guilt from wavering, and worst of all, the unique torture of watching her child suffer for something that she felt was arbitrarily imposed. That is, by submitting to the various forces of material and ideological compulsion, Cemre betrayed herself. In Ruddick's terms, she was inauthentically mothering.

Women's narratives reveal how they both internalize and externalize the forces of compulsion and ideologies of motherhood through and with other mothers that surround them in everyday life. To stake out and articulate their own authentic curriculum, other mothers often appear as antagonists in a battle that takes the form of appearance of the mommy wars. These moms, as individuals or as a generalized group, come to stand in for the abstract forces of domination not because the women are dupes misrecognizing the real relations in which they are embedded, but because material conditions are inscribed in subjects who then become their active or passive agents exerting pressure on women to mother in certain ways. That pressure is most visible and potent when it materializes in other mothers that love, care, and want the best for women and their children.

The spectacle of neoliberal motherhood is a force compelling intensified labors and contributes to the toxic affective states of neoliberal mothering. And there is no winning—not in submitting enthusiastically or ambivalently or in defiantly refusing. The irony of refusing the prescribed labors of intensive mothering is that, in many cases, it entails just as much or additional labors because its institutionalization ensures that it is the path of least resistance. For instance, Cemre's resistance of a high-pressure childhood entailed studying multiple other school systems and real estate listings to find a place that was not as oriented toward testing achievement, and then she single-handedly plotted a move in the middle of the school year, during winter, with an infant in tow (see Chapter 6). But here I emphasize the additional cognitive and affective labors of research and learning. It is perhaps universal that motherhood is a time of heightened and accelerated learning. Yet the enormous amount of contradictory and ever-shifting advice from econo-psy and neoliberal education complexes, coupled with its increasingly insecure futures translates to a profound existential uncertainty. The parenting industry, an appendage of the econo-psy and neoliberal education complexes, coerces intensified maternal labors and profits directly off this uncertainty in the forms of sales. Further, it keeps women occupied with sifting through the knowledge it produces, antagonized by other women, suffering from the weight of these negative affects, and then it delegitimizes and makes them second-guess their authentic knowledge. The parenting industry thus commits maternal epistemicide—the silencing of knowledge on how to care for children where life takes priority, a curriculum dangerous to the social order. While some thinkers have used language to suggest that such knowledge is innate to mothers or women, I maintain that it is available to any who have responsibility for and care for children.[33] To simply care for kids in a way they thought best within these toxic conditions, mothers had to fight against a host of forces personified in the women that surrounded them; endure feelings of inadequacy, guilt, and uncertainty; and perhaps worst of all, receive accusations that they were bad mothers.

Existential uncertainty, coupled with the various psychic pressures of opting in or out of intensive parenting, persists even for women with well-articulated critiques and developed authentic maternal thinking, as with Samantha, Cemre, and Alejandra. Alejandra, a forty-year-old woman who moved to New York City from Mexico in her early twenties, expressed this feeling when talking about how she differentiated her labors for her two children, her nine-year old daughter and five-year-old son. Her daughter was in an accelerated classroom, and she applied gentle pressure for her to achieve, whereas she did not do the same for her son:

> And [with] my son [it's] like, whatever they tell me, that's fine. And it's not that he's not smart, because he's doing very well. And sometimes I say to myself, do I push him a little more? But I don't want him to be unhappy either, I want him to have a good experience in school. But, I think, it's not, I wish I think they had it for everybody, because G&T [the gifted and talented program] to me, it doesn't say how smart is your kid. Because I know a lot of kids, they train them to pass the test and that's it, they're there for good. I know one of the moms, the teacher told her daughter, she should think

> about taking her out [of G&T]. Because she wasn't keeping up and she was unhappy. But the mother said, "No, I'm going to keep her there." Just because they say they're grandfathered [funneled] into [a highly rated middle school]. But I said to myself, "I don't think I want that for my child." You know, I want him to have a good experience, I think that's part of you know, learning too. You know, for me academics is a big thing, but if they're not happy, they're not going to succeed.

The conversation continued:

MARIA: I agree with you, you know.

ALEJANDRA: But sometimes I say to myself, am I doing wrong because I'm not pushing him that much? Because you know, I hear my surroundings, all I hear is like, "I want him to go to this specialized high school," and you know, they start from now. And I'm like, really? Am I not going to give a good opportunity to my kids? At the same time, I see some kids that are not showing any emotions because they're just, like, [there] to study. And when I see my kids smile and enjoying the childhood, I'm like, "No, I'm doing right." You know, it's like I'm mixing [mixed up]. Am I doing wrong? No, I'm doing right. Then, it's like I go back and forth. You know?

MARIA: This is like motherhood, we're always thinking, Should I be doing this?

ALEJANDRA: And you know, it's, everything I'm doing, I'm learning as I go. Because my sister-in-law, her kids are almost my age, so it's like a completely different stage, you know. My sisters, they don't have their kids here—they all live in Mexico, so it's like, it's a completely different system over there.

Alejandra's narrative echoes many themes in other women's narratives—the constant learning, the pressures, the other moms, the critiques of neoliberal childhood and schooling, competition, and scarcity. What she articulated most clearly of all my participants is the cloud of existential uncertainty that hangs over women's experiences as mothers, one that persists despite their informed resolve to do things a little bit differently, in order to do right by their kids. Alejandra rehearsed her internal dialogue at various points: "And sometimes I say to myself, do I push him more?" and "But sometimes I say to myself, am I doing wrong because I'm not pushing him that much?" Later she asks herself if she is denying her children chance in the future: "And I'm like, really? Am I not going to give a good opportunity to my kids?" She even questions her total approach: "I'm doing right. You know, it's like I'm mixing [mixed up]. Am I doing wrong? No, I'm doing right. Then, it's like I go back and forth. You know?" Alejandra's narrative captures something that is hard to perceive below the surface of bad mom talk—that women's struggles are very lonely ones. Care work—paid or unpaid—is indeed lonely, as feminist scholars have made abundantly clear. I wish to highlight that the particular kind of work in women's narratives—studying, analyzing, interpreting, evaluating, piercing contradictions, refusing, resisting, and critiquing of authoritative bodies of knowledge—is something that conventionally and ideally happens *with* others. Yet the material, ideological, and affective structures of neoliberal motherhood isolate mothers and pit them against one another and even themselves. This internal war is not a phantasm of hysterical women's brains. It is a defining characteristic of the schizophrenic maternal state, one that emerges from the material and ideological conditions of neoliberal capitalist reproduction.

Between a Psychic Rock and an Emotional Hard Place

While bad moms are readily available figures with which to think, good moms materialized much less frequently in my conversations with women. One of the rare occasions in which a good mom came up was in a conversation with Eugenia, also notable because it occasioned one of the more dramatic displays of emotional outpouring. Perhaps Eugenia's vulnerability slipped through because it was a more casual moment during a follow-up interview in which we were outside having a smoke while our kids played inside. This slip, I assert, reveals the intense negative feelings that many women must continually manage and contain behind a facade of emotional stability.

At the time I interviewed her, Eugenia was a thirty-eight-year-old teacher whose parents were born in Greece. She had a nine-year-old daughter and a three-year-old son. The good mom figure came up somewhat spontaneously when mentioning some gifts that arrived for her son from his godmother, a woman who lives in the suburbs of a Midwestern city. Eugenia was marveling about how the godmother managed to be such a good mom and recounted all the things the woman does for her own three kids—she was involved in their schooling and in the PTA, she encouraged participation in extracurriculars and ushering them to them. I asked, "Do you think she's a good mom because she doesn't have another job?" Eugenia stopped in her tracks for a few seconds before she simply said yes. She paused again and said, "A little bit." Finally, after another pause, she said: "For sure. So sad I'm going to fucking cry!" She sobbed while trying to laugh away the tears streaming down her face. "Turn this shit off!" she joked about my recorder. Eventually she regained composure and continued: "I don't know, yeah, she is always there, available. It's part of it, always available." I shrugged at the impossibility of that situation for many women like us and offered, "I mean . . ." Eugenia continued: "Very sad. But I'm saying, every single thing her kids do, and her kids do a million things, and she is there and doing all of the things. It's like *way* too much (sob laughs again). It's too much, it's a lot." I asked, "But is she there, like *there* there?" "No, she's *there*," Eugenia insisted. I conceded that the godmother is pulling off a difficult feat. I then admitted that I didn't even know how to get my child involved in sports and how I had recently become overwhelmed just trying to find a local soccer team for her and gave up. At this, Eugenia came to my defense to say that the godmother also had it easier because she didn't live in New York City. Try as we might to bring up the various factors that mitigated this woman's obstacles to the elusive good mother crown, or a better mom than us (she didn't work outside the home; she lives in a small town without the big city's competition and scarcity), Eugenia doubled down resignedly. This woman wasn't only good in the inauthentic style of her suburban neighbors (which I discuss later), Eugenia granted her the ultimate badge of authenticity: She is "the type of mom that, like, other kids want to go to your house."

In this conversation, like many others, I worked to reassure my interlocutor that she is indeed a good (enough) mom doing a good (enough) job. The reflexive strategies I used were similar to the women's, offering reasons this woman was able to do it, or to implicitly construct other women as bad moms. This was by no means premeditated. It was only in the analysis that I realized how I was responding to expressions of emotional difficulty that our conversations exposed and trying to find a way to assuage the women. It was rare for my participants to cast mothers who performs additional labors as good moms. It was as rare as the open display of defeat and vulnerability expressed in this conversation. Our conversation brings to the fore an easily overlooked point when thinking about a public sphere flooded with impossible and contradictory standards—that motherhood is saturated with psychic and emotional depths that differ radically from other identities, and that the sincere desire to do right by and for children becomes entangled with these ideologies. Indeed, that is why ideologies of mothering are so deeply embedded and felt, despite how much women may outwardly resist them.

Given that the emotional stakes of confronting a good or *better* mom are so fraught—the guilt of not doing enough for children's success, women reach for readily available bad mom figures to manage this conundrum. One strategy when faced with a mother who had taken on more labors than them was to portray their labors as excessive and to take their cue from the wider demonization of the scapegoat mother, casting their motives as selfish and the woman herself as a bad mother. Eugenia employed this tactic when she explained the drastic differences in her experiences since moving from one of the neighborhoods in my research to a wealthier Westchester County suburb. She painted an exaggerated portrait like that within movies or sitcoms, with a tight-knit crew of "alpha" mothers running school affairs and activities:

EUGENIA: Ugh, it's disgusting how parentally involved they are!
MARIA: Really?

EUGENIA: Can you go get a job, please?

MARIA: (Laughing) Are you serious?

EUGENIA: Oh God, you know the ones that are there, their names plastered on everything and the class mom reps that send you a million emails.

MARIA: Would you say it's like a small minority of superactive people or . . .

EUGENIA: The head honcho is like a parent of [child's] age, she's the head of the PTA, and they send out these letters in the beginning of who can volunteer. And I was home that year [on maternity leave], and they send out a thing [soliciting] who can do bulletin boards. And I wrote her a letter like "Please let me do the bulletin boards, I'm a teacher and this is my only time home." And she never even acknowledged my note, the bitch. Like who are you?! You're head of a PTA, you ain't head of shit!

The blatant act of disrespect from a "good" mom gave Eugenia an outlet, a clear target on which she could direct an anger that many women simply managed, suppressed, or turned inward as guilt. Eugenia was critical of the forces that compel maternal labors, but in this new upper middle class context, those forces became personified in a group of very visible women who embodied the intensive mom caricature. Eugenia relied on the mommy war battle lines of working mom versus stay-at-home mom, flipping the enshrining of the latter that reigned in this particular suburb. She comedically distanced herself from them by painting their maternal labors and entire lifestyles as serving a desperate need for attention and fulfillment in otherwise staid suburban domestic lives. "They have a fundraiser for this one big fair, and they like buy these booths just so they can have their freaking name on a booth or a freaking brick, a freaking brick!" She derided them for devoting themselves to meaningless labors that would ultimately void them of any identity of their own: "I wonder what's going to happen once their kids are older and out of school, like, are they going to melt and disintegrate? I think they're living vicariously; they must have been big losers when they were young, I on the other hand was very popular so I don't give a fuck." Eugenia's comedic and distanced scorn toward these women (pithily expressed by her conclusion) belies a much more ambivalent mix of feelings. These include her desire to be a good mom, too, although not exactly in the way expressed by these women. And it also included envy that these women could so easily manifest their ideal motherhood and be socially recognized as such. Her attitude toward these women and the way she expressed it was part of a specific classed stance. Eugenia's experience as a first-generation middle class person whose continued upward mobility landed her in an upper middle class, predominantly white suburban milieu is not uncommon. Her classed sensibility was the standpoint from which she scorned what she constructed as the carefully crafted cookie-cutter lives of "good moms." It was not unlike the experience of two other women who were also raised in racially diverse working and middle class Queens neighborhoods who were confronting intensive mothering not as part of sincere efforts to ensure children's opportunities and to give their kids things they felt they lacked in childhood, but as mere leisure pursuits and performances of femininity. Indeed, this is how Eugenia drew the line between good and bad mom—not in terms of "extra" labors but in terms of women's class trajectories. Some women like herself might engage in "extra" labors in sincere efforts to be good moms for children. Women's interpellation into motherhood positions them to other women in ways specific to geography and class that mediate the formation of gendered maternal subjectivities. Eugenia's class background functioned as a source to critique good mom ideologies and armor to defend herself from feelings of rejection and the sense of doubt about her own inability to measure up to the local ideal.

Sandwiched between scorn and sarcasm, Eugenia's vulnerability is present but submerged, and it revealed itself later in our exchange. Again, Eugenia brought up that her efforts were rebuffed, but without necessarily adding any new information. She seemed unable to let the situation go, even though it had transpired two years prior. The moment loomed so large because it crystallized her particular struggles to be a good mom. Through this caricatured good mom, Eugenia was able to deflect her anger and guilt and reflect on the impossibilities of being a good mom while being employed:

MARIA: So what do you participate in?

EUGENIA: Nothing. I pick up my kid from school. No, when I was off I did. I did do lunch duty. I tried to do bulletin boards, but that bitch didn't let me do it. And I wrote like a freakin' letter, like, "Please let me. I'm a teacher and I'm on maternity leave and this is my only year off."

MARIA: And she ignored you.

EUGENIA: And she ignored me.

MARIA: Damn. OK, to switch it up . . .

EUGENIA: No, wait, I'm trying to think what else I participate in, wait! Another thing that makes it so hard to participate is because everything is during the school day, any concern, any event is during schooltime, no concerts at night, nothing like that. Which is I guess good for the teachers but bad for the moms who work. But I'm going to assume most parents don't.

My question triggered Eugenia's guilt and activated her defense mechanisms. Her initial reply—"Nothing. I pick up my kid from school"—expressed defeat coupled with irony that distanced herself from the caricature Stepford-style moms she had painted. Underneath her outward rejection of this particular persona, Eugenia still desired to be a good mom in the double sense of doing right by her kid (picking her child up from school, something that was important for many children) and doing those arbitrary labors that are not necessarily connected to children's well-being. She began listing labors that would define her as such, and once again reached for the villain that personified her obstacles. I realized that I had inadvertently put her in this uncomfortable position with what I thought was a neutral question ("So what do you participate in?"). I tried to move past it, but Eugenia was determined to prove she did good mom things, more so for her own sake than mine. Racking her memory to come up with more things, she still came up short. The injunction "Wait!" gave her a chance to reconsider her analysis, moving from the obstacle of suburban mommy monster to that of the school's structure of parent participation. As a teacher in a New York City public school, Eugenia understood how difficult it is to be available for school events outside of the school day, so she didn't fall into the predictable position that pits parents against teachers. She recognized, as she had said earlier, that "everything sucks." The everything—the way capitalism structures our daily lives and made it increasingly difficult for most to provide care—is hard to identify and name as women juggle the various things they have to do by the prevailing standards of the day, and according to their authentic maternal curriculum. Flashes of insight amid everyday life represent partial recognitions that could serve as starting points for more robust critiques or changes in maternal practice. But amid the hustle of everyday life, it is simply easier to direct ire to other mothers. In fact, we are encouraged to do so.

Motherhood is a social relation to other mothers that is, within neoliberal capitalism, refracted through the spectacle of good, bad, and suffering mothers in the context of increasingly insecure presents and futures. Material and ideological structures condition how mothers encounter one another, making especially fraught encounters across structural locations, where some are more able to perform intensified labors than others. While cross-class encounters are the most obvious, within neighborhoods that are more or less class homogeneous, this fracture is sometimes expressed along the familiar battle lines of the so-called mommy wars; women employed in the labor force ("working moms") versus those who do not ("stay-at-home moms"). Women also expressed antagonisms that were less about one's privilege or ability to perform maternal labors and more about style or orientation to motherhood, and thus did not necessarily involve different positionalities vis-à-vis working a paid job nor the classed positionality regarding "choice." The caricature of the intensive mother within public culture and in some women's narratives was certainly classed and raced as white upper middle class. Because this talk takes certain cues from the mommy wars, it may appear as a straightforward case of "false consciousness," a misrecognition of forces coercing women's labors within neoliberal capitalism that recapitulates some of the worst stereotypes of women. Yet the repetitions, flows of topics, distancing, justifications, caricaturing, emotional bursts and seeps, injunctions like "Wait!"—all these signal a need to say something more that can't quite be said. This begs the question of what wants to be said and what it means in terms of how women understood their position within capitalist relations of reproduction. Certainly, bad mom talk expressed maternal ambivalence. But the term should not function as a gloss but signal a place to explore the psychosocial nexus of motherhood—the site where complex psychic and emotional states arise from the material conditions of neoliberal motherhood. Women are squeezed between a rock and a hard place by contradictory ideologies and punishing demands that chafed against their own knowledge and desires. Yet good mom ideologies also co-opt women's desires and rouse guilt and anxiety from their latent dormancy when provoked. Bad mom talk relieved some of this psychic pressure, and in the release, externalized ideologies that allowed women to partially recognize the impossible demands of neoliberal social reproduction and the damage they inflict, however temporarily.

The Unbearable, the Unsayable

In an essay about rewatching the family drama *The Sopranos* during the COVID-19 pandemic, Peter Coviello reflects on its powerful emotional resonance in providing a way to reflect on things "that, in the ordinary circuits of living, we cannot bear to know."[34] Although he writes about phenomena that seems distant from the women's concerns, he touches on something vital about the role of stories in helping us cope with the unbearable: "What does *The Sopranos* tell you, he asks, if not that there are things we cannot recognize, not straight on, because if we allowed them into our lives they would short the fuses, blow out all the delicate mazy wiring we need to conduct ourselves from one ailing day into the next?" Julia Kristeva made a related point—not in terms of things that are too much to bear, but in terms of the absence of language with which to bear them. She describes the work of feminist artists in late 1970s Italy who tried to express the particulars of women's experiences where there did not exist language in which to articulate it as "interwoven with the unsaid, riddled with repetitions, where women articulate, with the parsimony of their words and the ellipsis of their syntax, an innate gap of our monological culture: the saying of non being."[35] There is simply no available register or context to express contemporary mothering's emotional pulls, existential uncertainties, profound guilt, nagging doubts, sincere desires and hopes for alternatives, not even within small circles of radical feminist academic thought—and this is not my participants' language. Bad mom talk provided an oblique vocabulary to describe the profound ambivalence of neoliberal mothering, where women's labors and love devoted to children's flourishing are usurped, and it provided a space to attempt to come to terms with its ultimate tragedy: capital's bottomless appetite for value turning to children as strategic sources of investment, rendering mothers and children damaged subjects. Capitalism's abstract forms of domination are almost unthinkable outside specialist Marxist circles, and knowing that one's love, care, and work for children is ultimately in service for capital is unbearable. Neoliberal power relations make their mark on women's narratives, psyches, practices, and their relations to their children and other mothers – they face impossible labor demands, sacrifice their happiness for children's elusive futures, desire to be recognized as good moms. Yet subjectification is always and necessarily imperfect. In bad mom talk, material and symbolic relations of domination became the subject of reflection and critique, where the conditions of mothers and children were questioned as women tried to find relief from their demands and craft alternatives. Writing on parental regulation of children's academic, social, and imaginal lives within neoliberalism, Karen Lombardi writes that its demands "move us further away from the reflective thinking that allows us (parents and children) to live more fully and deeply, to claim our own thoughts and desires, to live through ourselves in ways that help us resist being caught up in the commodification machine."[36] Paradoxically, bad moms, the figures through which mothers themselves have been subject to regulation, became a vehicle for women to begin to partially apprehend the unbearable tragedy of mothering for capital.

CONCLUSION

Mothering Against Capital

Nurturing the Revolutionary Wellspring Within "the Child"

> The serious people accuse you of being a joker: Guilty.
> The jokers accuse you of being serious: Guilty.
> The adults accuse you of being a child: Guilty.
> The children accuse you of being an adult: Guilty.
>
> —*Subcomandante Marcos*

THE ONE THING I resolutely said I would not do through the years I was engaged in this project was give parenting advice. It is a requisite concluding move for anyone who has just written a book about it, as the genre nearly begs for it. And so compelled, I offer one humble, if absurdist, piece of parenting advice that is commensurate with the book's critique—a piece of advice that flips the genre on its head, that turns its pieties inside out, that laughs at its ends and means, that fans the flames of that indomitable revolutionary spirit that resides in each and every human, and that does so humorously, mischievously, playfully, childishly: "We should all mother against capital."

Each and every one of us—adult and child; mother, auntie, and sister; father, uncle, and brother; friend and cousin; comrade and accomplice—should fortify and nurture subjects against and beyond capital, nourish subjects that reject and refuse the forces that corrupt our collective human becoming and stifle our willfulness to remake the world, and nurture those qualities that prioritize the flourishing of life, conviviality, imagination, and emancipation in everyday activities, interactions, social relations, and most profoundly, in our psyches and spirit. The stakes require nothing less. The battleground of subjectivity is waged most profoundly in social reproduction, that arena that capital targets so stealthily. The most protracted struggles of our time are within everyday life, where the living subject struggles against that dreaded object.

The object here refers to what is finally the sole object across the Marxist critique of political economy—capital—the unprecedently massive force siphoned from our collective vitality thrusting to make value more by sucking human vitality hollow, insatiably and perpetually at ever-expanding scales. To those who don't connect the various compounding and exacerbating crises that humans face with capital's ferocious power to constantly remake the world in its image, Marxist analyses may seem to take a great deal of poetic license. Yet as Keston Sutherland insists, Marx's poetics are as essential as the logical and historical truths of his argument, necessary to make the "massively pressurized substance" that is "fundamentally inimical to life" resound throughout the critique.[1] For Beverley Best, capital's monstrous "gravitational force" holds at all times: It "invents a world—a mode of sociality," determines a "delimited range of forms" yet "appears not to be determinism."[2] For Peter Osborne, capital's insatiable fury to accumulate pulls, displaces, and refunctionalizes all social forms and activities toward its homogenizing and universalizing social relation.[3] For Samuel Fisher, capital is the invisible puppeteer pulling the strings that tighten the knots on our bodies and keep our jaws clenched as we spend our days at unsatisfying jobs to try to afford the things we need.[4] And as I've conveyed throughout this book, this stealthy power is ruthlessly unleashed into the most important processes and relations of childhood, distorting, stunting and disfiguring the development of subjectivity and routing it toward value's expansion. It's *not* the economy; it is capital penetrating and seeping everywhere to create a world in which life is subservient to capital, the fetish of fetishes.

For Marx, it was one of the greatest paradoxes and most telling contradictions of the capitalist order that the most powerful instruments for relieving human labor of onerous drudgery by reducing the time and strenuousness of work, within capitalism, undergo a "dialectical inversion" wherein humans are instead compelled to sacrifice more time, more energy, their freedom—even their children—to the now self-acting and self-willing force of capital.[5] On numerous occasions, Marx used the term "automaton" allegorically to convey this strange inversion of power within the modern factory as the quintessential site of capitalist labor at the time of his writing. Automatons are objects that, once set in motion by humans, operate independently of them. When Homer first used the term αὐτόματον (combining *auto*, or "self," with *matos*, or "thinking, acting, or willing"), it did not refer to the mechanics with which we now associate the term, but to the magic or witchcraft associated with the self-moving creations in the workshop of Hephaestus, the blacksmith of the gods.[6] Within the system of machines in the factory, workers must adapt their movements to the automaton's "unceasing motion," which confronts them as a "moving" or "alien power" that casts humans as "merely conscious linkages," mere "appendages of machinery."[7] The automaton taps into and sucks in human will, the powers of human cooperative relations, universal human attachments to community, and collective human knowledge, ingenuity, and creativity. It captures and reroutes them, perverting them to its own self-acting motion and will—the one globally dominant force, a force whose immense power is unprecedented in human affairs, one to which all must be subservient. Thus, the automaton is value itself, "the automatic subject," the "dominant subject" of capitalist society, "the capitalist socius as a whole."[8]

The automaton, Marx spelled out explicitly, is an autocrat.[9] Mothering for capital can best be understood through the frame of one vast machine of human capital theory casting each home, each mother and child, into appendages for creating value. The spectacle of motherhood, the disguise of the middle class project, the various crises of childcare, and the struggles of mothers and children in everyday life—all are manifestations of the radical restructuring of social reproduction in neoliberalism, mothers and children entrapped in endless alienating labors to construct children as the ultimate sacrifice and gift to capital. By subsuming social reproduction, capital reinscribes class, gender, and racialized divisions and legitimates them in the guise of "freedom"—the freedom to pursue the middle class project, a moral order whose primary obligations to the social are replaced by obligations to capital. Within social reproduction, capital drives us to bolster its undead reign by tapping into the wellspring of the developing human subject—the child, hijacking our elementary universal needs and desires to belong to human communities as valued members, and rerouting them to the global middle class project of not simply having but *becoming* value for capital.

A child value theory of maternal labor accounts for how capital's most treacherous weapons are deployed in this seemingly apolitical sphere—convincing, coaxing, and coercing mothers that the only way to ensure their child can participate in the global community of capital is to work, endlessly, tirelessly, cheerfully, toward augmenting their child as an embodiment and repository of value. Treacherous in its subtlety—transforming time for play, rest, leisure, dinner, bed, and free time, into so-called opportunities to augment and enhance the child's value and thus serve capital—the "silent compulsion of economic forces" seizes our "vital forces . . . at their very roots."[10] Treacherous in its cunning—presenting parents with promises of best practices, successful children, happy children, psychologically stable, calm, "well adjusted" children, productive children, "emotionally intelligent" children, future "leaders" who are self-regulated and socially aware, "investments in futures"—all distorted, perverted, bewitched so that individual moral, ethical, social, and professional development serve the community of capital as the only possible configuration of our collective global sociality. Economists, the "secular priesthood" of this global community of capital, prescribe to mothers more than to any other workers in the so-called labor force that they must serve; renounce their own needs and desires; sacrifice bodies, minds, souls, dreams, and fantasies for their child to belong to "society" by being well adapted to the only possible world, the community of capital.[11] Mothers, I emphasize, are the most vulnerable to capital's demands; they are veritable hostages because their labors are so crucial, caught in-between the present and future of capital's reproduction. Children are too curious, too imaginative, too playful, and therefore too willful to capture directly, and human willfulness is what Marx identified as capital's natural limits, and precisely what it drives to squelch.[12] Capital targets this revolutionary wellspring within each child through the emotional chains of motherly subjection. Thus, the social reproduction of the child is where capital wages its most protracted "organized suppression of individual vitality, freedom, and independence."[13] This is not "only" about mothers or children, however: The stakes are for virtually everyone as they concern how we are to be subordinated, always in new, unforeseen, and more intensive ways, to capital's reproduction. The autocrat drives, pushes, coerces, tricks, and blackmails mothers to snuff out the revolutionary will to life in each child and orient all of what's left to generating and expanding value.

Value, Marx finally concluded, is dead labor.[14] A society in which value is the dominant force is the rule of the undead over the living. The undead can rule only by sucking life hollow and depleting it. This undead force is personified in humans whether we are conscious of it or not, whether we like it or not—we must don the character masks of our categorical role in capital's unending drama of accumulating value or perish! We don't simply put these masks on at "work" and take them off when we come home—all of life is a social factory, reproduction time is productive time. We must always be better, fitter, rested just enough to make value more, to make ourselves into value. These masks seem to become "irremovable visages," grafted on to subjects who "embody and live" capital's desires, value becomes our "'inner eyes' which with we look through our physical eyes."[15]

Behind the overt and explicit directives to mothers to construct their children as self-managing and manageable subjects for capital, the autocrat implants and manifests itself in its subjects as profound emotional attachments to hierarchies and relations of domination, to fractures in social relations and fractured individual consciousness, to morbid attachments to what exists, to venerating capital's fetishes, to what looks like a second nature of scoffing at and thwarting desires and dreams of other worlds, to capturing and taming escape, to homogenizing unruly multilinear paths of human becoming, to extinguishing the flourishing of life, autonomy, and convivial collectivities. Value produces a profoundly antisocial sociality where the pursuit of "happiness" pits human against human, a sociality composed of deeply fractured subjects who are formed against their own selves, their own life, *life itself*. The object—capital—strives for unprecedented hold over the developing subject. That same force whose ruthless drive for expansion sends millions traveling across militarized borders and treacherous terrain, millions into the dark depths of the earth to mine its riches, depletes and pumps toxins into the soil rendering it scorched and barren, the land pockmarked, and the sea a whirl of plastic and poisons, with billions wheezing for fresh air and thirsting for clean water—that same force quietly sets its sights and takes aim at the will to live free when it is at its brightest and most fierce—the young child.

Where is the hope in any of this? Where is the humor?

It is in fact deeply funny to consider how, to the massive undead force of capital, any one child is a mighty, if tiny, force to reckon with. More than funny, it is gleeful to ponder that any and every single child poses a threat to capital, that each and every child is "in-and-against-and-beyond" capital and constitutes its crisis.[16] The colossal machine of human capital theory, the whole dismal science of the political economy of motherhood, the massive econo-psy complex and its neoliberal education industry—all are expressions of capital's crisis, manifested in the immense efforts on a global scale, the billions of dollars spent daily to target children, to homogenize their boundless and limitless creativity, and to hammer their willfulness into an exchangeable and measurable abstraction of value, to penetrate them through schools and nonprofits and, ultimately, through their mothers' love and care, offering those responsibilized with their future seemingly irresistible bargains, threatening them with abandonment and misery. And yet—kids still wriggle away, refuse, shout "NO!" They pretend, fib, escape. And most of the time, they don't even bother to thumb their noses at those of us tasked with constraining and disciplining their life force, homogenizing them, managing their labor, distorting their becoming, and deforming their willfulness toward value. They are simply too busy *doing* otherwise. This is uproariously funny!

And this joyous laughter expresses the subversive spirit of mothering against capital—nurturing the emancipatory and liberatory substances in the subject, the spontaneous critiques and imagining of other worlds, the flourishing of life, activities and dispositions and relations that fortify subjects in-and-against-and-beyond capital, the revolution of everyday life.

It's quite possible, likely even, that my parenting advice is being misunderstood as concerning what and how to teach children about being against and beyond capital. And this is funny too, though mischievously so, because it is precisely the reverse! Nearly everyone makes this mistake. It's one that has bedeviled radical thought for centuries—the most brilliant critics of capitalism, the fiercest revolutionaries—even, to use that most holy moniker—Marx *himself*. Who among us, the *we* who long for human emancipation, for making other worlds, who sincerely enjoy being with children, has not entertained the dream of molding children for those other more noble worlds, has not imagined instilling in children our own words of wisdom? I admit the joke is on me too. For the things we presume to teach, the traits and attitudes and dispositions we want to instill and nourish, and so much more—much, much more than we can attain, even in our wildest art or dreams—all already exist in children. In their very being, at their nerve endings, they feel and live them, in a big way. It is within us that these bold aspirations lie fallow, having been stifled and buried, with our own help, deep within us.

Mothering against capital means caring, relating, and being with children and one another in ways that nourish the willful unpremeditated emancipatory pulses that already reside with children. It means being in solidarity with children in ways we have never known, for it requires, as Madeline Lane-McKinley argues so passionately, being against adult supremacy, an ideology that is inherently anti-utopian.[17] To rephrase James Baldwin's insight about white identity for white supremacy: If you think you're an adult, there's no hope for you—it's "absolutely a moral choice."[18] Solidarity with children and the child-in-us entails treason to adulthood. And learning from children in a playfully serious and seriously playful way entails radical epistemic, moral, political, and imaginative leaps—it requires daring and discomfort. For the seemingly innocent practice of teaching children is built on a foundation of children's supposed "unknowing," their "underdeveloped" or "developing" status, a seemingly naturally subordinate relationship in which adult domination is good, necessary, and, more likely, unthinkable and absurd otherwise.

To propose learning from children entails unlearning our primary disposition toward capitalism's foundational and most entrenched form of domination, learned within familial relations. While children first learn about domination within the family, adults perhaps learn even more about domination in their relation to children. After all, adults are the ones who naturalize and cling to this authority, who cannot imagine a world where adults did not control children. Children every day denaturalize their subordinate status—and more! They unrelentingly question the most taken-for-granted truths and categories, flip the most cherished values of the social order—that is, they revert the bewitched truths and inverted ideals of capital, right side up. Furthermore, mothering against capital means nurturing the child within us, the child whose presence we stubbornly disavow and suppress. It means being childish, laughing at ourselves, playing, being absurd and "irrational" even. Being childish is also profoundly serious business—it means studying the world in an embodied way, confronting the unbearable, dwelling on irresolvable contradictions of caring in and for the world, destroying without the blueprint for rebuilding—much like children do every day.

The childish capacities of children and ourselves are crucial contributions to emancipatory theories and practice, and any and all that do not include the child are always already desiccated and half-dead. And although emancipatory theories begin with the autonomous subject, only a few intrepid thinkers have dared to include children in these projects, to allow children to present to us our upside-down world through their eyes, to learn from the endless reservoir of willfulness against the homogenizing and alienating rule of capital. Despite his ban on images (*Bilderverbot*) of utopia, Theodor Adorno saw in children that wellspring of utopian thought that was not yet tainted by the perverted social relations in which they are embedded.[19] For both Adorno and Ernst Bloch, whose utopian thought indelibly shaped Adorno, the ineffable absolute of utopia "shines into everyone's childhood."[20] Adorno's *Minima Moralia* contains more than a few gestures to children as always already against and beyond capital, and one of the only references where this fierce seemingly pessimistic critic of the "wrong life" mentions a right one. In play, "the child, by subterfuge, sides with use-value against exchange value," purposeless and useless activity that "remains true to their destiny" that does not "subserve the exchange relation that equally deforms humans and things . . . The unreality of games gives notice that reality is not yet real. Unconsciously they rehearse the right life."[21]

Day in and day out, children don't simply rehearse otherwise relations; they live them, practice the usefulness of uselessness, push against value, escape value, and live beyond value. Children make "utopian thought and practice more usable," as Toni Cade Bambara showed us in her exuberant fiction, laughing as they punch the deathly apparatuses of power in the nose and moving in the world as if it already were fundamentally alterable, as if they were already free.[22] Their incessant whys, unremitting nos, relentless "it's not fairs," their screams and refusals, the perpetual turning their backs to do their own things—these are the signs we should be reading as precise diagnoses of what is really wrong about this life. And despite incessantly confronting adults with such truths, critical theory does not bother to grapple with children's perspectives about how wrong this life is, or the millions of escapes and possibilities of living what might be called the right life. Further still, how we might nourish and route these playful, creative, subversive energies to further capital's crises—not teleologically oriented toward a monumental revolutionary event but in millions of everyday revolutions against the regime of value. We, every single one of us, somehow get pulled into an extraordinarily complex and powerful machinery that initiates subjects into value as the master signifier of our global order; we are all responsible for making value the inner and outer eyes through which we view self and others.

One need not have children to be automatically invested in the middle class project—the global form of the profoundly antihuman, antisocial, prohierarchical and hence protofascist war against life in which individual or family survival-cum-success depends on a material and ideological infrastructure legitimating a wide swath of the worlds' people suffering and struggling to eke out the most basic necessities for the false promise and illusion of security, convenience, and "standard of living" of the few. The autocracy of the automaton (capital) has transformed the means of our existence so that any and every innocent wish for individual comfort or success, any admiration for individual accomplishment or genius is necessarily the reproduction of a subjectivity that treasures accumulation and reveres hierarchy, and hence upholds a social order that worships death. Sadly, the middle class project and its hierarchical dispositions commonly persist and flourish in the very spaces where critical theories develop and anticapitalist practices are promoted—that is, in academia and activist circles—spaces where one might expect it to be otherwise. Rather than taking these misfortunes of adult life as a sign of despair, however, this project affirms that alternative worlds that prioritize life and love and care and rest and play assert themselves, persist, and sometimes thrive in the everyday lives of mothers and children, despite all efforts to keep them ensnared in capital's reproduction.

Children, I am not the first to propose, are already anarcho-communists. My work with four-, five-, and six-year-old kids demonstrated how they despised being homogenized and abstracted into value, despised being initiated into a hierarchy of humanness, despised the individualism and competition and scarcity of success, despised the instrumentalization of their activities and their time.[23] These spontaneous dispositions remind us what is truly at stake in emancipation, inviting us to extricate this force within ourselves, to route our anger (subdued, turned inward, or outward to others) toward the object in a way that fortifies our spirit and nourishes our collective conviviality to live freely.

Mothering for capital means looking at children's radical subjectivities and perspectives square in the face to rethink what it means to be human, to highlight what is fundamental and indispensable to our becoming human, to rupture the half-starved bio-economic notion of what it means to be human and symbolically nourish ourselves with new origin stories of our species. How we engage with children, relate to them and the child within is key to nourishing and engaging the multiple utopias that already exist and that spring forth anew with each child. *Autovalorizzazione*, or self-valorizing activities, de-linking or making power destitute, practicing hope in hopeless times, transforming phenomenological reality, all revolutionary traditions need to mother against capital—to incorporate the child into the rewriting, reimagining, and enacting multiple overlapping revolutions of everyday life.[24] Children are already convivial subjects—born with abilities and desires to enact the fundamental human condition of sociality. Children seek and create convivialities, they embody what Raoul Vaneigem defined as "radical subjectivity," the "consciousness that all people have the same will to authentic self-realisation and that their subjectivity is strengthened by the perception of this will in others."[25] They have not been "taught" these things, I underline, yet they can guide and nourish our imagination and our will.

The imperatives of capital's reproduction compel adults, and mothers most profoundly, to stamp out children's social and subjective orientation to life, to extinguish this open-ended conviviality and route this vitality toward the ends of producing value. Value tyrannizes children, and through children's suffering, their refusals, their practices and imaginings otherwise, and their joy-seeking life force, we can see anew our own submission to and complicity with tyranny, and thus intensify our resolve to refuse the yoke of this undead force that invisibly binds us, and strengthen our determination to make other worlds. To mother against capital means that adults should refuse the necrophilic drives to power, the cheap tricks and empty promises that lock us into the endless treadmill of capital's spiraling vortex. To mother against capital means that we nourish the qualities that fortify us for struggle, which is, most profoundly, against hierarchy and against value.

At the outset of this book, I averred that the question that underlay my project—what, then, is *for* children's own good and to what ends should love and work of care for children, ourselves, and others, be for?—could not be answered by it. While I have centered children in this conclusion, I must return to the women whose struggles are represented in this book, to their desires and longings. These women wanted simple things—time to be with their kids outside of work, time outside of managing children's work, time not cleaning up the damages of children's work, time to prioritize relations, time to exist outside or apart from their "jobs" as mothers, security for their children, a sense of comfort and freedom from fear of impoverishment. They wanted simple things, but these were simple things that would require "abolish[ing] the present state of things."[26] These women, who would ordinarily not be of interest to any academic or activist, and their humble gestures and longings and everyday practices, give me hope, because their mundane struggles confirm for me the most beautiful realization—everyone hates capital! What could be more joyful, then, than being engaged in practices and relations that further this hatred, deepen the love for children and life itself, and nurture the willful spirit that animates them both?

Appendix

NOTES ON METHODOLOGY

"Off to Pretend I'm a Good Mom"

THIS PROJECT BEGAN with my own estrangement from external demands to be a "good mom," feeling trapped into taking on a set of labors that seemed obligatory, labors that were depleting me, labors that often put me in an adversarial relation to my kid. The mothers around me similarly seemed to be struggling to keep their heads above water. I was further fueled to take on this project as a rejoinder to the scapegoat caricature of the "intensive mother" whose hyper-competitive status signaling and striving to keep up or get ahead of the Joneses is widely purported to exacerbate neoliberal austerity, deny opportunities to other children, and create an "arms race" of parenting. I was in the midst of a spectacle, but I did not quite understand what it concealed. When the opportunity for a research sabbatical arose, I devised a project that would allow me to scrutinize the "good mom" phenomenon and go beyond its surface form to the social relations of struggle beneath it. It was a project that would also allow me an opportunity to inhabit the "good mom," that is, engage in things I did not ordinarily have time to do as a university professor—from things that were important to my kid, like picking her up from school and hanging out while she played in the park, to things long associated with being a good mom, like being more attentive to her schooling and volunteering for events, and finally, performing the slew of new good mom practices that my own mother wouldn't recognize—attending "parent workshops" and adopting prescribed "partner teacher" activities in my home. At these times, I engaged in many informal conversations with mothers and caregivers that informed this project. Most ethnographers would agree that there is no clear separation between the participant and observer roles within ethnography's principal method. This is the case for this book as well. Its main source of data was participant observation, if an estranged participant, of my own and other women's circumstances and experiences trying to be a "good mom." I would occasionally joke about this double duty of mothering fieldwork that I was "off to pretend I'm a good mom."

My interlocutors are women who I encountered in my parenting milieu—that is, women I met through school events, extracurricular activities, parks, playgrounds, libraries, and through the snowball technique (see the introduction and Chapter 6 for more information about the women and the geographical setting). The racial and ethnic diversity of my participants, their recent middle-classness, and their concerted efforts to be "good moms"—moving into the area and paying inflated prices for housing so that their children could access "good schools"—meant that the maternal labors that are understood as "best practices" or maligned as "intensive mothering" were, in a sense, already defamiliarized. When inviting women for interviews, I asked if they would be willing to participate in my research about "the work of being a mom." The subsequent consent form was phrased as "how parents' care work shapes their own lives and their children's lives and how it is related to the neighborhood in which you live." I told women that we could meet anywhere convenient to them and gave choices of my home, theirs, a café, or walk and talk. Most women opted to meet me in my house, a few interviews were conducted in their homes, and one in a cramped PTA closet-office. Even if this was the first time we had spoken beyond a few casual words in public, these interviews very quickly became intimate affairs, and often very emotional. We sat for two to three and a half hours: The time flew by, and the interview usually came to a close because one or both of us had some child duty to attend. The instant intimacy was afforded by the positions I shared with many women—mother, neighborhood resident, first-generation US born. Although I am white, dialogues with nonwhite women were less guarded in terms of race than with white women because the women were aware of my professional profile as a race scholar (my first book was about kids learning race in New York City), and the intersections in our racial politics. Racial politics are quickly evident in any casual talk between parents, where almost every school and neighborhood issue is racialized or racially coded. These sometimes involved citywide hot-button issues (the debate about ending the city's "gifted and talented" programs pitting Asian and white parents against Black and Latine parents) to local not-quite issues where race emerged (rumors that school overcrowding was due to Asians using local addresses; a local high school no longer being "good" because it now served Black and Brown students from a high school that was shut down). Although it was not a premeditated strategy, upon reflection I can see how my reflexive decoding of coded speech and naming of how whiteness or racism structured a particular phenomenon enabled frank race talk with women of color within and outside the interview space.

Although I was hyperattuned to power dynamics of race and class (the latter because of status differences associated with educational attainment), I was not prepared to confront the most marked differential in interviews with long-term stay-at-home mothers. I naively believed that my agnosticism about women's so-called choice would be transparent to women. Although I was aware of the feminist scorn of women who stay at home, I had not reckoned with how profoundly the implicit injunction to "have it all" affected these women. And here I was, traipsing around doing "good mom" things while also conducting research—the very embodiment of having it all! Many of the women, with paid jobs or not, expressed some form of admiration of a career that evidently gave me flexibility to "have it all." My challenge was explaining that I did *not* have it all, without alienating women with my account. I found some way of expressing the truth to be the most effective, in short, that I too was "losing it" along with them. The various subtleties and missteps in my interviews represent the repair work that women have to perform to relate with women and build solidarity across manufactured antagonisms. To talk about motherhood is to tiptoe with trepidation across a minefield where one misstep can unintentionally level a profound insult that disregards a woman's struggles, including the existential ones that are the subject of this book.

Although fully prepared to document the intensified work of mothering, I was not prepared to document women's existential struggles, their unfathomable doubt, guilt, and anxiety that my interviews reveal. Women arrived bursting with their dramas, and I let conversations unfold organically. Unequivocally, the women determined the form and substance of our conversations and their own narratives. One woman spent two of our three hours talking about the tragic death of her first love, over fifteen years prior. I did not see this as a "failed" interview even though it did not generate much "data." In fact, I am gratified to have created a space that gave women what they needed at that moment. Rather than seeing the ethnographic encounter as principally a strategic method of "collecting data," I understand it as a human encounter based in relationality and respect. I describe the ethico-political stance that guides the encounter as one of "surrender—or a methodology of intellectual love," one that allows participants control over how our time together is spent, vis-à-vis the direction and flow of conversation, a practice that inevitably shapes the analysis and representation of phenomena.[1] This means that the analysis too was guided by the women's words and silences—the vicissitudes in the comfort of our talk, the shifts in emotion, the gentle twists and abrupt turns in themes. I followed their doubts, traced their inchoate fears, and intuited their hopes beyond what could be said. Most profoundly, surrendering to the women's narrative agendas reveals the depths of the transformations of mothering at the subjective, emotional, and psychic level. Indeed, honoring these women's experiences—their desires, fears, anxieties, small joys, victories, and hopes for their children—inspired my efforts to develop the somewhat unorthodox conceptual apparatus of this book. Although their children and my own child were not my participants, these kids and their struggles to *be a kid*, to play and explore and learn and grow in all the distinct ways that kids do, ways that bump against the dominating homogenizing hollowing power of capital, inevitably shaped this project. Their indomitable spirits hovered, goading me to keep going until I could convincingly demonstrate that their struggles are all our struggles—to be free.

ACKNOWLEDGMENTS

SHE'S NUMBER ONE on this list because she is the only person without whom this book would not exist, not in this form nor any form at all, my daughter, Markella. It's not that she made me a mother in the practical or even sentimental sense. Much more profoundly, I thank her for her fierce and staunch refusal of any of my attempts at "good mothering"—it is her fire that lies at the very center of this book. My deepest wish is for her to carry this fire forward with her and wield it in the good fight, forever, ftou ftou ftou.

I would like to thank my co-parent Daniel and my parents for their continued love and support with caring for M. I am grateful to my favorite people on earth, my nieces Joanna Pony Pone and little Georgie simply for existing. I also want to thank my spirit child, Meredith Fazzone, for caring for me as much as the reverse.

I thank my participants for the gift of their time, for their determination to make our conversation their own. While this book likely looks so different from what they may have imagined, I hope they recognize that its strange shape and language represent my most concentrated efforts to represent their struggles. They have my deep and enduring gratitude for sharing them with me.

The initial fieldwork research was made possible by a sabbatical award from William Paterson University, and I am so thankful. I was very fortunate to receive it, because what followed was a six-year period of austerity, including the elimination of any support for research, and the fear and insecurity of layoffs. I should also acknowledge those tasked with managing my labor through this time for inadvertently contributing to some of the book's key insights. Their efforts helped me discern how the alienating forces subjecting my professional labors were the very same ones subsuming my maternal labors. Further, the gusto with which they don capital's character masks underlined my insights about the irrationality of capital's drive.

I also thank my colleagues Lili, Murli, Vidya, Jason, Navyug, and Corey for their friendship and for brightening up the workplace. I am also grateful to the hundreds of students whose insights and enthusiasm shaped this project, especially those in my childhood course. I want to specifically acknowledge Oliver Bornheimer Briana Crudup, Ayana Harper, Nicole Visco, Yetunde Ojo, and Jess Philips.

Portions of this book were previously published in *Antipode* and *Capital & Class*; I thank the journals for permission to republish the material. I also thank the University of Chicago Press for permission to reprint figure 3.1.

I would be remiss if I did not shout out the Twitter gang (2019–2023) who sustained me in various ways during a significant chunk of time when this book was gestating. The Marxist gang whose humor and good spirits might even top their intellectual insights: Adam Ahlgrim, Nate DuFord, Sam Fisher, Nate Holdren, Dom Knowles, Kirsten Munro, and Chris O'Kane; Jeff Melnick, for being everyone's Twitter dad; Elisabeth Nicula, for bringing beauty and wisdom every day; the kid liberationists Carol Black, Idzie Desmarais, and Madeline Lane-McKinley; and the uncategorizable, singular Tim Clarke.

I am so grateful to Roberto Greco for the hours of conversation about childhood, schooling, technology, capitalism, and anything under the sun. I also thank him for sending me things he knew would get me seething (we snack for capital!). I am also grateful to eli thorkelson for the many hours talking about the weirdness of parenting and the irreducible weirdness of kids. Her endless insights marked this book in subtle yet profound ways. I also thank new mom and old friend Nadeen Thomas, and Jean Hunleth for organizing the writing retreats and for being a wonderful human and anthropologist extraordinaire.

Thank you to Joshy Poo, Lisa L., Jed B., Jed T., JP, and Christine for sticking around as my friends; to my sister Irene, cousins George, Anna, John, and Ali, Julie and Kirk, and Sandy and Dante for sticking around as my family; and to my beautiful dog baby Bea for everything!

So many thanks to Martha Lincoln for reading and commenting on an early draft of what is now Chapters 2 and 3; I appreciate her sharp insights that helped me develop those arguments and her friendship. I appreciate my conversations with Harry Cleaver during the writing of this book, and I am grateful for his insights and enthusiasm for the project. I so appreciate my cousin from another grandmother, Alexandros Orphanides, for his comments on an early draft of what is now Chapter 4, for being such a thoughtful friend throughout this project; his humor and laughter give me so much life.

So many thank-yous to the incomparable dynamo Gianna Mosser, for all of her efforts, her enthusiasm, for assembling an excellent team—Patrick, Jenna, and Joell—to Katherine Faydash for the wonderful work on the copyedits, and to the two reviewers for their thoughtful and generous comments. I am so grateful to have been able to hand over my baby to Gianna and to have been able to feel so confident and secure that it was in such good hands—this comfort was so important to me, thank you so, so much!

Finally, I thank Nicholas De Genova. What a joy it has been to share this journey with him. It would be inconceivable to express what and how much he has meant to this project—he read every word, probably thrice, and always came through with whatever I needed. What a joy to discuss each and every insight with him, to rap about "metaphysical subtleties and theoretical niceties," and to work alongside him while he pens the mighty MM. I won't go on and thankfully, he understands why, as he always does, my brilliant friend, ftou ftou ftou.

NOTES

Introduction

1. The ten-second video was posted on the social media site Twitter (now X), where it received over ten million views, thirty-six thousand "likes," and replies from over four hundred people, mostly mothers, echoing the importance and effectiveness of reading to newborns and fetuses, and some asking what more they could do. Wuori, "Read to Your Newborn." One man replied, "Absolutely the best tweet or x [he] had read all day. God Bless the Mom." For images of the caricature of the helicopter mom, see Pinsker, "Intensive Parenting"; Druckerman, "Bad News"; Strauss, "How to Know"; Kamentz, "Overparenting Crisis." The primal scream of the third panel in the triptych is from the *New York Times* report of the pandemic's effect on "working mothers"; Grose, "Primal Scream."
2. US Surgeon General, "Parents Under Pressure."
3. Hays provides one of the first early examples of feminist critique of intensive parenting in *Cultural Contradictions.* See O'Reilly's "Maternal Theory" for a constructive summary of this vast scholarship.
4. This mode of analysis is rooted in the Bourdieusian problematic of class reproduction via extraeconomic means of cultural capital and social capital. Bourdieu outlined how the specific lifeways and experiences of particular groups in society give rise to a set of knowledge, skills, and dispositions (cultural capital). In this perspective, the cultural and social capital of the middle class are valued and rewarded by dominant institutions (school and work) and help reproduce middle class status. Conversely, forms of capital of the working classes, however valuable in their social milieus, are devalued in dominant institutions and hamper chances of mobility into the middle class. Annette Lareau's *Unequal Childhoods* best exemplifies this interpretive vein, outlining the ways middle class mothers bequeath cultural, social (and later linguistic, symbolic, and even psychological) capital to ensure children's future middle class status or success. The book was declared an "instant classic" by its publisher, and inspired a so-called Lareau tradition on family and class reproduction, with over fourteen thousand citations to date in scholarship and media articles on parenting. For reviews, see Cooper and Pugh, "Families Across the Income"; Davies and Rizk, "Three Generations"; Kalil and Ryan, "Parenting Practices"; Nomaguchi and Milkie, "Parenthood and Well-Being."

5. Lareau, and others after her, construct blunt typologies of middle class versus working class parenting strategies, as "concerted cultivation" versus "accomplishment of natural growth," respectively, portraits that mirror caricatures of working class and middle class parenting circulating in the public sphere.
6. The so-called father of American sociology, Frank Lester Ward (1872), best exemplifies the normative, moral, and political thrust of traditional sociology in this quote, cited in Bowles and Gintis, *Schooling in Capitalist America*, 26–27, emphasis added. The Laureau tradition criticizes mothers for acting unfairly as conduits of (dis)advantages or, in more critical registers, the *way* the school system allocates slots on the basis of unfairly bequeathed maternal (dis)advantages. Inequality is a problem only insofar as how it is achieved is corrupted or unfair. That is, if children accrued advantages through their own efforts, skills, and capacities, equality of opportunity would reign, and inequalities would be based on fairly won and legitimate achievements.
7. E.g., Calarco, *Holding It Together*; Collins, *Making Motherhood Work*.
8. E.g., Bandelj and Spiegel, "Pricing the Priceless"; Bandelj, "Social Life of Money"; Griffen, "Economization of Early Life."
9. Garbes's recent bestseller, *Essential Labor*, is framed through a critique of capitalism and colonialism that devalues and makes the work of mothering "lonely." Montei's *Touched Out* focuses more directly on her tormenting bodily experience of mothering, which she describes as "created by bad policy and an exploitative economic system that relies on unpaid, underpaid, and unrecognized care work . . . foundational to capitalism" (43). The wide attention received by these books in popular culture can be seen in examples such as Tolentino, "Can Motherhood Be," and Wheeler, "Motherhood Radicalized Me."
10. Knott, *Mothering Is a Verb*. See also Gumbs, "M/Other Ourselves"; Lewis, "Mothering Against the World," on mothering as a verb. The emphasis on doing and experience in contemporary critical work is based on Adrienne Rich's foundational distinction between motherhood as institution and ideology versus mothering as experience. Rich, "Of Woman Born"; O'Reilly, "Maternal Theory," 19.
11. Heaney, "Introduction: Feminism Against Cisness," 1.
12. Marx, *Capital*, 460 (Reitter).
13. Marx, *Capital*, 372 (Reitter).
14. Marx, *Capital*, 899 (Fowkes); see recent elaborations of "silent" or "mute" compulsion in Bonefeld, *Critical Theory of Economic Compulsion*, and Mau, *Mute Compulsion*.
15. Marx, *Capital*, 61 (Reitter). The term *character mask* is not as widely known in English-language Marxism because in the most widely used translation of *Capital*, Ben Fowkes does not use the term. Baasch explains how Fowkes translated Marx's "ökonomischen Charaktermasken der Personen"—economic character masks of persons—as "the characters who appear on the economic stage." Baasch, "Theater of Economic Categories," 30. If the term had been used, the quotation would appear as such: "As we proceed to develop our investigation, we shall find, in general, that the *economic character masks* of persons are only the personifications of economic relations; it is as bearers of these economic relations that they come into contact with one another." Marx, *Capital*, 179

(Fowkes), emphasis added. Fowkes translates the other four instances of character masks as "role," "dramatis personae," "economic character," and "social mask." Marx, *Capital*, 170, 249, 711, 757. In his recent translation of *Capital*, Reitter translates it as the simple "economic actor's masks." Marx, *Capital*, 61, 122. Rodney Livingstone translates Adorno's use of Marx's term in the most arresting way as "economic character masks." Adorno, *History and Freedom*, 69. Adorno used Marx's term to emphasize that, even when humans appear to be in control "in the history they allegedly make," humans "continue to be determined by the universal," his term for capital's progressive rationality of dominating nature, including "inner nature" (subjectivity), an influence that he described definitively as "negative." Adorno, *History and Freedom*, 70.

16. O'Kane, "Critique of Real Abstraction."
17. Sutherland, "Poetics of Capital," 218.
18. Elson, "Value Theory of Labour," 174.
19. Baumann, "Adorno, New Reading," 70.
20. De Genova, "Toward a Marxian Anthropology," 133–34.
21. Virno, *Grammar of the Multitude*, 78.
22. It is important to state at this juncture that, although I emphasize how children are *made* subjects, in no way do I consider them "blank slates" with no agency in the central processes that are the focus here. Children, including infants, shape their own and others' trajectories and the contexts in which they are inserted, but far from "just as they please," as critical childhood scholars have pointed out. See S. Ferguson, "Children, Childhood"; Spyrou et al., "Introduction." While the field of critical childhood studies largely ignores psychoanalytic insights about the complexity of the child psyche, my perspective is informed by Melanie Klein's understanding of the richness of the young human's emotional and mental life in her "Development of a Child," "Psychoanalytic Play," and "Early Stages." Britzman elegantly summarizes Klein's work as revealing the infant's psychical life as "operatic: preludes without words, sounds and silences, and then, as rapidly changing scenes of protagonists and their nemeses sent on absurd missions and obeying inexplicable commands that defend against anxiety, suffering, loss, and the poignancy of thinking." Britzman, *Melanie Klein*, 2.
23. If capitalism launches new models of subjectivity the way the automobile industry launches new models of cars, then mapping how capital forges links between political economy and "subjective economy" becomes one of critical theory's urgent tasks. Guattari cited in Lazzarato, *Signs and Machines*, 8.
24. Cleaver, *Thirty-Three Lessons*.
25. Marasco, "There's a Fascist," 299.
26. Harvard Business Review, Emotional Intelligence.
27. Weeks, *Problem with Work*, 56.
28. This is Spinoza's ([1667] 2015) conatus, as defined in *Ethics*, pt. 3, proposition 6.
29. Capriglione, "Food & Nutrition"; Murkoff, "Play Music for Baby"; Loververy, "Play Kit"; Bedtime Math, "Bring Math to Life."
30. Griffen, "Economization Early Life," 181.
31. Slobodian, *Hayek's Bastards*, 23.
32. Roediger, *Sinking Middle Class*, 2–6.

33. Kalb's analysis focuses on how global institutions such as the World Bank, the National Intelligence Council, and the Organisation for Economic Co-operation and Development encourage the discourse of the "global middle class" as a way to neutralize the possibility that the masses would see themselves as part of a class struggle with global elite. Kalb, "Class," 160. Kalb deconstructs how "middle class" currently functions as an "empty sign" that includes virtually anyone who lives on more than five dollars a day and is not rich. For example of this hegemonic discourse, see Kharas, "Rise of the Global," who touts that the majority of people in the world are now "middle class."
34. Roediger, *Sinking Middle Class*, 6–7; Olin Wright, "Continuing Importance of Class."
35. Marx, *German Ideology*, 7.
36. Marx, *Eighteenth Brumaire*, 1.
37. Marx and Engels, *German Ideology*, 7.
38. Marx and Engels, *German Ideology*, 175.
39. G. Rose quotes St. Silouan the Athonite in the epigraph to *Love's Work*.
40. For analysis of how women's childhood memories of their mothers influenced their maternal labors, see Kromidas, "When I Was."
41. The Social Genome Project is a collaboration between the Brookings Institution's Center for Children and Families, the Urban Institute (another corporate and foundation funded nonprofit research organization), and Child Trends, the largest research organization focusing on childhood and youth. In its promotional material, the Social Genome is described as a tool for policy-makers and philanthropists who are "deciding whether and how to invest in programs, initiatives, and interventions"; it offers a "cost-efficient 'virtual laboratory' to understand how policy changes will affect children." All quotes here are from the Brookings Social Genome Project website unless otherwise noted.
42. Brookings's staff and board of trustees include members of the Federal Reserve, the Treasury Department, the Marine Corps. These government and business elite speak directly to members of the International Monetary Fund and the European Commission. See Alterman, "Altercations," for a critical take on Brookings's lobbying ties.
43. Reeves and Sawhill, "Introduction."
44. Deleuze, "What Is the Creative," 322.
45. Sawhill et al., "Pathways."
46. Marx, *Capital*, 899.
47. Fanon's original quote from *Wretched of the Earth* recommends stretching Marxism when "addressing the colonial problem" (5).
48. Arnall distinguishes "open and experimental" Marxism from "doctrinaire" approaches that take Marx's writings to be a "rigid set of beliefs" and "sacred and timeless axioms." Arnall, "Many Tasks," 101. What unites open Marxism is the method of analyzing concrete reality, the spirit of ruthless criticism, and its emancipatory politics. There is a recognized tradition of "open Marxism" inaugurated by the first eponymous edited volume, a tradition united by its "attitude" of "open and permanent critique of capital and the categories used to analyze it." Bonefeld et al., *Open Marxism*; Dinerstein, "Intricacies of Prefiguration," 215; Dinerstein et al., "Open Marxism."

49. "Psy complex" was coined by N. Rose, in *Psychological Complex*, and Ingleby, in "Professionals as Socialisers," who develops and applies Foucault's ideas to areas such as social work, education, and self-help. I. Parker, "Reflexive Research."
50. The term signals how schools are at the center of a multipronged political-economic infrastructure of institutions that include the multibillion-dollar industries of testing, real estate, tutoring, coaching, and private educational companies that provide services to both school systems and parents.
51. Roberts, *Torn Apart*.
52. In practice, there are no such sharp distinctions between these three forms of power in capitalist societies (violence, ideology, compulsion of economic relations); they are necessarily entangled, with violence ultimately undergirding the other two. See Mau, *Mute Compulsion*, 3–5. This is also the case within social reproduction.
53. Camatte, *Capital and Community*.

Chapter 1

1. Adorno, "Marx and the Basic Concepts"; Horkheimer, "Traditional and Critical Theory."
2. I opt to use "materialism" (rather than "historical materialism" or "dialectical materialism"), as in the explicit articulation of the first premises of the materialist method: Marx and Engels, *German Ideology*, 42. Marx's materialism is not a technological determinism, nor does it discount the force of ideas, discourses, consciousness, and subjectivity. It centers human practice and experience and necessarily includes how humans subjectively apprehend their world. Materialism names an orientation to the analysis of the social that embodies the spirit of Marx's oft-quoted "Men make history." Finally, materialism is an orientation toward the mode of production as primarily social and political, rather than simply economic, phenomena.
3. Seeing homologies in Marx's and Freud's conception of the drive as an insatiable demand, Tomšic uses the term "the capitalist unconscious" to describe capital's drive of self-valorization as a "fantasy of total subsumption of life-day under work-day and life-force under labour-force." Like Marx, Tomšic emphasizes how production for production's sake is distinct from miserly renunciation for enrichment. Capitalism's incessant demand for surplus value imposes an "infinite task" on subjects in the "guise of the universal imperative to renounce enjoyment . . . [and] every subject becomes a hostage of the system." Tomšic, "Psychoanalysis," 989.
4. M-C-M′ is Marx's formulation of capital's law of value, where money (M) buys commodities (C), including labor, to produce something sold for an additional amount of money (M′) that is reinvested and the cycle begins again—an endless, changing same. Marx, *Capital*.
5. Marx, *Capital*, 1003 (Fowkes).
6. Marx, *Capital*, 353, 342, 416, 302 (Fowkes).
7. Marx, *Capital*, 614 (Fowkes).

8. Bonefeld, *Critical Theory of Economic*; Mau, *Mute Compulsion.*
9. Marx, *Grundrisse*, 164; De'Ath, "Gender and Social Reproduction," 227.
10. Marx, *Capital*, 175 (Fowkes).
11. Marx, *Capital*, 95 (Fowkes).
12. Marx, *Capital*, 309 (Fowkes).
13. Marx, "Contribution to the Critique," 182.
14. Adorno, *History and Freedom*, 13; see O'Kane, "Society Maintains Itself," 2; O'Kane, "Critique of Real Abstraction."
15. Marx and Engels, *German Ideology*, 56.
16. Premise 2 has the advantage of immediately disaggregating mothering from a presumptively universal, unchanging, naturalized, and essentialized condition and instead establishes it as a historically specific social relation. Furthermore, it follows that there is no universal or eternal "family" as such and that the very form of the family as a patriarchal unit within an apparently bounded private sphere is always inherently the family under capitalism. Vogel, *Marxism and the Oppression*; 2013; Ferguson and McNally, "Capital, Labour-Power." In *The Communist Manifesto*, Marx and Engels famously asked, "On what foundation is the present family, the bourgeois family, based? On capital, on private gain" (28–29).
17. Munro, "Social Reproduction," 454.
18. Marx, *Capital*, 711, 716 (Fowkes).
19. See Ferguson, "Intersectionality," for an overview of different conceptions of reproductive labor. See also Bhattacharya, "Introduction"; Best, "Wages for Housework"; Ferguson and McNally, "Capital, Labour-Power"; Hensman, "Domestic Labor"; Munro, "Social Reproduction"; Vogel, *Marxism and the Oppression.*
20. Cleaver, *Thirty-Three Lessons*; Marx *Capital*, 274 (Fowkes).
21. Ferguson and McNally, "Capital, Labour-Power," xxix.
22. Vogel, *Marxism and the Oppression.*
23. Federici, *Revolution at Point Zero*; Dalla Costa, *Women and the Subversion*; Fortunati, *Arcana of Reproduction.*
24. Hennessy, *Profit and Pleasure*, 5.
25. Ferreira da Silva, "Before Man," 91; Wynter, "Unsettling the Coloniality," 309–11.
26. Robinson, *Black Marxism.*
27. Collins, *Black Feminist Thought*, 55.
28. Spillers, "Mama's Baby," 75; Hartman, "Belly of the World," 169. See also Davis, "Reflections", Hartman, *Lose Your Mother*; James, "Womb of Western"; Weinbaum, *Afterlife of Reproductive Slavery*. Spillers argues that the doctrine of *partus sequitir ventrem* (the child follows the womb) that ensured slavery's reproduction cast Black women as "ungendered" and threw gender into crisis, for enslaved African American women were "both mother and mother-dispossessed," an argument that forces the rethinking of white feminist theory. Spillers, "Mama's Baby," 80.
29. Hartman, "Belly of the World"; James, "Womb of Western."
30. Hartman, "Belly of the World," 7. The concept of the afterlives of slavery is not an "antiquarian obsession with bygone days . . . but because black lives are still imperiled and devalued by a racial calculus and political arithmetic that were entrenched centuries ago." Hartman, *Lose Your Mother*, 6.

31. Hartman, *Lose Your Mother*; Weinbaum, *Afterlife of Reproductive Slavery*; Sharpe, *In the Wake*.
32. Gilmore, "Race and Globalisation," 261; Melamed, "Racial Capitalism," 79.
33. In his letter to Engels about Eugene Dühring's review of *Capital*, vol. 1, Marx writes that Dühring and "the economists, without exception, have missed the simple point that if the commodity has a double character—use value and exchange value—then the labour represented by the commodity must also have a twofold character . . . This is, in fact, the whole secret of the critical conception." Marx, "Letter to Engels."
34. Marx, *Grundrisse*, 361.
35. Marx, *Economic and Philosophic*, 113; Marx, *Capital*, 286 (Fowkes). Oksala argues that an account of neoliberal subjectivation requires a dialogue with Marx and Foucault. Oksala points out Foucault's objection to what he saw as Marx's position that labor forms humans' essential nature, countering: "It is false to say, with certain famous post-Hegelians, that labor is man's concrete existence. The time and life of man are not labor by nature; they are pleasure, discontinuity, festival, rest, need, moments, chance, violence, and so on." Oksala citing Foucault, in "Neoliberal Subjectivation," 587–88.
36. Ferguson, "Intersectionality"; Ferguson, "Life-Making or Death."
37. For example, Katz et al., in "Demanding Life Work," emphasize "life-making" or "life's work" of social reproduction, and Munro, "Social Reproduction," 454, emphasizes how reproducing labor power reproduces our collective misery.
38. Marx, *Economic Manuscripts*, 92–93.
39. Marx, *Capital*, 1019–38 (Fowkes).
40. Marx, *Grundrisse*, 705, 694, 706.
41. Marx, *Grundrisse*, 705.
42. Marx, *Grundrisse*, 705, 712.
43. Clover, "Subsumption and Crisis," 1567.
44. Tronti's *Workers and Capital* is the inspiration for scholarship on the "social factory," although he did not use that term. See, e.g., Cleaver, *Thirty-Three Lessons*; Cox and Federici, *Counter-Planning*; Dalla Costa, *Women and the Subversion*; Federici, *Revolution at Point Zero*. For overview of debates about the meaning of the fragment, see Pitts, "Beyond the Fragment"; Thoborn, *Deleuze, Marx*; Heinrich, "Fragment on Machines," for what he understands as the "misapplication" of autonomous readings of the fragment; Wright, *Storming Heaven*; and Tomba and Bellofiore, "Fragment on Machines," for an overview of interpretations within Italian autonomous Marxism.
45. Dalla Costa, *Women and the Subversion*; Cox and Federici, *Counter-Planning*.
46. Dalla Costa, *Women and the Subversion*, 29.
47. Comitato Padova, "Operaie Della Casa."
48. Federici, *Caliban and the Witch*, 8.
49. Cox and Federici, *Counter-Planning*, 12.
50. Portella and Busk, "Formal and Real," 355.
51. My general stance on this (and other) debates about Marx's "original" meaning is agnostic; I am instead interested in particular concepts' analytic and political utility in terms of understanding the struggle of life against capital in everyday life. Arnall persuasively argues for *translating* Marx's concepts when they are

used in contexts that "elude their traditional formulation," rather than "strictly and methodically" preserving them. Arnall, "Capitalist Slavery," 10; Arnall, "Many Tasks," chapter 1, n. 44. Long-standing debates about the formal characteristics of reproductive labors chiefly revolve around whether such labors are productive or unproductive. Marx's distinction of productive and unproductive labor does not revolve around the content, nature, or utility of labor, but apprehends it from the standpoint of capital, wherein productive labor is labor that generates surplus value. For the purposes established here, I find it useful to follow Marx's spirit, if not his letter, and propose that there can be no a priori list of productive or unproductive labors because these oppositions are produced *within* processes of valorization, and further, the distinction itself is rigid and relies on "productivist, wage-centric understandings of exploitation." Mezzadri, "Value of Social Reproduction," 2. Value itself is a dynamic concept, and the law of value is "nothing other than capital's struggle to, first, reduce all human activity to labour, and to make all labour productive," Harvie, "Value Production," 27. The productive-unproductive distinction is thus historical, political, contestable, emerging, and contingent upon struggle and antagonistic social relations in everyday life—at the workplace, in public space, at school, and in the home. Analyzing reproductive activities as *labor* is a theoretical leap within Marxist critique of political economy that further overcomes the reified forms of appearance of a gendered division of labor within capitalism—in this case, the apparent separation of production from reproduction, work from non-work, creation of value from creation of non-value—and instead demonstrates how they are different moments in the unitary movement of value within capitalism. Alessandrini, "Immaterial Labour"; Dalla Costa, *Women and the Subversion*; Mezzadri, "Value of Social Reproduction." For more on this debate, interested readers can consult the various instances when Marx could be seen to support either position regarding the (un)productive character of reproductive labors in *Capital*, 509, 1038–40 (Fowkes), and *Theories of Surplus Value*, 153, 393, or they could consult the secondary literature in Marxist feminism, which takes an unproductive stance, arguing that reproductive labor is not commodified, nor does it produce a commodity (e.g., Vogel, *Marxism and the Oppression*), or the stance that reproductive labor generates surplus value by coproducing labor power that will be exploited, albeit in the future. See, e.g., Fortunati, *Arcana of Reproduction*; Mezzadri "Value of Social Reproduction."

52. Gonzalez and Neton, "Logic of Gender," 65.
53. Dalla Costa, *Women and the Subversion*, 74, emphasis added. The "wages for housework" call was a tactical demand for wages *against* housework and against capitalism. As Cox and Federici averred in *Counter-Planning* in an early statement defending the movement, "Ultimately, when we say we produce capital, we are saying that *we can and want to destroy it*" (6).
54. Best, "Wages for Housework," 899.
55. Best, "Wages for Housework," 899.
56. Claussen, "Critical Theory," 77.
57. There is a rich history of integrating Marxist and psychoanalytic approaches, including a recent resurgence of work synthesizing key elements that speaks

to our present conditions. However, very little of this work, past or current, is grounded in everyday life outside the clinic.

58. Marx, *Capital*, 61 (Reitter).
59. Lefebvre, *Critique of Everyday Life*, 167.
60. In "Dialectically Constituted," Ogden claims that Freud's subject was always "created, sustained (and decentered) through the dialectical interplay of consciousness and unconsciousness" (23).
61. Sexton, "Antidoting," 19.
62. In the past decade or so, this tradition been revived in productive ways from psychoanalytic thinkers engaging with Marx (e.g., Tomšič, *Capitalist Unconscious*; B. Fong, *Death and Mastery*), to the field of Afro-pessimism (Sexton, "People-of-Color-Blindness"; Spillers, "All the Things"), to a resurgence of interest in the psychoanalytic elements of the Frankfurt school (Allen, *Critique on the Couch*), and to engagements with Wynter's articulation of Fanon's sociogeny (Wynter, "Towards the Sociogenic"; Wynter and McKittrick, "Unparalleled Catastrophe").
63. Samo Tomšič reads Marx through Lacan to posit that Marx's critique of the subject rejected the concept as a bourgeois fiction and provided the tools to distinguish "the fiction of the subject from the real subject of politics"—a "decentralized, de-individualized, and de-psychologized" subject—the latter by which he means moving away from a "knowing" subject as in Lukacs notion of class consciousness. Tomšič, *Capitalist Unconscious*, 29–30.
64. Deleuze and Guattari, *Anti-Oedipus*, 38.
65. Both unconscious desires and the maternal invite biologized notions of drives and feminine "instincts" that materialist approaches should reject. Melanie Klein, the psychoanalyst most closely related to object relations theory, explains how the infant's unconscious develops in and through interaction with the mother, and she provides an account of the intersubjective and intrapsychic aspects of experience. In *Critique on the Couch*, Allen argues that Klein fully rejects biologized notions of the drives arising from some readings of Freud.
66. Allen, *Critique on the Couch*, 37.
67. Laplanche, "Other Within," 36.
68. Allen, *Critique on the Couch*, 19–21.
69. Fong in Allen *Critique on the Couch*, 37.
70. Rich, *Of Woman Born*; O'Reilly, "Maternal Theory."
71. Rose, *Mothers*.
72. Munro, "Welfare State," 200.
73. Bonefeld, "State as Political Form."
74. Bonefeld, "Capitalist State," 207.
75. Wacquant, "Three Steps," 68, 76.
76. Adkins, "Contingent Labour"; Brown, *Ruins of Neoliberalism*; Cooper, *Family Values*.
77. Marx and Engels, *Communist Manifesto*, 24.
78. Lewis, *Abolish the Family*; O'Brien, "Abolish the Family"; Weeks, "Abolition of the Family."
79. Weeks, "Abolition of the Family," 6.

80. Comitato per il Salario al Lavoro Domestico di Padova, "Operaie Della Cassa."
81. Weeks, "Abolition of the Family," 439.
82. King, "Black 'Feminism,'" 75.
83. King, "Black 'Feminism," 75; Nash, "Political Life"; Collins, *Black Feminist*; Gilmore, *Golden Gulag*.
84. Nash, "Political Life," 702.
85. Vasquez-Tokos and Yamin, "Racialization of Privacy". See also Briggs, *Taking Children*; Spillers, "Mama's Baby."
86. K. Fong, "Getting Eyes"; Roberts, "Prison, Foster Care"; Roberts, *Torn Apart*; Tazzioli and De Genova, "Kidnapping Migrants."
87. Munro, "Welfare State," 200–201.
88. Donzelot, *Policing of Families*.
89. Hochschild, "Global Care Chains."
90. Bhattacharya, "Introduction," 79; Cox and Federici, *Counter-Planning*, 3.
91. Briggs, *How All Politics*.
92. Hennessy, *Profit and Pleasure*, 5.
93. Hennessy, *Profit and Pleasure*, 6.
94. See Wright's "Continuing Importance" for a conceptualization of managers as occupying "contradictory location within class relations."
95. Dreier, "Alone and Exploited."
96. Bowles and Gintis, *Schooling in Capitalist America*; Willis, *Learning to Labour*.
97. Ayotte, "Soon as You're Born"; Caffentzis, "Throwing Away the Ladder"; Cleaver, "Comradely Appropriation"; Wages for Students, "Wages for Students."
98. Kromidas, *City Kids*, chs. 3–4.
99. Kromidas, *City Kids*, 105.
100. Ferguson, "Children, Childhood," 113.
101. Katz, *Growing Up Global*, 14; "Childhood as Spectacle"; "Angel of Geography."
102. Katz, *Growing Up Global*, 15; Ferguson, "Children, Childhood," 112.
103. Lane-McKinley, "Idea of Children"; *Solidarity with Children*; Lewis, *Abolish the Family*.
104. Buck-Morss, *Dialects of Seeing*.
105. Kromidas, "'Agent of Revolutionary Thought.'"

Chapter 2

EPIGRAPH. Becker here directly responds to Ewald's claim that human capital theory asks "people to see themselves as dogs in a Pavlovian experiment" in a conversation between the two about Foucault's ideas concerning Becker's theoretical legacy. See Becker et al., "Becker on Ewald," 17.

1. This is a *détournement* of the first sentences of Marx's *Capital*, vol. 1, with italicized terms in the text replacing the commodity in the original: "The wealth of societies in which the capitalist mode of production prevails appears as 'an immense collection of *commodities*'; the *individual commodity* appears as its elementary form. Our investigation therefore begins with the analysis of the *commodity*" (125 [Fowkes]).

2. This is not an arbitrary array of commodities but the ones Marx includes in his equation explaining how individual substances shed their irreducible sensuous qualitative identities as use-values and acquire uniformity within exchange: "(20 yards of linen = 1 coat or = 10 lb. tea or = 40 lb. coffee or = 1 quarter of corn or = 2 ounces of gold or = 1 ton of iron or = etc.)." Marx, *Capital*, 155 (Fowkes).
3. World Bank Group, "Human Capital Project."
4. Brown, *Undoing the Demos*, 33, 24.
5. Foucault, *Birth of Biopolitics*, 226. I would read this with gender-neutral pronouns "they" and "their" rather than Foucault's "him" and "his."
6. Marx, *Capital*, 899 (Fowkes).
7. Marx, *Capital*, 380 (Fowkes).
8. I am inspired here by Sutherland's argument that Marx's poetics are necessary to capture the unprecedented state of things in capitalism. Sutherland, "Poetics of Capital," 209.
9. Much has been made of the child's pricelessness as the constitutive feature of the "modern" child since Zelizer argued in *Pricing the Priceless* that nineteenth-century notions of the child's economic utility transformed in the twentieth century to the "sacred child" as economically useless but "emotionally priceless." Bandelj and Spiegel argue that the dominant notion of the child's "social value" has once again transformed in the twenty-first century, what they call the "priceless child 2.0" that is an "economically useful-to-be human capital investment." Bandelj and Spiegel, "Pricing the Priceless," 20. In contrast, I argue that both notions of the child exist in dialectical tension, as priceless and as having a present value that is pregnant with potential for appreciation, a double character imbued with tension, contradiction, and struggle. See especially Chapter 2 for more on Marx's double-sided conception of labor.
10. Gilmore, *Abolition Geography*.
11. Katz, "Accumulation, Excess, Childhood."
12. Marx, *Capital*, 270 (Fowkes); Marx, *Capital*, 292 (Reitter).
13. While so-called expert parent advice to raise well-adjusted children is a centuries-old gambit, neoliberalism has given rise to a new emphasis on intelligence, and then more recently on children's developing brains. Bandelj and Spiegel, "Pricing the Priceless"; Macvarish, *Neuroparenting*; Wrigley, "Do Young Children?" While they may not be familiar with term "neuroparenting," any parent or parent-to-be is familiar with the concern with the "developing brain" and the "claims about the 'critical significance' of what they do in pregnancy and the 'early years' of their child's life for his or her long-term prospects." Macvarish, *Neuroparenting*, 2. Images of earphones pumping Bach strapped onto pregnant torsos and toys for infants labeled with their educational or brain development benefits are not unfamiliar in the parenting public sphere.
14. Mincer, "Investment in Human Capital"; Schultz, "Investment in Human Capital"; Becker, "Investment in Human Capital"; Becker, "Human Capital."

15. Mincer, "Investment in Human Capital.
16. Marx, *Capital*, 532 (Fowkes).
17. Burns, "Marx's *Capital*"; Ramirez, "Marx and Ricardo on Machinery."
18. There are two ways to pump more surplus value from labor—increase the time (absolute surplus value) or increase the intensity of laboring (relative surplus value). Outlining the production of relative surplus value, Marx wrote more generally about the tendency for capital to assume greater control over the production process as it develops historically through social and technological means (division of labor, science and technology, scale). Marx's historical discussion of the struggles over the workday is recounted in his analysis of the production of absolute surplus value. Labor's success in this arena led to capital's intensification of labor through technology (machines) and management, and Marx discusses these struggles in his analysis of the production of relative surplus value. *Capital*, 340–416 (Fowkes).
19. Marx, *Capital*, 799 (Fowkes).
20. Cleaver, *Thirty-Three Lessons*, 3.
21. In an early critique of the concept of human capital, Bowles and Gintis wrote: "One gets the uneasy feeling that the operation was successful, but the patient vanished!" Bowles and Gintis, "Problem with Human Capital," 74.
22. Marx, *Capital*, 270 (Fowkes).
23. De Genova, "Toward a Marxian Anthropology," 135.
24. Marx, *Capital*, 128 (Fowkes).
25. Marx, *Grundrisse*, 164.
26. Marx, *Capital*, 135 (Fowkes); Bonefeld, *Critical Theory of Economic*; De'Ath, "Hidden Abodes"; Sohn-Rethel, *Intellectual and Manual.*
27. Bonefeld, *Critical Theory of Economic.*
28. Marx's full quote: "As the objective basis of the whole of the system of production, already in itself implies compulsion over the individual, since his immediate product is not a product for him, but only *becomes* such in the social process, and since it *must* take on this general but nevertheless external form; and that the individual has an existence only as a producer of exchange value, hence that the whole negation of his natural existence is already implied; that he is therefore entirely determined by society; that this further presupposes a division of labour etc., in which the individual is already posited in relations other than that of mere *exchanger*, etc." Marx, *Grundrisse*, 247–48.
29. Marx, *Capital*, 280 (Fowkes).
30. De Genova, "Reply," 286, De Genova, "Management of Quality."
31. De'Ath, "Hidden Abodes"; Elson, "Value Theory."
32. Marx, *Grundrisse*, 690–712. Within Italian Marxist workerist thought (*postoperaismo*), Marx's machines fragment has been interpreted as leading to a heightening of capitalism's contradictions, and thus a kind of prophecy for communism's emergence. In short, the machines fragment outlines the tendency that, as capital absorbs the general intellect that workers generate in their free time to then turn the technology against labor, increases in productivity decreases socially necessary labor time and concomitantly increases surplus labor time (also known as a decrease in free time), and thereby "undercuts" capital's potential to further accumulate. T. Smith, "General Intellect," 3.

33. Adamson, "Human Capital Strategy"; Caffentzis, "Throwing Away the Ladder"; Harvie and de Angelis, "Cognitive Capitalism"; Federici and Caffentzis, "Notes on the Edu-factory."
34. Read, "Genealogy of Homo Economicus," 33.
35. Jappe, "Sohn-Rethel," 8; Camatte, *Capital and Community*, 57; Clover, "Subsumption and Crisis," 1572.
36. De Genova, "Racial Theory of Labour," 221–22.
37. The position that slavery served as the foundation of capitalism rather than as a historically aberrant variation of it has been reanimated in recent scholarship under the racial capitalism frame. Robinson, *Black Marxism*.
38. Becker in Jauregui, "Foucault on Becker," 40.
39. Morgan, *Reckoning with Slavery*, 19.
40. In *Specters of the Atlantic*, Baucom argues that the world historic catastrophe of slavery provided a "theory of value" that made finance capital possible (7, 17).
41. Hartman's *Scenes of Subjection* imaginatively reads the links between fungibility and anti-Blackness to emphasizes how, counterintuitively, fungibility is also open and elastic, symbolically dispersing anti-Blackness throughout the social body. Recent work develops this analytic thread in various ways, including most notably work registered as Afro-pessimist (Sexton, "People-of-Color-Blindness"; Wilderson, *Red, White & Black*) and work that takes different analytic paths (King, "Black 'Feminisms'"; King, "Labor's Aphasia"; Weinbaum, *Afterlife of Reproductive Slavery*; Winnubst, "Many Lives of Fungibility").
42. Hartman, *Lose Your Mother*. See also Sharpe, *In the Wake*.
43. Hartman, *Lose Your Mother*, 6.
44. J. James, "Womb of Western Theory"; Morgan, *Reckoning with Slavery*; Weinbaum, *Afterlife of Reproductive Slavery*.
45. Morgan, *Reckoning with Slavery*, 10; 17.
46. For Black studies accounts of how fungibility extends the symbolic capacities of enslavement throughout the social imaginary, see King, "Labor of (Re) Reading"; Garba and Sorentino, "Slavery Is a Metaphor"; Wilderson, *Red, White & Black*. The total domination and ownership inherent in enslavement's subjection was forever joined to its "opposite" in freedom, thus structuring the political imaginary. Hartman, *Lose Your Mother*. Wilderson argues that within this political ontology, white "human" subjects appear to be free from domination and face only "contingent violence" that "kicks in when s/he resists, or is perceived to resist, the disciplinary discourse of capital" as opposed to Black subjects continual and necessary "subsumption by violence." Wilderson, *Red, White & Black*, 3.
47. The distinctions between environment and heredity in key forms of human capital—most notably health and intelligence—are increasingly blurred by science. Jacob Mincer, one of the first economists to bring the concept of human capital into the field relied on Francis Galton's conception of intelligence as hereditary that is normally distributed (i.e., bell curve) throughout the population and linked to income distribution. Mincer, "Investment in Human Capital."
48. Ewald, in Becker et al., "Becker on Ewald," 5.
49. Foucault, *Birth of Biopolitics*, 221.
50. Feher, "Self-Appreciation," 28, emphasis added.

51. Feher, "Self-Appreciation," 26.
52. Foucault, *Birth of Biopolitics*, 229.
53. To date, there are few considerations of how human capital theory has intervened in children's development (what I call children's becoming) in the family. The work of Ba' is an important exception; he forcefully argues that human capital theory dominates childhood socialization and the contemporary domestic sphere is dedicated toward children's "becoming human capital." Ba', "Critique of Sociology," 77, 74. A considerable body of recent Marxist scholarship outlines how human capital theory increasingly subsumes teaching and learning in neoliberal schooling. Adamson, "Human Capital Strategy"; De Lissovoy, *Education and Emancipation*; Slater and Seawright, "Putting Homo Economicus." For analyses mapping how students take up this subject form, see Kromidas, "Learning Hierarchy"; Nxumalo et al., "Lunch Time." Critical scholarship in early childhood education reveals how human capital theory opens up the field for neuroscience-based interventions. Millei and Joronen, "(Bio)Politicization of Neuroscience"; Roberts-Holmes and Moss, *Neoliberalism and Early Childhood*.
54. Becker, "Human Capital and the Economy," 89.
55. Foucault, *Birth of Biopolitics*, 223, 229.
56. Foucault, *Birth of Biopolitics*, 229–30.
57. Feher, "Self-Appreciation," 30.
58. Wynter, "No Humans Involved," 44.
59. Wynter, "Unsettling the Coloniality," 318; Wynter, "Towards Sociogenic," 66.
60. Kromidas, "'Savage' Child"; Kromidas, "Towards the Human"; Kromidas, "Becoming Convivial."
61. Bernstein, *Racial Innocence*.
62. Kromidas, "Towards the Human"; Nxumalo and Cedillo, *Decolonizing Place*.

Chapter 3

1. Goldstein, "Research Shows"; Jacobs, "COVID Learning Loss"; World Bank Group, "Learning Losses."
2. Hanushek and Woessmann, "Economic Impacts," 3.
3. Case and Deaton 2023a.
4. The headlines reporting on the "widening mortality gap" for those without a college education include Case and Deaton, "Without a College Degree, Life Is Staggeringly Shorter" (*New York Times*); Nietzel, "Americans Without College Degrees Live Shorter Lives" (*Forbes*); Matherly, "Americans Without College Degrees Die Younger" (*Chronicle of Higher Education*); and Rubin, "Life Expectancy Gap in America Widens Depending on College Education" (*Axios*).
5. Hays, *Cultural Contradictions*; Jensen, *Parenting the Crisis*; Nelson, *Parenting out of Control*; O'Reilly, "Maternal Theory."
6. Marx, *Capital*, 174 (Fowkes).
7. Elson, "Value Theory of Labour," 123.
8. Ewald claims that Foucault situated human capital economists as liberalism's "sole thinkers." Ewald, in Becker et al., "Becker on Ewald," 5.
9. There is a growing emphasis on "economization" or how the "economic style of reasoning" has come to dominate different fields in sociology. Hirschman

and Berman, "Do Economists Make?"; Griffen and Panofsky, "Ambivalent Economization." In *Thinking Like an Economist*, Berman traces how an "economic style of reasoning" came to dominate US politics and public policy in the 1960s–1980s. I put "economization" in scare quotes because, as there are many different types of economic thinking, the term is imprecise and should be qualified as capitalist economic thinking or bourgeois economics thinking. Analytic frames of "economization" are limited precisely because they are grounded in traditional theory that takes key features of capitalist political economy for granted. See Chapter 1 for a critique of paradigms grounded in traditional theory in their incapacity to account for key power relations of capitalist society.

10. Oster, *Family Firm.*
11. Milkie et al., "Amount of Time," 368.
12. Yglesias, "News Study Says."
13. Valenti, "Don't Stress Out."
14. Justin Wolfers is one-half of an "economic power couple" with partner Betsey Stevenson. The pair regularly make their rounds on the public circuit to translate economics to parenting and coupledom ("lovenomics" they call it). They successfully leverage the media and social media to teach the public and promulgate economists' vision of the world with "findings" such as "money really does lead to a more satisfying life." Wolfers, "Money Really Does."
15. Wolfer's first article appeared in the *New York Times*' data-visualization rich website *Upshot*, and the second was a more detailed debunking of the original study. Wolfers, "Why a Claim"; Wolfers, "Yes, Your Time."
16. Wolfers, "Yes, Your Time."
17. Bonefeld, "Bringing Critical Theory," 5.
18. Schultz, "Fertility and Economic Values," 3.
19. Schultz, "Fertility and Economic Values," 9.
20. Becker, "Investment in Human Capital."
21. Marx explains that the continual existence of a "free worker in the market selling his own labor-power" is the "one historical condition" that must hold in order for the "buying and selling of labor-power" and capital itself to exist. Marx, *Capital*, 143–44 (Reitter).
22. Marx, *Capital*, 342 (Fowkes).
23. Cox and Federici, *Counter-Planning*, 12.
24. Cox and Federici, *Counter-Planning*, 6.
25. Marx, *Capital*, 143 (Reitter). While Marx seems to discount or take for granted women's reproductive labors, he can be read to be taking the view of capital, for which those labors are free and necessarily must be so.
26. Marx, *Capital*, 309 (Fowkes).
27. Schultz, "Fertility and Economic Values," 12.
28. Brilli, "Mother's Time Allocation," 2.
29. del Boca et al., "Household Choices," 137. See also Agostinelli and Sorrenti, "Money vs. Time"; Bigoni et al., "Parental Investments"; del Bono et al., "Early Maternal Time"; Flood et al., "Inequality in Early Care."
30. Brilli, "Mother's Time Allocation," 12.
31. Agostinelli and Sorrenti, "Money vs. Time," 3.
32. Martin, "Curse of 2022."

33. Normanton, "Why Can't Our Children."
34. Normanton, "Why Can't Our Children."
35. Martin's "Curse of 2022" was authored by a chief executive officer. While there were many critical comments directed at the BBC article on Twitter (now X) that targeted the deficit approach to children's incoming skills, many from educators and academics, none commented on the enlisting, policing, condemnation, or attempt to subordinate mothers' labors.
36. Christakis, "Dangers of Distracted."
37. American Academy of Pediatrics, "Changing Landscape."
38. Christakis, "Dangers of Distracted."
39. Klass, "Guilty Secret."
40. Harris, "Just Too Much."
41. Hainer, "My Son Thinks."
42. Braff, "How to Get". See also Harris, "Just Too Much."
43. Chancellor of the NYC Department of Education, "I'm amazed," tweet.
44. The World Bank Group (2021) estimated nearly $17 trillion in learning losses from school closures. The Federalist (2021) reported a nearly $1 trillion in learning loss for US students.
45. Dorn et al., "COVID-19 and Student Learning."
46. Williamson, "Counting Learning Loss." President Biden then gave $190 billion to US schools to offset the pandemic learning losses. In "Huge in Learning Loss," MacGillis critically evaluates educational tech companies' "cashing in" on the pandemic learning losses.
47. Goldstein, "Research Shows Students."
48. DeParle, "Disadvantaged Students"; Goldstein, "Research Shows Students"; Kim, "Remote Schooling."
49. Harris, "Just Too Much."
50. Perelman, "COVID-19 Economy."
51. See, e.g., Alon et al., "Impact of COVID-19"; Collins et al., "COVID-19 and the Gender Gap"; Landivar et al., "Early Signs"; Lyttleton et al. 2020.
52. Gogoi, "Stuck at Home Moms."
53. Ferguson, "Life-Making."
54. Leibowitz's chapter is the most cited one in the volume and was simultaneously published in the *Journal of Political Economy*.
55. Leibowitz, "Home Investments in Children," 434.
56. Leibowitz, "Home Investments in Children."
57. Leibowitz, "Home Investments in Children," 432.
58. For example, Attanasio et al., "Early Childhood Development"; Cunha et al., "Econometrics of Early Childhood," Flood et al., "Inequality in Early Care"; Kalil et al., "Education Gradients"; Nicoletti et al., "Mothers Working." The maternal science literature concerning mothers and children in poverty is a major source that contributes to racialized notions of maternal "quality," but it is too vast to review here.
59. Brilli, "Mother's Time Allocation," 233; 262.
60. Brilli, "Mother's Time Allocation," 262.
61. Agostinelli and Sorrenti, "Money vs. Time"; Caucutt et al., "Child Skill Production."
62. King, "Black 'Feminisms.'"

63. Slobodian, "Unequal Mind," 84.
64. Slobodian, "Unequal Mind," 74; 75.
65. Murphy traces how the conception of human capital is at the center of the global development apparatus and of aid targeted to educating girls in the Global South, linking fertility, childhood, education, and economic development. In the logic of Lawrence Summers, then chief economist of the World Bank, educating girls is cheaper than directly distributing contraception. Murphy, *Economization of Life*, 113–24.
66. One of Brookings's leading economists, Isabell Sawhill, has penned various tracts about fertility. For example, Sawhill wrote a commentary "Should We Worry?" about how low fertility may aid upward mobility in the US and another coauthored piece suggesting that abortion bans exacerbate the price of already expensive childcare. Sawhill et al., "Getting More Expensive."
67. Reeves and Howard, *Parenting Gap*.
68. Foucault, *Birth of Biopolitics*, 227–28.
69. Foucault, *Birth of Biopolitics*, 229.
70. E.g., Hainer, "My Son Thinks."
71. E.g., DeParle, "Disadvantaged Students"; Brooks, "Children Need."
72. Goldstein, "Research Shows Students."
73. Goldstein, "Research Shows Students."
74. DeParle, "Disadvantaged Students."
75. Harris, "Just Too Much."
76. Brooks, "Children Need."
77. Gilbert et al., "Racial and Ethnic."
78. Gilbert et al., "Racial and Ethnic."
79. Anderson, "Out of Your Mind"; Anderson, "Why Black Parents"; Gilbert et al., "Racial and Ethnic."
80. Mott Children's Hospital, "Top Health Concerns."
81. Brooks, "Children Need."
82. Goldstein, "Research Shows Students."
83. Collins, *Black Feminist Thought*.
84. On how the family becomes a target of neoliberal governance, see Brown, *Undoing the Demos*; Brown, *In the Ruins of Neoliberalism*; Cooper, *Family Values*; Garrett et al., *We Need to Talk*; Giles, "Mothering".
85. Cooper, *Family Values*. Cooper's work outlines how both neoliberals and neoconservatives see the family as a site to reconstruct moral and political order. She describes how human capital economists like Howard Becker mourned how the welfare state (public education included) interfered with "the bonds of family obligation" and the family's ideal state of "natural altruism," "mutual dependence and self sufficiency." Concerted state policies by neoliberals and neoconservatives have responded to this crisis of the family with efforts to "preserve" the family and reinforce it as the "primary source of economic welfare" in a "world of ever-diminishing public goods." Cooper, *Family Values*, 60, 49.
86. Adkins, *Time of Money*, 70.
87. It is important to note that both Cooper and Adkins discuss the state's massive disinvestment from higher education, but neither discusses how the state has rerouted resources to early education, in line with the new econo-psy

complex understanding that one obtains larger "returns on investment" when children are younger because of their supposed "neuroplasticity." See Bandelj and Spiegel, "Pricing the Priceless Child," for a discussion of the recent trends of increases in federal investment in earlier and earlier schooling, and Griffen, "Economization of Early Life," for how this interest in early childhood connects to economists and policy-makers taking up research in the fields of neurobiology, developmental psychology, and epigenetics on children.

88. Katz, "Angel of Geography."
89. Marx, *Grundrisse*, 711–12, emphasis added.
90. Vaneigem, *Revolution of Everyday Life*, 227.
91. The Italian term *autovalorizzazione* is central to Italian autonomous Marxism, a term first appropriated by Antonio Negri from Marx's conceptualization of the "self-valorization" of capital, that signals autonomia's perspectival flip, whereby the working class is analytically and historically prior to capital and at its core is about the development of radical subjectivities. Cleaver, "Self-Valorization"; Cleaver, "Inversion of Perspective." For a discussion of the political relevance of the concept for creating what C. L. R. James called the "future in the present," see Cleaver, "Self-Valorization."
92. Marx, *Capital*, 367 (Fowkes).
93. Dalla Costa, *Women and the Subversion*; Fortunati, *Arcana of Reproduction.*

Chapter 4

1. The particular "social and emotional skills" assessment tool is the Devereaux Student Strengths Assessment built by the educational technology company Aperture Education, and acquired by the educational technology company Riverside Insights. In 2021, the New York City Department of Education entered a three-year, $18 million contract with the company to measure students "competencies." All quotes come from material from my child's school or links from Aperture's "Parent Portal."
2. Books in Harvard Business Review's Emotional Intelligence series are meant to be "uplifting and practical" and teach the "social skills that are critical for ambitious professionals to master."
3. Weeks, *Problem with Work*, 69–71.
4. Marx, *Capital*, 614 (Fowkes).
5. Clover, "Subsumption and Crisis," 1572.
6. Chancellor of the NYC Department of Education, "I'm amazed," tweet.
7. New York City Public Schools, "Parent University."
8. In 2010, Arne Duncan served as secretary of education under Obama. Duncan, "Looking in the Mirror."
9. Federici, *Wages Against Housework.*
10. "Family engagement" is a key component of recent federal reforms in educational policy, and the Every Student Succeeds Act of 2015 requires any school receiving Title I (federal) funds to use at least 1 percent of its allocated funds to develop policies and programs to get families involved in efforts to boost student achievement; it guides all schools to develop such policies, as did

the previous No Child Left Behind Act of 2001. See New York State Education Department, *Guidance.*

11. Garcia et al., "Toolkit of Resources."
12. A Google Scholar search of "parent involvement schools" shows the dramatic increases in publication. From 1950 to 1960, there are 1,480 results; from 1960 to 1970, 10,300 results; from 1970 to 1980, 17,200 results; from 1980 to 1990, 23,000 results; from 1990 to 2000, 103,000 results; from 2000 to 2010, 216,000 results; from 2010 to 2020, 253,000 results. Mapp discusses how the evolution of preferred terms, from "parent involvement" to "family engagement," marks a different parental relationship to schooling, where the latter entails "shared responsibility" and is "continued across the life span." Mapp, "Title I," 2.
13. Critical race scholars criticize the term "achievement gap" for obfuscating how the gap emerges from structural causes. Some opt for the term "opportunity gap," while others borrow from Ladson-Billings to think in terms of the "educational debt" owed Black students. The former term directs attention to resources, while "educational debt" frames the issue in terms of how whiteness structures US schooling at every level. Ladson-Billings, "Achievement Gap"; Ross, "Anti-Blackness in Education."
14. The scholarship criticizing the power dynamics, normative assumptions and regulatory functions of "parent involvement" programs is vast. Baquedano-López et al., "Equity Issues"; Ciblis, "Discourse of Parental Involvement"; McCarthy Foubert, "Damned If You"; Nygreen, "Neoliberal Reform." It is important to note that, though directly targeted as subjects of reform and regulation, Black and Brown mothers have taken up school "involvement" in alternative, including more authentically empowering ways. For instance, Black mothers were key in community takeover of New York City schools in the late 1960s. Erickson and Morrell, *Educating Harlem.*
15. Spillers, "Mama's Baby," 66; R. Ferguson, *Aberrations in Black*, 123. See also King, "Black 'Feminisms.'"
16. Black Power activist intellectuals like Stokely Carmichael countered caricatures of Black mothers and families: "They called conferences about our mamas and told us that's why we were where we were at. Some people were sitting up there talking with [President] Johnson while he was talking about their mamas. I don't play the dozens with white folks. To set the record straight, the reason we are in the bag we are in isn't because of my mama, it's because of what they did to my mama. That's why I'm where I'm at. We have to put the blame where it belongs. The blame does not belong on the oppressed but on the oppressor, and that's where it is going to stay." Not all responses from within the Black community were of outrage. In "Black 'Feminisms,'" King discusses how some Black nationalists recommitted to a Black patriarchal model. See also R. Ferguson, *Aberrations in Black*. Black womanists' counterassertions have also put forth rich radical alternatives to thinking about motherhood as politically empowering practice, one that is not necessarily directed to one's own children (othermothering); Gumbs, "M/Other Ourselves"; hooks, *Feminist Theory*, O'Reilly, *Toni Morrison and Motherhood.*
17. Baquedano-López et al., "Equity Issues"; Briggs, *Taking Children*; K. Fong "Getting Eyes"; Roberts, *Torn Apart.*

18. Lazzarato, *Everyone Hates Capital*, 8.
19. Iasevoli, "This Isn't Your Mom's."
20. One of the key instruments through which New York City determines school quality, the annual "School Survey" sent to parents, positions the school-home connection as primary. The first two items in the survey are "School staff regularly communicate with me about how I can help my child learn" and "Teachers and parents/guardians think of each other as *partners* in educating children." School quality reports are purportedly "designed to support a dialogue among all members of the school community about how to make the school a better place to learn." New York City Public Schools, "School Quality." While it is possible that the school survey authentically reflect parents' understandings of school quality, I argue that schools actively shape the understanding of school quality through such seemingly neutral forms of communication.
21. Next Generation Science Standards for States, by States, "Understanding the Standards."
22. Marx, *Capital*, 270 (Fowkes).
23. Williamson, "Psychodata," 1.
24. Williamson, "Decoding ClassDojo," 450.
25. Quotes from this section come from material from my child's school and the RULER website. Ruler, "Resources for Families."
26. Aperture Devereaux Student Strengths Assessment, "Parent Portal."
27. C. Stearns, "Responsive Classroom?"; C. Stearns, "Unruly Affects"; P. Stearns, "Happy Children". See also Ahmed, *Promise of Happiness*.
28. Atkins and Salzhauer, *Kindness Advantage*.
29. Phrases such as "last a lifetime" are typical within this discourse. In research touting the benefits of SEL in early childhood, economists argue that there is "a 'fade up' of cognitive and social emotional skills that persist through life" (rather than a fading out). This research was published through the Heckman Foundation, named after a University of Chicago economist and the founder of the so-called Heckman equation, one of the more influential economists to focus on the economic potential of early childhood (including birth to age three) education. The institute is funded by the Pritzker Children's Initiative and the Buffett Early Childhood Fund. See Heckman, "Fadeout Toolkit."
30. Williamson, "Psychodata," 1.
31. Template from a series of documents titled "HELP! With [specific skill]," sent home by my child's school and sourced from websites such as Reading Rockets (www.readingrockets.org); K12 Reader (www.k12reader.com); and Understood (www.understood.org).
32. Khatib, "Time of Capital."
33. Benjamin, "Theses."
34. Myers, "Becoming 'Babies.'"
35. The concept of libidinal economy appropriates Freud's understanding of unconscious libidinal energies to understand the movement of fantasies and desire throughout the social. Lyotard, *Libidinal Economy*.
36. Cooper, *Family Values*.
37. Leeming, *Myth*. Wynter uses Leeming's definition of cosmogony in her articulation of how humans are instituted as genre-specific beings by the dominant

order of knowledge within a society, and more specifically as she tracks the shift from a theocentric to the secular biocentric and ratiocentric cosmogony inaugurated by the Darwinian revolution. "We are only enabled to do so [tell ourselves who we are] . . . because it is by the very means of these *genre*-specific cosmogonies that we are enabled to fictively construct and performatively enact ourselves as the *who* of the *what* that we-are." Wynter, "Ceremony Found," 196.

38. Tomšič, "Psychoanalysis," 999.

Chapter 5

1. In the spring of 2021, due to the COVID-19 pandemic, the New York City Public Schools distributed state tests on a limited basis that were not supposed to "count"—that is, were not the basis of admissions criteria or sorting into homogeneous groups. Whether schools used these results on a less formal basis, and whether larger bodies used data from them to make decisions or whether they have or will be used in certain contentious conversations about "learning loss" is uncertain.
2. Kathi Weeks coins this apt neoliberal amalgam of "simultaneously self-directed and manageable" in her discussion of the contradictions of autonomy and command in post-Fordist or "post-Taylorist" work. Weeks, *Problem with Work*, 56.
3. Terms such as "affective labor" and "emotional labor" refer to the types of work that have to do with managing emotions and are key aspects of subject making. There are subtle yet important differences between the two terms, and they arise from different intellectual traditions. "Affective labor" is a concept that arose in socialist feminist traditions to account for a considerable part of women's domestic work that was invisibilized, while "emotional labor" was popularized by Arlie Hochschild to refer to the management of customer's emotions in the feminized field of working class service jobs, although the term has now been popularized to include activities far outside its intended usage. Weeks, "Life Within and Against Work"; Hochschild, "Housework." See Oksala's "Affective Labor" for a critical review of such conceptions for critical feminist politics.
4. I set aside the issue of how these profound struggles are often glossed with such simple invocations as if one can simply "teach" compliance, passivity, and compliance to authority rather than a long protracted struggle of subjection that is never total.
5. Bowles and Gintis, *Schooling in Capitalist America*, 39.
6. Marx, *Grundrisse*, 692.
7. Lazzarato, "Immaterial Labour," 137. Weeks, *Problem with Work*, 56–57.
8. Marasco, "Fascist in the Family," 795, 793. Marasco reappraises early critical theory's position that the bourgeois family is the site where the "authoritarian personality" is reproduced, and that "fascism begins in the family."
9. Klein, "Psycho-analytic Play."
10. Dalla Costa, *Women and the Subversion*, 52.
11. Holloway and Pimlott-Wilson, "Parental Involvement," "Schools, Families."
12. Harvie, "Value Production."

13. In "Value Production," Harvie elaborates: "Teachers (co-)produce new labour power. But this new labour power—new workers—will in turn be employed to produce value and surplus value, i.e. to produce and reproduce capital, the very social relation that exploits human beings, including teachers. Thus, the 'product' of teachers' labour is turned against them: they become alienated from the product of their labour" (12).
14. Healthline, "Reading to Children."
15. Solar, "Importance of Reading."
16. C. Stearns, "Unruly Affects," 9; C. Stearns, "Let Them Get Mad."
17. C. Stearns, "Responsive Classroom"; C. Stearns, "Consent in the Childhood Classroom"; P. Stearns, "Happy Children."
18. Women's initial response that they don't assist with homework or "only" check it is likely due to the invisible nature of these labors as labor, and because such an admission might undermine their children's abilities, such that they themselves would appear as the caricature of mothers who do their child's homework for them. Either way, asking about after-school routines was more neutral and a concrete way to elicit specific responses.
19. Fraad, "Exploitation in the Labor of Love."
20. Fraad, "Exploitation in the Labor of Love," 69.

Chapter 6

1. Ranganathan and Bonds, "Racial Regimes"; Bhandar and Toscano, "Race, Real Estate"; Wyly et al., "New Racial Meanings."
2. Aggarwal, "Ideological Architecture"; Coughlan, "Divergent Trends"; Makris, "Chimera of Choice"; Roda, "School Choice"; Yoon et al., "Geography of School Choice."
3. Boterman, "Deconstructing Coincidence"; Devine, "Class Reproduction."
4. Coughlan et al., "Tensions Between School Choice"; Cucchiara, "Doing Damage"; Lareau and Goyette, *Choosing Homes.*
5. Harris, "Whiteness as Property"; Aggarwal, "Ideological Architecture"; Dixson and Rousseau, "Critical Race Theory."
6. Lareau and Goyette, *Choosing Homes*; Ewing, "Choosing Homes," 291.
7. Ranganathan and Bonds, "Racial Regimes of Property, 198.
8. Green et al., "School Finance"; Lipsitz, "Possessive Investment"; Taylor, *Race for Profit*; Wyly et al. "New Racial Meanings."
9. Gibbons, City of Segregation; "Toscano and Bhandar, "Race, Real Estate"; Chakravartty and da Silva, "Accumulation, Dispossession."
10. Bonefeld, *Critical Theory of Economic*, 24.
11. Marx, *Capital*, 61 (Reitter).
12. Neoliberal high-stakes testing and accountability reforms have decimated public education with disparate effects on schools serving students in poverty and/or racialized minorities is vast. See Au, "High-Stakes Testing"; de Lissovoy, *Education and Emancipation*; Slater and Seawright ,"Putting Homo Economicus."
13. Slater and Seawright, "Putting Homo Economicus," 371.
14. Bonefeld, *Critical Theory of Economic*, 36.

15. Kromidas, "Learning Hierarchy."
16. de Lissovoy, *Education and Emancipation.*
17. Kromidas, "Mothering and the Racialised Production," 297.
18. Barnum and LaMarr LeMee, "Looking for a Home?"
19. Karp, "Buyer's and Renter's."
20. Venture capital firms and philanthropists with interests in school privatization have invested enormous resources into datafication to shape education policy. Barnum and LaMarr LeMee, "Looking for a Home?"; Williamson, "Decoding ClassDojo."
21. Hasan and Kumar, "Digitisation and Divergence." School ratings websites that factor in parent reviews in their ratings also magnify racial and class segregation. Gillani et al., "Parents' Online."
22. Yoshinaga and Kamenetz, "Race, School Ratings." See also Barnum and LaMarr LeMee, "Looking for a Home?"
23. Wall, "Latest Upper West."
24. Wall, "Latest Upper West."
25. Kucsera and Orfield, "New York State."
26. Mader et al., "Paradox of Choice."
27. Sattin-Bajaj and Roda, "Opportunity Hoarding," 25.
28. "Opportunity hoarding," a term coined by Charles Tilly is defined as "behavior that reserves for one's own children the best possible educational opportunities," with an "inevitable flip side . . . excluding others from those same good opportunities." Sattin-Bajaj and Roda, "Opportunity Hoarding," 5; Tilly, *Durable Inequality*. Rather than simply a vehicle to transfer resources, school choice is productively conceived as a highly charged arena in which to articulate one's politics and aspirations, an important site at which class and raced subjectivities are formed. Various activists groups, parents, social justice advocates, community members, students, and educators verily shape this highly charged arena, continually challenging the way the New York City Public Schools' choice policies and their implementation (among other policies and practices) reproduce race and class inequalities. The work of the New York City Alliance for School Integration and Desegregation, New York Appleseed, and the youth-led Integrate NYC is vocal in its resistance to policies that entrench racial divisions in schools, with school choice policies often a key target. Parents who benefit from neoliberal reforms increasingly position themselves as "engaged and collective activists" resisting reforms such as choice policies. Rubin et al., "Parental Action." While Rubin et al., in "Parental Action," include the widespread opting out of high-stakes standardized tests, I found that many women who opted out did so not out of any commitment to social justice but for the benefit of their child.
29. Mader et al., "Paradox of Choice."
30. Bowles and Gintis, *Schooling in Capitalist America.*
31. The demographics for New York City are Asian, 13 percent; Black, 22 percent; Hispanic, 29 percent; white, 32 percent; and two or more races, 2 percent.
32. See Lung-Amam's *Trespassers* for an analogous analysis of white flight and resistance to Asian American place making in Silicon Valley.
33. Hemphill, *Best Public Elementary*, 236.

34. Hemmings and Treacher, "Feminist Subject."
35. Jarvis et al., "Cities and Gender"; B. Parker, "Feminist Forays."
36. New York City educational activists have long claimed that the city's "gifted and talented" program exacerbates class and race inequalities and racial segregation. Mayor de Blasio capitulated to these pressures at the end of his tenure. The decision sparked equally passionate resistance and erupted into one of the most heated educational controversies to grip the city in my adult life. In the geographical context of my research, where there are many "gifted and talented" programs, the issue took on starkly racialized dynamics, which pitted Asian and white parents against Black and Latino parents. Then Mayor Eric Adams reinstated the program in 2022, his first year of office.
37. Noble, *Algorithms of Oppression*.
38. Joffe Walt, "Nice White Parents."
39. Nguyen-Hoang and Yinger, "Capitalization of School Quality."
40. Schwartz et al., "Do Choice Schools?"
41. Campagna, "Do Homebuyers Care?"
42. Connolly, *World More Concrete*, 7.
43. Wynter, "Ceremony Found," 199–200. Black studies as a field has theorized Black life both as the "negative ontological ground" of Western humanism, as well as its world-making capacities. Weheliye, *Habeas Viscus*, 5; Sharpe "In the Wake."
44. Kromidas, "Towards the Human."
45. Bhandar, "Registering Interests," 295.
46. Au, "High Stakes Testing," 21.
47. Kromidas, "Towards the Human."

Chapter 7

1. Watson, *Juggling Mother*, 4; Wilson and Yochim, *Mothering Through Precarity*.
2. "Read what was never written" is Hugo van Hofmannsthal's phrase that Walter Benjamin cites in "Theses on the Philosophy of History," 338.
3. Scholars of motherhood date the origin of the media hype around the "mommy wars" to the 1980s. See Steiner and Lachover, "Mommy Wars." In "Deconstructing the 'Mommy Wars,'" Zimmerman et al. critique talk and reality shows of this period for making "mommy wars" a spectacle that diverted attention from structural issues mothers faced, such as health care, childcare, and racial justice.
4. Currently, the divide in the mommy wars encompasses various practices (e.g., breast or bottle feeding) and philosophies (e.g., attachment versus conventional parenting), and is increasingly fought in the "mommysphere." Abetz and Moore, "Welcome"; Mustosmäki and Sihto, "'F*** This Shit"; Wilson and Yochim, *Mothering*.
5. Rose, *Mothers*, 18, 24.
6. Zeavin, "Hot and Cool," 54.
7. Jensen, "Against Resilience," 76.
8. Rose, *Mothers*, 17.
9. Rose, *Mothers*, 26–27.

10. While both are intensive mothers, there are differences between the tiger and the helicopter mother. The figures are racialized as Asian and white respectively, and this guides how their associated suite of parenting practices are represented. The tiger mom is caricatured as too cold and disciplining, whereas the helicopter mom is too warm and obsessively coddling. See Zeavin, "Hot and Cool," for a theory of maternal fitness that emerged from midcentury psychology.
11. Druckerman, "Bad News."
12. Kamentz, "Overparenting Crisis"; Pinsker, "Intensive Parenting"; Rosin, "Overprotected Kid"; Petersen, "Overprotected American Child." The latter two are accompanied by photographs of cosseted boys, one bubble wrapped and the other strapped in pillows.
13. Druckerman's "Bad News" did not mention Lareau but focused on the recent book of two economists, Doepke and Zilibotti's *Love, Money, and Parenting*, a work that picks up Lareau's dichotomization of parenting styles and zeroes in on Lareau's claim that middle class professional mothers spend more "quality time" with children, which they verify and quantify through time-use studies. They see mothers' education level, rather than work status, as the key difference in the "time gap." "More-educated women" spend an average of four more hours a week on childcare, an equation balanced by their reports of four hours less of leisure time. Doepke and Zilibotti, *Love, Money, and Parenting*, 130.
14. Roediger, *Sinking Middle Class*.
15. Rose, *Mothers*.
16. Berlant, *Desire/Love*, 51.
17. Wilson and Yochim, *Mothering*, 161.
18. Ruddick, *Maternal Thinking*, 347.
19. Rich, *Of Woman Born*, 275.
20. Ruddick *Maternal Thinking*, 103. See also O'Reilly, "Maternal Theory."
21. Adorno's summary ethical proposition about our "choices" within capitalism is his oft-quoted: "Wrong life cannot be lived rightly." Adorno, *Minima Moralia*, 39.
22. Lazarre, *Mother Knot*, xxiii.
23. Lowy, *Maternal Experience*, 2–3; Takševa, "Mother Love," 1–2; Tuval-Mashiach and Shaiovitz-Gourman, "Maternal Ambivalence, 357.
24. Freud, "Notes upon a Case"; Freud, *Totem and Taboo*; Klein, "Development"; Klein, "Mourning."
25. Watson, *Juggling Mother*, 4.
26. Mustosmäki and Sihto, "'F*** This Shit,'" 225.
27. Gill, "Affective, Cultural, and Psychic," 610; Smyth, "Postfeminism, Ambivalence."
28. Freud, "Screen Memories," 315.
29. Kromidas, "When I Was."
30. Jackson, "Phenomenological Psychopathology," 1.
31. Psychoanalytic theory suggests that dialogue with women about maternal ideologies can help women develop liberatory models of parenting. Even acknowledging maternal ambivalence can be significant for mothers' psychological and emotional growth. Tuval-Mashiach and Shaiovitz-Gourman, "Maternal Ambivalence." Such conversations can function as interventions where women can discuss how to resolve some of their dilemmas, not to better

"fit" into or better perform the labors they are obliged to do, but to alleviate the psychic stress, and to deepen critiques from which they may collectively refuse the structural forces that bind them to them.

32. Jackson, "Phenomenological Psychopathology."
33. For instance, in "Uses of the Erotic," Audre Lorde discusses the "deepest and non-rational knowledge" (53) that women are taught to distrust that could be put to use to enrich life for women and children.
34. Coviello, "Anthony and Carmela," 254.
35. Kristeva, in Casavecchia, "Taci, Anzi, Parla."
36. Lombardi, "New Ties," 282.

Conclusion

1. Sutherland, "Poetics of *Capital*," 209.
2. Best, *Automatic Fetish*, 9, 11, 2, 5.
3. Osborne, "Introduction," 10.
4. Fisher, "Abstract Models."
5. Marx, *Capital*, 546, 532 (Fowkes).
6. In *Capital* Marx referred to Hephaestus's workshop in Homer's *Iliad* (532; Fowkes).
7. Marx, *Grundrisse*, 692, 693; Marx, *Capital*, 544, 147 (Fowkes).
8. The phrase "dominant subject" appears twice in *Capital*, first in a passage about the movement of value in different forms, and the second in a passage referring to work within factories. Marx, *Capital*, 255, 544 (Fowkes). "Automatic subject" appears in the same passage as the first use of "dominant subject." Marx, *Capital*, 255 (Fowkes); Thoborn, *Deleuze, Marx*, 63.
9. Marx, *Capital*, 544 (Fowkes).
10. Marx, *Capital*, 899; 380 (Fowkes).
11. Wynter, "Ceremony Found," 26, refers to economists as the "secular priesthood" of our global order.
12. Marx, *Capital*, 372 (Fowkes).
13. Marx, *Capital*, 460 (Fowkes).
14. Sutherland discusses how Marx is more tentative or open in the *Grundrisse*, where capital is variously described as "stored up," "accumulated," or "objectified" labor, wherein the "critical terminus" of *Capital*, capital is described through one predicate, "it is 'dead' labour once and for all." Sutherland, "Poetics of Capital," 210.
15. Johnston, *Infinite Greed*, xvii, xviii; Wynter, "No Humans Involved," 44.
16. Holloway argues that revolutionary thought and practice must not only emphasize the "presence of the object in the subject," but "the destructive force of the subject within the object, the presence of the subject in-and-against-and-beyond the object as its crisis. We have to make explicit that our struggles are the crisis of capital." Holloway, "The Train," 176.
17. McKinley, *Solidarity with Children*, 125.
18. Baldwin, "On Being White," 92.
19. Roessler, "Utopianism in Pianisimo," 230.

20. Bloch in Roessler, "Utopianism in Pianisimo," 230.
21. Adorno, *Minima Moralia*, 228.
22. Gordon, *Hawthorn Archives*, 34. See also Kromidas, "'Agent of Revolutionary Thought.'"
23. Kromidas, "Learning Hierarchy."
24. Cleaver, "Self-Valorization"; Tronti, "Destituent Power"; Holloway, *Hope in Hopeless Times*; Hemmens, "Radical Subjectivity," 256.
25. Vaneigem, *Revolution of Everyday Life*, 196.
26. Marx and Engels, *German Ideology*, 57.

Appendix

1. Kromidas, *City Kids*, 14–17.

BIBLIOGRAPHY

Sources from the Parenting Public Sphere

REFERENCES TO MEDIA, POPULAR WRITING, WEBSITES, AND OTHER PARENTING ARTIFACTS CITED IN THE TEXT.

American Academy of Pediatrics. "Changing Landscape of Media Has Multiple Impacts on Children, Teens." *AAP News*, October 23, 2016. https://www.aappublications.org/news/2016/10/23/Peds21102316.

Anderson, Melinda D. "Why Black Parents Aren't Joining the Push to Reopen Schools." *Mother Jones*, March 18, 2021. https://www.motherjones.com/politics/2021/03/why-black-parents-arent-joining-the-push-to-reopen-schools/.

Anderson, Melinda D. "'You're Out of Your Mind If You Think I'm Ever Going Back to School.'" *International New York Times*, October 28, 2020. https://www.nytimes.com/2020/10/28/opinion/virtual-school-racism.html.

Aperture Devereaux Student Strengths Assessment. "Parent Portal." https://info.apertureed.com/parent-portal.

Atkins, Dale, and Amanda Salzhauer. *The Kindness Advantage: Cultivating Compassionate and Connected Children.* Simon and Schuster, 2018.

The Atlantic. "Helicopter Parents: Are Helicopter Parents Ruining a Generation?" April 11, 2018. https://www.theatlantic.com/video/index/557696/home-school-episode-1/.

Barnum, Matt, and Gabrielle LaMarr LeMee. "Looking for a Home?" *Chalkbeat*, December 5, 2019. https://www.chalkbeat.org/2019/12/5/21121858/looking-for-a-home-you-ve-seen-greatschools-ratings-here-s-how-they-nudge-families-toward-schools-wi/.

Bedtime Math. "Bring Math to Life So Kids Want to Learn It." https://bedtimemath.org/.

Braff, Danielle. "How to Get Your Kids to Treat You as a Teacher" *New York Times*, April 21, 2020. https://www.nytimes.com/2020/04/21/parenting/coronavirus-home-schooling-children.html.

Brookings Institution. "The Social Genome Project" (accessed September 1, 2024). https://www.brookings.edu/the-social-genome-project/.

Brookings Institution. N.d. "About Us." https://www.brookings.edu/about-us/.

Brooks, David. "Children Need to Be Back in School Now." *New York Times*, January 28, 2021. https://www.nytimes.com/2021/01/28/opinion/coronavirus-schools-unions.html.

Capriglione, Amanda. "Food & Nutrition to Boost Your Baby's Brain Development While Pregnant." May 6, 2024. https://feedmomandme.com/blogs/mama-blog/nine-foods-to-boost-your-babys-brain-development-while-pregnant.

Case, Anne, and Angus Deaton. "Accounting for the Widening Mortality Gap Between American Adults with and Without a BA." *Brookings Papers on Economic Activity* (Fall 2023): 1–45.

Case, Anne, and Angus Deaton. "Without a College Degree, Life Is Staggeringly Shorter." *New York Times*, October 3, 2023. https://www.nytimes.com/2023/10/03/opinion/life-expectancy-college-degree.html.

Chancellor of the NYC Department of Education (@DOEChancellor). "I'm Amazed by the Resilience." Twitter, April 28, 2020. https://twitter.com/DOEChancellor/status/1255172139461812224?s=20.

Christakis, Erika. "The Dangers of Distracted Parenting." *The Atlantic*, July–August 2018. https://www.theatlantic.com/magazine/archive/2018/07/the-dangers-of-distracted-parenting/561752/.

Collins, Kaitlyn. "The Real Mommy War Is Against the State" *New York Times*, February 9, 2019. https://www.nytimes.com/2019/02/09/opinion/sunday/the-real-mommy-war-is-against-the-state.html.

DeParle, Jason. "Disadvantaged Students More Likely to Be Learning Remotely, Study Finds." *New York Times*, December 24, 2020. https://www.nytimes.com/2020/12/24/us/remote-learning-student-income.html.

Dorn, Emma, Bryan Hancock, Jimmy Sarakatsannis, and Ellen Viruleg. "COVID-19 and Student Learning in the United States: The Hurt Could Last a Lifetime." *McKinsey & Company* 1 (2020): 1–9.

Dreier, Hannah. "Alone and Exploited, Migrant Children Work Brutal Jobs Across the US." *New York Times*, February 5, 2023. https://www.nytimes.com/2023/02/25/us/unaccompanied-migrant-child-workers-exploitation.html.

Druckerman, Pam. "The Bad News About Helicopter Parenting: It Works." *New York Times*, February 7, 2019. https://www.nytimes.com/2019/02/07/opinion/helicopter-parents-economy.html.

Duncan, Arne. "Looking in the Mirror." Keynote address of Secretary Arne Duncan to the MOM Congress on Education, 2010. https://permanent.fdlp.gov/gpo15120/looking-mirror.htm.

The Economist. "Choose Your Parents Wisely." July 25, 2014. https://www.economist.com/united-states/2014/07/25/choose-your-parents-wisely.

Fluker, Dominique. "According to This Stay-at-Home Mother and Wife, the #Tradwife Trend Is Problematic." *Essence*, March 22, 2023. https://www.essence.com/lifestyle/tradwife/.

Garbes, Angela. *Essential Labor: Mothering as Social Change*. Harper Wave, 2023.

Garcia, Maria Elena, Kay Frunzi, Ceri B. Dean, Nieves Flores, and Kirsten B. Miller. "Toolkit of Resources for Engaging Families and the Community as Partners in Education: Part 4: Engaging All in Data Conversations." National Center for Education Evaluation and Regional Assistance, Institute of Education Sciences, US Department of Education, and REL Pacific: Regional Educational Laboratory at McREL International, September 2016. https://ies.ed.gov/sites/default/files/migrated/rel/regions/pacific/pdf/REL_2016153.pdf.

Gilbert, Leah K., Tara W. Strine, Leigh E. Szucs, Tamara N. Crawford, Sharyn E. Parks, Danielle T. Barradas, Rashid Njai, and Jean Y. Ko. "Racial and Ethnic Differences in Parental Attitudes and Concerns About School Reopening During the COVID-19 Pandemic—United States, July 2020." *Morbidity and Mortality Weekly Report* 69 (2020): 1848–52. http://dx.doi.org/10.15585/mmwr.mm6949a2.

Gogoi, Pallavi. "Stuck-at-Home Moms: The Pandemic's Devastating Toll on Women." *NPR*, October 28, 2020. https://www.npr.org/2020/10/28/928253674/stuck-at-home-moms-the-pandemics-devastating-toll-on-women.

Goldstein, Dana. "Research Shows Students Falling Months Behind During Virus Disruptions." *New York Times*, June 5, 2020. https://www.nytimes.com/2020/06/05/us/coronavirus-education-lost-learning.html.

Grose, Jessica. "The Primal Scream: America's Mothers Are in Crisis" *New York Times*, February 4, 2021. https://www.nytimes.com/interactive/2021/02/04/parenting/working-moms-coronavirus.html.

Hainer, Michelle. "My Son Thinks I'm His Teacher." *New York Times*, November 6, 2020. https://www.nytimes.com/2020/11/06/parenting/remote-learning-parent-boundaries.html.

Hanushek, Eric, and Ludger Woessman. "The Economic Impact of Learning Losses." Organisation for Economic Cooperation and Development, 2020.

Harris, Elizabeth A. "'It Was Just Too Much': How Remote Learning Is Breaking Parents." *New York Times*, April 27, 2020. https://www.nytimes.com/2020/04/27/nyregion/coronavirus-homeschooling-parents.html.

Harvard Business Review, Daniel Goleman, Annie McKee, Bill George, and Herminia Ibarra. Emotional Intelligence (series). https://store.hbr.org/books/hbr-emotional-intelligence-series/.

Healthline. "Reading to Children: Why It's So Important and How to Start." 2020. https://www.healthline.com/health/childrens-health/reading-to-children#benefits.

Heckman Foundation. "Fadeout Toolkit." 2024. https://heckmanequation.org/resource/fadeout-toolkit/.

Hemphill, Clara. *NYC's Best Public Elementary Schools: A Parent's Guide.* 2016.

Iasevoli, Brenda. "This Isn't Your Mom's Parent Teacher Conference." *Education Week*, July 12, 2017. https://www.edweek.org/leadership/this-isnt-your-moms-parent-teacher-conference/2017/07.

Iglesias, Matt. "A New Study Says It Doesn't Matter How Much Time You Spend with Your Kids." *Vox*, March 31, 2015. https://www.vox.com/2015/3/31/8320233/time-spent-with-kids.

Jacobs, Christopher. "Covid Learning Loss Could Cost American Kids 900 Billion in Lost Income." *The Federalist*, November 28, 2021. https://thefederalist.com/2022/11/28/covid-learning-loss-could-cost-american-kids-900-billion-in-lost-income/.

Joffe Walt, Chana. *Nice White Parents*. Podcast, Serial Productions and New York Times, 2020.

Kamentz, Anya. "The Overparenting Crisis in School and Home." *NPR Ed*, July 24, 2018. https://www.npr.org/sections/ed/2018/07/24/628042168/the-over-parenting-crisis-in-school-and-at-home.

Karp, Jennifer White. "The Buyer's and Renter's Guide to the NYC's Public and Private Grade Schools." *Brick Underground*, August 25, 2023. https://www.brickunderground.com/blog/2013/03/buyers_and_renters_guide_to_NYC_grade_schools.

Kharas, Homi. *The Rise of the Global Middle Class: How the Search for the Good Life Can Change the World*. Brookings Institution Press, 2023.

Kim, Juliana. "Remote Schooling Brings Bigger Losses for Children Still Learning to Speak English." *New York Times*, December 29, 2020. https://www.nytimes.com/2020/12/29/world/remote-schooling-brings-bigger-losses-for-children-still-learning-to-speak-english.html.

Klass, Perri. "The Guilty Secret of Distracted Parenting." *New York Times*, March 20, 2017. https://www.nytimes.com/2017/03/20/well/family/the-guilty-secret-of-distracted-parenting.html.

Lovevery. "The Looker Play Kit." https://lovevery.com/products/the-play-kits-the-looker.

MacGillis, Alec. "We're Huge in Learning Loss!" Cashing in on the Post-Pandemic Education Crisis." *ProPublica*, July 24, 2023. https://www.propublica.org/article/education-technology-covid-pandemic-crisis-schools.

Mader, Nicole, Clara Hemphill, and Qasim Abass. *The Paradox of Choice: How School Choice Divides New York City Elementary Schools*. Center for New York City Affairs, May 2018. https://www.centernyc.org/the-paradox-of-choice.

Mapp, Karen L. "Title I and Parent Involvement: Lessons from the Past, Recommendations for the Future." Paper presented at the conference Tightening Up Title I, Center for American Progress and American Enterprise Institute, March 11, 2011. https://cdn.americanprogress.org/wp-content/uploads/events/2011/03/av/parental_involvement.pdf.

Martin, Gary. "It's the Curse of 2022: Distracted Parenting." LinkedIn, August 19, 2022. https://www.linkedin.com/pulse/its-curse-2022-distracted-parenting-martin-faim-face.

Matherly, Charlotte. "Americans Without College Degrees Die Younger." *Chronicle of High Education*, October 3, 2023. https://www.chronicle.com/article/americans-without-college-degrees-die-younger-heres-what-the-latest-research-tells-us.

Montei, Amanda. *Touched Out: Motherhood, Misogyny, Consent, and Control.* Beacon Press, 2023.

Montei, Amanda. "When I Became a Mother, I Lost My Body and Realized It Never Belonged to Me." *The Guardian*, September 11, 2023. https://www.theguardian.com/lifeandstyle/2023/sep/11/motherhood-parenting-body-autonomy .

Mott Children's Hospital. "Top Health Concerns for Kids in 2020 During the Pandemic." *National Poll on Children's Health* 37, no. 4 (2020). https://mottpoll.org/reports/top-health-concerns-kids-2020-during-pandemic.

Murkoff, Heidi. "Should I Play Music for My Baby in the Womb?" What to Expect, October 18, 2025. https://www.whattoexpect.com/pregnancy/ask-heidi/week-20/influences-on-the-womb.aspx.

New York City Public Schools. "Parent University: Classes for NYC Families." https://parentu.schools.nyc/.

New York City Public Schools. "School Quality." https://www.schools.nyc.gov/about-us/reports/school-quality.

New York State Education Department. *Guidance: Parent and Family Engagement: Title I, Part A.* Office of ESSA-Funded Programs, June 2019.

Next Generation Science Standards for States, by States. "Understanding the Standards." https://www.nextgenscience.org/understanding-standards/understanding-standards.

Nietzel, Michael. "Americans Without College Degrees Live Shorter Lives." *Forbes*, October 3, 2023. https://www.forbes.com/sites/michaeltnietzel/2023/10/03/americans-without-college-degrees-live-shorter-lives-brookings-study-finds/.

Normanton, Kim. 2019. "Why Can't Our Children Talk?" *BBC*, February 11, 2019. https://www.bbc.co.uk/programmes/m0002bmv.

Oster, Emily. *The Family Firm: A Data-Driven Guide to Better Decision Making in the Early Schools Years.* Penguin, 2022.

Perelman, Deb. "In the COVID-19 Economy, You Can Have a Kid or a Job. You Can't Have Both." *New York Times*, July 2, 2020. https://www.nytimes.com/2020/07/02/business/covid-economy-parents-kids-career-homeschooling.html.

Petersen, Andrea. "Overprotected American Child." *Wall Street Journal*, July 1, 2018. https://www.wsj.com/articles/the-overprotected-american-child-1527865038.

Pinsker, Joe. "Intensive Parenting Is Now the New Norm in America." *The Atlantic*, January 16, 2019. https://www.theatlantic.com/family/archive/2019/01/intensive-helicopter-parenting-inequality/580528/.

Reeves, Richard, and Kimberly Howard. *The Parenting Gap*. Center on Children and Families at the Brookings Institution, 2013.

Reeves, Richard V., and Isabell V. Sawhill. "Introduction: A New Contract with the Middle Class." Future of the Middle Class, September 2020. Brookings Institution. https://www.brookings.edu/articles/a-new-contract-with-the-middle-class-introduction/.

Rosin, Hannah. "The Overprotected Kid." *The Atlantic*, April 2014. https://www.theatlantic.com/magazine/archive/2014/04/hey-parents-leave-those-kids-alone/358631/.

Rubin, April. "Life Expectancy Gap in America Widens Depending on College Education." *Axios*, October 16, 2023. https://www.axios.com/2023/10/16/life-expectancy-educated-adults-mortality-rate.

Ruler. "RULER Resources for Families." https://rulerapproach.org/ruler-resources-for-families/.

Sawhill, Isabel V. "Should We Worry About Low Fertility?" *Commentary*, Brookings Institution, December 17, 2014. https://www.brookings.edu/blog/social-mobility-memos/2014/12/17/should-we-worry-about-low-fertility/.

Sawhill, Isabel V., Morgan Welch, and Chris Miller. "It's Getting More Expensive to Raise Children. And Government Isn't Doing Much to Help." *Commentary*, Brookings Institution, August 30, 2022. https://www.brookings.edu/blog/up-front/2022/08/30/its-getting-more-expensive-to-raise-children-and-government-isnt-doing-much-to-help/.

Sawhill, Isabel V., Scott Winship, and Kerry Searle Grannis. "Pathways to the Middle Class: Balancing Personal and Public Responsibilities." Center on Children and Families at the Brookings Institution, September 20, 2012. https://www.brookings.edu/articles/pathways-to-the-middle-class-balancing-personal-and-public-responsibilities/.

Skenazy, Leonore. "Parents, You Can Stop Helicoptering." *Wall Street Journal*, March 29, 2018. https://www.wsj.com/articles/parents-you-stop-helicoptering-1522364378.

Solar, Laura. "The Importance of Reading to Children." *Patch* (Half Hollow Hills, NY), December 7, 2017. https://patch.com/new-york/halfhollowhills/importance-reading-aloud-children.

Strauss, Elissa. "How to Know If You're a 'Helicopter Parent' and Why It Matters." *CNN*, March 22, 2019. https://www.cnn.com/2019/03/22/health/helicopter-parenting-strauss/index.html.

Tolentino, Jia. "Can Motherhood Be a Mode of Rebellion?" *New Yorker*, May 8, 2022. https://www.newyorker.com/books/under-review/can-motherhood-be-a-mode-of-rebellion.

U.S. Surgeon General. "Parents Under Pressure: The US Surgeon General's Advisory on the Mental Health & Well-being of Parents." 2024.

Valenti, Jessica. "Don't Stress Out. Our Kids Are Just Fine When Their Mothers Work Late." *The Guardian*, April 1, 2015. https://www.theguardian.com/commentisfree/2015/apr/01/dont-stress-out-our-kids-are-just-fine-when-their-mothers-work-late.

Wall, Patrick. "Latest Upper West Side Rezoning Battle Renews Debate Over How Best to Integrate Schools" *Chalkbeat New York*, June 16, 2016. https://www.chalkbeat.org/newyork/2016/6/16/21100565/latest-upper-west-side-rezoning-battle-renews-debate-over-how-best-to-integrate-schools/.

Wheeler, Sarah. "Motherhood Radicalized Me." *The Cut*, September 12, 2023. https://www.thecut.com/2023/09/amanda-montei-touched-out-interview.html.

Wolfers, Justin. "Money Really Does Lead to a More Satisfying Life." *New York Times*, April 24, 2018. https://www.nytimes.com/2018/08/24/business/money-satisfaction-lottery-study.html.

Wolfers, Justin. "Why a Claim About the Irrelevance of Parenting Time Doesn't Add Up." *New York Times: The Upshot*, April 2, 2015. https://www.nytimes.com/2015/04/03/upshot/why-a-claim-about-the-irrelevance-of-parenting-time-doesnt-add-up.html?_r=0.

Wolfers, Justin. "Yes, Your Time as a Parent Does Make a Difference." *New York Times: The Upshot*, April 1, 2015. https://www.nytimes.com/2015/04/02/upshot/yes-your-time-as-a-parent-does-make-a-difference.html.

World Bank Group. "The Human Capital Project: Frequently Asked Questions." March 19, 2019. https://www.worldbank.org/en/publication/human-capital/brief/the-human-capital-project-frequently-asked-questions#HCP7.

World Bank Group. "Learning Losses from COVID-19 Could Cost This Generation of Students Close to $17 Trillion in Lifetime Earnings." Press release, December 6, 2021. https://www.worldbank.org/en/news/press-release/2021/12/06/learning-losses-from-covid-19-could-cost-this-generation-of-students-close-to-17-trillion-in-lifetime-earnings.

World Economic Forum. "Why Having It All Is a Myth—For Men and Women." November 6, 2015. https://www.weforum.org/agenda/2015/11/why-having-it-all-is-a-myth-for-men-and-women/.

Wuori, Dan (@DanWuori). "Read to Your Newborn . . ." Twitter, July 31, 2023. https://x.com/DanWuori/status/1685978193881153542?s=20.

Yoshinaga, Kendra, and Anya Kamenetz. "Race, School Ratings, and Real Estate: A Legal Gray Area." *NPR Ed*, October 10, 2016. https://www.npr.org/sections/ed/2016/10/10/495944682/race-school-ratings-and-real-estate-a-legal-gray-area.

Scholarly Sources

Abetz, Jenna, and Julia Moore. "'Welcome to the Mommy Wars, Ladies': Making Sense of the Ideology of Combative Mothering in Mommy Blogs." *Communication Culture & Critique* 11, no. 2 (2018): 265–81.

Adamson, Morgan. "The Human Capital Strategy." *Ephemera* 9, no. 4 (2009): 271–84.

Adkins, Lisa. "Contingent Labour and the Rewriting of the Sexual Contract." In *The Post-Fordist Sexual Contract: Working and Living in Contingency*, edited by Lisa Adkins and Maryann Dever. Palgrave Macmillan, 2016.

Adkins, Lisa. *The Time of Money*. Stanford University Press, 2018.

Adorno, Theodor. *History and Freedom: Lectures 1964–1965*. 1964. Translated by Rodney Livingstone. Polity, 2008.

Adorno, Theodor. "Marx and the Basic Concepts of Sociological Theory." 1962. *Historical Materialism* 26, no. 1 (2018): 154–64.

Adorno, Theodor. *Minima Moralia: Reflections on a Damaged Life*. 1951. Translated by E. F. N. Jephcott. Verso, 2005.

Aggarwal, Ujju. "The Ideological Architecture of Whiteness as Property in Educational Policy." *Educational Policy* 30, no. 1 (2016): 128–52.

Agostinelli, Francesco, and Giuseppe Sorrenti. "Money vs. Time: Family Income, Maternal Labor Supply, and Child Development." Working Paper No. 273, Department of Economics, University of Zurich, 2021.

Ahmed, Sarah. *The Promise of Happiness*. Duke University Press, 2010.

Alessandrini, Donatella. "Immaterial Labour and Alternative Valorisation Processes in Italian Feminist Debates: (Re)Exploring the 'Commons' of Re-production," *feminists@law* 1, no. 2 (2012): 1–28.

Allen, Amy. *Critique on the Couch: Why Critical Theory Needs Psychoanalysis*. Columbia University Press, 2021.

Alon, Titan, Matthias Doepke, Jane Olmstead-Rumsey, and Michèle Tertilt. "The Impact of COVID-19 on Gender Equality." *Political Economy* 9 (2020): https://digitalcommons.wcl.american.edu/wlpeconomy/9.

Alterman, Eric. "Altercation: Is Brookings a 'Liberal' Think Tank or a Big Money Lobbyist?" *American Prospect*, June 17, 2022. https://prospect.org/power/altercation-is-brookings-liberal-think-tank-or-big-money-lobbyist/.

Arnall, Gavin. "Capitalist Slavery and Its Afterlives: On Commodification, Racialization, and Social Reproduction." *Small Axe* 29, no. 1 (2025): 147–58.

Arnall, Gavin. "The Many Tasks of the Marxist Translator. Approaching Marxism as/in/with Translation from Antonio Gramsci to the Zapatistas." *Historical Materialism* 30, no. 1 (2022): 99–132.

Attanasio, Orazio, Sarah Cattan, and Costas Meghir. "Early Childhood Development, Human Capital, and Poverty." *Annual Review of Economics* 14, no. 1 (2022): 853–92.

Au, Wayne. "High-Stakes Testing: A Tool for White Supremacy for over 100 Years." In *What's Race Got to Do with It: How Current School Reform Policy*

Maintains Racial and Economic Inequality, edited by Edwin Mayorga and Bree Picower. Peter Lang, 2019.

Ayotte, Wendy. *As Soon as You're Born, They Make You Feel Small*. Pamphlet, 1986.

Ba', Stefano. "The Critique of Sociology of Childhood: Human Capital as the Concrete 'Social Construction of Childhood.'" *Power and Education* 13, no. 2 (2021): 73–87.

Baasch, Kyle. "The Theater of Economic Categories: Rediscovering *Capital* in the Late 1960s." *Radical Philosophy*, no. 208 (2020): 18–33.

Baldwin, James. "On Being White . . . and Other Lies." *Essence* 14, no. 2 (1984): 90–92.

Bandelj, Nina. "The Social Life of Money for Children." *British Journal of Sociology* (2025): 1–21. https://doi.org/10.1111/1468-4446.13176_1.

Bandelj, Nina, and Michelle Spiegel. "Pricing the Priceless Child 2.0: Children as Human Capital Investment." *Theory and Society* 52, no. 5 (2023): 805–30.

Baquedano-López, Patricia, Rebecca Anne Alexander, and Sera J. Hernandez. "Equity Issues in Parental and Community Involvement in Schools: What Teacher Educators Need to Know." *Review of Research in Education* 37, no. 1 (2013): 149–82.

Baucom, Ian. *Specters of the Atlantic: Finance Capital, Slavery, and the Philosophy of History*. Duke University Press, 2005.

Baumann, Charlotte. "Adorno, the New Reading of Marx, and Methodologies of Critique." In *Adorno and Marx: Negative Dialectics and the Critique of Political Economy*, edited by Werner Bonefeld and Chris O'Kane. Bloomsbury Academic, 2022.

Becker, Gary. "Human Capital." *The Concise Encyclopedia of Economics*, edited by David R. Henderson. Liberty Press, 1964.

Becker, Gary. "Human Capital and the Economy." *Proceedings of the American Philosophical Society*, 136, no. 1 (1992): 85–92.

Becker, Gary S. "Investment in Human Capital: A Theoretical Analysis." *Journal of Political Economy* 70, no. 5 (1962): 9–49.

Becker, Gary S., François Ewald, and Bernard E. Harcourt. "'Becker on Ewald on Foucault on Becker': American Neoliberalism and Michel Foucault's 1979 'Birth of Biopolitics' Lectures." *University of Chicago Institute for Law & Economics Olin Research Paper* 614 (2012): 1–20.

Benjamin, Walter. "Theses on the Philosophy of History." 1940. In *Illuminations*. Translated by Harry Zohn. Mariner Books, 2019.

Berlant, Lauren. *Desire/Love*. Punctum Books, 2012.

Berman, Elizabeth Popp. 2022. *Thinking Like an Economist: How Efficiency Replaced Equality in US Public Policy*. Princeton University Press.

Bernstein, Robin. *Racial Innocence: Performing American Childhood and Race From Slavery to Civil Rights*. NYU Press, 2011.

Best, Beverley. *The Automatic Fetish: The Law of Value in Marx's Capital*. Verso, 2024.

Best, Beverley. "Wages for Housework Redux: Social Reproduction and the Utopian Dialectic of the Value-Form." *Theory & Event* 24, no. 4 (2021): 896–921.

Bhandar, Brenna. "Registering Interests: Modern Methods of Valuing Labour, Land and Life." In *Searching for Contemporary Legal Thought*, edited by Justin Desautels-Stein and Christopher Tomlins. Cambridge University Press, 2017.

Bhattacharya, Tithi. Introduction to *Social Reproduction Theory: Remapping Class, Recentering Oppression*, edited by Tithi Bhattacharya. Pluto Press, 2017.

Bigoni, Maria, Stefania Bortolotti, Margherita Fort, Annalisa Guarini, Daniela Iorio, Chiara Monfardini, Alessandra Sansavini, Davide Sansone, and Chiara Suttora. "Parental Investments and Engagement: New Measures from a Parental Time Use App." *Review of Economics of the Household* 23 (2025): 1–27.

Bonefeld, Werner. "Bringing Critical Theory Back In at a Time of Misery: Three Beginnings Without Conclusion." *Capital & Class* 40, no. 2 (2016): 233–44.

Bonefeld, Werner. "The Capitalist State: Illusion and Critique." In *Revolutionary Writing*, edited by Werner Bonefeld. AK Press, 2003.

Bonefeld, Werner. *A Critical Theory of Economic Compulsion: Wealth, Suffering, Negation*. Routledge, 2023.

Bonefeld, Werner. "On the State as Political Form of Society." *Science & Society* 85, no. 2 (2021): 177–84.

Bonefeld, Werner, Richard Gunn, and Kosmas Psychopedis. *Open Marxism: Dialectics and History*. Pluto Press, 1992.

Boterman, Willem R. "Deconstructing Coincidence: How Middle-Class Households Use Various Forms of Capital to Find a Home." *Housing, Theory and Society* 29, no. 3 (2012): 321–38.

Bowles, Samuel, and Herbert Gintis. "The Problem with Human Capital Theory—A Marxian Critique." *American Economic Review* 65, no. 2 (1975): 74–82.

Bowles, Samuel, and Herbert Gintis. *Schooling in Capitalist America*. Basic Books, 1976.

Briggs, Laura. *How All Politics Became Reproductive Politics: From Welfare Reform to Foreclosure to Trump*. University of California Press, 2017.

Briggs, Laura. *Taking Children: A History of American Terror*. University of California Press, 2020.

Brilli, Ylenia. "Mother's Time Allocation, Childcare, and Child Cognitive Development." *Journal of Human Capital* 16, no. 2 (2022): 233–72.

Britzman, Deborah. *Melanie Klein: Early Analysis, Play, and the Question of Freedom*. Springer, 2016.

Brown, Wendy. *In the Ruins of Neoliberalism: The Rise of Antidemocratic Politics in the West*. Columbia University Press, 2019.

Brown, Wendy. *Undoing the Demos: Neoliberalism's Stealth Revolution*. MIT Press, 2015.

Buck-Morss, Susan. *The Dialectics of Seeing: Walter Benjamin and the Arcades Project*. MIT Press, 1991.

Burns, Tony. "Marx's Capital and the Concept of Super-Exploitation." *Capital & Class* 48, no. 3 (2024): 335–55.

Caffentzis, George. "Throwing Away the Ladder: The Universities in Crisis." *Zerowork* 1 (1975): 128–42.

Calarco, Jessica. *Holding It Together: How Women Became America's Safety Net*. Penguin, 2024.

Camatte, Jacques. *Capital and Community*. Translated by David Brown. Unpopular Books, 1988.

Campagna, John I. "Do Homebuyers Care About Good Grades? Evaluating the Effect of NYC School Accountability Program on Housing Values." Master's thesis, Hunter College, City University of New York, 2018.

Carmichael, Stokely. *We Want Black Power*. Student Nonviolent Coordinating Committee, 1966.

Casavecchia, Barbara. "Taci, Anzi, Parla." *South as a State of Mind* 14, no. 7 (2016): https://www.documenta14.de/en/south/463_taci_anzi_parla.

Caucutt, Elizabeth M., Lance Lochner, Joseph Mullins, and Youngmin Park. "Child Skill Production: Accounting for Parental and Market-Based Time and Goods Investments." Working Paper No. 27838, National Bureau of Economic Research, 2020.

Chakravartty, Paula, and Denise Ferreira Da Silva. "Accumulation, Dispossession, and Debt: The Racial Logic of Global Capitalism—An Introduction." *American Quarterly* 64, no. 3 (2012): 361–85.

Ciblis, Lilia. "The Discourse of Parental Involvement and the Ideologies of Motherhood." *Counterpoints* 439 (2017): 53–78.

Claussen, Detlev, and Jordi Maiso. "Critical Theory and Lived Experience: Interview with Detlev Claussen." *Radical Philosophy* 2, no. 6 (2019): 63–82.

Cleaver, Harry. "Comradely Appropriation." In *Commoning with George Caffentzis and Silvia Federici*, edited by Camille Barbagallo, Nicholas Beuret, and David Harvie. Pluto Press, 2019.

Cleaver, Harry. "The Inversion of Perspective in Marxian Theory: From Valorisation to Self-Valorisation." In *Open Marxism Volume II: Theory and Practice*, edited by Werner Bonefeld, Richard Gunn, and Kosmas Psychopedis. Pluto Press, 1992.

Cleaver, Harry. *Self-Valorization in Mariarosa Dalla Costa's "Women and the Subversion of the Community."* https://la.utexas.edu/users/hcleaver/357k/HMCDallaCostaSelfvalorizationTable.pdf.

Cleaver, Harry. *Thirty-Three Lessons on Capital: Reading Marx Politically*. Pluto Press, 2019.

Clover, Joshua. "Subsumption and Crisis." In *The Sage Handbook of Frankfurt School Critical Theory*, edited by Beverley Best, Chris O'Kane, and Werner Bonefeld. Sage, 2022.

Collins, Caitlyn. *Making Motherhood Work: How Women Manage Careers and Caregiving*. Princeton University Press, 2019.

Collins, Caitlyn, Liana Christin Landivar, Leah Ruppanner, and William J. Scarborough. "COVID-19 and the Gender Gap in Work Hours." *Gender, Work & Organization* 28 (2021): 101–12.
Collins, Patricia Hill. *Black Feminist Thought*. Cambridge, 2000.
Comitato per il Salario al Lavoro Domestico di Padova. "Le Operaie Della Casa, Jan—April 1977." Translated by Sam Pinto and Steve Wright. Reprinted in *Viewpoint Magazine*, October 31, 2015, https://viewpointmag.com/2015/10/31/excerpts-from-le-operaie-della-casa.
Connolly, Nathan D. B. *A World More Concrete: Real Estate and the Remaking of Jim Crow in South Florida*. University of Chicago Press, 2014.
Cooper, Marianne, and Allison J. Pugh. "Families Across the Income Spectrum: A Decade in Review." *Journal of Marriage and Family* 82, no. 1 (2020): 272–99.
Cooper, Melinda. *Family Values: Between Neoliberalism and the New Social Conservatism*. Zone Books, 2017.
Coviello, Peter. "'Anthony and Carmela Get Vaccinated.'" In *Is There God After Prince?* University of Chicago Press, 2023.
Coughlan, Ryan W. "Divergent Trends in Neighbourhood and School Segregation in the Age of School Choice." *Peabody Journal of Education* 93, no. 4 (2018): 349–66.
Coughlan, Ryan, Molly V. Makris, and Allison Roda. "Tensions Between School Choice and Neighborhood Schools Research." *Peabody Journal of Education* 93 (2018): 345–48.
Cox, Nicole, and Silvia Federici. *Counter-Planning from the Kitchen*. New York Wages for Housework Collective and Falling Wall Press, 1975.
Cucchiara, Maia. "'Are We Doing Damage?' Choosing an Urban Public School in an Era of Parental Anxiety." *Anthropology & Education Quarterly* 44, no. 1 (2013): 75–93.
Cunha, Flavio, Eric Nielsen, and Benjamin Williams. "The Econometrics of Early Childhood Human Capital and Investments." *Annual Review of Economics* 13, no. 1 (2021): 487–513.
Dalla Costa, Mariarosa. *Women and the Subversion of the Community: A Mariarosa Dalla Costa Reader*. 1972; PM Press, 2019.
Davies, Scott, and Jessica Rizk. "The Three Generations of Cultural Capital Research: A Narrative Review." *Review of Educational Research* 88, no. 3 (2018): 331–65.
Davis, Angela. "Reflections on the Black Woman's Role in the Community of Slaves." *Black Scholar* 12, no. 6 (1981): 2–15.
De Genova, Nicholas. "The Management of 'Quality': Class Decomposition and Racial Formation in a Chicago Factory." *Dialectical Anthropology* 34, no. 2 (2010): 249–72.
De Genova, Nicholas. "A Racial Theory of Labour: Racial Capitalism From Colonial Slavery to Postcolonial Migration." *Historical Materialism* 1 (2023): 1–33.

De Genova, Nicholas. "Reply to Mishler, Harney, and Roediger: Production, Class, Race . . . and Labor as Subject." *Dialectical Anthropology* 34, no. 2 (2010): 283–86.

De Genova, Nicholas. "Toward a Marxian Anthropology? Bare, Abstract, Mobile, Global." *Dialectical Anthropology* 40, no. 2 (2016): 125–41.

De'Ath, Amy. "Gender and Social Reproduction." In *The SAGE Handbook of Frankfurt School Critical Theory*, edited by Beverley Best, Werner Bonefeld, and Chris O'Kane. Sage, 2018.

De'Ath, Amy. "Hidden Abodes and Inner Bonds: Literary Study and Marxist-Feminism." In *After Marx: Literature, Theory, and Value in the Twenty-First Century*, edited by Lye, Colleen, and Christopher Nealon. Cambridge University Press, 2022.

Del Boca, Daniela, Christopher Flinn, and Matthew Wiswall. "Household Choices and Child Development." *Review of Economic Studies* 81, no. 1 (2014): 137–85.

Del Bono, Emilia, Marco Francesconi, Yvonne Kelly, and Amanda Sacker. "Early Maternal Time Investment and Early Child Outcomes." *Economic Journal* 126, no. 596 (2016): F96–F135.

Deleuze, Gilles. "What Is the Creative Act?" In *Two Regimes of Madness: Texts and Interviews 1975–1995*, edited by David Lapoujade and translated by Ames Hodges and Michael Taormina. MIT Press, 2009.

Deleuze, Gilles, and Félix Guattari. *Anti-Oedipus: Capitalism and Schizophrenia*. Viking Press, 1977.

De Lissovoy, Noah. *Education and Emancipation in the Neoliberal Era: Being, Teaching, and Power*. Palgrave Macmillan, 2015.

Devine, Fiona. "Class Reproduction and Social Networks in the USA." In *The Way Class Works: Readings on School, Family, and the Economy*, edited by Lois Weis. Routledge, 2009.

Dinerstein, Ana Cecilia, and María José Ventura Alfaro. "Intricacies of Prefiguration: A Conversation About Hope, Resistance, Critical Theory, Open Marxism, and Weaving." *Ephemera: Theory & Politics in Organization* 24, no. 1 (2024): 215–45.

Dinerstein, Ana Cecilia, Henry Pitts, and Patricia Zanoni. "Open Marxism." In *Encyclopedia of Critical Political Science*, edited by Clyde W. Barrow. Edward Elgar, 2023.

Dixson, Adrienne D., and Celia K. Rousseau, eds. *Critical Race Theory in Education: All God's Children Got a Song*. Taylor & Francis, 2006.

Doepke, Matthias, and Fabrizio Zilibotti. *Love, Money, and Parenting: How Economics Explains the Way We Raise Our Kids*. Princeton University Press, 2019.

Donzelot, Jacques. *The Policing of Families*. Translated by R. Hurley. John Hopkins University Press, 1997.

Elson, Diane. "The Value Theory of Labour." In *Value: The Representation of Labour in Capitalism*, edited by Diane Elson. CSE Books, 1979.

Erickson, Ansley T., and Ernest Morrell, eds. *Educating Harlem: A Century of Schooling and Resistance in a Black Community*. Columbia University Press, 2019.

Ewing, Eve. "Choosing Homes, Choosing Schools." *Harvard Educational Review* 85, no. 2 (2015): 279–93.

Fanon, Frantz. *Black Skin, White Masks*. Monthly Review Press, 1967.

Fanon, Frantz. *The Wretched of the Earth*. 1961; Grove Press, 2004.

Federici, Silvia. *Caliban and the Witch*. Autonomedia, 2004.

Federici, Silvia. *Revolution at Point Zero: Housework, Reproduction, and Feminist Struggle*. PM Press, 2012.

Federici, Silvia. *Wages Against Housework*. Power of Women Collective and Falling Wall Press, 1975.

Federici, Silvia, and George Caffentzis. "Notes on the Edu-factory and Cognitive Capitalism." *The Commoner* 12, no. 2007 (2007): 63–70.

Feher, Michel. "Self-Appreciation; or, The Aspirations of Human Capital." *Public Culture* 21, no. 1 (2009): 21–41.

Ferguson, Roderick A. *Aberrations in Black: Toward a Queer of Color Critique*. University of Minnesota Press, 2004.

Ferguson, Susan. "Children, Childhood, and Capitalism: A Social Reproduction Perspective." In *Social Reproduction Theory: Remapping Class, Recentering Oppression*, edited by Tithi Bhattacharya. Pluto Press, 2017.

Ferguson, Susan. "Intersectionality and Social-Reproduction Feminisms: Toward an Integrative Ontology." *Historical Materialism* 24, no. 2 (2016): 38–60.

Ferguson, Susan. "Life-Making or Death-Making?" *Midnight Sun*, Oct. 17, 2021. https://www.midnightsunmag.ca/life-making-or-death-making/.

Ferguson, Susan, and David McNally. "Capital, Labour-Power, and Gender Relations: Introduction to the Historical Materialism Edition of Marxism and the Oppression of Women." In *Marxism and the Oppression of Women: Toward a Unitary Theory*, edited by Lise Vogel. Brill, 2013.

Ferreira da Silva, Denise. "Before Man: Sylvia Wynter's Rewriting of the Modern Episteme." In *Sylvia Wynter: On Being Human as Praxis*, edited by Katherine McKittrick. Duke University Press, 2015.

Fisher, Samuel. "Abstract Models, Concrete Frictions: On Mau's *Mute Compulsion*." *Spectre Journal*, 2024.

Flood, Sarah, Joel McMurry, Aaron Sojourner, and Matthew Wiswall. "Inequality in Early Care Experienced by US Children." *Journal of Economic Perspectives* 36, no. 2 (2022): 199–222.

Fong, Benjamin Y. *Death and Mastery: Psychoanalytic Drive Theory and the Subject of Late Capitalism*. Columbia University Press, 2016.

Fong, Kelley. "Getting Eyes in the Home: Child Protective Services Investigations and State Surveillance of Family Life." *American Sociological Review* 85, no. 4 (2020): 610–38.

Fortunati, Leopoldina. *The Arcana of Reproduction: Housework, Prostitution, Labor and Capital*. Autonomedia, 1981.

Foucault, Michel. *The Birth of Biopolitics: Lectures at the Collège de France, 1978–79*. 1978; Palgrave Macmillan, 2008.

Fraad, Harriet. "Exploitation in the Labor of Love." In *Class and Its Others*, edited by Julie Katherine Gibson-Graham, Stephen A. Resnick, and Richard D. Wolff. University of Minnesota Press, 2000.

Freud, Sigmund. "Notes upon a Case of Obsessional Neurosis." 1909. In *The Standard Edition of the Complete World of Sigmund Freud*, translated by James Strachey, vol. 10. Hogarth Press, 1953–1974.

Freud, Sigmund. "Screen Memories." 1899. In *The Standard Edition of the Complete World of Sigmund Freud*, translated by James Strachey, vol. 3. Hogarth Press, 1953–1974.

Freud, Sigmund. *Totem and Taboo*. 1912. In *The Standard Edition of the Complete World of Sigmund Freud*, translated by James Strachey, vol. 13. Hogarth Press, 1953–1974.

Garba, Tapji, and Sara-Maria Sorentino. "Slavery Is a Metaphor: A Critical Commentary on Eve Tuck and K. Wayne Yang's 'Decolonization Is Not a Metaphor.'" *Antipode* 52, no. 3 (2020): 764–82.

Garrett, Roberta, Tracey Jensen, and Angie Voela, eds. *We Need to Talk About Family: Essays on Neoliberalism, the Family and Popular Culture*. Cambridge Scholars Publishing, 2016.

Gibbons Andrea. *City of Segregation: 100 Years of Struggle for Housing in Los Angeles*. Verso, 2018.

Giles, Melinda Vandenbeld. *Mothering in the Age of Neoliberalism*. Demeter Press, 2014.

Gill, Rosalind. "The Affective, Cultural and Psychic Life of Postfeminism: A Postfeminist Sensibility 10 Years On." *European Journal of Cultural Studies* 20, no. 6 (2017): 606–26.

Gillani, N., E. Chu, D. Beeferman, R. Eynon, and D. Roy. "Parents' Online School Reviews Reflect Several Racial and Socioeconomic Disparities in K–12 Education." *AERA Open* 7 (2021): https://doi.org/10.1177/2332858421992344.

Gilmore, Ruth Wilson. *Abolition Geography: Essays Toward Liberation*. Verso, 2022.

Gilmore, Ruth Wilson. "Race and Globalisation." In *Geographies of Global Change: Remapping the World*, edited by Ronald John Johnston and Michael John Watts. Blackwell, 2002.

Gilmore, Ruth Wilson. *Golden Gulag: Prisons, Surplus, Crisis, and Opposition in Globalizing California*. University of California Press, 2007.

Gonzalez, Maya, and Jeanne Neton. "The Logic of Gender: On the Separation of Spheres and the Process of Abjection." In *Contemporary Marxist Theory: A Reader*, edited by Andrew Pendakis, Jeff Diamanti, and Nicholas Brown. Bloomsbury, 2014.

Gordon, Avery. *The Hawthorn Archives: Letters from the Utopian Margins*. Fordham University Press, 2017.

Green, Preston C., III, Bruce D. Baker, and Joseph O. Oluwole. "School Finance, Race, and Reparations." *Washington and Lee Journal of Civil Rights and Social Justice* 27, no. 2 (2021): 483–558.

Griffen, Zachary Webster. 2024. "The Economization of Early Life: Human Capital Theory, Biology, and Social Policy." *Science, Technology, & Human Values* 49, no. 1 (2024): 175–205.

Griffen, Zachary, and Aaron Panofsky. "Ambivalent Economizations: The Case of Value Added Modeling in Teacher Evaluation." *Theory and Society* 50 (2021): 515–39.

Gumbs, Alexis Pauline. "M/Other Ourselves: A Black Queer Feminist Genealogy for Radical Mothering." In *Revolutionary Mothering: Love on the Front Lines*, edited by Alexis Pauline Gumbs, China Martens, Mai'a Williams, and Loretta J. Ross. PM Press, 2016.

Harris, Cheryl I. 1993. "Whiteness as Property." *Harvard Law Review* 106, no. 8 (1993): 1707–91.

Harvie, David. "Value Production and Struggle in the Classroom: Teachers Within, Against and Beyond Capital." *Capital & Class* 88 (2005): 1–32.

Harvie, David, and Massimo De Angelis. "'Cognitive Capitalism' and the Rat-Race: How Capital Measures Immaterial Labour in British Universities." *Historical Materialism* 17, no. 3 (2009): 3–30.

Hasan, Sharique, and Anuj Kumar. "Digitisation and Divergence: Online School Ratings and Segregation in America." *SSRN*, 2019. https://doi.org/10.2139/ssrn.3265316.

Hartman, Saidiya. "The Belly of the World: A Note on Black Women's Labors." *Souls* 18, no. 1 (2016): 166–73.

Hartman, Saidiya. *Lose Your Mother: A Journey Along the Atlantic Slave Route*. Farrar, Straus, and Giroux, 2007.

Hartman, Saidiya. *Scenes of Subjection: Terror, Slavery, and Self-Making in Nineteenth-Century America*. Oxford University Press, 1997.

Hays, Sharon. *The Cultural Contradictions of Motherhood*. Yale University Press, 1996.

Heaney, Emma. "Introduction: Feminism Without Cisness." In *Against Cisness*, edited by Emma Heaney. Duke University Press, 2024.

Heinrich, Michael. "The 'Fragment on Machines': A Marxian Misconception in the *Grundrisse* and Its Overcoming in *Capital*." In *In Marx's Laboratory: Critical Interpretations of the Grundrisse*, edited by Riccardo Bellofiore, Guido Starosta, and Peter D. Thomas. Brill, 2013.

Hemmens, Alastair. "Radical Subjectivity: Considered in its Psychological, Economic, Political, Sexual and, Notably, Philosophical Aspects." *The Situationist International: A Critical Handbook*. Pluto, 2020.

Hemmings, Clare, and Kabesh Amal Treacher. "The Feminist Subject of Agency: Recognition and Affect in Encounters with 'the Other.'" In *Gender, Agency and Coercion*, edited by Sumi Madhok, Anne Phillips, Kalpana Wilson, and Clare Hemmings. Palgrave Macmillan, 2013.

Hennessy, Rosemary. *Profit and Pleasure: Sexual Identities in Late Capitalism*. Routledge, 2000.

Hensman, Rohini. "Domestic Labor and the Production of Labour-Power." In *The SAGE Handbook of Marxism*, edited by Beverley Skeggs, Sara R. Farris, Alberto Toscano, and Svenja Bromberg. Sage, 2021.

Hirschman, Daniel, and Elizabeth Popp Berman. "Do Economists Make Policies? On the Political Effects of Economics." *Socio-Economic Review* 12, no. 4 (2014): 779–811.

Hochschild, Arlie Russell. "Global Care Chains and Emotional Surplus Value." In *On the Edge: Living with Global Capitalism*, edited by Will Hutton and Anthony Giddens. Jonathan Cape, 2000.

Hochschild, Arlie. "Housework Isn't Emotional Labor." Interview by Julie Beck. *The Atlantic*, 2018.

Holloway, John. *Hope in Hopeless Times*. Pluto Books, 2022.

Holloway, John. "The Train." In *Open Marxism 4: Against a Closing World*, edited by Ana Cecilia Dinerstein, Alfonso Garcia Vela, and John Holloway. Pluto Press, 2020.

Holloway, Sarah L., and Helena Pimlott-Wilson. "Parental Involvement in Children's Learning: Mothers' Fourth Shift, Social Class, and the Growth of State Intervention in Family Life." *The Canadian Geographer / Le Géographe Canadien* 57, no. 3 (2013): 327–36.

Holloway, Sarah L., and Helena Pimlott-Wilson. "Schools, Families, and Social Reproduction." In *Geographies of Schooling*, edited by Holger Jahnke, Caroline Kramer, and Peter Meusburger. Springer International Publishing, 2019.

hooks, bell. *Feminist Theory: From Margin to Center*. South End Press, 1984.

Horkheimer, Max. "Traditional and Critical Theory." In *Critical Theory: Selected Essays*, translated by Matthew J. O'Connor et al. Continuum, 1972.

Ingleby, David. 1985. "Professionals as Socialisers: The 'Psy Complex.'" *Research in Law, Deviance and Social Control* 7 (1985): 79–109.

Jackson, Jake. "Phenomenological Psychopathology and America's Social Life-World." In *Oxford Handbook of Phenomenological Psychopathology*, edited by Giovanni Stanghellini, Andrea Raballo, Matthew Broome, Anthony Vincent Fernandez, Paolo Fusar-Poli, and René Rosfort. Oxford Handbooks Online, 2018.

James, Joy. "The Womb of Western Theory: Trauma, Time Theft, and the Captive Maternal." *Carceral Notebooks* 12, no. 1 (2016): 253–29.

Jappe, Anselm. "Sohn-Rethel and the Origin of 'Real Abstraction': A Critique of Production or a Critique of Circulation?" *Historical Materialism* 21, no. 1 (2013): 3–14.

Jarvis, Helen, Jonathan Cloke, and Paula Kantor. *Cities and Gender*. Routledge, 2009.

Jauregui, Iker. "Foucault on Becker on Neoliberalism." *Cultural Critique* 127, no. 1 (2025): 56–81.

Jensen, Tracey. "Against Resilience." In *We Need to Talk About Family: Essays on Neoliberalism, the Family and Popular Culture*, edited by Roberta Garrett, Tracey Jensen, and Angie Voela. Cambridge Scholars Publishing, 2016.

Jensen, Tracey. *Parenting the Crisis: The Cultural Politics of Parent-Blame*. Policy Press, 2018.

Johnston, Adrian. *Infinite Greed: The Inhuman Selfishness of Capital*. Columbia University Press, 2024.

Kalb, Don. "Class." In *A Companion to Urban Anthropology*, edited by Don Nonini. John Wiley and Sons, 2014.

Kalil, Ariel, Susan E. Mayer, William Delgado, and Lisa A. Gennetian. "Education Gradients in Parental Time Investment and Subjective Well-Being." *Review of Economics of the Household* 23, no. 2 (2025): 661–706.

Kalil, Ariel, and Rebecca Ryan. "Parenting Practices and Socioeconomic Gaps in Childhood Outcomes." *Future of Children* 30, no. 1 (2020): 29–54.

Katz, Cindi. "Accumulation, Excess, Childhood: Toward a Countertopography of Risk and Waste." *Documents d'Anàlisi Geogràfica* 57, no. 1 (2011): 47–60.

Katz, Cindi. "The Angel of Geography: Superman, Tiger Mother, Aspiration Management, and the Child as Waste." *Progress in Human Geography* 42, no. 5 (2018): 723–40.

Katz, Cindi. "Cultural Geographies Lecture: Childhood as Spectacle: Relays of Anxiety and the Reconfiguration of the Child." *Cultural Geographies* 15, no. 1 (2008): 5–17.

Katz, Cindi. *Growing Up Global: Economic Restructuring and Children's Everyday Lives*. University of Minnesota Press, 2004.

Katz, Cindi, Sallie A. Marston, and Katharyne Mitchell. "Demanding Life's Work." In *Precarious Worlds: Contested Geographies of Social Reproduction*, edited by Katie Meehan and Kendra Stauss. University of Georgia Press, 2015.

Khatib, Sami. "The Time of Capital and the Messianicity of Time: Marx with Benjamin." *Studies in Social and Political Thought* 20 (2012): 46–69.

King, Tiffany Lethabo. "Black 'Feminisms' and Pessimism: Abolishing Moynihan's Negro Family." *Theory & Event* 21, no. 1 (2018): 68–87.

King, Tiffany Lethabo. "The Labor of (Re)Reading Plantation Landscapes Fungible(ly)." *Antipode* 48, no. 4 (2016): 1022–39.

King, Tiffany Lethabo. "Labor's Aphasia: Toward Antiblackness as Constitutive to Settler Colonialism." *Decolonization: Indigeneity, Education & Society* 10, no. 10 (2014): https://decolonization.wordpress.com/2014/06/10/labors-aphasia-toward-antiblackness-as-constitutive-to-settler-colonialism/.

Klein, Melanie. "The Development of a Child." 1921. In *Love, Guilt and Preparation and Other Works, 1921–1945: The Writings of Melanie Klein*, vol. 1. Free Press, 1975.

Klein, Melanie. "Early Stages of the Oedipal Conflict." 1928. In *The Selected Melanie Klein*, edited by Juliet Mitchell. Free Press, 1986.

Klein, Melanie. "Mourning and Its Relation to Manic-Depressive States." 1940. In *Love, Guilt and Reparation and Other Works, 1921–1945: The Writings of Melanie Klein*, vol. 1. Free Press, 1975.

Klein, Melanie. "The Psycho-Analytic Play Technique: Its History and Significance." 1955. In *The Selected Melanie Klein*, edited by Juliet Mitchell. Free Press, 1986.

Knott, Sarah. *Mother Is a Verb: An Unconventional History*. Sarah Crichton Books, 2019.

Kromidas, Maria. "'Agent of Revolutionary Thought': Bambara and Black Girlhood for a Poetics of Being and Becoming Human." *Jeunesse: Young People, Texts, Cultures* 11, no. 1 (2019): 19–37.

Kromidas, Maria. "Becoming Convivial with Child: Dismantling the Race/Child/Human Assemblage." In *Childhoods in More Just Worlds: An International Handbook*, edited by Timothy Kinard and Gaile Cannella. Myers Education Press, 2021.

Kromidas, Maria. *City Kids: Transforming Racial Baggage*. Rutgers University Press, 2016.

Kromidas, Maria. "Learning Hierarchy and Displacing Conviviality: Time and Subjectivity in the Neoliberal Kindergarten." *Pedagogy, Culture & Society* 30, no. 4 (2022): 491–51.

Kromidas, Maria. "Mothering and the Racialised Production of School and Property Value." *Antipode* 54, no. 1 (2022): 284–304.

Kromidas, Maria. "The 'Savage' Child and the Nature of Race: Posthuman Interventions from New York City." *Anthropological Theory* 14, no. 4 (2014): 422–41.

Kromidas, Maria. "Towards the Human, After the Child of Man: Seeing the Child Differently in Teacher Education." *Curriculum Inquiry* 49, no. 1 (2019): 65–89.

Kromidas, Maria. "'When I Was a Kid': Childhood Memories, Care Work, and Becoming Mom." *Subjectivity* 14, no. 1 (2021): 36–52.

Kucsera, John, and Gary Orfield. "New York State's Extreme School Segregation: Inequality, Inaction, and a Damaged Future." Civil Rights Project, University of California, Los Angeles, 2014. https://civilrightsproject.ucla.edu/research/k-12-education/integration-and-diversity/ny-norflet-report-placeholder.

Lane-McKinley, Madeline. "The Idea of Children." *Blindfield Journal*, 2018. https://blindfieldjournal.com/2018/08/02/the-idea-of-children/1/6.

Lane-McKinley, Madeline. *Solidarity with Children: An Essay Against Adult Supremacy*. Haymarket, 2025.

Landivar, Liana Christin, Leah Ruppanner, William J. Scarborough, and Caitlyn Collins. "Early Signs Indicate That COVID-19 Is Exacerbating Gender Inequality in the Labor Force." *Socius* 6 (2020): 1–3.

Ladson-Billings, Gloria. "From the Achievement Gap to the Education Debt: Understanding Achievement in US Schools." *Educational Researcher* 35, no. 7 (2006): 3–12.

Laplanche, Jean. "The Other Within: Rethinking Psychoanalysis." *Radical Philosophy* 102 (2000): 31–42.

Lareau, Annette. *Unequal Childhoods: Class, Race, and Family Life*. University of California Press, 2011.

Lareau, Annette, and Kimberly Goyette, eds. *Choosing Homes, Choosing Schools*. Russell Sage Foundation, 2014.

Lazarre, Jane. *The Mother Knot*. Duke University Press, 1997.

Lazzarato, Maurizio. *Capitalism Hates Everyone: Fascism or Revolution.* Semiotext(e), 2021.

Lazzarato, Maurizio. "Immaterial Labor." In *Radical Thought in Italy: A Potential Politics*, edited by Paolo Virno and Michael Hardt. University of Minnesota Press, 1996.

Lazzarato, Maurizio. *Signs and Machines: Capitalism and the Production of Subjectivity*. Translated by Joshua David Jordan. Semiotext(e), 2014.

Leeming, David. *Myth: A Biography of Belief.* Oxford University Press, 2002.

Lefebvre, Henri. *Critique of Everyday Life*. 1947; Verso, 1991.

Leibowitz, Arleen. "Home Investments in Children" In *Economics of the Family: Marriage, Children, and Human Capital*, edited by Theodore Schultz. University of Chicago Press, 1974.

Lewis, Sophie. *Abolish the Family: A Manifesto for Care and Liberation.* Verso, 2022.

Lewis, Sophie. "Mothering Against the World: Doula Work, Xenohospitality, and the Idea of the Momrade." *Feminist Theory* 24, no. 1 (2023): 68–85.

Lipsitz George. *The Possessive Investment in Whiteness: How White People Profit from Identity Politics*. Temple University Press, 2006.

Lombardi, Karen L. "The New Ties That Bind: Helicopter Parenting and Surveillance." In *We Need to Talk About Family: Essays on Neoliberalism, the Family and Popular Culture*, edited by Roberta Garrett, Tracey Jensen, and Angie Voela. Cambridge Scholars Publishing, 2016.

Lorde, Audre. "Uses of the Erotic: The Erotic as Power." In *Sister Outsider*. Crossing Press, 1984.

Lowy, Margo. *The Maternal Experience: Encounters with Ambivalence and Love*. Routledge, 2020.

Lung-Amam, Willow. *Trespassers: Asian Americans and the Battle for Suburbia*. University of California Press, 2017.

Lyotard, Jean-Francois. *Libidinal Economy*. Translated by Iain Hamilton Grant. Indiana University Press, 1974.

Lyttleton, Thomas, Emma Zang, and Kelly Musick. "Parents' Work Arrangements and Gendered Time Use During the COVID-19 Pandemic." *Journal of Marriage and Family* 85, no. 2 (2023): 657–73.

Macvarish, Jan. *Neuroparenting: The Expert Invasion of Family Life*. Palgrave Macmillan, 2016.

Makris, Molly Vollman. "The Chimera of Choice: Gentrification, School Choice, and Community." *Peabody Journal of Education* 93, no. 4 (2018): 411–29.

Marasco, Robyn. "There's a Fascist in the Family: Critical Theory and Antiauthoritarianism." *South Atlantic Quarterly* 117, no. 4 (2018): 791–813.

Marx, Karl. *Capital Volume I*. 1867. Translated by Ben Fowkes. Vintage/Random House, 1976.

Marx, Karl. *Capital Volume I*. 1867. Translated by Paul Reitter. Princeton University Press, 2024.

Marx, Karl. "A Contribution to the Critique of Hegel's Philosophy of Right: Introduction." 1844. In *Collected Works*, by Karl Marx and Friedrich Engels, vol. 3. Lawrence & Wishart, 1975.

Marx, Karl. *Grundrisse: Foundations of the Critique of Political Economy.* Translated by Martin Nicolaus. 1858; Vintage/Random House, 1973.
Marx, Karl. *Economic and Philosophic Manuscripts of 1844.* International Publishers, 1964.
Marx, Karl. *Economic Manuscripts of 1857–58.* In Marx and Engels, *Collected Works*, vol. 28. Lawrence & Wishart, 1986.
Marx, Karl. *The Eighteenth Brumaire of Louis Bonaparte.* 1852; International Publishers, 1970.
Marx, Karl. 1868. "Letter to Engels." January 8. https://www.marxists.org/archive/marx/works/1868/letters/68_01_08.htm.
Marx, Karl. *Theories of Surplus Value.* 1862. In Marx and Engels, *Collected Works*, vol. 31. Lawrence & Wishart, 1969.
Marx, Karl, and Friedrich Engels. *The Communist Manifesto.* 1848; Penguin, 1967.
Marx, Karl, and Friedrich Engels. *The German Ideology.* 1846; International Publishers, 1970.
Mau, Søren. *Mute Compulsion: A Marxist Theory of Economic Power of Capital.* Verso, 2023.
McCarthy Foubert, Jennifer L. "'Damned If You Do, Damned If You Don't': Black Parents' Racial Realist School Engagement." *Race Ethnicity and Education* 25, no. 5 (2022): 647–64.
Melamed, Jodi. "Racial Capitalism." *Critical Ethnic Studies* 1, no. 1 (2015): 76–85.
Mezzadri, Alessandra. "On the Value of Social Reproduction: Informal Labour, the Majority World and the Need for Inclusive Theories and Politics." *Radical Philosophy* 2, no. 4 (2019): 33–41.A
Millei, Zsuzsa, and Mikko Joronen. "The (Bio)Politicization of Neuroscience in Australian Early Years Policies: Fostering Brain-Resources as Human Capital." *Journal of Education Policy* 31, no. 4 (2016): 389–404.
Milkie, Melissa A., Kei M. Nomaguchi, and Kathleen E. Denny. "Does the Amount of Time Mothers Spend with Children or Adolescents Matter?" *Journal of Marriage and Family* 77, no. 2 (2015): 355–72.
Mincer, Jacob. "Investment in Human Capital and Personal Income Distribution." *Journal of Political Economy* 66, no. 4 (1958): 281–302.
Morgan, Jennifer L. *Reckoning with Slavery: Gender, Kinship, and Capitalism in the Early Black Atlantic.* Duke University Press, 2021.
Munro, Kirstin. "'Social Reproduction Theory,' Social Reproduction, and Household Production." *Science & Society* 83, no. 4 (2019): 451–68.
Munro, Kirstin. "The Welfare State and the Bourgeois Family-Household." *Science & Society* 85, no. 2 (2021): 199–206.
Murphy, Michelle. *The Economization of Life.* Duke University Press, 2017.
Mustosmäki, Armi, and Tiina Sihto. "'F*** This Shit': Negotiating the Boundaries of Public Expression of Mother's Negative Feelings." *NORA: Nordic Journal of Feminist and Gender Research* 29, no. 3 (2021): 216–28.
Myers, Casey Y. "Becoming 'Babies' in Real Time: Temporal Emergence in the Classroom Mangle." *Contemporary Issues in Early Childhood* 17, no. 4 (2016): 421–30.

Nash, Jennifer C. "The Political Life of Black Motherhood." *Feminist Studies* 44, no. 3 (2018): 699–712.

Nelson, Margaret K. *Parenting Out of Control: Anxious Parents in Uncertain Times*. New York University Press, 2012.

Nguyen-Hoang, Phuong, and John Yinger. "The Capitalization of School Quality into House Values: A Review." *Journal of Housing Economics* 20, no. 1 (2011): 30–48.

Nicoletti, Cheti, Kjell G. Salvanes, and Emma Tominey. "Mothers Working During Preschool Years and Child Skills: Does Income Compensate?" *Journal of Labor Economics* 41, no. 2 (2023): 389–429.

Noble, Saffiya U. *Algorithms of Oppression: How Search Engines Reinforce Racism*. New York University Press, 2018.

Nomaguchi, Kei, and Melissa A. Milkie. "Parenthood and Well-Being: A Decade in Review." *Journal of Marriage and Family* 82, no. 1 (2020): 198–223.

Nxumalo, Fikile, and Stacia Cedillo. "Decolonizing Place in Early Childhood Studies: Thinking with Indigenous Onto-Epistemologies and Black Feminist Geographies." *Global Studies of Childhood* 7, no. 2 (2017): 99–112.

Nxumalo, Fikile, Veronica Pacini-Ketchabaw, and Mary Rowan. "Lunch Time at the Child Care Centre: Neoliberal Assemblages in Early Childhood Education." *Journal of Pedagogy* 2, no. 2 (2011): 195–223.

Nygreen, Kysa. "Neoliberal Reform and Family Engagement in Schools: An Intersectional Gender Analysis." *Policy Futures in Education* 17, no. 2 (2019): 205–21.

O'Brien, M. E. "To Abolish the Family: The Working-Class Family and Gender Liberation in Capitalist Development." *Endnotes* 5 (2020): 361–417.

O'Kane, Chris. "The Critique of Real Abstraction: From the Critical Theory of Society to the Critique of Political Economy and Back Again." In *Marx and Contemporary Critical Theory: The Philosophy of Real Abstraction*, edited by Antonio Oliva, Ángel Oliva, and Iván Novara. Springer, 2020.

O'Kane, Chris. "'Society Maintains Itself Despite All the Catastrophes That May Eventuate': Critical Theory, Negative Totality, and Crisis." *Constellations* 25, no. 2 (2018): 287–301.

Ogden, Thomas. "The Dialectically Constituted/Decentred Subject of Psychoanalysis." In *Psychoanalysis at Its Limits: Navigating the Postmodern Turn*, edited by Anthony Elliott and Charles Spezzano. Routledge, 2000.

Oksala, Johanna. "Affective Labor and Feminist Politics." *Signs: Journal of Women in Culture and Society* 41, no. 2 (2016): 281–303.

Oksala, Johanna. "Neoliberal Subjectivation: Between Foucault and Marx." *Critical Inquiry* 49, no. 4 (2023): 581–604.

O'Reilly, Andrea. "Maternal Theory: Patriarchal Motherhood and Empowered Mothering." In *The Routledge Companion to Motherhood*, edited by D. Hallstein, Lynn O'Brien, Melinda Vandenbeld Giles, and Andrea O'Reilly. Routledge, 2019.

O'Reilly, Andrea. *Toni Morrison and Motherhood: A Politics of the Heart*. State University of New York Press, 2004.

Osborne, Peter. "Introduction: Capitalism, Concept, Idea, Image." In *Capitalism: Concept, Idea, Image. Aspects of Marx's Capital Today*, edited by Peter Osborne, Eric Alliez, and Eric John-Russell. CRMEP Books, 2019.

Parker, Brenda. "Feminist Forays in the City: Imbalance and Intervention in Urban Research Methods." *Antipode* 48, no. 5 (2016): 1337–58.

Parker, Ian. "Reflexive Research and Grounding of Analysis: Psychology and the Psy-Complex." In *Critical Discursive Psychology*, edited by Ian Parker. Springer, 2015.

Pitts, Frederick Harry. "Beyond the Fragment: Postoperaismo, Postcapitalism and Marx's 'Notes on Machines,' 45 Years On." *Economy and Society* 46, nos. 3–4 (2017): 324–45.

Portella, Elizabeth, and Larry Alan Busk. "The Formal and Real Subsumption of Gender Relations: Challenging the Transhistorical Status of 'Patriarchy.'" *Historical Materialism* 32, no. 3 (2024): 353–84.

Ramirez Miguel D. "Marx and Ricardo on Machinery: A Critical Note." *European Journal of the History of Economic Thought* 26, no. 1 (2019): 81–100.

Ranganathan, Malini, and Anne Bonds. "Racial Regimes of Property: Introduction to the Special Issue." *Environment and Planning D: Society and Space* 40, no. 2 (2022): 197–207.

Read, Jason. "A Genealogy of Homo Economicus: Neoliberalism and the Production of Subjectivity." *Foucault Studies* 6 (2009): 25–36.

Rich, Adrienne. *Of Woman Born: Motherhood as Institution and Experience*. W.W. Norton, 1976.

Roberts, Dorothy E. "Prison, Foster Care, and the Systemic Punishment of Black Mothers." *UCLA Law Review* 59 (2012): 1474–500.

Roberts, Dorothy. *Torn Apart: How the Child Welfare System Destroys Black Families—and How Abolition Can Build a Safer World*. Basic Books, 2022.

Roberts-Holmes, Guy, and Peter Moss. *Neoliberalism and Early Childhood Education: Markets, Imaginaries and Governance*. Routledge, 2021.

Robinson, Cedric J. *Black Marxism: The Making of the Black Radical Tradition*. 1983; University of North Carolina Press, 2020.

Roda, Allison. "School Choice and the Politics of Parenthood: Exploring Parent Mobilization as a Catalyst for the Common Good." *Peabody Journal of Education* 93, no. 4 (2018): 430–49.

Roediger, David. *The Sinking Middle Class: A Political History of Debt, Misery, and the Drift to the Right*. Haymarket Books, 2022.

Roessler, Jonathan. "'Utopianism in Pianissimo': Adorno and Bloch on Utopia and Critique." *Critical Horizons* 23, no. 3 (2022): 227–46.

Rose, Gillian. *Love's Work*. New York Review Books, 2011.

Rose, Jacqueline. *Mothers: An Essay on Love and Cruelty*. Farrar, Straus, and Giroux, 2018.

Rose, Nikolas S. *The Psychological Complex: Psychology, Politics, and Society in England, 1869–1939*. Routledge & Kegan Paul Book, 1985.

Ross, K. M. "Anti-Blackness in Education and the Possibilities of Redress: Toward Educational Reparations." *Amerikastudien / American Studies* 66, no. 1 (2021): 229–33.

Rubin, Julia Sass, Ryan M. Good, and Michelle Fine. "Parental Action and Neoliberal Education Reform: Crafting a Research Agenda." *Journal of Urban Affairs* 42, no. 4 (2020): 492–510.

Ruddick, Sara. *Maternal Thinking: Towards a Politics of Peace*. Beacon Press, 1989.

Sattin-Bajaj, Carolyn, and Allison Roda. "Opportunity Hoarding in School Choice Contexts: The Role of Policy Design in Promoting Middle-Class Parents' Exclusionary Behaviours." *Educational Policy* 34, no. 7 (2020): 992–1035.

Schultz, Theodore, ed. *Economics of the Family: Marriage, Children, and Human Capital*. University of Chicago Press, 1974.

Schultz, Theodore. "Fertility and Economic Values." In *Economics of the Family: Marriage, Children, and Human Capital*, edited by Theodore Schultz. University of Chicago Press, 1974.

Schultz, Theodore. "Investment in Human Capital." *American Economic Review* 51, no. 1 (1961): 1–17.

Schwartz, Amy E., Ioan Voicu, and Keren Mertens Horn. "Do Choice Schools Break the Link Between Public Schools and Property Values? Evidence from House Prices in New York City." *Regional Science and Urban Economics* 49 (2014): 1–10.

Sexton, Jared. "People-of-Color-Blindness: Notes on the Afterlife of Slavery." *Social Text* 28, no. 2 (2010): 31–56.

Sexton, Jared. "Antidoting." *Black Scholar* 51, no. 3 (2021): 5–24.

Sharpe, Christina. *In the Wake: On Blackness and Being*. Duke University Press, 2016.

Slater, Graham B., and Gardner Seawright. "Putting Homo Economicus to the Test: How Neoliberalism Measures the Value of Educational Life." In *The Wiley Handbook of Global Educational Reform*, edited by Kenneth J. Saltman and Alexander J. Means. Wiley, 2018.

Slobodian, Quinn. *Hayek's Bastards: Race, Gold, IQ and the Capitalism of the Far-Right*. Zone Books, 2025.

Slobodian, Quinn. "The Unequal Mind: How Charles Murray and Neoliberal Think Tanks Revived IQ." *Capitalism: A Journal of History and Economics* 4, no. 1 (2023): 73–108.

Smith, Tony. 2013. "The 'General Intellect' in the *Grundrisse* and Beyond." *Historical Materialism* 21, no. 4 (2013): 235–55.

Smyth, Sarah Louise. "Postfeminism, Ambivalence and the Mother in Lynne Ramsay's *We Need to Talk About Kevin* (2011)." *Film Criticism* 44, no. 1 (2020): 1–16.

Sohn-Rethel, Alfred. *Intellectual and Manual Labour: A Critique of Epistemology*. Translated by Martin Sohn-Rethel. Humanities Press, 1978.

Spillers, Hortense. "All the Things You Could Be by Now If Sigmund Freud's Wife Was Your Mother: Psychoanalysis and Race." *Critical Inquiry* 22, no. 4 (1996): 710–34.

Spillers, Hortense. "Mama's Baby, Papa's Maybe." *Diacritics* 17, no. 2 (1987): 64–81.

Spinoza, Benedictus de. *Ethics Part 3*. 1667. Dossier Press, 2015.

Spyrou, Spyros, Rachel Rosen, and Daniel Cook. "Introduction: Reimagining Childhood Studies. Connections . . . Relationalities . . . Linkages" In *Reimagining Childhood Studies*, edited by Spyros Spyrou, Rachel Rosen, and Daniel Cook. Bloomsbury Academic, 2019.

Stearns, Clio. *Consent in the Childhood Classroom: Centering Student Voices Across Early Years and Elementary Education*. Routledge, 2022.

Stearns, Clio. "Let Them Get Mad: Using the Psychoanalytic Frame to Rethink SEL and Trauma Informed Practice." Bank Street Occasional Paper Series No. 43, article 3 (2020).

Stearns, Clio. "Responsive Classroom? A Critique of a Social Emotional Learning Program." *Critical Studies in Education* 57, no. 3 (2016): 330–41.

Stearns, Clio. "Unruly Affect in the Kindergarten Classroom: A Critical Analysis of Social-Emotional Learning." *Contemporary Issues in Early Childhood* 19, no. 1 (2018): 8–19.

Stearns, Peter. "Happy Children: A Modern Emotional Commitment." *Frontiers in Psychology* 10, no. 5 (2019): 1–8.

Steiner, Linda, and Einat Lachover. "The Mommy Wars: On the Home Front and Waged Abroad." *Feminist Media Studies* 16, no. 5 (2016): 869–85.

Sutherland, Keston. "The Poetics of Capital." In *Capitalism: Concept, Idea, Image. Aspects of Marx's Capital Today*, edited by Peter Osborne, Eric Alliez, and Eric John-Russell. CRMEP Books, 2019.

Takševa, Tatjana. "Mother Love, Maternal Ambivalence, and the Possibility of Empowered Mothering." *Hypatia* 32, no. 1 (2017): 152–68.

Taylor, Keeanga-Yamahtta. *Race for Profit: How Banks and the Real Estate Industry Undermined Black Homeownership*. University of North Carolina Press, 2019.

Tazzioli, Martina, and Nicholas De Genova. "Kidnapping Migrants as a Tactic of Border Enforcement." *Environment and Planning D: Society and Space* 38, no. 5 (2020): 867–86.

Thoborn, Nicholas. *Deleuze, Marx, and Politics*. Routledge, 2003.

Tilly, Charles. *Durable Inequality*. University of California Press, 1998.

Tomba, Massimiliano, and Riccardo Bellofiore. "The 'Fragment on Machines' and the *Grundrisse*: The Workerist Reading in Question." In *Beyond Marx: Theorising the Global Labour Relations of the Twenty-First Century*, edited by Marcel van der Linden and Karl Heinz Roth. Brill, 2014.

Tomšič, Samo. *The Capitalist Unconscious: Marx and Lacan*. Verso, 2015.

Tomšič, Samo. "Psychoanalysis." In *The Sage Handbook of Marxism*, vol. 2, edited by Sara R. Farris, Alberto Toscano, and Svenja Bromberg. Sage, 2022.

Toscano, Alberto, and Brenna Bhandar. "Race, Real Estate and Real Abstraction." *Radical Philosophy* 194 (2015): 8–17.

Tronti, Mario. "On Destituent Power." Translated by Andreas Petrossiants. *Ill Will*, May 21, 2022. https://illwill.com/on-destituent-power.

Tronti, Mario. *Workers and Capital.* Translated by David Broder. 1966; Verso Books, 2019.

Tuval-Mashiach, Rivka, and Shaiovitz-Gourman Shirit. "Maternal Ambivalence and 'Ideal Mothering.'" In *Mothering and Psychoanalysis: Clinical, Sociological and Feminist Perspectives*, edited by Petra Bueskens. Demeter Press, 2014.

Vandenbeld, Melinda Giles. "Mothering, Neoliberalism, and Globalization." In *The Routledge Companion to Motherhood*, edited by D. Lynn O'Brien Hallstein, Melinda Vandenbeld Giles, and Andrea O'Reilly. Routledge, 2020.

Vaneigem, Raoul. *The Revolution of Everyday Life.* Translated by Donald Nicholson-Smith. 1967; Rebel Press, 2001.

Vasquez-Tokos, Jessica, and Priscilla Yamin. "The Racialization of Privacy: Racial Formation as a Family Affair." *Theory and Society* 50, no. 5 (2021): 717–40.

Virno, Paolo. *A Grammar of the Multitude: For an Analysis of Contemporary Forms of Life.* Semiotext(e), 2004.

Vogel, Lise. *Marxism and the Oppression of Women: Toward a Unitary Theory.* 1983; Brill, 2013.

Wacquant, Loïc. "Three Steps to a Historical Anthropology of Actually Existing Neoliberalism." *Social Anthropology/Anthropologie Sociale* 20, no. 1 (2012): 66–79.

Wages for Students. "Wages for Students." Pamphlet, 1975.

Watson, Amanda D. *The Juggling Mother: Coming Undone in the Age of Anxiety.* UBC Press, 2020.

Weeks, Kathi. "Abolition of the Family: The Most Infamous Feminist Proposal." *Feminist Theory* 24, no. 3 (2023): 433–53.

Weeks, Kathi. "Life Within and Against Work: Affective Labor, Feminist Critique, and Post-Fordist Politics." *Ephemera: Theory & Politics in Organizations* 7, no. 1 (2007): 233–49.

Weeks, Kathi. *The Problem with Work: Feminism, Marxism, Antiwork Politics, and Postwork Imaginaries.* Duke University Press, 2020.

Weheliye, Alexander G. *Habeas Viscus: Racializing Assemblages, Biopolitics, and Black Feminist Theories of the Human.* Duke University Press, 2020.

Weinbaum, Alys Eve. *The Afterlife of Reproductive Slavery: Biocapitalism and Black Feminism's Philosophy of History.* Duke University Press, 2019.

Wilderson, Frank B., III. *Red, White & Black: Cinema and the Structure of US Antagonisms.* Duke University Press, 2010.

Williamson, Ben. "Counting Learning Losses." *Code Acts in Education* 24 (2021): 3–13.

Williamson, Ben. "Decoding ClassDojo: Psycho-Policy, Social-Emotional Learning and Persuasive Educational Technologies." *Learning, Media and Technology* 42, no. 4 (2017): 440–53.

Williamson, Ben. "Psychodata: Disassembling the Psychological, Economic, and Statistical Infrastructure of 'Social-Emotional Learning'" *Journal of Educational Policy* 1–26 (2021): 129–34.

Willis, Paul. *Learning to Labour: How Working Class Kids Get Working Class Jobs.* Columbia University Press, 1977.

Wilson, Julie A., and Emily Chivers Yochim. *Mothering Through Precarity: Women's Work and Digital Media.* Duke University Press, 2017.

Winnubst, Shannon. "The Many Lives of Fungibility: Anti-Blackness in Neoliberal Times." In *Biopolitics, Necropolitics, Cosmopolitics: Feminist and Queer Interventions*, edited by C. L. Quinan and Kathrin Thiele. Routledge, 2021.

Wright, Erik Olin. "The Continuing Importance of Class Analysis." In *The Way Class Works*, edited by Lois Weis. Routledge, 1997.

Wrigley, Julia. "Do Young Children Need Intellectual Stimulation? Experts' Advice to Parents, 1900–1985." *History of Education Quarterly* 29, no. 1 (1989): 41–75.

Wright, Steve. *Storming Heaven: Class Composition and Struggle in Italian Autonomist Marxism.* Pluto Press, 2017.

Wyly, Elvin, C. S. Ponder, Pierson Nettling, Bosco Ho, Sophie Ellen Fung, Zachary Liebowitz, and Dan Hammel. "New Racial Meanings of Housing in America." *American Quarterly* 64, no. 3 (2012): 571–604.

Wynter, Sylvia. "The Ceremony Found: Towards the Autopoetic Turn/Overturn, Its Autonomy of Human Agency and Extraterritoriality of (Self-)Cognition." In *Black Knowledges / Black Struggles: Essays in Critical Epistemology*, edited by Jason R. Ambroise and Sabine Broeck. Liverpool University Press, 2015.

Wynter, Sylvia. "'No Humans Involved.' An Open Letter to My Colleagues." *Forum N.H.I.: Knowledge for the 21st Century*, 1, no. 1 (1994), 42–71.

Wynter, Sylvia. "Towards the Sociogenic Principle: Fanon, Identity, the Puzzle of Conscious Experience." In *National Identities and Socio-Political Changes in Latin America*, edited by M. F. Durán-Cogan and A. Gómez-Moriana. Routledge, 2001.

Wynter, Sylvia. "Unsettling the Coloniality of Being/Power/Truth/Freedom: Towards the Human, After Man, Its Overrepresentation—An Argument." *CR: The New Centennial Review* 3, no. 3 (2003): 257–337.

Wynter, Sylvia, and Katherine McKittrick. "Unparalleled Catastrophe for Our Species? Or, To Give Humanness a Different Future: Conversations." In *Sylvia Wynter: On Being Human as Praxis*, edited by Katherine McKittrick. Duke University Press, 2015.

Yoon, Ee-Seul, Christopher Lubienski, and Jin Lee. "The Geography of School Choice in a City with Growing Inequality: The Case of Vancouver." *Journal of Education Policy* 33, no. 2 (2018): 279–98.

Zeavin, Hannah. "Hot and Cool Mothers." *Differences* 32, no. 3 (2021): 53–84.

Zelizer, Viviana. *Pricing the Priceless Child: The Changing Social Value of Children.* Princeton University Press, 1985.

Zimmerman, Toni Schindler, Jennifer T. Aberle, Jennifer L. Krafchick, and Ashley M. Harvey. "Deconstructing the 'Mommy Wars': The Battle over the Best Mom." *Journal of Feminist Family Therapy* 20, no. 3 (2008): 203–19.

INDEX

www.ingramcontent.com/pod-product-compliance
Lightning Source LLC
LaVergne TN
LVHW041133061026
849616LV00029B/206
9780826500564